THE
POWER
OF THE
ACTOR

THE
POWER
OF THE
ACTOR

The Chubbuck Technique

Ivana Chubbuck

Avery
an imprint of Penguin Random House
New York

AVERY

an imprint of Penguin Random House LLC
1745 Broadway, New York, NY 10019
penguinrandomhouse.com

Library of Congress Cataloging-in-Publication Data

Names: Chubbuck, Ivana, author.
Title: The power of the actor: the Chubbuck technique / Ivana Chubbuck.
Description: New York: Avery, 2025. | "Previous edition published © 2004"—
    Title page verso.
Identifiers: LCCN 2024044697 (print) | LCCN 2024044698 (ebook) |
    ISBN 9780593716816 (trade paperback) | ISBN 9798217047673 (epub)
Subjects: LCSH: Acting.
Classification: LCC PN2061 .C573 2025 (print) | LCC PN2061 (ebook) |
    DDC 792.02/8—dc23/eng/20250131
LC record available at https://lccn.loc.gov/2024044697
LC ebook record available at https://lccn.loc.gov/2024044698

Printed in the United States of America
1st Printing

The authorized representative in the EU for product safety and compliance is Penguin Random House Ireland, Morrison Chambers, 32 Nassau Street, Dublin D02 YH68, Ireland, https://eu-contact.penguin.ie.

For Claire
You gave my journey purpose

CONTENTS

Introduction

· · · · · · · · · · · · · · · · · ·

Acting is a complex and elusive art to define. Yet almost everyone can tell good acting from bad acting—or good acting from brilliant acting. Why can one actor be riveting in a play and another actor be dull and boring in the very same play, doing the same character, the same lines? If it were just the script, the beauty of its language, the artful turn of a phrase, we would need only readings. But the words are not just read with sterility from the page. They are performed and brought to life by actors.

Every actor knows that discovering and understanding your personal pain is an inherent part of the acting process. This has been true since Stanislavski. The difference between the Chubbuck Technique and those developed in the past is that I teach actors how to use their emotions not as an end result, but as a way to empower a goal. My technique teaches actors how to win.

If you look closely at virtually all drama and comedy—in fact, all literature— you will find that the will to win is the one constant element. In every story, a character wants or needs something regarding love, power, value, absolution, revenge . . . or something that boils down to a simple human primal need. The story documents the way in which the character attempts to win that specific need. How the character precisely tries to win is defined in many ways and takes many forms, shapes and behaviors. But in every case, a character's dramatic struggle is about fighting to overcome the conflicts and obstacles getting in the way of accomplishing that win.

Archaeologists have found objects and cave drawings that indicate early man played games of contest and sport. Acting began a couple thousand years ago in Ancient Greece. Let's do the math: The need for man to "win" is millions of years old; the theater is a couple thousand years old.

I teach actors how the concept of winning can be layered into their emotional constructs. Interesting and dynamic people go after what they want in interesting and dynamic ways, creating greater emotion and intensity in realizing these goals. They do this subconsciously, whereas actors must be aware and work to discover them. The "win" factor is essential in re-creating fundamental human needs for our script analysis and makes our work more compelling. The Chubbuck Technique not only stimulates the search for rich inner emotional information, but also helps to proactively and effectively activate our emotions to accomplishment.

The Chubbuck Technique grew out of my search to understand and overcome my own personal traumas and how they impacted both my acting and my personal life. I grew up with a distant/dysfunctional/workaholic father (a good man but emotionally unavailable) and a physically violent and emotionally abusive mother. My mother was never officially diagnosed, but my brother Joe Gottfried, who is a psychiatrist, has said that the following disorders would make sense of her behaviors: "social anxiety disorder, mixed personality disorder heavy with narcissistic and histrionic traits, and Complex PTSD." The assumption was that the Complex PTSD came from severe childhood traumas. (Our mother was sexually abused by a family member when she was a young teen, then beaten and blamed by her parents when she informed them.) She also was a severe hoarder, so my six siblings and I shared our home with vermin that lived happily among the piles of moldy, mulchy junk that had long ago stopped serving a purpose. As a result of her abuse and the absence of my father to protect me, I developed all kinds of ways to self-loathe and self-destruct. As an adult and as an actress, I wallowed in my childhood and adolescent horrors. As any actor would strive to be, I was truly in touch with my emotional pain.

But I began to wonder, "To what end am I feeling all of this? How do the feelings and emotions from my past shape my work as an actor?" As a working actress, I would see so many actors who were "honestly" dredging up deep, painful emotions, but whose work seemed self-indulgent. I realized that having deep and profound feelings didn't necessarily make me a deep and profound actor. I saw that coddling one's pain—in life and onstage—created almost the opposite effect. It came across as self-involved, self-pitying, and weak, the key characteristics of a victim. Not the most compelling choice for an actor to make.

I began investigating how to put the legacy of emotions I had inherited to better, more effective use in my work. When I examined the lives of successful people, I noticed that they seemed to use their physical and emotional traumas as a stimulus, not to self-indulgently suffer, but to *inspire* and *drive* their great achievements.

I suspected that very same formula could be applied to actors and their approach to their work. I watched the great actors of our time and I saw in their performances the same emotional drive to overcome adversity and, in fact, to use those very obstacles to necessitate achievement of a goal and win. In their performances, great actors were instinctively mirroring the behavior and nature of great people.

I needed to create a system that would reflect and guide this process. A system to replicate real, dynamic human behavior. A system that, once the actor committed to making fearless choices, would guide and empower the actor to use their own pain to win their character's goal. A system that would also provide a way to craft risky choices that would allow an actor to *break the rules* and *make new rules*, inspiring exceptional work and characters. A system that would create an emotionally heroic character rather than a victim.

I realized that an actor must identify their character's primal need, goal or OBJECTIVE. With this OBJECTIVE in mind, the actor must then find the appropriate personal pain that can effectively drive this OBJECTIVE. After working with this idea for a while, I understood that the pain must be powerful enough to inspire an actor to fearlessly commit to doing *whatever it takes* to WIN their OBJECTIVE. If the emotions were not strong enough, then there wasn't enough there to motivate the actor to sustain their fight to win. But when the appropriate personal pain is paired with an OBJECTIVE, it connects the actor to their character's predicament, making winning the OBJECTIVE real and necessary for them as a person, not just as an actor playing a part. With this new approach, my cutting-edge technique was born.

I began working to refine this theory of overcoming personal pain to empower a performance into a technique. I had to figure out how to help actors find a way to psychologically personalize and feel their character's drive to win as their own.

Once I began applying these concepts, I found the process so personally enriching that it literally took over my life. I began teaching seven days a week, many hours a day. Because I primarily taught and coached working actors, word spread through the professional-acting community quickly. I opened an acting studio. Shortly thereafter, the studio had a rather lengthy waiting list. I never advertised and refused to do any promotion or have my school listed in any of the trade publications for actors. I didn't even have a website. In fact, for a number of years, my studio's telephone number was unlisted. I wasn't being snobby or arrogant, I just figured that if an actor really wanted to find me, they would. Some people went to great lengths to get into my class, sometimes taking months just to get the school's phone number. As a result, I attracted those who were truly dedicated to the craft—whether they were a writer, director or actor. I truly believe that the quality of my students, the majority of whom are committed to working hard and taking risks, has been a part of elevating and advancing my technique.

I have coached thousands of actors on thousands of parts in literally thousands of movies, television shows and plays. These actors are a living (and acting) research lab for my acting technique. I have seen, firsthand, what works and what doesn't. Over time, I have identified the common denominators of what is most effective. When I would see certain approaches succeed again and again, I would develop, explore and refine them until they were easily reproducible. When my actors would get parts or win great reviews and awards, I found that it frequently came from using similar fundamental tools, all rooted in psychology, behavioral science and cultural anthropology—you know, *science*.

Another pattern I've observed over time is that my acting technique has a tendency to bleed into an actor's personal life. To actually *use* adversity as a way to overcome it and win is so inspiring and effective that many of my actors unconsciously incorporate this way of being into their lives, becoming more personally realized and empowered. They take the victimization out of their lives, as they do for a scripted character.

This book will give you the precise methodology for the Chubbuck Technique, which is ultimately a rigorous, step-by-step, nuts-and-bolts script-analysis system. A script-analysis system that will help you to access your emotions and give you a way to not just feel them, but to *use* them with dimension and power. *The Power of the Actor* will show you how to take your conflicts, challenges and pain and turn them into something positive, both from the standpoint of the character you are portraying and the human being behind the character.

Throughout my career as a teacher, I have received from my students many cards, notes and letters expressing their gratitude for the technique, which seems to always change an actor's, writer's and director's life and career. Let this book be my way of saying "Thank you" right back. For I've learned just as much, if not more, from my students—through who they are as people and their diverse life experiences—as they have from me.

PART I

· · · · · · ·

The 12-Step Chubbuck Acting Technique

An actor who merely feels tends to turn his performance inward and does not energize or inspire himself or an audience. An actor who does *anything and everything* to override pain in an attempt to accomplish a goal or an OBJEC-TIVE puts an audience on the edge of their seats, because the outcome becomes alive and unpredictable. Taking action results in risk and therefore an unexpected journey. It's not enough for an actor to be honest. It's the actor's job to make the kinds of choices that motivate exciting results. You can paint a canvas using real oil paint, but if the final painting isn't a compelling image, no one will want to look at it.

This technique will teach you how to use your traumas, emotional pains, obsessions, fears, needs, desires and dreams to fuel and drive your character's achievement of a goal. You'll learn that the obstacles of your character's life are not meant to be accepted but to be overcome, in heroic proportions. In other words, my technique teaches actors how *to win*.

More than two thousand years ago, Aristotle defined the struggle of the individual to win as the essence of all drama. Overcoming and winning against all the hurdles and conflicts of life are what make dynamic people. Martin Luther King Jr., Stephen Hawking, Susan B. Anthony, Albert Einstein, Beethoven, Mother Teresa and Nelson Mandela all had to overcome almost insurmountable struggles in their lives to achieve their goals. Indeed, the greater the obstacles and the more passion these people brought to overcoming their obstacles, the more profound the achievement or contribution they made. They didn't become amazing, accomplished people despite their challenges, but because of them. These are qualities we want to duplicate in characterizations. It's much more captivating to watch someone who's trying to win against the odds than someone who's content to put up with life's travails. A winner doesn't have to actually win to be a winner—a winner tries to win; a loser accepts defeat.

The better you know yourself, the better an actor you'll be. You need to understand what makes you tick, profoundly and deeply. The following twelve acting tools and exercises will help you to dig into your psyche, allowing for discovery and a way to expose and channel all those wonderful demons that we all have. Your dark side, your traumas, your beliefs, your priorities, your fears, what drives your ego, what makes you feel shame and what initiates your pride are your colors, your paints to create with as an actor.

. . . .

The twelve tools:

1. **OVERALL OBJECTIVE:** What your character wants from life more than anything that considers all the scenes in the entire script. The OVERALL OBJECTIVE is phrased as a universal human need or mission. The OVERALL OBJECTIVE is always a primal need, one that is relatable and emotionally driven. This means, in some way, the heart has to be in jeopardy.

2. **SCENE OBJECTIVE:** What your character wants from the other character over the course of an entire scene. This must support the OVERALL OBJECTIVE. The SCENE OBJECTIVE, different from the OVERALL OBJECTIVE, is always phrased as wanting to get something from the other character. In this way, you will always be proactive in your attempt at achieving your SCENE OBJECTIVE.

3. **OBSTACLES:** The physical, emotional and mental hurdles that make it difficult for your character to achieve his or her OVERALL and SCENE OBJECTIVES. You first consider the character on the page's OBSTACLES, and then when doing your personalizations (the next steps), add your personal OBSTACLES that make sense to those choices.

4. **SUBSTITUTION:** Endowing the other actor in the scene with a person from your real life who makes sense to your OVERALL OBJECTIVE and/or your SCENE OBJECTIVE and who will add more history, urgency and desperation. This way you have all the rich and diverse layers that a real need from a real person will give you.

5. **INNER OBJECTS:** The images you see in your mind about a <u>person, place, thing or event</u>—there's always a natural movie that passes behind our eyes when we speak or when we listen. The images you use should make sense to the OBJECTIVES and SUBSTITUTION. Everything must be filled in with INNER OBJECTS so we are activating a true human response.

6. **BEATS and ACTIONS:** A BEAT is a thought. Every time there's a change in thought, there's a BEAT change. ACTIONS are the mini-OBJECTIVES attached to each BEAT that support the SCENE OBJECTIVE and therefore the OVERALL OBJECTIVE. An ACTION is phrased as trying to get the other person to do or feel something so that you can accurately respond to whether or not you are getting it. BEATS and ACTIONS provide different tactics in getting what you want.

7. **MOMENT BEFORE:** The event that happens before you begin the scene, which gives you a place to move from, both physically and emotionally. It provides the how and why, triggering with great urgency and desperation the need to get your SCENE OBJECTIVE. You choose an event that emanates from information based in the script, but you use your real life in executing the MOMENT BEFORE. It should support and make sense to the personalizations you've made in your inner work.

8. **PLACE and FOURTH WALL:** Using PLACE and FOURTH WALL means that you endow the physical environment with attributes from a PLACE from your real life to create privacy, intimacy, history, meaning and reality. The PLACE and FOURTH WALL you choose must support and make sense with your personalizations.

9. **DOINGS:** The handling of props, which produces behavior that allows for us to regroup, find safety, make a statement, expose or hide what we are really thinking, reveal a character's weaknesses and vices, etc. DOINGS also add weight to the scene, because when we are in high-stakes circumstances, it's hard to be still.

10. **INNER MONOLOGUE:** The dialogue that's going on inside your head that you don't—and in most cases shouldn't—speak out loud. Essentially anything you can't say out loud without some version of consequences. The INNER MONOLOGUE must be voiced in your head with detail and in full sentences and generally is informed by your INNER OBJECT choices.

11. **PREVIOUS CIRCUMSTANCES:** A person's history. The accumulation of life experiences that determines who they are—*why* and *how* they operate in the world. First, you do this for the character; then you personalize the character's PREVIOUS CIRCUMSTANCES with what makes sense to your life, thus comprehending more fully—and without judgment—the layers of what makes a human being do what they do.

12. **LET IT GO:** Once you've completed all the steps, you have to trust the work you've done and then . . . LET IT GO. This will allow for organic impulses and surprises of thought and behavior so you have the freedom to truly become, in full glory, the character. And this is where the fun begins.

· · · · · · ·

These twelve acting tools create a solid foundation that will keep you present and inspire a raw, profound, dynamic and powerful performance.

My work with Halle Berry in *Monster's Ball* is a good example of how this technique works. Using one pivotal scene, I'll give you a glimpse of how we used some of the elements of my technique. In this scene, I'll show how we used just a few of the acting tools from my script-analysis system. Keep in mind, we used all twelve steps in the final performance, but to break down each scene using all twelve tools would be a book in itself. So here's a taste, using a few of the tools to illustrate how effective the technique can be.

Monster's Ball is an extremely heartrending story, and Halle's character, Leticia, is a tragic woman. We had to find a way to prevent Halle, as Leticia, from being a victim of her circumstances and thereby becoming resigned to the multitude of tragedies that her character has suffered. In the film, the heartbreak begins with Leticia taking her obese son to his last visit with his father (her husband), who is on death row and about to be executed. Shortly after her husband's death, her son is killed in a car accident, and then Leticia is fired from her job and evicted from her home. As the story evolves, Leticia discovers that her new boyfriend—her one hope—has a horribly racist father. And as if all this wasn't enough, at the end of the film, she learns that her boyfriend was a part of her husband's death and never told her. Leticia is incensed and overwhelmed.

How was Halle going to take these events and not give up? What personal experiences did she have that would relate to her character? How could we possibly make this oppressive story hopeful, thereby allowing her character to win in the end? Once someone gives up the struggle to win, the story is over, leaving an audience unfulfilled. We applied the twelve tools, starting with determining her character's OVERALL OBJECTIVE. Then we found Halle's personal pain that emotionally duplicated Leticia's, and set out to overcome these issues within her performance.

Betrayal Scene

Illustrating the use of OVERALL OBJECTIVE (tool #1), SCENE OBJECTIVE (tool #2) and INNER MONOLOGUE (tool #10).

- The scene: The betrayal is established when Leticia discovers that Hank played a role in her husband's execution and never told her.
- Leticia's OVERALL OBJECTIVE: *"to be loved and taken care of."*

With all that Leticia has experienced in her past and present life, what she needs more than anything is the feeling of safety and support that comes from being loved and taken care of. The SCENE OBJECTIVE has to support the OVERALL OBJECTIVE in order to complete an arc to the entire script and a focused journey for the actor, the character and the audience. This is the last scene in the movie, so she must resolve her journey by defeating her OBSTA-CLES and achieving and *winning* her OVERALL OBJECTIVE. To make this happen, her SCENE OBJECTIVE can't be about the betrayal but how she gets what she wants, which is love. This makes . . .

- Leticia's SCENE OBJECTIVE: *"to make me feel safe in your love."*

The last scene of *Monster's Ball* opens with Leticia discovering her dead husband's drawing of her boyfriend, Hank, in Hank's belongings. The drawing indicates that Hank knew her husband, probably while her husband was on death row, and has never told her. The intention of Marc Forster, the director, was to have an unresolved ending, nothing that was too pat. Although independent and art movies often have dark endings, it is my belief that everyone, even someone who's a part of the art-house crowd, wants to feel hope (*the win*) at the end of a movie. In other words, provide moviegoers with an experience that will allow them to anticipate a joyful resolution in their life dramas the same way Leticia has found one in hers. We couldn't change the script, which didn't support a happy ending, so it was up to Halle's performance to infuse a sense of hope and possibilities.

Hank's omission is a huge betrayal, yet another heartbreak to add to Leticia's long list. For Leticia, this deceit is the straw that breaks the camel's back. She explodes with fury. We wonder if she's going to kill him or herself or both (keeping in line with the director's ideas). By using INNER MONOLOGUE that supported the SCENE OBJECTIVE of *"to make me feel safe in your love"* (not *"I need to feel angry and desperate"*—what person in their right mind wants that?), we changed the ending without changing the director's vision, as it's important that the actor, writer, and director are telling the same story.

To find the INNER MONOLOGUE, we had to personalize Leticia's painful discovery, which helped Halle create her intense rage. In the film, the rage in her face says, "How can he do this to me?!" To make her INNER MONOLOGUE produce a transition from rage to a place of hope, Halle and I talked about Leticia's survival instinct. In this scene, she must fight for Hank's love to be real or she'll die. Leticia could view the discovery as an evil betrayal, which would mean that she would suffer an emotional death, possibly even a physical death. Because of her need to be loved by Hank, she is forced to find a way to perceive his lie differently. It's possible that Hank's motivation for lying wasn't an act of deception, but rather an action taken that expressed an ultimate sacrifice of love. Leticia could rationalize Hank's behavior by thinking, "He could've loved me so much, he was afraid to tell me for fear of losing me once I found out. He was willing to live and be oppressed by his guilty secret because he loved me so deeply. He didn't think he could live without me, so he didn't act out of deceit but out of a great love for me. . . ."

Thus, without words said out loud, strictly by Halle using INNER MONOLOGUE, the audience was able to see exactly what she was thinking and feeling. The arc that was created by her INNER MONOLOGUE began with:

- The surprise of the discovery . . .
- Which turned into a murderous rage . . .
- Which turned into hurt and confusion . . .
- Which turned into a survival need to find a way to change the horror of what she'd discovered . . .
- To actually finding the solution by viewing the betrayal as something positive . . . which allowed her to feel unconditionally loved (a feeling she'd never had before).

All of this is played out in Halle's facial expressions and behavior. In the film, she processes all this before Hank returns. So when Hank comes home and feeds her a spoonful of ice cream on the front porch, she is able to look at him with love in her eyes and to say in her INNER MONOLOGUE, "After all that I have suffered in my life, your love is going to make it all better." Then she looks up at the heavens and, through her INNER MONOLOGUE, thanks God for giving her someone who can love her so well. In this way, we created a fulfilling journey for Leticia as well as giving the audience the feeling that no matter how much tragedy befalls you, there's always hope for change and happiness.

· · · · · · ·

I hope that relating this specific story of the work Halle and I did together in *Monster's Ball* has given you a clearer understanding of the technique. In the same way, I have found in my years of teaching that using case histories from my work with various actors has helped to create a visual that exponentially aided in the comprehension of a particular tool or aspect of the technique. In the following explanations of the twelve tools I will do the same, utilizing a broad range of stories—from actors with Academy Award status, to television, theater and soap opera actors, to up-and-coming actors from my class.

CHAPTER 1

Tool #1:
OVERALL OBJECTIVE

What your character wants from life more than anything that considers all the scenes in the entire script. The OVERALL OBJECTIVE is phrased as a universal human need or mission. The OVERALL OBJECTIVE is always a primal need, one that is relatable and emotionally driven. This means, in some way, the heart has to be in jeopardy.

The OVERALL OBJECTIVE is the tool that gives a script a beginning, middle and end. It defines the journey for the actor as well as for the audience. All the other acting tools must serve and support the OVERALL OBJECTIVE.

To be a poignant and powerful actor, you must duplicate the true behavior of dynamic, powerful people. And these compelling people are always, in one form or another, goal oriented. Many actors fall into the trap of believing that just being real or having real, deep emotional feelings is acting—it is not. Too many actors feel that if they have reached real tears in their work, they have successfully fulfilled the role. It's how you use those emotions to fuel your goal that makes the art of acting exciting to play as well as to watch. Without the goal, without the struggle to win, the purely emotional actor will lack purpose and be a victim to the circumstances of the script, and no one likes to watch a victim be a victim. We want to watch a person change their life, not accept abuse.

An actor must learn to use emotions, not as an end result, but as a
tool to provide the passion to overcome the conflict of the script.

Beyond providing the actor and the audience with something to root for and a journey to travel on, the OVERALL OBJECTIVE also infuses the action with a sense of urgency. As you know, time flies when you're busy trying to get something done. Because the actor is going for his or her goal in the moment and with great passion, it compresses the actor's as well as the audience's sense of time, causing the minutes to tick away faster, making everything a more exciting, anything-can-happen experience. The better the actor is at accessing his life experiences as a way of creating urgency and passion for the goals in the script, the higher the art.

Ask yourself, "What does my character want from life?"
"What is the primal goal?"
This is the OVERALL OBJECTIVE.

The OVERALL OBJECTIVE is the main *need* that drives your character. Your OVERALL OBJECTIVE should always be a basic human need, a primal goal such as *"soulmate love,"* or *"getting my power back,"* or *"being valued,"* or *"to have self-worth,"* or *"to have legacy,"* or *"family."*

All the subsequent tools are there to support the journey (your OVERALL OBJECTIVE) as well as to make it deeper, more crucial, detailed, significant and truthful. Man's survival instinct makes us goal oriented. Our emotional lives come *only* as a result of getting or not getting our goals. Say the OVERALL OBJECTIVE is *"to find love without pain"*—simply said, if you win your goal (OVERALL OBJECTIVE), then you'll be happy; if you lose your goal (OVERALL OBJECTIVE), then you'll be sad and angry.

Emotions are a reaction to an action, not the other way around.

Finding your OVERALL OBJECTIVE first keeps you from having to pump up emotions before you begin acting, and it allows the emotions to emerge in a more natural, human way. It's a lot easier than spending an hour before performing remembering some awful past memory and trying to keep it alive. If you're attempting to pump up emotions from some disconnected place, the result is emotional vomit. And as in life, throwing up is pleasant neither for the participant nor the viewer. It becomes an emotional explosion, accomplishing nothing.

More important, working scene to scene to win your OVERALL OBJEC-TIVE creates real behavior in every scene. As you fight for your character to overcome every obstacle, to achieve the OVERALL OBJECTIVE, real and unique behavior will instinctively emerge in your journey to achieve your goal. Your pure concentration on accomplishing a goal makes you unaware of what you look like, and allows your naturally distinctive mannerisms and quirks to come forward. It's this kind of real behavior that generates in-the-moment tension that makes an audience breathlessly watch and cheer for your character. The audience gets to watch the unresolved emotional and physical OVERALL OBJECTIVE become resolved before their eyes and to relate to it as if it is their own resolution. People will be more likely to support another person if they feel their struggle is the same as their own.

Several years ago, Catherine Keener was studying with me. She has an amazingly rich emotional life to draw from, but at the time, she was using it without the benefit and motivation of an OVERALL OBJECTIVE. In class, week after week, scene after scene, she would put up emotionally wrought performances. But while her classmates and I could see her pain, we couldn't relate to it. We, as her audience, couldn't find a way to understand her feelings, because all of those wonderfully profound and accessible emotions were not attached to a reason—a need to win a goal. Catherine felt that to go after a goal without reservation would result in making her characters manipulative and unlikable. But I see manipulation as a strong and conscious effort to get what one wants. Using manipulation as a way to win an important OVERALL OBJECTIVE actually makes the character effective, and effective people are always very appealing. Just think of Elizabeth Taylor in *Who's Afraid of Virginia Woolf?* or Jude Law in *The Talented Mr. Ripley.* I told her, "Once you know that it's okay to manipulate in your work, *this* is when you'll be truly recognized for your work." At this point, Catherine had a solid acting career, but without public recognition.

As it turned out, it was playing the role of the enthusiastically *manipulative* sexpot Maxine in *Being John Malkovich* that made audiences and critics notice her. Catherine's character was imbued with such a calculated sense of winning and desire that she had to embrace her character's OVERALL OBJECTIVE and I-don't-care-about-anything-else-but-winning attitude. And Catherine's worry that going after an OBJECTIVE without mercy would make audiences hate her was completely unfounded. In fact, it had quite the opposite effect. The audience didn't care that Maxine was a bitch, because Maxine had a justifiable reason to ruthlessly go after her goal, something they could relate to: her OVERALL OBJECTIVE of *"to get my power back."* Audiences identified with her longing, and cheered for her willingness to do anything, to completely debase herself, to claw her way to getting that power back—because clearly her need for present power was a reaction to being made to feel powerless in her past. Because Catherine made the decision to win Maxine's OVERALL OBJECTIVE, she was able to embody and behave as the character of Maxine. As a result, for the first time in her career, Catherine was nominated for an Academy Award and a Golden Globe, and she won the Independent Spirit Award for Best Actress. But beyond the awards, she learned how crucial it was to pursue an OVERALL OBJECTIVE, and it changed her career.

For an actor, the OVERALL OBJECTIVE fills in aspects of plot and gives them a high-stakes, viable way to personalize the role. The OVERALL OBJECTIVE essentially constructs a journey for the actor and the audience. At the beginning of a play or a film, the character (and actor) starts at A, at ground zero. This is where they need to establish the goal they need to accomplish. The rest of the play or film shows how that particular character goes about accomplishing the goal to ultimately earn the right to get to Z.

The script informs the raw material to be analyzed, providing the specific information that makes a character do what he or she has to do. This includes the character's socioeconomic background and history of traumatic events; the geographical location in which the character was born and raised; the time period; the character's history of personal and professional success and failure; the character's dreams; the character's modus operandi; how the character sees themself; and how the other characters view him or her. Then the actor personalizes, duplicating these elements from his or her own life. This will organically generate idiosyncratic speech patterns and behavior.

Your character's OVERALL OBJECTIVE must be worded in a way that establishes a change in their life that is necessary for physical and/or emotional survival.

These are big-picture, universally human issues that can drive a character's journey of an entire script, whether it takes place over the course of one day or spans a lifetime. Examples of OVERALL OBJECTIVES that include basic human needs are:

- To get my power back
- To have children
- Family (for example, to have . . . , to fix . . . , to belong to . . .)
- To find absolution of guilt
- To have legacy
- To be worshipped
- To have self-worth
- To be valued
- To be empowered
- To find purpose (why am I on this planet?)
- To right wrongs
- To be a force of nature

If it's about love, it can't just be "to find love," which is too generic and too large a concept. It must have a specification.

- To find love without pain
- To be loved and taken care of
- To get love in order to get my power back
- To be loved without judgment
- To get love without abandonment
- To be loved in spite of what I did
- To be loved in spite of and because of my flaws
- To find friendship love
- To get love with proof that I won't get hurt (this is in the testing-people category)

If dying and death are what the script is about, that must be verbalized in the OVERALL OBJECTIVE.

- To find love before I die
- To resolve my relationship with my father/mother/sister/brother/
wife/husband/etc. before I die
- To be absolved of my guilt before I die
- To have family before I die
- To make my parent proud before I die

OVERALL OBJECTIVE is not about plot. George Bernard Shaw said that there are no new plots, only new ways for people to negotiate and create relationships. And since every person is unique, *how* they negotiate and create relationships will be special and one of a kind. *How* your character attempts to win their OVERALL OBJECTIVE, which is based in an essential human need, is the journey.

We don't need an actor's interpretation to provide plot.
The script gives us that.

You have to always keep in mind that an audience goes to the theater or the movies or watches television to see human relationships take place. It doesn't matter if the plot takes us to the nonexistent planet of Nebulosa or to a battle in World War II or tells the story of giant roaches wreaking dirty havoc—an audience can always relate to the human element of people attempting to establish, build or negotiate a relationship. This is true no matter what locale or venue it happens to take place in.

In the movie *Out of Time*, Eva Mendes played a cop named Alex, who works side by side with her ex-husband and fellow cop, Matt, played by Denzel Washington, to solve a murder. As she works to solve the murder, it looks more and more like Denzel's character has committed the crime. The story ends with the revelation that he was framed, and they reconcile.

Eva could have worked with the plot's OVERALL OBJECTIVE: *"to solve the crime."* This would be dry, cold and passionless and lacking what an audience really cares about—a human connection. The human equation would be missing. Instead, Eva and I tackled her character using the OVERALL OBJECTIVE *"to get Matt* (Denzel's character) *back and loving me again."* This made it imperative that she solve the case for two reasons. One, she needed to impress him with her prowess as a cop. And two, disregarding her feelings that he might be guilty, she needed to help to clear his name. This OVERALL OBJECTIVE makes Eva's character indispensable in his life—both career-wise and love-wise. In this way, it *earns* her the way to get him back in her life, not just *wanting* him back, but taking viable actions to *get* him back. This also inspired more emotional reactions for her, because every little turn that takes place in the plot creates more conflict for her to overcome in reaching her OVERALL OBJECTIVE of getting him back. This is how the complexities and texturing are infused into a performance. She must confront all of the plot's twists and turns and still be able to accomplish her OVERALL OBJECTIVE. These complexities can emerge only if the OVERALL OBJECTIVE is driven by a simple and basic human need. This enables the actor to keep the experience from being a cerebral, intellectual process and instead turns it into something that is felt in your body.

The OVERALL OBJECTIVE Should Be Simple, Basic and Active

Keeping the OVERALL OBJECTIVE simple and human also creates an arena in which the actor can stop acting and really be in the scene. The most common mistake people make is to make the OVERALL OBJECTIVE too complicated and therefore too complicated to play.

When I was coaching Jessica Biel for her starring role in the remake of *The Texas Chainsaw Massacre*, we faced this very problem. It could have been easy to state her OVERALL OBJECTIVE as *"to want to get away from the crazy guy and keep my friends and myself alive because the murderer is out of control and bloodthirsty and we're just a bunch of young people, and I'm also pregnant and my boyfriend doesn't know. . . ."* It's hard to act out such a complicated, plot-driven goal. Keeping it simple, we came up with the OVERALL OBJECTIVE *"to protect my unborn child."* This allowed her to have an urgent need to survive, because if she died, so would her baby. She could also act from a place that was desperate, hyperaware and primal (it doesn't get any more primal than protecting your unborn child). This OVERALL OBJECTIVE also created more tension and reality in her relationship to the others, especially to her boyfriend, because she thought she couldn't reveal her pregnancy until she felt the future infant would be emotionally safe in the hands of her friends and the father of the child. A simple OVERALL OBJECTIVE allowed her more dimension in what would otherwise have been a hokey horror story.

In the final editing of the remake of *The Texas Chainsaw Massacre*, they cut all references to Jessica's character being pregnant. But although she wasn't pregnant in the version that audiences saw, Jessica, using the OVERALL OBJECTIVE of protecting her unborn child, gave the performance a primal urgency to survive and to save those around her. It didn't matter that we the audience were not privy to her pregnancy, because we interpreted her moves as a dire need to protect her friends and to stay alive. As a result, her acting in what could have been viewed as a generic-horror-film performance was instead heralded, and Jessica received the kind of movie offers (and salary) that she had never received before.

Don't intellectually decide your OVERALL OBJECTIVE.

Instead, decide on three or four—determined from the circumstances of the script—and try them all in rehearsal. By the end of the second page of dialogue, the simplest and most effective choice for OVERALL OBJECTIVE will become obvious.

Hedda Gabler is one of theater's most complex characters. She is often played as an evil, calculating, unsympathetic woman. Judith Light came to me looking for a way to avoid this frequent interpretation. She was preparing for a run at the Kennedy Center in Washington, D.C. Judith and I stepped back and looked at the circumstances of Hedda's life. Hedda's father is a major general who wanted a son to continue the family's military legacy. Of course, at that time, it was impossible for a woman to have anything to do with the military. Having his daughter, Hedda, meant less than nothing to him.

It made sense then to assume that throughout Hedda's childhood, she had overheard her father ardently discuss war strategy and tactics and play war games, all the while ignoring young Hedda. Any child who is shunned by a parent is going to become obsessed with changing that relationship to one of pride, acceptance and, most important, love. Her OVERALL OBJECTIVE was *"to get my father's love."* This OVERALL OBJECTIVE gives a sympathetic rationale for Hedda's harsh and calculating behavior. She is trying to become, even after her father dies, the kind of person her father *could* have loved: a major general.

To accomplish this, I had Judith behave like the major general of the house. With every interaction, conversation and gesture she was at war, moving troops, engaging in subterfuge, spying, convincing Mrs. Elvsted to destroy evidence, etc. The behavior may have been evil, but because Judith worked with a righteous, primal reason—to get a father's love—the audience and critics saw Hedda as a real and vulnerable woman doing what was necessary to win, rather than a calculating woman incapable of love. We found the driving OVERALL OBJECTIVE that would make the most sense for the given circumstances, one that would give her a primal reason to behave so badly. Even the most vicious criminals have a sympathetic reason for their behavior. It's up to the actor to find it.

The OVERALL OBJECTIVE has to be a simple, bottom-line, primal need that will make sense throughout the script.

It doesn't matter how long or short the time frame is in a script (whether it's in real time or spans a lifetime . . . and all that lies in between), your OVERALL OBJECTIVE must provide a coherent and focused "through line." Where your character begins and where your character ends up provide clues as to what your OVERALL OBJECTIVE might be. The OVERALL OBJECTIVE must make sense to every scene that your character is in. This simplifies figuring out what your character's OVERALL OBJECTIVE is by focusing on what drives the character throughout; the best OVERALL OBJECTIVE will be one that supports even scenes without dialogue—every scene counts.

In my work with Aubrey Plaza on the award-winning series *White Lotus*, we had to figure out what her character's OVERALL OBJECTIVE over eight episodes would be—and it had to be true for every scene that she was in. The whole season involved her character, Harper, trying to fix her problematic marriage. We needed to boil that down to a primal reality people everywhere could relate to, and not everyone is married or connected to someone in a similar way. The choices we make should be relatable to anyone watching. And one thing I know from coaching people all over the world is that human beings are human beings, no matter their country, culture, religion, political beliefs, etc. We all have the same issues: fear of abandonment, loneliness, feeling misunderstood, feeling abused, being overlooked, lack of self-worth, etc. And so many people have suffered some version of trauma, like sexual, mental or physical abuse; inappropriate connections with authority figures; deaths of loved ones, etc. Just about any issues you can name, people from across the world have also probably suffered from them. This is why we need the OVERALL OBJECTIVE to be something that everyone everywhere can relate to. It will make your audience, no matter their background, especially engaged and eager to watch you.

What we decided on for Harper's OVERALL OBJECTIVE, which would encompass her entire journey and be a primal need, was *"to be loved again."* Everyone's had the experience of finding love and then losing it in some way. It doesn't have to come from a lover; it could come from the lost love of a parent, a sibling, a friend, etc. Thus, this OVERALL OBJECTIVE is highly relatable. It positions Aubrey as the character of Harper to become an emotional hero as she finds her way through the thicket of problems that her marriage has, and it can bring her husband lovingly back to her. Problems like her husband seeming to like his friend better than her, making the friend more important than she is through most of the episodes. Their sex life has atrophied to the point where he seems to enjoy pornography a lot more than her company. She wonders if he cheated on her. He seems bored and over it. Their problems are obstacles that will become insurmountable unless she pulls out the big guns. Anything to save her marriage and the love of her life.

Even though Harper seemed caustic at times (which makes sense for a woman who needs to be in an emotionally protective mode), we loved and supported her because any behavior—including making her husband wonder if she cheated on him with his friend—was righteous behavior since she was on a mission to get her husband back! It also gave her vulnerability underneath that was so strong; no matter how cynical or sarcastic she seemed, it was all drawn from her love for him and her feelings of abandonment. (Of course, we personalized it to make it even more of a monumental OVERALL OBJECTIVE for Aubrey as Harper to win.)

Harper, who feels unheard and misunderstood, might come off as acerbic, which can result in the character being "unlikable." To avoid that, we also made her needs come from a childlike place—after all, a child will do anything to win and will not be judged for it. For instance, if a child really wants a toy, that child will charm, negotiate, complain, accuse, become the victim, have a tantrum, and in general be a brat . . . and we forgive this behavior because it stems from innocence, a purity of spirit. To go after her OVERALL OBJECTIVE from a childlike place gave Aubrey the innocence to make Harper a sympathetic character. If an adult maintains childlike need and behavior, we are more likely to forgive them. Look at Jack Nicholson in the movie *As Good as It Gets*. He, too, created a character from a childlike place, a character that easily could have been viewed as abusive and cruel if he had played it as an adult. All of this made us root for Harper to accomplish her OVERALL OBJECTIVE with support and love.

Read the Entire Script More Than Once

To find the OVERALL OBJECTIVE for your character in a script, it's important to read the entire script more than once. By doing so, you can determine more specific elements about your character and begin to think about how the other characters relate to and talk about your character, even when you're not there.

Without having read and reread the script for *The Silence of the Lambs*, Anthony Hopkins would never have understood that his OVERALL OBJECTIVE as Hannibal Lecter wasn't about becoming an even more dangerous serial killer; it was to gain the friendship of Agent Clarice Starling (Jodie Foster). The script opens with Lecter testing Clarice to determine if she is worthy of his advice and camaraderie. Hopkins used his character's bizarre and scary behavior as a very effective way to test her—intellectually, emotionally and physically. Hannibal Lecter is a very damaged man, damage that almost always comes from severe childhood abuse. His testing of Clarice becomes necessary as a way to ensure that she won't become an abuser, too. His strange testing tactics are truly the only way to emotionally protect himself. She passes his stringent test. How? Not only does she prove her intellectual and emotional strength, but more important, they come to realize that they have similar emotional demons in their lives to overcome. Both of them have the same "screaming lambs" in their heads but have found opposing solutions to over-coming them—her by saving others, him by killing. The commonality of pain bonds them, and a friendship is formed—a friendship so strong that the audience came to trust that no matter what, Hannibal Lecter would never hurt or harm her. In fact, the bond created by the actors was so effective that at the end of the movie when Hopkins' character quips to Clarice, "I'm having an old friend for dinner," the audience laughs rather than being appalled, even though we know he is going to literally eat his guest. Why? Because the OVERALL OBJECTIVE—"*friendship love*"—made this final comment acceptable and even funny: It was a friend talking to a friend rather than an accomplished and flesh-starved cannibal talking to a rookie FBI agent. Anthony Hopkins' relationship-based OVERALL OBJECTIVE made *The Silence of the Lambs* a movie about friendship between two unlikely people rather than yet another typical thriller film. His OVERALL OBJECTIVE effectively raised the com-merciality, the relevance and the integrity of the film.

It's important to note that Anthony Hopkins also didn't see his character of Hannibal Lecter as a bad man. Hopkins didn't judge his character. He saw his character as someone injured by the PREVIOUS CIRCUMSTANCES of his life, and his serial killing as a retributional reaction to a horrible and painful past. Because Hopkins wasn't burdened by moral judgments, he was allowed the freedom to explore all the facets of a very complex man, therefore creating a very complex performance.

Never Judge Your Character's OBJECTIVES

Noël Coward said, "You can't judge art." Likewise, you can't judge your char-acter or his or her OBJECTIVES. A stupid person never thinks they're stupid. An evil person doesn't think they're evil—they always have a righteous reason for doing what they do. A pimp/prostitute/stripper doesn't necessarily hate what they do for a living or think it's sleazy or wrong. You can't contaminate your canvas with moral doctrines and societal values. Nurturing your values takes energy and focus away from your character and their goals. Art needs room to breathe, with the freedom to discover without restraint. The colors you use in your work have to include a buffet of attributes. This consists of the good, likable parts of who you are, but it also includes the parts that make you bad, the darker elements that reside in all of us. It may make you feel smarmy, but really, it's the darker parts of being human that usually drive us to seek a goal with vengeance, passion and urgency—making the journey taken by the OVERALL OBJECTIVE a more exciting one.

When determining your OVERALL OBJECTIVE, don't be afraid to investigate and use the ugly, darker parts of who you are. You may be playing someone who might, by society's standards, be considered a bad person, but that person feels that what he or she is doing is right. This needs to be reflected in your OVERALL OBJECTIVE. For instance, if the character is a rapist, the OVERALL OBJECTIVE isn't *"to rape people"* but rather *"to get my power back"* from the primal person who, through abuse, took it away. As we'll explore later on in this book, abusers, rapists and killers usually see their victims as symbols or representations of the original person who raped or abused them. So when they act—abuse, rape and kill—they feel they are getting revenge and hurting the person who cruelly took their power away. Striking back at a symbolic tormentor is often the only way the rapist/abuser/killer can cope with their horrible childhood abuse. It's a means for the rapist/abuser/killer to stop feeling like a victim to the childhood abuse and instead feel empowered. This makes the act of raping/killing in a performance justified.

This is true even with the issue of suicide—you can't judge it. To some it is a viable solution to overwhelming and untenable pain. *Leaving Las Vegas* is a story about Ben (played by Nicolas Cage), a man who wants to commit suicide by drinking himself to death and then comes across the path of Sera, a prostitute (played by Elisabeth Shue). I worked with Elisabeth on both her audition as well as the actual movie.

First, we had to get past the audition, which was difficult because the director, Mike Figgis, didn't think Elisabeth was right for the role. His reasoning wasn't groundless. Before this movie, Elisabeth had always played good girls, the girl-next-door type. But Elisabeth really wanted the part and Figgis finally agreed to meet with her. We knew that, at best, it was a charity meeting. It was up to us to change his mind and see Elisabeth as the perfect Sera.

Based on the script, it seemed like Sera's OVERALL OBJECTIVE was *"to *keep Ben from committing suicide and make him want to live."* However, this OVERALL OBJECTIVE judged the act of suicide as something amoral and wrong, which, as you may have guessed, went against my belief about not judging characters and their actions. We played around with a few ideas and then I asked Elisabeth, "What if your Sera saw suicide as a solution for herself, as well, and instead of trying to get Ben to stay alive, she connects with him because they have both found the exact same solution to their pain?" Her OVERALL OBJECTIVE then became *"to find soulmate love,"* a love that emanates from two people sharing the same extreme solution to their unbearable emotional agony. This would change *Leaving Las Vegas* from a depressing, maudlin story about suicide to a great love story. It would be a love story about two people who are going to die soon and who have the urgency to fit what might normally be fifty years of a loving relationship into a few weeks. This made the question that Sera asks Ben in the scripted dialogue—"Why do you want to commit suicide?"—an entirely different issue. Instead of meaning, "Why would you want to do something like that?" which implies judgment, her question means, "Do you have the same reason for committing suicide that I do?" which makes it more about how similar they are and provides for further bonding. Staying in the nonjudgmental mindset, we also made the choice that she really liked being a prostitute—this occupation, after all, would be the only way a person like Sera could experience power in her life, and that's always a good thing.

Elisabeth auditioned and presented our vision of the script to Mike Figgis. This interpretation surprised and intrigued him. He had seen several other actresses and they had all presented the OVERALL OBJECTIVE of Sera as someone trying to save Ben, essentially a hooker with a heart of gold. The result of such an OBJECTIVE is patronizing and demeaning to Ben's course of action. Figgis couldn't get this new vision of Sera out of his head. He not only hired Elisabeth to play Sera against type, but also rewrote the script with her OVERALL OBJECTIVE in mind—two people who find great love fueled by a mutual need to commit suicide. Elisabeth was also able to bring true love and hope to a potentially relentless story of addiction, prostitution and rape. In fact, in his review of the film, Peter Travers of *Rolling Stone* magazine wrote, "The film, directed by Mike Figgis from an autobiographical 1991 novel by John O'Brien, is a tragedy that unspools with astonishing buoyancy and sneaky wit, as if no one told the lovers their story should be depressing." In fact, most of the reviewers echoed one critic's opinion that the film "is a strangely uplifting story about suicide." Elisabeth Shue was nominated for an Oscar, Nicolas Cage won the Oscar, and Mike Figgis was nominated for Best Director and Best Screenplay.

You must analyze the psyche of the character and find a way of making your character feel righteous in his behavior by investigating the probable primal issue(s) that makes your character behave the way he or she does today. You look at the character's psyche and then find out how that duplicates itself emotionally in your life, thereby making the character's amoral, outrageous behavior actually make good sense.

The character of Blanche DuBois in *A Streetcar Named Desire* is one of the most celebrated antiheroes of American theater. Her OVERALL OBJECTIVE is *"to get Stella* (her sister) *away from Stanley* (Stella's husband) *and back to me."* In her attempt to win her sister back, she's willing to lie and steal, but worst of all, she has sex with Stanley, her brother-in-law, by seductively driving him to rape her. Why push your brother-in-law to go this far? Blanche does *anything* and *everything* to win her OVERALL OBJECTIVE, because if she doesn't, she will die. And not just in the spiritual sense—if she can't get Stella to leave Stanley and be with her, she will be penniless, homeless and utterly alone.

Personalize Your Character's OVERALL OBJECTIVE

I worked with Travis Fimmel, who played Ragnar Lothbrok, the legendary character of Viking lore, on the hit series *Vikings*. I find that usually when an actor is doing multiple seasons, their OVERALL OBJECTIVE can, and often does, change season to season. I also find that when personalizing your own OVERALL OBJECTIVE at the time you are acting in the show, the writers will often subconsciously take that into consideration while writing future episodes. The writers intuit your inner work—your specific and triggering personalizations—and write a storyline that lends itself to continuity with your inner work. Originally Ragnar Lothbrok was written as someone who was ambitious and, in the Viking world, wanted to be the leader and worshipped. Exploring and conquering the world for glory. This has never been Travis' personal journey, so we decided to make his OVERALL OBJECTIVE be "*family*." It helped make Ragnar's journey more relatable to the world that we live in today, but it also gave validity to the Viking world where there is very little practical knowledge from written history about the Vikings regarding their existence and motivations. Doing this allowed the viewer to see the Vikings as a substantial culture that viewers could connect with and feel empathetic understanding of.

First, we analyzed the character as written on the page (always step #1). Ragnar has a wife, a son, and a daughter. He wants to make his family proud of his accomplishments. We looked at Ragnar's inherent ambition as achieving success for his family—he wants to be seen as a role model. His family can witness with love and pride Ragnar's exploration and conquering of foreign lands, which no one in Viking history had ever accomplished before. Using Ragnar's familial losses—which include his young daughter's death, his wife's miscarriage of a very wanted baby and the ending of the first season when his wife leaves him taking their young son to a faraway unknown place—made Ragnar/Travis' OVERALL OBJECTIVE of "*family*" make sense. The tearing apart of his family becomes more significant because of his OVERALL OBJECTIVE of "*family*." This leaves Ragnar beyond devasted, as it's not just loss of family, but loss of his ability to prove his value as a father and husband. This gave the creator and writer, Michael Hirst, the ability to be able to build an even richer depiction of a Viking persona. The actor, the writer and the director should always work together as a team—whether subliminally or consciously. After all, the actor, the writer and the director should be telling the same story.

Using Family as the OVERALL OBJECTIVE also allowed for the creation of a very important friendship-love story between Ragnar and the Christian monk Athelstan, who started out as a captured enemy. Athelstan could be Ragnar's friend without judgment, and Ragnar could learn the Christian ways, not necessarily to become a Christian, but to understand the ways of the world. To stay inquisitive would make him more of the type of leader he wants to be, more of a father-figure king (again supporting the OVERALL OBJECTIVE of "*family*") than a figure that inspires fear and terror. This also allows Ragnar to be a mentor to his children and protector of his wife. The scene where Ragnar offers his wife to Athelstan to have a three-way sexual union isn't about sex at all; we saw it more as a way of bringing Athelstan into the family fold. Again, this supports the OVERALL OBJECTIVE of *"family"* and also makes it a more unique and interesting choice for the actor (and audience). Athelstan was supposed to be a small story arc, but these choices made him so important to Ragnar's path of finding his way in the world that he became an integral part of the show over many seasons.

It is important you make decisions first for the character. Then, and only then, do you personalize it.

Ragnar's OVERALL OBJECTIVE could have been *"get my power back,"* *"to be worshipped,"* or *"family."* They all fit. Travis and I chose *"family"* because it replicated his own personal OVERALL OBJECTIVE in life. Therefore, it became easier and more meaningful to the telling of the story.

More than wanting money, or fame, or power, Travis wanted a family to love and to nurture. True art involves making choices; it's up to you to make the most effective ones to explore the hidden truth of the character.

OVERALL OBJECTIVE can also be an opportunity to make a bigger statement, an underlying message that gives the opportunity for universal change.

Creating a truthful performance is important, but sometimes there's even more we can do: We have the platform to change the world through the arts. With OVERALL OBJECTIVE, dealing with a universal problem can be a way to find a solution. Actors have the ability to empower the audience (and ourselves) through our choices.

When I worked with Beyoncé Knowles on *Dreamgirls,* her OVERALL OBJECTIVE served a vital and pertinent mission, as well. Using plot points to guide us, we determined that the OVERALL OBJECTIVE for her character, Deena Jones, would be *"female empowerment."* An essential plot point of the script was that the women in the all-female singing group were being controlled by a man in a male-dominated business. Curtis, their manager, was actively working to destroy Deena's long-term friendship with Effie, who was the lead singer in their original group. His first point of business was to make Deena the lead singer instead of Effie in a divide-and-conquer power move. Curtis was also having sex with Effie while flirting very publicly with Deena. Curtis eventually fires Effie, the coup de grâce in destroying Deena's friendship with Effie. He has shattered the support system that female friendship creates, keeping Deena away from anyone who could love and protect her, which puts her in a position in which she has to rely on him even more. Deena marries Curtis, who proceeds to up the ante of abuse by controlling her every move both at home and onstage. With the music business being in the hands of men in the 1960s, Deena feels she is powerless to do anything about her situation.

All of this leaves Deena isolated and in despair, feeling there is no way out. But for a strong performance, we couldn't allow defeat to be the endgame. By using the OVERALL OBJECTIVE of *"female empowerment,"* she makes the choice to overcome Curtis' abuse and win. This gives the character a solid way to resolve, evolve and earn the right to a satisfying future of her own making. This OVERALL OBJECTIVE also informs her leaving Curtis and her ability to reunite with Effie in the most glorious way, in front of their fans and with spirited music. It makes a powerful statement of empowerment and self-worth not only for Beyoncé as Deena, but also for anyone watching this performance.

• • • • • • • •

Speaking of music, just as a sidebar:

When Beyoncé and I worked on the songs in *Dreamgirls*, we broke each down using the twelve steps. We explored the lyrics as if the song were a monologue. We already had the OVERALL OBJECTIVE and did a proper script analysis of the "monologue" (lyrics) as if it were a regular scene. Using all the tools, we continued to tell the story through the songs as well as through the dialogue. I would hold up a photo of Beyoncé's SUBSTITUTION (tool #4), and she would do her inner work aloud to the photo, then speak the lyrics in the same way an actor does when performing a monologue.

A monologue should be thought about in the same way as dialogue, the difference being the other person isn't vocally responding, although the need to get a response is still there. When we had worked on it enough for Beyoncé to feel truly connected, then, and only then, was it time to add the music. This substantiated the songs as more than just momentary interruptions to the drama of the script, but integral parts of telling the story. Nothing in a script is a throwaway. All can be broken down into making a more important story using script analysis.

And as a sidebar to the sidebar: The thought process of working on a song as a monologue first can be used even if you are singing songs that aren't a part of a script. A couple weeks before Beyoncé's "Single Ladies" came out, from her first album about women's empowerment, she called me and told me to get the album. She wanted me to know that she was proud of how she'd applied the work we had done together. She hoped that this album would help women see that they had been undervalued for far too long. It was something I said again and again in our time creating Deena—that the statement she was making in playing this character was just as essential as being truthful. Artists need to give people hope through choices they make in their work, and pain can be a path to prosperity, emotional or otherwise.

Indeed, it really did resonate with the world as a statement being made to empower those who feel powerless. "Single Ladies" was Beyoncé's first foray into really seeing the bigger picture of change through art, and the success of this album is proof that people embraced it.

The OVERALL OBJECTIVE and SCENE OBJECTIVE are the driving forces of my script analysis technique.

Without OVERALL OBJECTIVE and SCENE OBJECTIVE (which is the focus of the next chapter), there's no need, no point, no consequence, no path and, most important, no beginning, middle or end of a story.

CHAPTER 2

Tool #2:
SCENE OBJECTIVE

> What your character wants from the other character over the course of an entire scene. This must support the OVERALL OBJECTIVE. The SCENE OBJECTIVE, different from the OVERALL OBJECTIVE, is always phrased as wanting to get something from the other character. In this way, you will always be proactive in your attempt at achieving your SCENE OBJECTIVE.

The SCENE OBJECTIVE has to support the OVERALL OBJECTIVE. Each SCENE OBJECTIVE cannot negate the OVERALL OBJECTIVE of the entire script. This is because each scene is a consecutive link, collectively building into one chain that completes the arc of the entire story. If the OVERALL OBJECTIVE for your character is *"soulmate love,"* each successive scene is going to shape your character's path to getting that love. This means that even if your character asks another character to marry your character in one scene, but in a later scene asks that same character for a divorce, the OVERALL OBJECTIVE is still being served. How? Because the second SCENE OBJECTIVE is motivated by your character's OVERALL OBJECTIVE. Your character is not getting soulmate love in his current marriage, so his circumstances have led him to seek love elsewhere. So the divorce doesn't negate the OVERALL OBJECTIVE of *"soulmate love."* It fulfills it.

A SCENE OBJECTIVE is the specific drive of intercommunication between you and the other character within a scene, whereas the OVERALL

OBJECTIVE is the broad strokes of what your character seeks throughout the whole script. The SCENE OBJECTIVE is the precise way that you're going to achieve the OVERALL OBJECTIVE, informed by the dialogue and activity of the particular scene that you're breaking down.

In *Patton*, the OVERALL OBJECTIVE of George C. Scott—who played the title character of General Patton, a major player in World War II—was *"to get his power back"* over anyone, be it his enemy or his troops. In the monologue he made famous, Scott stands in front of an American flag and uses a SCENE OBJECTIVE of *"to empower and inspire you* (the troops)." This motivates Patton's troops to do whatever he asks of them, including die for him. Inspiring this kind of loyalty can't help but make Scott as Patton a more powerful man, thereby making the act of empowering his men to come back at him twofold. By using SCENE OBJECTIVE, a symbiotic relationship is formed in which everyone benefits. Scott could have easily talked *at* his troops, but instead he made this monologue about intercommunication and forging human relationships. This is why it remains one of the most memorable scenes in any war film.

Your SCENE OBJECTIVE Should Be Worded in a Way That Requires a Response

For instance, *"to get you to be my friend."* In other words, something you can *get* from the other person in the scene. Going after your SCENE OBJECTIVE should *include* the other person, which prevents you from talking *at* the other actor—instead, it makes you talk *to* him. In this way you are looking for a re-action, not a sounding board. You must answer the question "Have I worded my SCENE OBJECTIVE in a way that generates a response?" You have to bottom-line your needs, taking out the intellect and wording the SCENE OB-JECTIVE so that it is basic, needy and primal. This will allow you to act from your body, not from your brain. When you are being rational, you are in con-trol. But when the stakes are high—whether you're incredibly angry or sexu-ally charged—your rational brain goes out the window, your body and emotions take over and you end up behaving in a way that often surprises you. "Where did that come from? I'm usually never like that" is the thought that should arise as a result of a good bottom-line, high-stakes, basic, needy and primal SCENE OBJECTIVE. Two examples of a cerebral and rational thought process for SCENE OBJECTIVE are:

- *"I want to figure out how your mind works so that I can see if we have enough in common to fall in love."*

or
- *"I need you to understand why I do the things I do because I was abused as a child and I wonder if you can relate to that."*

As you can see, this kind of phrasing for a SCENE OBJECTIVE becomes too heady and confusing to create a straightforward journey. Stay away from esoteric or overintellectualized concepts. No matter how smart or stupid your character is, primal needs are always the same—they're primal. Albert Einstein and the mentally challenged character of Lenny in *Of Mice and Men* have the same primordial human drives, such as a need to be loved. They just manifest them differently.

You can avoid overintellectualizing your SCENE OBJECTIVE by trying three or four SCENE OBJECTIVES with the dialogue. The one that seems to make the most sense, the one that includes your body and emotions as you're saying the words out loud, is the right one. It will be obvious because the most effective SCENE OBJECTIVE will fit like a glove.

The SCENE OBJECTIVE never changes midway through the scene.

If the SCENE OBJECTIVE changes or feels like it changes somewhere in the scene, you have picked the wrong SCENE OBJECTIVE. A SCENE OBJECTIVE has to make just as much sense at the beginning of the scene as it does at the end in order to have a scene with a beginning, middle and end.

The SCENE OBJECTIVE should be a simple thought process—one that doesn't take a right turn with a new direction and new thoughts by using more than one SCENE OBJECTIVE. The complexities of your acting come from how that particular character manifests his needs. In other words, *how* the part is played will change radically depending upon the unique background, experiences, personality and priorities emanating from the character *and* the actor who is playing the part. It's the who-am-I of the character as well as who you are as a person that brings in the nuances of individual behavior for that character.

The SCENE OBJECTIVE has to be something you can process from your mind, heart, gut and sexuality—simple human needs. And it must be phrased to get the other person to do or feel something, thus creating communication and a proactive forward motion. Examples:

- To get you to fall in love with me
- To make you love me in spite of and because of my flaws
- To get you to love me in spite of what I did
- To make you love me without judgment
- To make you believe in me
- To make you my ally or support system
- To get you to make me feel good
- To get you to give me my power back
- To make you wrong so I can be right
- To make you take the blame so I don't have to
- To make you the bad guy so I can be the good guy
- To get you to give me hope
- To get you to worship me
- To get you to comfort me
- To challenge you to challenge me
- To get you to let me go
- To be the winner over you (make you admit defeat)
- To get you to absolve my guilt
- To empower you to empower me
- To make you fix the relationship (if you feel the other person broke it)
- To get you to prove to me you can love me without hurting me (to test you . . .)
- To get you to prove to me that you can love me without abandoning me (to test you . . .)
- To get you to prove that you are my equal (to test you . . .)

Wording is so important in SCENE OBJECTIVE as it can activate a scene, or just have you sit in your need.

The wrong approach for the SCENE OBJECTIVE would be phrased like this:

- I want love
- I need support
- I need an ally
- I want power
- I want to be right
- I want hope
- I want comfort
- I want to be worshipped
- I want empowerment
- I want to be guilt-free

The second set of examples is wrong because the structure and conceptualization of the wording do not demand a response. You're not affecting the other actor with a SCENE OBJECTIVE worded this way.

Acting is the interplay between people.

There is a powerful difference between someone saying, "I want love," and someone saying to you, "I'm going to get *you* to love *me*." With the first statement, you can shrug your shoulders and say, "Fine, great, good luck, don't we all?" Whereas the second statement *changes* the other person. They are forced to react. They may be ecstatic, destroyed, afraid, but the response will be real. It helps to think about SCENE OBJECTIVE as an affective action you need to take in order to establish a human relationship of some kind.

You have to change the other person to ultimately get what you want.

Your SCENE OBJECTIVE *must* be phrased to require a response. It must affect the other actor in a manner that generates a need within him to give a response. The back-and-forth interplay of two actors trying to win what they need from each other is as exciting as watching a good boxing match. The more powerful the SCENE OBJECTIVE you choose, the more powerful the response and thus the more powerful the scene. Going after a SCENE OBJECTIVE that requires a reaction will always keep you present, because you have no idea how the other actor is going to react. And based on that unknown reaction, you don't know how you're going to respond. It makes the acting work you're doing truly a moment-to-moment experience.

In fact, it might help to actually think about acting as a kind of boxing match. If you're in the ring, you don't know what moves the other boxer is going to use to try to win the match. You only know what the other boxer is going to do when he actually does it. You start the bout with your best punch. The other boxer will respond with, say, an uppercut. You then respond to his uppercut by first taking it in and then countering it with the best counterpunch you've got, trying for the winning edge. The other boxer takes in your response to his uppercut and responds with his own countermove that will hopefully enable him to win and so on. All of the action is present and in the moment.

OBJECTIVE (Whether It's OVERALL or SCENE) Is Your Most Important Acting Tool

Yes, your emotional life is important. But without the sense of movement that an OBJECTIVE gives you and without using the emotions to fuel a goal (OBJECTIVE), your emotions just lie there, a quivering mass of useless feelings. When an actor just emotes, the audience experiences it as a self-indulgent performance. Inner work by itself, without an OBJECTIVE, creates a static emotional arena and scene, because emotions by themselves have no forward motion. Emotions are the *reaction* to an event or stimulus. What you do with those emotions to achieve your SCENE OBJECTIVE is what creates a powerful performance. Let the emotions be the impetus, or motivation, to achieve your SCENE OBJECTIVE, not the end itself.

The first time I worked with Gal Gadot was in a workshop/masterclass I held in Israel. I assigned her a scene from the movie *Hitman* where her character, Nika, was an abused lover of the main antagonist. The other character in this scene was Agent 47—though seemingly the bad guy, he ultimately falls in love with her and saves her life. They don't end up together because Agent 47 was facilitating Nika's ability to feel her value (without having sex, as was her abuser's M.O.) but rather to help her get away and have a new, more empowered life. We determined Nika's OVERALL OBJECTIVE was *"to get my power back"* and the SCENE OBJECTIVE was *"to get you to fall in love with me to get my power back."* This way, we weren't making her the damsel in distress who needs a man to save her; instead, she could use her cleverness to rightfully get what she needs for herself. We saw it as a way to drive what happens to her in the script, instead of letting the circumstances of the script drive her. No matter what circumstances your character is in—good or bad—it's crucial that you drive the end result. Therefore, you must never judge the outcome, but find the strength and empowerment in anything that befalls your character. Being proactive always makes for a more dynamic journey. We watch the driver, not the passenger as a general rule. Especially in a male-driven movie like this, we wanted to make the lone main female character as fully charged as all her male counterparts. These OBJECTIVES allow her to embody that.

The insights that come from using the OVERALL OBJECTIVE of *"getting my power back"* and SCENE OBJECTIVE of *"I want you to give me my power back"* came up again and again in many of the private coaching sessions we were doing, as well. It was something Gal needed to discover, too. Let's face it. It is not unusual for people from all walks of life to have the problem of giving away their power—whether in love or at work or both. Once an actor can understand the importance of empowered inner choices, then it becomes easier to make a more dynamic overall journey. We want to see someone who has hit rock bottom yet finds a way to win in spite of and because of the obstacles.

Coincidentally (or not?) with all the work we did together in making empowered choices via OBJECTIVES that were power based, Gal's star-making role became Wonder Woman.

Always Make the SCENE OBJECTIVE About Relationship—Don't Play the Plot

If all an audience wanted to see was plot, then we wouldn't need actors. We'd just put the script on the screen and let people read. Actors exist to interpret the script by bringing in humanity. This boils down to creating a relationship of one kind or another. Even when someone has a gun to your head, you need to create a relationship with the gun bearer or that person will shoot you as soon as you try to run away. The movie *Misery* exemplifies this. James Caan has been drugged and tied up by a crazy, obsessed, homicidal fan played by Kathy Bates. When he tries to fight her or berate her it only makes her angrier and causes him further physical damage. His character realizes that the only way he is going to survive is by making her believe that he likes her, relates to her and trusts her. By creating a relationship with her, he saved his life.

In the series *The West Wing*, actress Janel Moloney was originally hired as a onetime, possibly recurring guest star to play the character Donnatella Moss, assistant to Josh Lyman. The dialogue on the page was nonrelationship work-place chatter and plot driven. Janel, however, did not see her scenes with her "boss" as a way to be good at her job at the White House (plot) but created the relationship-driven SCENE OBJECTIVE of *"to get you to fall in love with and be sexually attracted to me"* instead. She brought in sexuality because it's a pri-mal need that *everyone* relates to. This is something Janel learned over and over again while doing scene work in my class. Making the SCENE OBJECTIVE involve sex and love opened up a whole can of worms to play with—there's the employee-boss relationship dynamic, which is always risky and dangerous for both because you risk losing your job and having a hard time getting another; then there's the risk that he's married and she's not, which brings the wife in as a potent enemy; and of course, there's the getting your job done properly, which becomes more of a challenge when your mind keeps wandering to thoughts of the flesh. This SCENE OBJECTIVE enabled Janel to take a sim-ple, uneventful character and turn her role into one that was complex, layered and multifaceted, and her character into someone we all could relate to. As a result, she turned that onetime guest-star role into a regular role on a hit series and two Emmy nominations.

SCENE OBJECTIVE gives the scene a beginning, a middle and an end.

SCENE OBJECTIVE gives the scene a focused through line and journey: a beginning, a middle and an end. It also gives a scene a reason for being—it answers the question "Why does this scene exist?" SCENE OBJECTIVE makes the material make more sense by giving each character movement and direction for the emotions and ideas in the scene. Pure emotions by themselves are not part of the human spirit; they evolve from our need to gain or accomplish something. When Djimon Hounsou, who starred in *Amistad* and *Gladiator* and was an Oscar nominee for his role in *In America*, came to me soon after he had just arrived in the United States from Africa (he's originally from Benin in West Africa), he could speak English, but it was not his native language. In class, his scene work was incomprehensible due to his heavy African accent. I knew he was talented and his emotional life was full, but who cares when the audience—the class and I—doesn't understand what the heck he is saying? The breakthrough came when he did a scene from the play *Women of Manhattan*. The scene was about a blind date where Djimon's character, Duke—an African American man—meets his date, a white woman who was never told that Duke was Black. The first run of the scene was confusing because what he was saying was once again incomprehensible due to his exceptionally heavy dialect. He might as well have been speaking Latin. Apparently, Djimon was solely playing his inner work of being uncomfortable with his date's seemingly racist attitude without the aid of a SCENE OBJECTIVE. I told him he needed to have a SCENE OBJECTIVE to make the story make sense. The SCENE OBJECTIVE was *"to make you love me in spite of and because of who I am"*— which would be an effective way to overcome and use his date's bigotry and earn the right to the sex they have at the end of the evening. He did the scene again, but this time really going after his SCENE OBJECTIVE. He used charm, humor, sexuality, availability and challenge. Somehow the accent didn't seem to be a hindrance anymore; the class and I knew precisely what was going on and he got numerous laughs (the play is a comedy) where he had previously gotten nothing but baffled gawking. The point is you can even be speaking a foreign language, but if you have a strong SCENE OBJECTIVE, the other actor(s) and the audience will get it.

Figure Out Where and How the Particular Scene Fits into the Entire Script

A SCENE OBJECTIVE must support the OVERALL OBJECTIVE in order to enable your character to take a journey that begins at A and logically ends at Z. The path must be straightforward and easy to follow for both the actor playing the character and the audience viewing it. This requires you to consider exactly where that particular scene fits into the whole script. Does it take place in the beginning, middle or end? As time progresses in the script, the drama and the stakes rise exponentially. The best way to understand this scene-by-scene buildup is to think about the way a relationship evolves. Let's look at a first date that ultimately ends up in marriage. Say the first scene is the first date. There isn't as much heat in this scene because there is no history between the two characters. On the first date, the stakes come from previous hurtful relationships, not from events that have taken place between the two people on the date. On this first date, the characters are looking at each other, asking, "How are you like my ex who hurt me?" Another scene takes place six months later. The characters are moving in together. Now they have a shared history. There's fear of commitment, fear of getting hurt and tension created from the battles that have happened over those six months. The stakes are higher because each party is capable of hurting the other, potentially causing much more emotional pain than they could have in their first month together. The next scene takes place after they move in together. The woman finds out that the man has been cheating on her, yet she wants to continue their relationship. Now the stakes have become even higher because they both have a tremendous number of obstacles to overcome in order to keep their relationship going. Somehow, this happens. The next scene is the night before the wedding. The stakes are even higher. Marriage is a big commitment. It's forever. All the what-ifs become cruelly apparent: What if he cheats again? What if we have no money? What if I find somebody better? What if he changes? What if she becomes her mother?! As you can see, knowing exactly where a scene takes place helps you more accurately analyze it with the proper minutiae of that moment in time.

Carrie-Anne Moss learned how to see a scene in relationship to an entire script while she was doing scene work in class and put it to great use in her audition scene for *The Matrix*. She had to read a scene that takes place at the beginning of the script, the scene in the film where her character recruits Keanu Reeves' character, Neo, at a nightclub. First, she looked at the entire script and determined her OVERALL OBJECTIVE, which was *"to be empowered."* Then she looked at the scene. Although the scene's dialogue was pure recruitment speak and science fiction technobabble, she made the SCENE OBJECTIVE *"to empower you to empower me."* This enabled Carrie-Anne to establish the beginning of her journey, which would eventually lead her to accomplish her OVERALL OBJECTIVE. Since it took place in the beginning of the script, where the characters of Trinity and Neo have yet to share a history together, her SCENE OBJECTIVE manifested itself in behavior that was emotionally powerful. She made her SCENE OBJECTIVE a human need that required a response, which generated a human interaction. She was one of a handful of actresses who auditioned who didn't play the science fiction plot but established the beginning of a powerful relationship instead. She got the job over hundreds of other hopefuls.

Earn the Right to Get to the End of the Script

An actor also has to keep in mind how the script ends, and earn the right—scene by scene—to get there. If the script ends with you being together with the other character, every scene has to be, in some form, about going after the love. If the end of the script finds you split up, then you must earn the right to break up. In the movie *The Way We Were*, the characters played by Barbra Streisand and Robert Redford end up estranged. Thus, even in the earliest scenes in which they are together, there must be apparent insurmountable differences. In the film, we watch them as they try to address these differences, which need to be dealt with and overcome in order for them to have a healthy relationship. He's a W.A.S.P., refined, gorgeous, and everything comes easily for him. She's Jewish, loud, opinionated, coarse and has had to work very hard to accomplish anything. In their attempt to come together, they find themselves having to give up too much, which contradicts both of their innate needs to grow and evolve as human beings. In other words, they're bad for each other. They both find themselves overcompensating in word and deed and trying to do the impossible: mix oil and water. In one scene, Redford's character goes to

Streisand's character's house to break up with her. However, Streisand's character is doing everything she can to keep him in her life. She offers to change the way she looks; to learn "Gentile" cooking; to live in Los Angeles, which she finds disagreeable; and to be a part of the film industry, which she feels is selling out. When you look at this scene as a separate entity, without seeing it in the context of the full script, it looks as though Barbra's character's SCENE OBJECTIVE would be *"to get you to fall in love with me."* But because they don't end up together and she must earn the right to be separated at the end of the film, the SCENE OBJECTIVE instead becomes *"to make you stay with me at any cost."* This SCENE OBJECTIVE earns the right because it implies that, in time, she's going to grow dissatisfied and resentful of him (and he of her), because they have to change and give up so much of who they are as people to be together. By including the at-any-cost idea in the SCENE OBJECTIVE, it is inevitable that, eventually, the cost will be too high and the only way either of them will emotionally survive will be to separate.

Even if your character dies, it's often the case that you must earn the right to die.

In other words, as opposed to seeing your character as a victim, you can find a way to make your character's death a choice. In this way the character constructs a death with dignity. You also have to use the knowledge of your character's looming death for the SCENE OBJECTIVE in the scene when the character is dying or dies. I worked with Cody Fern on *The Assassination of Gianni Versace: American Crime Story*, where he played David Madson, the boyfriend of Andrew Cunanan, the man who killed Versace.

Andrew Cunanan ultimately kills David Madson. Cody and I both agreed that he wouldn't play David Madson as simply a victim of homicide. We could've focused solely on the true fear David experienced, but we wanted David to be an empowered person by making it his choice to be killed by Andrew. David's journey in the script includes Andrew forcing him to watch as he brutally murders a man who had a crush on David. There are later scenes when they are in a bar eating, in hotel rooms hiding, driving in a car together—all essentially a journey for David that most actors would make as one of fear and terror. We decided to view his death as something that could (through personalizations) resolve some specific shame-inducing issues for Cody. By playing someone who seeks to be killed, he is killing off the shame that was getting in Cody's way. (This is the concept of ENERGY KILLS, which is discussed in more detail in chapter 16, Playing a Killer or Someone Who Is Killed.)

We established that Cody's SCENE OBJECTIVE in the scene where David is actually killed was *"I need you to kill me."* And in preceding scenes we built up to that with OBJECTIVES like *"I want you to fall in love with me so I can break your heart"* and *"I need you to want to kill me"* (which worked because David broke Andrew's heart in the previous scene, which would motivate Andrew to want to harm him). This creates a story arc that leads us to the last SCENE OBJECTIVE for the main scene of *"I need you to kill me."*

Cody's choices were undeniable, and the writers subsequently felt the need to write more in for him. What started as a one-episode part became a role that carried throughout half the season! They also wrote a lovely memory scene inspired by Cody's inner choices for David/Cody as David is dying. This made the death scene one of heartfelt resolution and peace. All this from inner choices Cody made to take the victim out of playing a victim, and from using actions normally considered depressing and sad as a way to celebrate the human spirit, showing that even when the worst happens, you can spin anything into something to prosper from. Especially in the world of fantasy and art, since no one is killing anyone and no one is actually dying—it's just acting.

You're probably wondering, "Well, what if my character doesn't know he's going to die at the end? How can my character know they will be in an accident, or get terminal cancer, or die from any type of impending death that isn't obvious?" While it's clear that actors must use their five senses to re-create human behavior, they must also rely on their sixth sense, which is an honest and viable tool. Somehow, we always know when danger or tragedy is about to strike. An actor must develop and use their sixth sense in tandem with the other senses to create the fullest performance. If some huge tragedy befalls your character, have some sense that it's going to happen and make those adjustments to your SCENE OBJECTIVE. In *The Godfather II*, Fredo, Michael Corleone's brother, is murdered at Michael's request. While alive, Fredo has to be constantly aware that Michael is capable of killing even his own brother. He thinks about this every time he screws up, which in Fredo's case happens a lot. A SCENE OBJECTIVE like *"Love me in spite of what I did"* might just help to keep his brother from fitting him with cement shoes. An actor playing Fredo must maintain conscious contact with the idea that he could be murdered at any and every turn. This SCENE OBJECTIVE will cause intensified feelings of fear and panic (which are justified in a Mafia environment), which would, in turn, create more dramatic results even in the brothers' large group scenes where Fredo's follies are not the focus. This enables the character to stand out in a scene, even if it's a scene that isn't in any way about the character. Never think that any scene is a throwaway because it's not "written" about you. If your character is in the scene, there's a reason for it. It's up to you to *find* it.

If you kill someone, you must earn that, too.

David Mamet's play *Edmond* is material I frequently use in class because it is a good illustration of how to play a serial killer (the kind of character that seems to be in so many movies and television shows). In one scene, the character of Edmond has sex with a girl he's just picked up. After the sex, Edmond tries to provoke her, to push her buttons so that she'll become enraged, say horrible things, act out terribly and therefore deserve to be killed. The SCENE OBJEC-TIVE is *"to get you to deserve to die."* He tries being bigoted, violent, conde-scending, and making her feel stupid. None of it works. Finally, he puts her down for never having worked as an actress even though she calls herself one. Under the guise of helping his victim face her reality, Edmond says, "Say it: 'I am a waitress. . . . I am a waitress. . . .'" But Edmond's true intention is to goad her to explode with rage. And lo and behold, it works—she becomes a human cherry bomb. She furiously and viciously acts out (just as he in-tended), thereby justifying Edmond's SCENE OBJECTIVE. From his point of view, she now deserves to be killed, and he's just the guy to do it. (This is also discussed in more detail in chapter 16, Playing a Killer or Someone Who Is Killed.)

Don't Judge Your SCENE OBJECTIVE

Don't contaminate your choices with societal views, morality or personal issues. That judgment becomes a form of censorship. And censorship contradicts art.

Sometimes what looks like a horrible situation can be viewed as something positive. If your character gets beaten up at the end of a scene, there's a really good chance that he or she wanted it that way. In *Raging Bull* there's a scene where Jake LaMotta questions his wife, Vikki, about where she's been all afternoon. She lies. They're obvious lies that intimate she's cheating on him. Vikki doesn't have to lie. She wasn't cheating and has witnesses to prove it. Yet she tells the kind of insinuating lies that she knows will make Jake's blood boil. Why? She wants him to hit her because after the beating, they'll have sex, violent sex—just the way they like it. It's the game they play, their special game that makes their relationship thrive . . . for them. And because the abuse will help her get what she wants, it becomes a positive act. Her SCENE OBJECTIVE is *"to provoke you to violence to inspire lovemaking."*

Even when you're playing someone who appears to be a shy, unassuming character whose behavior seems inactive, you must use SCENE OBJECTIVE.

The character of Laura in the classic play *The Glass Menagerie* illustrates this. At first glance, Laura looks like a shy, put-upon woman who doesn't want anything. But if you read deeper, you'll see that Laura has great desires and actually uses her shyness to get what she wants. Throughout the play she accomplishes a great deal by utilizing her timidity: She gets out of going to her typing class; she keeps her brother living at home with her; she makes her mother continue to financially support her; and she gets a date with a guy she's always had a crush on. She gets all this done by using her incapacity, her fear and the victimization of her crippled leg to make people take care of her and love her. In the gentleman-caller scene she is victorious in her SCENE OBJECTIVE of *"to get you to love me to make me feel special."* He talks to her, he gives her advice, he opens up to her, he tells her he likes her, he dances with her and he kisses her. She gets what most women would consider to be a successful date. Laura's success is driven by her ability to use her supposed weaknesses to get what she wants.

There's always a goal, or a SCENE OBJECTIVE, when you are communicating and conversing with someone else. Always.

Your SCENE OBJECTIVE will never be *"to get you to leave me alone"* or *"to make the other person leave."* If a conversation is more than two sentences, then you must have a reason to want to engage in dialogue with that person. Think about how you behave in your own life. If you really want to leave, you leave. If you want to split up with someone and your mind is made up, the easiest way out is to send a letter, e-mail or text, something that doesn't require being there emotionally or physically. That's how I extricated myself from my first husband: I left a letter on his bureau while he was away having one of his multitudinous affairs. If you bother to have a long, involved conversation, then it's clear that there's something more that needs to be resolved. Perhaps you don't want to split up after all (S.O.: *"to make you want me back"*), perhaps you want closure or peace of mind (S.O.: *"to make you take the blame so I don't have to"* or *"to get you to give me my power back"*), or perhaps you want that person to suffer—payback, of sorts (S.O.: *"to make you feel guilty"*). In any of these cases, there's a reason to stay in the room or need the other person to stay.

Always Make Selfish Choices

We always do more to get something when it involves something for ourselves rather than for someone else. To help another selflessly can make you feel good, but it doesn't have heat to it because there's nothing personally at risk for you. You can be helping a friend with a problem with the SCENE OBJECTIVE of *"to make you feel better."* But what do *you* get out of it? However, the SCENE OBJECTIVE *"to get you to feel better so you'll love me"* gives you something in return for all your hard work. It also gives you the possibility of failure. If you can't make the other person feel better, then there's a good chance that person won't like you. The apprehension that your attempt at gaining your SCENE OBJECTIVE may or may not succeed keeps you anticipating the worst, and therefore you keep trying harder and harder. This takes the ordinary and turns it into something extraordinary. Joan of Arc is a historical figure who has been realized again and again in art, theater and film. The essence of this woman's story is that she hears voices from God and believes that she's been put on this Earth to connect God to the masses. Imagine watching two hours of a performance that reveals Joan of Arc as a woman who is fully confident in her voices and her belief that she's there to help people by bringing them religion. It makes Joan of Arc seem patronizing and superior. That's because, in this light, there's no vulnerability, no human side to seeing her story. Conversely, imagine that same woman who, through painful life experiences, has become so desperate to make people love her that she *needs* to believe in those voices, *needs* people to follow and worship her—in fact, her *needs* are so dire that she's even willing to die the horrible death of burning at the stake to realize her SCENE OBJECTIVE of *"to make you* (everyone she comes across) *worship me."* This brings in the possibility that she might personally question her voices, but won't allow herself to disbelieve, because not being connected to God would eliminate any reason for people to adore her. And that simply cannot happen. Now, that's dramatic!

SCENE OBJECTIVE works for commercials, sketch comedy and cartoon voices.

If you are acting using a SCENE OBJECTIVE, you are creating a relationship. It doesn't matter what the medium is—from high drama to sketch comedy, a commercial or even a cartoon. SCENE OBJECTIVE will make the sketch funnier, the commercial more effective and the cartoon voice more real, because it brings in the human equation, thereby making it universally appealing.

When Rob Schneider was on *Saturday Night Live*, he had a very popular recurring character: Rich the Copyboy. Basically, Rich would sit by the copy machine waiting for a coworker to enter his enclave, and then chat away. If, for example, the coworker was named Sandy, Rich would welcome her with, "Sandy! The Sandster . . . making copies . . . Sandarama . . . Sandana . . . needing a Xerox . . ." and on and on until Sandy would get annoyed and walk away. When I discussed this character with Rob, we didn't address his behavior as a bigger-than-life comedic character, but as a frightened and very lonely man. We decided that the character of Rich is a guy who goes home alone, lives alone and dines nightly on home delivery—not for the food but for the company. One can imagine Rich answering the door and exclaiming, "Pizza Man, delivering a pizza! The Pizza Manster! The Pizza Pie-arama! . . ." until the pizza man flees, eardrums aflame from Rich's constant babble. Now this is a lonely guy. I told Rob that Rich was acting out because of his terrifying loneliness.

Rich's only human contact was when someone would come to him to make a copy, so he had to make the most of each short visit. The humor of these sketches emanated from his desperation and his willingness to do *anything* (no matter how silly or strange) to get his SCENE OBJECTIVE of *"to get you to be my best friend."*

There is a SCENE OBJECTIVE in every scene—NO EXCEPTIONS!
And with that in mind...

OVERALL OBJECTIVES and SCENE OBJECTIVES are the most important tools!

All the following tools that you're about to read and learn are solely to make your OBJECTIVES more real and more urgent. You must figure out your OVERALL OBJECTIVE and then each SCENE OBJECTIVE before filling in any of your other choices. In this way, you are driving a scene by a goal, making it active and interactive.

Do NOT do your inner work first and then try to layer
OBJECTIVES on top of it—cart before the horse, as they say.
If you do this, the SCENE OBJECTIVE ceases to drive the scene.

Once you've figured out the best, most effective OVERALL OBJECTIVE and correlating SCENE OBJECTIVES, the rest of the choices you make regarding the other acting tools will be easy—they'll fall into place in a logical manner.

CHAPTER 3

Tool #3:
OBSTACLES

> The physical, emotional and mental hurdles that make it
> difficult for your character to achieve his or her OVERALL
> and SCENE OBJECTIVES. You first consider the character
> on the page's OBSTACLES, and then when doing your per-
> sonalizations (the next steps), you add the OBSTACLES that
> make sense to your personal choices.

OBSTACLES give power and intensity to your OBJECTIVES by making your goal harder to accomplish. If your OBJECTIVES have risks to them, then they bring physical and emotional jeopardy and danger to the goal. Climbing Mount Everest is a much more exciting story to play (and to watch) than climbing a hill on a sunny day. Mount Everest has the danger of avalanches, thin air, and a misplaced foot that could bring death to the player. The hill on a sunny day has virtually no risk. While they are both goals, one has much bigger and more compelling OBSTACLES.

Winning is only satisfying when there is a possibility of failure.
The possibility of failure emanates from OBSTACLES.

First, you must figure out the OBSTACLES that make sense to the charac-ter in the script and your OVERALL and SCENE OBJECTIVES. Then you can go back through the scene and personalize them, making the OBSTACLES make sense to *your* life. For example, if you're working with a seduction scene, the character's OBSTACLES might be rejection, specific sexual inadequacies, self-worth issues, body insecurities or a history of past hurts from other mates or lovers. Once you've identified your character's OBSTACLES, then you must find personal OBSTACLES that correlate to your personal and unique history, which might include rejection, sexual fears, body image. (The part of your body that you hate the most—breasts, chest, legs, arms, whatever. Pick one. The worst one.) Are you shy, overbearing or submissive? How does it get in your way? Do you have weight issues, a chronic bladder infection or smelly feet? OBSTACLES are both internal and external. They are *anything* and *everything* that get in the way of your OBJECTIVES.

Attempting to overcome OBSTACLES, large and small, to finally achieve your OVERALL and SCENE OBJECTIVES is what generates heat and the stakes in your acting and the script.

Using OBSTACLES Creates the Challenge

The more difficult and risky it is for you to realize your OVERALL and SCENE OBJECTIVES, the greater the journey for you as an actor as well as for your audience. The more OBSTACLES you put in a scene, the harder you work to get your SCENE OBJECTIVE. A scene begins. Your character begins to confront and try to overcome the innate OBSTACLES in their SCENE OBJECTIVE's path. The scene progresses. Your character continues to attempt to overcome the many OBSTACLES that come up along the way. As the scene progresses, the more your character tries to overcome the OBSTACLES but can't, the harder they're going to try. This effort creates the "arc" of a scene. Working with OBSTACLES keeps the intensity growing, driving the need and meaning of the scene, which eventually brings it to the crescendo that all scenes must have. It's also true that the more difficult it is to achieve a goal, the more satisfying it is to accomplish it and to watch the character doing so.

OBSTACLES generate the difficulty that makes
for a more dramatic result.

Think of the snake scene in *Indiana Jones and the Raiders of the Lost Ark*. The character of Indiana Jones was deathly afraid of snakes, yet he had to cross mounds of large, scaly, writhing serpents to escape. Without the audience's knowledge that Jones had a horrifying phobia of snakes (physical and emotional OBSTACLE), his crossing of them would have been uneventful. Yet bringing in the fear of these gruesome and often misunderstood creatures made the scene terrifying and Indiana Jones heroic.

It would be fruitless (and endless) to list every possible OBSTACLE you may encounter in script analysis. Anything and everything that is a hurdle or creates conflict is an OBSTACLE. Nonetheless, most OBSTACLES fit into one of three categories: physical, mental and emotional.

Physical OBSTACLES

- **Physical disability:** Broken limbs, limps, paralysis, palsy, tics, blindness or visual impairment, deafness, impotence.
- **Race and religion:** Racism, religious issues, religious rivalry.
- **Physical-size extremes:** Short, too tall, fat, skinny, penis too large or too small, breasts too large or too small, nose too large.
- **Appearance:** A burn victim, ugly or too beautiful and therefore unapproachable, too old, too young, body dysmorphia, age differences.
- **Financial:** Too rich, too poor.
- **Mind altered:** Are you stoned, drunk or high? Do you have an addiction—such as to heroin, cocaine or alcohol—that needs to be overcome?
- **Medical:** Are you dying or is someone you love dying? Organ problems? Genetic health issues? Do you have to overcome the death of a loved one, the loss of a limb, an abortion, a degenerative disease?
- **Professional:** Dangerous professions such as being a cop, prostitute, secret agent, member of the military, drug dealer, gangster, bank robber. Or high-stress occupations such as a job in high finance, politician, big business executive, actor, lawyer, sports player, student, salesman, doctor, teacher, journalist, psychiatrist.

- **Social status:** Being an immigrant, member of a different class, homosexual, victim of gossip.
- **Place:** A haunted house, a dark imposing alley, a concentration camp, a place that contains a killer, a place riddled with physical hurdles, a place that reminds you of a traumatic event, an unfamiliar and faraway locale.
- **Event:** War, giving birth, graduation, a high school reunion, a deadline for owing money to a loan shark or drug dealer, gang war, a wake, kidnapping, unintentional homicide, rape, vengeance, a birthday, a contest, unwanted pregnancy, getting married, divorce, an affair, the Depression, dying on death row, getting caught for a crime.

Mental OBSTACLES

- **Brain capacity:** Too smart, too analytical, too stupid, developmentally disabled, overanalytical, on the spectrum.
- **Political beliefs and principles:** Fighting the system, being true to your ideals, pushing the envelope, risking your job, stability and life in standing by your character's beliefs.
- **Mental illness:** Phobias, split personality, schizophrenia, depression, OCD, paranoia.
- **Secrets and lies:** Having a secret, keeping up the lies.
- **Formal education or lack thereof:** Educational disparity—one character is educated; the other is not.

Emotional OBSTACLES

- **Relationship issues:** Intimacy issues, history of love gone wrong, history of family problems, history of problems with a friend, history of problems in the marriage, pent-up rage, sibling rivalry, history of problems with the ex-mate, obsession, racial issues where there is love involved, jealousy, history of parental problems, incongruent personalities, history of cheating or being cheated on, unrequited love, ruthless rivalry with someone of the same gender.

- **Personal problems:** Greed and extreme ambition, shyness, self-loathing, overbearing and controlling, feeling like a loser, abandonment issues, history of promiscuity, guilt, overwhelming anger, being a virgin at an older age, being antisocial, loneliness, history of self-sabotaging behavior, paranoia, fear of being judged.
- **Deviancy:** Homicidal tendencies; incest; violent tendencies; incestuous obsessions; issues stemming from past abuse, rape or molestation; other people's perceptions of a sexually deviant predilection.

· · · · · · · ·

Anything that creates a hurdle, conflict, barrier or a stumbling block to accomplishing your OVERALL and SCENE OBJECTIVES is fodder for being an OBSTACLE.

The Graduate is riddled with OBSTACLES in all the categories for both Mrs. Robinson and Benjamin.

Mrs. Robinson's OVERALL OBJECTIVE: To Have Self-Worth

Mrs. Robinson's OBSTACLES.

- Benjamin might reject her. (The possibility of failure, the possibility that you might not get what you want, will always be an OBSTACLE in every script you analyze.)
- She's much older than Benjamin, which means that she's going to feel uncomfortable about her body. She'll compare herself to someone his age who would have an unlined, firm, lean body with perky breasts versus her wrinkles, sagging skin and cellulite.
- Her husband hasn't touched her in a long time, making her needy for some male attention. This combined with her age issues makes for a very real fear of becoming that genderless age when women go from beautiful to "handsome."

- Benjamin is her neighbor and best friend's son. If this doesn't work out perfectly, Benjamin could tell others. As a result, she would lose her husband and social standing and generally become ridiculed.
- Benjamin falls in love with her daughter, Elaine. This heightens the risk of Elaine finding out about the affair. It would destroy Mrs. Robinson's relationship with her daughter.
- She may be discovered by friends, neighbors or a nosy acquaintance at the hotel where the sexual rendezvous takes place.
- She becomes attached to him. Maybe even falls in love with him, making it extremely difficult to give him up or to endure his love for her daughter.
- Her love for Benjamin also makes her jealous of his love for her daughter. It is not uncommon for jealousy to be an integral part of a mother-daughter relationship.

Mrs. Robinson's attempt to overcome all these OBSTACLES substantiates her OVERALL and SCENE OBJECTIVES.

Benjamin's OVERALL OBJECTIVE: To Be Worthy of Love

Benjamin's OBSTACLES (with regard to Mrs. Robinson).

- Possible rejection.
- He's much younger than Mrs. Robinson. He is intimidated by her sexual experience and knowledge and his comparative lack of it. Will he ejaculate too quickly? Will he be able to get an erection? Will he touch her in a way that doesn't seem mature and intelligent?
- His lack of knowledge. What will they talk about? Will he seem idiotic and naive?
- She's his mother's best friend, which makes having sex with Mrs. Robinson almost incestuous.

- She's watched him grow up. She knows way too much about him. She knows every embarrassing moment and event that has happened in his life—if he was a bed wetter or was considered a nerd by his peers or spent his childhood eating boogers, she'd know.
- His fear of their affair being discovered by Mrs. Robinson's husband, Benjamin's parents and Mrs. Robinson's daughter, Elaine.
- When he falls in love with her daughter, Mrs. Robinson wages an all-out war against him.

As you can see, Benjamin's OBSTACLES coincide with Mrs. Robinson's, but come from a different point of view. When you are breaking down a script and looking for OBSTACLES, find as many of them as you can—physical, emotional and mental—because the more OBSTACLES a character has to overcome, the more intricate the performance.

The OBSTACLES you infuse into your work should always be the hardest, the most demanding, problematic and challenging.

The more difficult it is to win, the more satisfaction you feel when you have achieved the goal. The OBSTACLES give you the difficulty factor. A challenging OBSTACLE makes you fight more passionately. You'll do more if you have a mountain of OBSTACLES to overcome, making your journey to reach your OVERALL OBJECTIVE, through your arc of SCENE OBJECTIVES, that much more moving.

OBSTACLES produce desperation, and desperation creates comedy.

OBSTACLES are there to heighten and intensify the drama, and the more OBSTACLES you have to overcome in realizing your SCENE OBJECTIVE, the more desperate you'll be in going after that SCENE OBJECTIVE. In the name of wanting something really badly, we often find ourselves behaving in a silly, crazy and outlandish manner. Think about that date you had when you really, really liked a person and wanted to impress them. Of course, the slicker and cooler you tried to be, the more awkward and stupid you became: tripping, bumping into walls, using the wrong doors, blurting out inane comments, spilling on yourself and/or the other person, breaking something and on and on.

Even something as seemingly trivial as passing gas can, in the wrong circumstances, be devastating—a potent OBSTACLE, if you will. Michael Richards' character of Kramer on *Seinfeld* had all kinds of comic behavior. But his motivation wasn't to be funny. His behavior came from his urgent and desperate desire to accomplish his character's frequently used SCENE OBJECTIVE of *"to make you* (Jerry) *love me."* While they were taping one episode, Richards passed gas while in character as Kramer. Jerry was across the room when it happened, so Richards felt it was safe to stop clenching and let 'er rip. Unfortunately, Jerry decided to come over to Kramer's side of the room at the exact time of the gaseous detonation. Knowing that his silent-but-deadly gas bomb would turn Jerry off, Richards, staying in character as Kramer, frantically and frenetically began to fan the air behind his rear end. Each time Jerry tried to get near Kramer, Kramer scooted away and fanned his behind. Humorous behavior was created by Kramer's desperate need to overcome a reeking OBSTACLE in order to attain his SCENE OBJECTIVE.

Just think about Jim Carrey's high-comedy role as Lloyd in *Dumb and Dumber*. Everything was an OBSTACLE, because everything was hard for Lloyd to do, because he had to overcome the OBSTACLE of being dumb(er).

OBSTACLES help you better understand the motivations of your character.

When I began to work with Kat Graham on the hit TV show *The Vampire Diaries*, the producers were ready to kill off her character, Bonnie, mid–season one. Her part was written as a weak woman who, though she had the power of a witch, seemed never to use it for her own benefit. She was always selflessly helping others and sacrificing herself for her friends—and with very little gratitude from the other characters. Bonnie didn't have a love interest to obsess over or who obsessed over her (as most of the other main characters did).

Kat made the choice, as most actors would given a similar role, to accept the weakness of the character. It is not unusual for actors who play characters who are written as powerless to find the truth in that weakness as a flaw that they simply must portray. And that is what Kat was doing, a truthful, heartfelt and honest portrayal of a young woman who was dealing quietly with the hand that she had been dealt. The problem with that thought process is that it doesn't excite an audience. We revel in watching a person attempting to overcome such things. This is where OBSTACLES come in.

Instead of leaving her to be crushed under the weight of what had become Bonnie's cross to bear, we made all the elements that expressed her powerlessness into OBSTACLES in her quest to overcome and accomplish her OVERALL OBJECTIVE. The OVERALL OBJECTIVE that helped her journey to overcome her character's weakness was *"to find empowerment and value."* What Bonnie had to endure didn't have to be her destiny. Bonnie could now see these OBSTACLES as motivation to find solution and resolution. She could see that whatever was attempting to destroy her was unacceptable. Instead of Kat having Bonnie accept her fate, she played her as motivated to change that certain path of destruction into a path of empowerment. Once she started playing it this way, she became an emotional hero for all those fans who feel that they, too, have suffered at the hands of others; and she created a strong and devoted international fan base and a mainstay character for the duration of the long-running show. Watching Bonnie do something about her situation—or at least try to, since it's the effort we applaud—gave fans of *The Vampire Diaries* hope that they could do the same.

All of Your Character's OBSTACLES Are Not Necessarily Written in the Script

When determining your character's OBSTACLES, some will be obvious—they'll be written in black and white on the pages of the script. Others you'll find by conjecture and supposition based on the facts of the script. But even when it seems that your character has no OBSTACLES, it's up to you to find them. Without OBSTACLES and conflict, your character's journey to accomplish the OVERALL OBJECTIVE and SCENE OBJECTIVE will be too easy and therefore unsatisfying. It's stimulating to watch a storm and very dull to watch the calm.

When I was working with Tasha Smith on Tyler Perry's *Why Did I Get Married Too?* her character, Angela, was written as a loud woman who was overwhelmed with jealousy. But Angela's behavior was crazier than her backstory, making for a character who could easily have come off as an irritating hot mess.

Sure, Angela was jealous—her husband, Marcus, had cheated in the past, leading to her unraveling. But the intensity of Angela's actions was far beyond anything that would be motivated by mere jealousy. What's on the page has to be substantiated by OBSTACLES that help her outrageous behavior make sense, allowing the audience to support her and maybe even laugh with recognition. We needed to find more OBSTACLES buried within the plot facts in the script.

- **FACT:** Angela is a hair stylist who owns her own shop. The shop hasn't been doing very well.
  - **Assumed OBSTACLE:** Marcus (her husband) gets a job as an on-air host of a successful sports TV show. Comparatively, she feels like a loser. Why would Marcus want a loser for a wife?

- **FACT:** Marcus was a football player, and like most sports figures, he had rabid fans.
  - **Assumed OBSTACLE:** He cheated when he was a football player, so now that he has an even more visible top-tier job, it's likely to happen again. How can she compete?

- **FACT:** One of her best friends, Patricia, is a famous author and psychologist.
  - **Assumed OBSTACLE:** Yet again, Angela feels like a loser. Both her husband and her best friend are respected public figures, and people must think she is just a hanger-on. She feels invisible. Being loud and out of control keeps that from happening. She thinks along the lines of: "I may be in the shadow of these stars, but you can't ignore my presence. No matter how hard you try."

- **FACT:** Angela is a woman in her forties. Age is always an issue, especially for women. Men often see youth as value and therefore a young woman is worth more.
  - **Assumed OBSTACLE:** The fear that Marcus will leave her for someone younger, or at least not find her attractive anymore. Also, if Marcus does leave her, Angela's options to regroup and find another love are limited. She's terrified. Thus, all the

obnoxiousness can really be the actions of a terrified person. Fear can make people act out.

- **FACT:** Not only has Marcus cheated in the past, but he won't give her the password to his phone.
  - **Assumed OBSTACLE:** Angela has trust issues. It might seem over-the-top to make this one thing—Marcus stubbornly not giving her the password to his phone—such a big deal. I mean, she talks about this throughout most of the movie. But because she's been cheated on and has no self-worth or successful job, she finds herself obsessing about it.

- **FACT:** Angela (and Tasha) was born and raised in Camden, New Jersey, which is referred to in the movie as a "ghetto." By its very nature, a ghetto is rife with poverty, oppression and bigotry.
  - **Assumed OBSTACLE:** Responding to her oppressive childhood environment, she was always in survival mode, resulting in her confrontational behavior.

In addition to finding OBSTACLES, we can gather from these facts that an effective OVERALL OBJECTIVE for Angela would be *"to be a force of nature."* This also allows us to support her and see her wild behaviors as justified.

It's always essential to look beyond the OBSTACLES that are clearly written in the script. Be a detective, glean from the facts of the plot and from the reactions of others to your character's behaviors. You can always create more layers and richness, but you must be inquisitive in your investigation of your character.

> *Once you've identified the most challenging OBSTACLES,*
> *never give up on your SCENE OBJECTIVE, even if*
> *the OBSTACLES seem impossible to overcome.*

Don't ever admit defeat. There's always a possibility that you will be able to overcome an OBSTACLE. Even if the chances are small, know that there's always hope. The person who gives up too easily is often perceived by the audience as a loser. You always want to act from a winning, anything's-possible point of view. The scene ends when your fight to overcome OBSTACLES to accomplish your SCENE OBJECTIVE ceases. This means if the scene isn't over and your fight to overcome conflict stops, the forward motion is arrested and the audience will cease to care. So always keep in mind that *it's not over 'til it's over*. Continue the struggle to overcome your OBSTACLES even a few BEATS after you exit, the director says "Cut" or the curtain comes down.

OBSTACLES: The Practical Application

It may sound obvious, but the first step when identifying OBSTACLES for a scene is to read the scene with a pencil in hand and to note them as you go along. Then you can go back through and add another layer, and another. OBSTACLES should be written directly onto the script in pencil (this gives you a chance to erase if you change your mind).

Do not solely consider your scenes or your lines when reading for OBSTACLES, because many of your OBSTACLES will be the results of the actions and words of other characters.

In this chapter, we've explored how to identify your character's OBSTACLES, which you must find in the script or presume would make sense to your character. The next step is to make it personal to you and your life. Personalization of your OBSTACLES can be specifically determined only by the choice you make for your SUBSTITUTION (the next chapter, tool #4). And your choice of SUBSTITUTION will change the choices you make to personalize the OBSTACLES.

The initial order for script analysis goes as follows:

1. Find your OVERALL OBJECTIVE.
2. Find your SCENE OBJECTIVES.
3. Find the OBSTACLES that make sense to the script and the character on the page.

The first three tools need to be examined from the point of view of the character on the page. Then and only then can you start to personalize.

CHAPTER 4

Tool #4:
SUBSTITUTION

> Endowing the other actor in the scene with a person from your real life who makes sense to your OVERALL OBJECTIVE and/or your SCENE OBJECTIVE and who will add more history, urgency and desperation. This way you have all the rich and diverse layers that a real need from a real person will give you.

We will explore how to identify and apply the best SUBSTITUTION choice. Once you have found your SUBSTITUTION, I will show you how to take your character's OBSTACLES and, considering your SUBSTITUTION choice, make them personal and relevant to your life. In other words, first, you will find the most compelling and appropriate SUBSTITUTION. Then you will learn how to personalize those OBSTACLES you've already identified in the script (tool #3) to make sense to your SUBSTITUTION choice.

Applying and Identifying SUBSTITUTION

SUBSTITUTION gives you an immediate history with another character or problem and all the layered emotional responses that come with it. Using SUBSTITUTION enables you to attach emotions—emotions that have the depth and complexity that usually take years to develop—to another actor. You may have known an actor you are working with only for a few days, yet your character has an intricate, lengthy relationship with the other actor's character in the script. With SUBSTITUTION you can endow the actor playing, for instance, your mother with the involved history you have with your real mother—her love; the certainty or uncertainty of her love for you; and memories, both joyful and painful. Working with your real mother as the SUBSTITUTION will make your interplay with the other actor as nuanced and complex as your relationship with your real mother—in every line, glance and gesture. In other words, SUBSTITUTION creates a truly human relationship, not an acted-out interpretation that is merely motivated by a cerebral source.

We have all noticed that we act differently around different people. Likewise, a performance can change radically depending upon whom you are thinking about and responding to (your SUBSTITUTION). Think about it. You are different around your child, your mother, your lover, your crush, your husband or wife, your nemesis, your friend and your boss. We have a multitude of emotional responses to each person we come in contact with. Most actors, left to their imaginations, will take something like a love scene and just attempt to produce the feelings of love. This results in a one-note performance. Nobody *just* loves someone. Real-world love has moments of anger, pain, competition, jealousy, hate and sadness attached to it. Few of the complexities and minutiae—the layers of history and emotions—of a real loving relationship can emerge by acting a loving relationship from our imaginations. SUBSTITUTION is effective because we have such unique responses to each individual we come into contact with. Different aspects of our personalities are drawn out when we encounter different people. Each SUBSTITUTION choice will provide different reactions and stimuli.

> *It's important to use real people in your acting work*
> *because you don't know how you'll really behave in front of a*
> *person when there's a lot at risk. You think you do, but you don't.*

After the first reading of a script, it's common for an actor to have a picture of precisely how a scene should look and operate. Then the actor tries to create this picture as precisely as he sees it in his imagination. However, life rarely goes as we see it. Think about the disgruntled wife or husband who's been cheated on or lied to and wants their mate to change their ways. They imagine how they are going to confront their dishonest mate. They think to themselves, "I'm going to march right up, and this time, I'm going to be strong. And I'm going to say, 'I'm great, I'm special, without me in your life you'd be screwed. So stop lying to me or I'm leaving. Really! This time I'm really outta here!'" In the disgruntled wife's or husband's fantasy, the mate is hugely intimidated by this hard-line approach, realizes the depth of their wrongdoing, gets on his or her hands and knees and, with tears in their eyes, begs for forgiveness. Now, this is the picture in their mind of exactly how it's all going to occur in their I-refuse-to-be-a-victim-to-you-anymore scene. But as you know, it never goes this way. Ever. The disgruntled husband or wife may begin the confrontation with this picture in their mind, but when faced with the *actual person* who holds their future in their hands, the *actual person* who has the power to exile the husband or wife to a potential life of loneliness, all that strength goes out the window. The disgruntled husband's or wife's imagination may have pumped them up, but ultimately, their fear wins. They'll often accept their mate's hateful behavior because it's still better than being alone. An actor's fantasy of what a scene should look like functions the same way. Rather than acting from these pictures, which are rarely accurate, SUBSTITUTION personalizes your work so that your actions and reactions are from your heart and body. In other words, SUBSTITUTION makes your behavior real.

SUBSTITUTION grounds an actor's work, providing them with real people to react and interact with. This leads to appropriate, real and original behavior, which even to you, the actor, will often be a surprise. Why? We think we know how we will act around specific people, but how we really behave around them is always quite different from what we imagine. We're weak when we think we'll be strong; we're seductive when we think we'll be standoffish; we're playful when we think we'll be boring. Using a SUBSTITUTION from your real life creates an arena for you to be whoever it is that you are around that person—with all the layers that naturally emerge.

Before we explore how to find and make your SUBSTITUTION choices, you need to understand how SUBSTITUTION works on a practical and physical level.

SUBSTITUTION: The Practical Application

In creating this SUBSTITUTION you would begin by finding one thing about the other actor's face that reminds you of the person you're using as the SUBSTITUTION. It can be anything—the eyes, eyebrows, skin color, nose, lips, cheekbones, forehead, etc. It's very important to use one specific feature, because our minds have a hard time latching on to vague ideas. Once you decide what it is, then concentrate on that one feature until the feeling of the person comes to you in your gut. No, you don't want to look cross-eyed until you see your SUBSTITUTION. You should simply wait to feel that person's essence in front of you. As you do this, remember key events (both traumatic and joyful) with the person you are using as your SUBSTITUTION while looking at that one facial feature. This entire exercise should take only a few seconds.

Working this way may seem awkward at first, but after trying it a few times, you'll find that this process will become as easy and natural as breathing.

Identifying Who to Use as a SUBSTITUTION

You must find the person (SUBSTITUTION) who provides the appropriate emotional and physical reactions. How do you find that person? Your SCENE OBJECTIVE answers this question. If the SCENE OBJECTIVE is *"to get you to fall in love with me,"* who is it that you need love from the most? Your mother, brother, ex-wife, ex-boyfriend or estranged friend? Don't worry about the appropriateness of the script's character to your SUBSTITUTION choice. Work from your SCENE OBJECTIVE. Because our psyches are strange, complicated and frequently incomprehensible, we aren't always aware of what we truly feel and need from the people in our lives. It's important to try every person that feels even slightly right in answering the question of who best represents the need expressed in your SCENE OBJECTIVE. In rehearsal, try each possibility, going as far as the first half page of the dialogue.

The SUBSTITUTION choice that generates the most powerful and fitting emotions for the scene, and therefore the SUBSTITUTION that you will most likely want to use, will quickly become clear.

Or maybe your SCENE OBJECTIVE is *"to get you to give me my power back."* Here an appropriate SUBSTITUTION might be a director who gave you trouble on your last film, your unforgiving mother, a wretched in-law, the person who abused you in some way, an ex, a mean sorority sister, that guy who beat you in a fight, an unreasonable teacher or a team member who ruthlessly competes with you. The issue of power comes in many shapes. Don't get stuck in the physical world—make choices that make emotional sense. The results are much more effective.

Don't be literal about your SUBSTITUTION choice—
look at it from an emotional point of view.

Just because the scene is about your lover doesn't mean that you have to use a person from your life who is, or has been, your lover. You want to find a SUBSTITUTION that you have similar emotional issues with.

Say you have a scene where your character's SCENE OBJECTIVE is *"to make you prove you can love me without hurting me,"* and in the script, this SCENE OBJECTIVE is directed toward a lover. Your first instinct may be to use a past or present lover as your SUBSTITUTION. But what if your life circumstances include a father who abandoned you when you were eight? For most people, an event like this has a higher emotional charge than anything that ever happens with their lovers. By using your father as a SUBSTITUTION for your mate character in the to-make-you-prove-you-can-love-me-without-hurting-me scene, you are more capable of finding a richer, more empowered and more profound emotional base to your SCENE OBJECTIVE. Besides, more often than not, we get involved with a mate who is, in psychological terms, a parental substitute. It's a simple psychological concept that most of us are more likely to be attracted to and attached to a mate who embodies the same unresolved issues that we have with one or both of our parents than with someone else who does not push these emotional buttons. It's just as legitimate to use your parent in a scene about a girlfriend-boyfriend situation as it is to use an actual lover.

Your SUBSTITUTION is not always going to be a linear or literal path from the character in the script.

I once assigned a scene from *The Hustler* for a pair to perform in class. The film tells the story of Fast Eddie, a brash pool shark who challenges the best pool player in town, loses and falls into a sea of self-pity and the arms of a woman named Sarah. In the scene I selected, Fast Eddie is telling Sarah that he's leaving, that he doesn't know for how long but that he's definitely coming back to her. Sarah gets angry, doesn't believe that he'll come back and uses every tactic she can think of to accomplish her SCENE OBJECTIVE: *"to prove that you love me by staying."* Shawna, the student playing Sarah, was doing a good job of going after her SCENE OBJECTIVE, but her performance was missing something. I didn't feel that her emotional life was in enough jeopardy if Fast Eddie did go and stayed away. Shawna was using her boyfriend as a SUBSTITUTION. I didn't think he provided Shawna with high enough stakes. If she lost her boyfriend, she, a gorgeous and smart woman, could easily find another guy. I also knew that when Shawna was young, her parents had divorced and her father abandoned her. Now, this was a much more dramatic and traumatic event, filled with high stakes and pain. I thought it was safe to assume that she still possessed a fear of abandonment because of this event. I told her to go to the primal source of her fears and use her real father as her SUBSTITUTION. Let's just say the tears flowed freely, as did her passion to win. The second time through the scene, the class and I *felt* Sarah's need to get Fast Eddie to stay. She was wildly, desperately, vulnerably, violently, powerfully trying to get him *"to prove that you love me by staying."* It made the class and me want her to win her goal. We rooted for her to win because we truly felt her goal *needed* to be accomplished for survival.

Your family members will often be your
SUBSTITUTION choice.

In an interview with the *New York Times* regarding his performance in *Creed*, Sylvester Stallone discussed his process:

To prepare for his role, Mr. Stallone hired a full-time acting coach, Ivana Chubbuck; his skill set, he said, "had basically atrophied." When production

*began, he was still paralyzed by the devastation of losing his oldest son, Sage,
who had a fatal heart attack in the summer of 2012 at 36.*

*He figured his grief would be off-limits, but Ms. Chubbuck forced him
to drill deep. "You just feel responsible," he said, of Sage's death. "That you
weren't there. Here you save all these fictitious people, and you can't even
save your son." Once that floodgate opened, he said, his emotions streamed
out, shifting both his performance, and his mourning. "It helped," Mr.
Stallone said. "I can talk about it now. There's some solace in that."*

On the NPR program *The Frame*, Stallone said that preparing with me
utilizing the philosophy of my technique "was very cathartic."

Normally I don't reveal what my actors are using for their SUBSTITU-
TION. It is our private and secret time together, much like a therapeutic relationship, and secrets create a rich underbelly for inner work. But because
Sylvester Stallone revealed this information in a *New York Times* article, I can
tell you that we were using the death of his son Sage in his work on that film,
and discuss how we used it within the confines of the storyline of the script.

Let's start with the reality that the most devastating loss any parent could
suffer is the death of their child. The role became a way for Stallone not only
to make the most dynamic and truthful choices for his performance, but also
to find catharsis and personal closure. Viewers with trauma might also find
some kind of resolution in their own lives by relating to Rocky and his painful
journey to find closure—making it an even more profound experience.

In the script of *Creed*, Rocky has lost his wife, his best friend, and his
trainer (who was a mentor to him). Rocky's relationship with his son is strained
and has been for a long time. When Creed's son, Adonis, shows up, it becomes
a second chance for Rocky to become a better father through his father-son-
like relationship with Adonis. We made the choice that when Rocky gets the
news that he will die of cancer if he doesn't do chemo treatment, he wouldn't
be devasted by the news, because he feels he doesn't have much to live for, as
most of his important loved ones have passed. Maybe he even sees it as an opportunity to meet up again in the afterlife with those he has lost. This helped
to justify how Rocky handles Adonis' reaction to his diagnosis: We made the
choice, as well, for the character of Rocky, that since dying wasn't such a bad
thing, he would use it to make Adonis rise to the occasion of being a great

fighter and stop whining about how bad his life is. Using tough love, Rocky lets Adonis know that he will do chemo, and decide to live, only if Adonis works harder and has a true fighter's attitude (in and out of the ring). In order to duplicate such a catastrophic event, we needed something from Stallone's personal life that could replicate it.

Since Stallone never got the chance to have any resolution with his own son before he died, using Sage as the SUBSTITUTION for Adonis gave Stallone a second chance to be the father he always wanted to be for Sage. Instead of causing more pain, the movie allowed for Stallone to find that second chance that most people never get. This could've easily been depressing, but seeing it in this light made the experience transformative for Stallone.

When we met to start our script analysis, we talked about Sage. I told Stallone to pick any scene to try out this SUBSTITUTION. The only way you know you have the most resonating choice is to try it. I told Stallone to think over some of the things he never got to say to Sage and then begin the scene. I was reading/acting the part of Adonis, and let's just say that both of us were crying within a couple lines, letting us know this was definitely a good choice. Both for Stallone's heart and his art.

The big epiphany we found through using this personal work was that the pivotal fight for Rocky in *Creed* was not in the actual ring, but rather it was the fight in life, for life. This garnered him much deserved critical acclaim for being brave enough to tackle in his art the very things he needed to overcome in his own life.

You don't know if it will work until you try it.

The best SUBSTITUTION choices are people who are currently important to your life and are emotionally charged. This keeps you in the present and stops you from trying to regurgitate something that has already been resolved and that you have few feelings for or about. This doesn't mean you can use a person as a SUBSTITUTION only if they're presently in your life. Sometimes we have strong feelings for someone in our past, but these feelings remain current because they're unresolved. Now here's the tricky part: We don't always know which relationships are resolved and unresolved. Often, we feel we're done with a relationship when, in fact, we're not. The feelings reside hidden in our subconscious mind. Because our subconscious doesn't play fair; it rarely communicates with our conscious mind truthfully. Because only our subconscious knows, the only way we can know if a SUBSTITUTION will work or not is to try it.

Several years ago, when I was working as an actress, I needed a SUBSTITUTION for a character that I was supposed to passionately love. I wasn't dating anyone special at the time, so this was a daunting task. I tried a multitude of guys I had crushes on. None of them worked. Ex-boyfriends were next. Nothing. My father, who was often a potent SUBSTITUTION didn't trigger me. I was at my wit's end and decided, out of desperation, to try my ex-husband. He was someone I hadn't thought about for years (I swear!), and on those rare occasions when I did think about him, all that ever consciously emerged were thoughts of how good he'd look boiling in oil, his skin peeling off, and yet that good-for-nothing bastard was not apologetic for all the nasty, abusive things he had done to me (okay . . . I need to take a breath). It was a long shot. I needed a SUBSTITUTION that would work for love, and I was trying a guy I had nothing but hate for? But to my great surprise, it worked. Through using my ex-husband as my SUBSTITUTION, I realized that I still had a lot of unresolved feelings for him. I also discovered that you can't hate that much unless you love that much. To go along with this fortune-cookie wisdom, I discovered a SUBSTITUTION that worked for me in this material and again and again in other projects. So, you just don't know what will work until you try it. Art is rarely rational. Don't intellectually make your choices. Like me, most people are unaware of what is resolved and what is not. Are your issues with that SUBSTITUTION resolved and therefore unusable? The only way you'll know is if you try it. If you feel connected, it is the right choice; if you don't feel connected, it is the wrong choice. It's as simple as that.

Not all scenes require a SUBSTITUTION.

SUBSTITUTION is a tool that's there if you need it. Sometimes the person you're acting with (including a casting director in a casting setting) already provides you with the motivation to accomplish your SCENE OBJECTIVE, and you can use the person who's right in front of you.

When I first started helping Jessica Capshaw prepare for her role on the television show *The Practice*, we found that she didn't need a SUBSTITUTION in her scenes with Camryn Manheim. Jessica's character, Jamie Stringer, a relatively new lawyer on the block, is supposed to be intimidated and feel naive around Camryn Manheim's character, Ellenor Frutt, a lawyer who has many cases under her belt. Because Jessica held Camryn's acting abilities and experience in high esteem, her need to please Camryn paralleled her character's need to please Ellenor. She didn't need a SUBSTITUTION to feel deferential.

SUBSTITUTION is a tool that you use if you need emotional history.

For instance, for sexual connection you wouldn't use a SUBSTITUTION; you would use the actor who's right in front of you. Why? Because using a SUBSTITUTION takes away the intimacy. A SUBSTITUTION is there to provide a strong emotional connection, not a physical one. Sexual connections are what help create chemistry between two actors—which is essential in making a movie, television show or play a hit. I don't care how well written the script is, if the chemistry isn't there, the relationship is not worth your audience rooting for. (Refer to the discussion in chapter 14, Creating Chemistry, for a full how-to exercise.)

You'll find that there are only a handful of people in your life who are powerful enough to use as SUBSTITUTIONS.

Only a few people really shape and affect our emotional lives. For most of us, these people are our families—mother, father and siblings. And as life progresses, this core group may expand to include a life partner, children and exes. Because there are so many layers to these relationships that need to be resolved and understood, these people can and should be used again and again as SUBSTITUTIONS. Jack Nicholson frequently uses his mother as a SUBSTITUTION. Why? Because Jack's relationship with his mother is so complex.

As Jack was growing up, he was led to believe that a woman named June was his sister and a woman named Ethel was his mother. When his "sister" June was dying, Jack was offered a part in Mike Nichols' *The Fortune*. He told June that he wouldn't leave her, that being with her as she was dying was much more important than any acting job. June assured him she was okay. She said that she'd be alive when he came back and that he should just go and do the part. He left. A few days later, June died. Devastated, Jack returned home. And to further his shock, he later discovered that June wasn't his sister. She was his mother. And Ethel, the woman he thought was his mother, was his grandmother. Ethel had died a few years earlier and now June was dead. There was no one for Jack to talk to or ask, "Why?" Jack was left to unravel this mystery himself—both emotionally and mentally. He had to investigate what had happened and why. And one of the ways he does this is by using his mother/sister as a SUBSTITUTION in his work. His unresolved feelings of anger, love and power make for a powerful SUBSTITUTION. Instead of feeling sorry for himself, which is a common response to trauma like this, Jack used his pain to fuel his work. The result: full, ever-present and terrifically oddball characters. Jack's personal stamp makes his roles so "Nicholson" that they are impossible to duplicate.

SUBSTITUTION provides catharsis.

Acting allows us to do things we can't normally do because real events or convention keep us from experiencing them. Death takes away a relationship, but in our acting fantasy, we can keep that person alive. That fantasy can extend to many issues. Whatever we dream of or truly want to be or do is doable in our acting. Because it's not truly real, in our acting fantasy, we can kill people (who we think deserve to die), get married (even though you're not dating anyone), have children (even if you can't conceive), hate (those who are not politically correct to disparage), be divorced (from that person you can't leave) and be gay or straight. Acting allows our fantasies to take form. For Natasha Gregson Wagner, the daughter of the late (and great) Natalie Wood, the fantasy of having a mother was huge for her and the SUBSTITUTION work she did had a very positive effect on her life.

Natasha was very close to her mother. So when Natalie died, Natasha, who was only eleven, was overwhelmed and in excruciating pain. In the years I've worked with her, we've discovered that her mother is a powerful SUBSTITUTION for Natasha. Clearly, her thoughts about her mother are infused with the kind of powerful issues that a SUBSTITUTION needs to have: abandonment, loss and great love. Because Natasha is an actress, she can do what a lot of people can't. Using her work, Natasha can live out the fantasy of what her life would be like if her mother were still alive. For instance, if she's playing a role where love and loss is the issue, she will often use her mother as a SUBSTITUTION. And this SUBSTITUTION work allows her to connect with her mother in a way that she never had the opportunity to do because her mother died when Natasha was so young. Some may view this as unhealthy, but keeping her mother alive in her work, as corny as it may sound, keeps her alive in Natasha's heart.

Every time you use a SUBSTITUTION that is infused with a loaded subject, the unresolved relationship gets worked out a little more in both your conscious and subconscious mind. Things you'd like to say or do to a high-stakes person in your past and/or present life—but *can't* do in real life—you can do in your acting.

Be Open to Change

When a new crisis enters our lives, our minds cannot veer from thinking about the trauma at hand. Yesterday's dramas take a back seat to today's dramas. If, as you are doing a play, movie or television show, something more distressing, crucial or relevant happens in your life and it introduces a better SUBSTITUTION choice, by all means change your SUBSTITUTION. This was the case when I was working with Charlize Theron on the film *Mighty Joe Young*. This movie tells the story of Jill Young (Charlize's character), who is left to care for a baby gorilla when her father, an American researcher, is killed by poachers in Africa. Charlize's character must raise this ape and make sure that he thrives, even when he is taken from his native Africa to a sanctuary in California. Jill feels she must protect the two-ton ape, Joe, from the perils of modern civilization. We had decided on a SUBSTITUTION for Joe and had done extensive work on her role when, just a few days into filming, Charlize's brother died in an automobile accident. Naturally, this new and very traumatic event over-shadowed everything else in her life. Like many people who lose family members, particularly siblings, Charlize felt helpless after her brother's death. She wondered what she could have done to keep him alive. What should she have told him before his death that she'd never get a chance to say? What would never get resolved or accomplished? When she went back to work, she switched her SUBSTITUTION for Joe to her brother. By using her brother as a SUBSTI-TUTION, Charlize used her work as a second chance to take care of the un-finished feelings she had about her brother. Not only did it make her acting present and eventful, but it was also cathartic. In every scene, she got to bring her brother back and fight for him to stay alive, alleviating the helplessness that she was experiencing in her real life.

Of course, death isn't the only high-stakes event that can change your choices. Others include getting divorced, getting sued, getting caught doing something illegal or immoral, being in a big fight with a loved one, being sexually harassed, being lied to, or getting pregnant, just to name a few.

Take Risks with Your Choices

As you've probably noticed, I really believe in taking risks. If I got a nickel for every time I've said to an actor, "Always, always take risks!" I'd have to buy a very large piggy bank. To create risk there must be huge, risky OBSTACLES to overcome. If you make a SUBSTITUTION choice that allows you to easily gain your SCENE OBJECTIVE, there's no real need to do anything exciting to get what you want. Let's look at how we behave with our friends. We often have two kinds of friends. There's the one who you know will do anything on your behalf—take a bullet if necessary—and then there's the friend that you try too hard for—try to be extra smart, helpful or funny, because you're still trying to win their approval and love. You can see how in a friendship scene the friend you try too hard for is going to be the more compelling SUBSTITU-TION choice. As with all the tools:

There must always be inherent OBSTACLES attached to your SUBSTITUTIONS.

When making a SUBSTITUTION choice, always ask yourself:

- Whom do I most need to get my SCENE OBJECTIVE from?

And from that list . . .

- Who is most *un*likely to give it to me?

This brings the possibility of failure into the equation, which will create unpredictability for you, the other actor and the audience. The possibility of failure also allows your personal flaws to emerge, which will create affectations and mannerisms that are unique to you.

Finding Your SUBSTITUTIONS

Begin with the SCENE OBJECTIVE to help you figure out who the best and most effective SUBSTITUTION is to add reality and depth to your performance. Let's look at how this works for the character of Bonasera in the opening scene of *The Godfather*. The film opens, and it's Don Corleone's daughter's wedding. According to the story's tradition, on the day of a daughter's wedding, the Don of a family must receive and be open to requests. Bonasera the undertaker has a request for the Godfather. He is seated in front of the Don's desk.

THE GODFATHER
by Mario Puzo and Francis Ford Coppola
© 1972 Paramount Pictures

BONASERA
I believe in America. America has made my
fortune. And I raised my daughter in the American
fashion. I gave her freedom, but—I taught her
never to dishonor her family. She found a
boyfriend; not an Italian. She went to the movies
with him; she stayed out late. I didn't protest. Two
months ago, he took her for a drive, with another
boyfriend. They made her drink whiskey. And then
they tried to take advantage of her. She resisted.
She kept her honor. So they beat her, like an
animal. When I went to the hospital, her nose was
a'broken. Her jaw was a'shattered, held together
by wire. She couldn't even weep because of the
pain. But I wept. Why did I weep? She was the
light of my life—beautiful girl. Now she will never
be beautiful again.

[He breaks down]
Sorry . . .
I—I went to the police, like a good American.
These two boys were brought to trial. The judge
sentenced them to three years in prison—

> suspended sentence. Suspended sentence! They
> went free that very day! I stood in the courtroom
> like a fool. And those two bastards, they smiled at
> me. Then I said to my wife, "For justice, we must
> go to Don Corleone."

Bonasera hoped to get justice on behalf of his daughter, who, in his mind, had been raped three times. Twice by men and then again by the American legal system, a system he once dearly believed in. Feeling powerless to do anything about the men who hurt someone he loved so dearly, he went to the Godfather to seek vengeance.

- Bonasera's SCENE OBJECTIVE: *"to get you* (Don Corleone) *to murder for me."*

When picking your SUBSTITUTIONS, always consider the script's OBSTACLES, which in this case are:

1. Possible rejection.
2. Fear of the Godfather. As an undertaker, Bonasera knows firsthand what Don Corleone is capable of.
3. Fear of being beholden to the Godfather.
4. If the Godfather doesn't grant the request, Bonasera will be left with horrible guilt and feelings of massive inadequacy.
5. In the story, Bonasera has gone out of his way to not socially connect to Don Corleone, which infuriates Don Corleone. Don Corleone feels particularly disrespected in this case because Corleone's wife is Bonasera's daughter's godmother. Therefore, Don Corleone is less inclined to grant Bonasera his request.
6. Corleone's going to do whatever he wants. Bonasera must be submissive to him. Bonasera has a feeling of utter weakness.
7. His desperate desire for justice through retribution.
8. If Corleone doesn't grant his request, Bonasera has no other options.

After thinking about your SCENE OBJECTIVE, *"to get you to murder for me,"* and the OBSTACLES attached to it, you then find out how this is true in your life by asking yourself, "Whom in my personal life do I currently need a huge favor from but I'm intimidated by them because the power base is so uneven?" Or, "Whom would it be emotionally painful to need anything from?"

As you look at the people that have come up as answers to the above questions, you have to decide who in your life would affect you the *most* as a SUBSTITUTION. Frequently, three or more names of people might come up as conceivably suitable SUBSTITUTIONS for the other character in the script. Because acting is a physical art form, you should never intellectually decide who the best SUBSTITUTION choice is. I repeat: The choices have to be actually tried out—on your feet, speaking the dialogue. It becomes clear upon trying each of your possible SUBSTITUTION choices which one affects you the most. Look for these reactions:

- Touching you emotionally.
- Giving you passion to succeed in achieving your SCENE OBJECTIVE.
- Having inherent OBSTACLES.
- It triggers your body to be involved.

Someone may come to mind immediately and you might feel you have the perfect choice. Even so, you still must come up with at least two more alternative SUBSTITUTION choices, because we are not always aware, until we try it, who in our life affects us the most. Don't assume the most obvious SUBSTITUTION choice will work—sometimes it's someone you least suspect who will motivate the most passion to win your SCENE OBJECTIVE.

Here are possible SUBSTITUTION choices for Don Corleone:

- **Your father:** One common son-father dynamic is for a son to feel intimidation and fear toward his father. A son will put his father on a pedestal and feel that, no matter what he's accomplished, he has, in some way, disappointed his father. This makes the son constantly attempt to make his father proud and, at the same time, to feel that whatever he does, it's never enough. Or if the father exhibits abusive tendencies, the son's need to overcome the abuse to get his father's love is limitless. A primal choice like a parent sets up an uneven power struggle, which is inherent in a parent-child relationship.

- **Your mother:** Perhaps in your family dynamic, your mother is the powerhouse. As with the father SUBSTITUTION, a son will put his mother on a pedestal and feel that, no matter what he's accomplished, he has, in some way, disappointed his mother. This makes the son constantly attempt to make his mother proud and feel like it's never enough. And if the mother is overdemanding or verbally or physically abusive, the son's need to overcome the abuse to get his mother's love is limitless. Again, a primal choice like using a parent sets up an uneven power struggle, which is inherent in a parent-child relationship.

- **Your stepmother or stepfather:** Children often have problems with the person who steps in as an authority but hasn't earned it through blood ties. And they often blame this person for tearing the original family unit apart. A stepmother or stepfather relationship is wrought with issues, whether real or imagined (to a child, there's no difference). A common problem is the power struggle to capture the biological parent's attention and focus. The child often loses this battle because the blood parent will often side with the person who shares their bed. As a result, having to ask this person for anything can be painful.

- **A teacher:** It's common for a person who's thrust into a position of power and authority to abuse that power. Some teachers thrive on making students feel stupid, untalented, unliked, sexually harassed or ridiculed. If you have had a teacher like this, they can be a viable SUBSTITUTION.

- **A casting director, director, producer, agent, etc.:** These people can make an actor's dreams come true. When a person holds this much power over people's hopes and desires, it's difficult not to feel tempted to abuse the people they have power over. This dynamic makes for an optimal SUBSTITUTION. What will you have to give up to get your request: your dignity, your morality, your ethics? Are you expected to give unjustifiable adulation or sexual favors to make this request happen? Note that for this SUBSTITUTION to work, you must have a *real* problematic personal history with a *specific* individual holding a high-powered position in the industry.

- **Your ex-mate:** Exes are our exes for a reason: We have major issues with them—especially power struggles. Who made more money? Who gave more to the relationship? Were you disempowered by an affair? Was your ex-mate physically and/or verbally abusive? Was your ex-mate condescending? To request something—anything—from an ex is humbling.

- **A sibling:** Obviously, this choice is about sibling rivalry. The pain of spending an entire childhood dealing with a sibling possibly beating you up, tattling on you and mocking you doesn't easily go away just because you're both grown up and currently the best of friends.

- **A family member like an uncle/aunt or grandfather/grandmother:** In some families, an uncle or grandmother may take on a more active, involved and complicated role. In cases such as these, family members have the responsibility and authority of a parent. As a result, your issues with this relative will embody a parental dynamic. Your power struggles will then be the same as they might have been with your mother or father.

- **Your present mate:** This SUBSTITUTION can be used only if there are major problems in your relationship. If all is well, barring the occasional flare-ups that plague all couples, there will be no conflict and nothing to really overcome to get your SCENE OB-JECTIVE. But if the relationship is on its way out or there are *huge* issues, like your mate is having an affair or has a tendency toward emotional castration, then you've got something to work with. Eating crow in order to ask your detestable mate to do anything for you would make eating a rat seem like a doable alternative.

- **An abusive friend:** No matter how emotionally healthy we claim our friend relationships to be (I've often heard from students, "Oh, I don't have any friends like that. I got rid of them long ago. . . ."), most of us seem to retain at least one abusive friend. You know the one. The friend that your other friends ask you, "*Why* are you friends with that person anyway?!" What makes the friendship even worse is that the power struggle with the abusive friend has a friendly veneer to it. And then there's the fact that the abusive friend wins the power struggles most of the time, which infuriates you. This can be a powerful SUBSTITUTION, because these relationships are so complex and usually tap into our parental issues, as well.

• **A person who sexually abused you (a babysitter, uncle, neighbor, teacher, etc.):** This person took your power away in the most heinous way, especially if it happened when you were a child and you didn't have the tools either to understand it or to fight it. Asking a favor of someone like this might be devastating. Yet if your daughter (or some loved one) had to be protected and the molester was the only one capable of doing this, you'd be forced to do so. This would create amazing drama, as the push and pull of the scene would be palpable.

Of course, there are many other possibilities for SUBSTITUTIONS, but these suggestions will give you an idea of how far you can go in making SUBSTITUTION choices that make sense emotionally and to the script, and that will further aid in making a character like Bonasera *live* inside of you.

Once you've determined your SUBSTITUTION, you can personalize the script's OBSTACLES. The personalization of OBSTACLES will be determined by whom you are using as a SUBSTITUTION. The conflicts or problems that exist are unique to each person in your life. Thus, it's important to understand who your SUBSTITUTION is before you can analyze any of your inner work, because it will change radically depending upon whom you're talking to. After you've determined your SUBSTITUTION, it's time to personalize the script's OBSTACLES.

Personalizing OBSTACLES:
The Practical Application

The first thing you do to personalize the script's OBSTACLES is to review the OBSTACLES you've already listed and defined that are established from the script itself. Then, with your SUBSTITUTION in mind, determine what similar OBSTACLES exist within your relationship with your SUBSTITUTION.

For the purposes of explaining how to personalize your OBSTACLES, let's say that I've been cast to play the role of Bonasera in *The Godfather*.

In the script, Bonasera's key OBSTACLES are:

1. Possibility of rejection.
2. Disparity of power.
3. Intimidation.
4. Fear of the person he's talking to.
5. A history of problems in the relationship.
6. The request is enormously important.
7. There are probably severe repercussions if the request is perceived as a sign of disrespect.

After I consider these OBSTACLES, the SUBSTITUTION of my mother seems apropos. Let's take a closer look at how this SUBSTITUTION affects the OBSTACLES.

- **My mother:** She abused me as a child. So in our relationship, there's a history of abuse. And although I'm an adult now, a kernel of the *fear and intimidation* of her still lives inside of me. Primal emotions like this die hard.

  My mother is also not particularly mentally stable. I fear that if I push her too hard (like asking a favor as big as Bonasera's), she might lose it and be extremely abusive verbally, emotionally and/or physically. Also, as I'm already hardwired to feel guilty, I would have to live with the massive guilt for driving her over the edge. *Severe repercussions.*

  The *disparity of power* is intrinsic to our relationship, as she's the parent and I'm the child. This dynamic will never emotionally change, no matter what I've accomplished or how dependent on me she becomes in her old age.

Based on this SUBSTITUTION, my request would be that I would ask my mother to become more financially dedicated to the needs of my mentally handicapped brother. She is my brother's caretaker. My father failed to set up any kind of trust for him before he died. My mother spends money extravagantly, rewarding any wayward salesman who rings her doorbell with unnecessary purchases. However, when it comes to my brother's expenses, she becomes Scrooge. If my brother doesn't get her financial support, he'll physically lose the roof over his head, the food to feed himself and the mental health care he so desperately needs. *An important request.*

Notice that the personal OBSTACLES still echo the OBSTACLES of the character in the script. In using my mother as a SUBSTITUTION example, the OBSTACLES include an imbalance of power, fear of the other person, a history of problems and a request that has a lot at stake. Personalizing OBSTACLES creates a more powerful and intimate investment in the material and adds need, heat and substance to your performance.

**The OBSTACLES that need to be personalized
are not always obvious or written in the script.**

For many years, I worked with Adrian Paul on his role as Duncan MacLeod in the television series *Highlander*. Although he was playing a superhero, we had to create OBSTACLES to humanize his character so that the audience could relate to him. In one episode, Duncan was trying to help a friend who was a raging alcoholic. I told Adrian that people with addictions rarely can or will listen to someone who hasn't had similar problems. If his character hadn't experienced any kind of addictive behavior, then his alcoholic friend would feel that Duncan's attempt to help him was judgmental and patronizing. And as you know, no one likes to be patronized. Even though the idea of Duncan being an addict of some kind wasn't in the script, we had to create this OBSTACLE for his character and then personalize it for Adrian so that he and his character could truly commiserate with this alcoholic character. We invented a backstory for Duncan: Somewhere in his four-hundred-year life, he, too, had suffered from alcoholism. But when we began to personalize the OBSTACLE, we had a new problem: Adrian Paul had never had a problem with alcohol. We had to find a different vice. You may be in denial, but everyone has at least one vice—sex, drugs, cutting, food issues, social media, etc. People who have chosen show business as a career often have an array of vices to choose from. It's nothing to be ashamed of. It's what makes you an artist. With Adrian's personal vice infused into his characterization of Duncan MacLeod, he could now truly relate to his character's friend's obsessive and addictive behavior. This allowed Adrian, as Duncan, to truly understand his alcoholic friend, which made this performance about empathy, not about charity.

Dig deep. Look below the surface to those dark, tortured and hidden places that reside inside of you.

When you personalize a script's OBSTACLES, it requires you to look at your demons—especially those places we're often in denial about. Finding the appropriate SUBSTITUTION and personalizing a script's OBSTACLES ask you to dig deep within yourself and be rigorously honest about who you are and who and what pushes your buttons. There'll also be personal discovery. When you try different choices, it's sometimes really surprising what works and what doesn't. Issues you think you've resolved are not. People you think no longer hold any power over you still prevail in your heart. What is effective in your work is the *real truth* of what you feel. That's why it's important to try many choices, even the ones that seem wrong, because underneath, in your heart and gut, there may be residual unresolved feelings—no matter how much your conscious mind may fight them. Working this way not only gives you a better performance; it gives you a better understanding of yourself.

The SUBSTITUTION you choose colors and changes what choices you make for *all* the inner work, including the mental images that are created by *what* it is you are talking about and *what* it is you are hearing. These are your INNER OBJECTS, the next acting tool.

CHAPTER 5

Tool #5:
INNER OBJECTS

The images you see in your mind about a <u>person, place,</u> <u>thing or event</u>—there's always a natural movie that passes behind our eyes when we speak or when we listen. The images you use should make sense to the OBJECTIVES and SUBSTITUTION. Everything must be filled in with INNER OBJECTS so you are activating a true human response.

In life, there's a natural movie that passes behind our eyes when we talk and listen. These rolling images are associations we make based on our past and present experiences. Likewise, any character you play must also have a movie behind their eyes. But because your character's words and life are not yours but those of the writer, you need to make your own personal and appropriate associations to find the right pictures. This is so that when you say or hear dialogue, the visuals and pictures that come up should feel like they are emanating from your own personal life. If you don't have clear associations to the words, they will seem and feel meaningless. It's your job as the actor to personalize the words that come from the author's mind, and make it appear and feel as though they come from *your* mind. Using INNER OBJECTS makes this happen.

Our INNER OBJECTS are never random. Think about how we learn to speak. First, a baby sees a picture and then forms the words. Often, our first words are Ma Ma and Da Da. We learn these words first because these pictures are key to our survival, as well as the first important images that an infant perceives. Similarly, when we're learning a new language, we need a picture attached to the foreign word to recall it. That is why we often learn the words for things like bathroom, bed and various food items first.

Our INNER OBJECT movie plays constantly. Your mind never goes blank. *Ever.* Every person, place, thing or event you talk about or hear another person talk about must have INNER OBJECTS attached to it. Why? Because we are always thinking. To evoke any sense of reality, you have to have your mind continuously generating images that will inspire your character's reality and feelings. The best illustration of our mind's ticker tape of activity is when someone says to you, "I've got something to tell you. . . ." It's rare when this statement precedes good news. If you have good news, you usually just blurt out the good news: "Hey! I've won the lottery!" You don't say, "I've got something to tell you. . . . I've won the lottery!" Yet when hearing "I've got something to tell you," most actors wait for the news with a blank expression and an empty head. The reality is that when someone says, "I've got something to tell you. . . ." you suspect it's something bad and your thoughts race, trying to figure out what the bad news could be. If these words are coming from a mate, you might think, "Oh, my God, he's cheating on me!" or "She's leaving me!" or "He's gay!" or "He's not gay!" or "She's pregnant!" or "He's dying!" and so on. The pictures and thoughts of the anticipated bad news you've come up with may be right or totally off base, but it doesn't matter as long as the thoughts and pictures are plentiful and profuse. Your job as an actor is to have pictures and thoughts going on in your head as you talk and as your costar lays out whatever news they have to tell you. This means that there should be INNER OBJECTS for every person, place, thing or event in the script.

The SUBSTITUTION choice you've made will determine your choices for the INNER OBJECTS. This means that if you're using your mother, your INNER OBJECTS should relate to your experiences with her. This way your work will track, filling out the larger inner story you're creating. Do not use one SUBSTITUTION and then work with INNER OBJECTS that relate to another person. It's too confusing to keep track of and ultimately creates a befuddled and unfocused performance. If you find that you're saying to yourself, "What am I thinking about now?" then you've made the wrong INNER OBJECT choices. Your INNER OBJECTS should flow, fitting together with your SUBSTITUTION, OBSTACLES, SCENE OBJECTIVE and OVERALL OBJECTIVE like a good jigsaw puzzle.

In *Gone with the Wind,* Scarlett O'Hara often speaks of her home, Tara. Actors who don't work with INNER OBJECTS will try to picture some generic plantation mansion rather than a home that means something to them. The results of generic choices like this will be vague and generic. A generic plantation mansion has no personal meaning, relevance or emotional connection. Even if you happen to be from the South and you've seen many plantation mansions, the picture in your head is not infused with all the joys, traumas and real-life events that are attached to the places that have a real emotional history for you. Instead, you can use INNER OBJECTS and make charged choices. For instance, say you're doing a scene opposite Scarlett's archrival, Melanie, and you've chosen your mother as the SUBSTITUTION for Melanie. The INNER OBJECT (picture) you might use for Tara is the home you grew up in with your mother. Or perhaps you're doing a scene opposite Rhett Butler and you've chosen your ex-mate as your SUBSTITUTION. The INNER OBJECT that you choose for Tara is going to change because your thoughts, needs and history are quite different from how they would be with your mother. With your ex-mate in mind, Tara is now pictured in your head as the home you lived in with your ex.

Your INNER OBJECT Choices Should Be Made on an Emotional Level, Not on a Physical Level

The character of Bubba in *Forrest Gump* constantly refers to a shrimp boat. If you were playing Bubba and needed an INNER OBJECT, the idea wouldn't be to come up with the best boat reference you could think of. Bubba saw the shrimp boat not as a boat, but as something that symbolized his dream career, a reason to survive the Vietnam hell he was living in and an inspiration for him to get through his tour of duty. So, if you were playing Bubba, you might use the idea of getting a starring movie role opposite your favorite actor as an INNER OBJECT for the shrimp boat. Or the shrimp boat could be getting that dream house for your mother before she dies. There are no right or wrong choices, just more effective or less effective ones. When breaking down a script for INNER OBJECTS, just make sure the INNER OBJECT visuals relate to the SUBSTITUTION you're using and that the choices you make are the ones that hold the greatest value to you emotionally.

INNER OBJECTS should have inherent OBSTACLES attached to them.

The more specific and angst ridden your choices for the INNER OBJECTS are in a scene, the more they will evoke an emotional response for you, the other actor and the audience. Generally, high stakes are created by conflict—if a choice is unproblematic, it becomes too easy to assimilate and therefore not particularly interesting. The point is not only to concern yourself with finding INNER OBJECTS that make your performance the most honest, but to find the pictures that are the most precarious and risky. If the dialogue is "I feel sick," you should use your worst nightmarish fear. The picture in your head shouldn't be of you being laid up with the flu, but rather of you in bed in the final throes of cancer, the cancer that your grandma died from, the cancer that your mother has been diagnosed with, the cancer you might get because cancer can be hereditary. Using something like cancer as your INNER OBJECT choice is based on a *real* fear. If the choices you make for your INNER OB-JECTS aren't infused with history and high stakes, then they won't naturally emerge when it comes time for performance. The hotter the choices you make, the more likely you'll organically remember your images without having to think about them.

*It's not just your own dialogue that requires
INNER OBJECTS—the other actor's words must be
attached to pictures that mean something to you.*

People *hear* in pictures. Using INNER OBJECTS when the other person is talking also enables you to react more honestly. One of the biggest complaints that directors and casting directors have is that actors don't listen. They just wait to speak their dialogue. That doesn't imply that you as the actor aren't hearing the words from the other character—you're probably hearing every single word. But if the words don't mean anything to you and aren't summoning pictures in your head, then you're not effectively listening.

*When we listen, we don't try to imagine another
person's life; we relate everything we hear
to our own world.*

When we hear other people speak, we don't try to imagine what their pictures look like, even if we casually know the person, place, thing or event they're talking about. We listen with our own personal pictures because they mean something to us. Say your friend is talking to you about the recent death of his mother. You don't picture his mother dying. Instead, you recall an important death you've experienced, or you imagine what it would feel like if your own mother were to die. To duplicate how we listen as we do in life, we naturally match the other person's thoughts to relatable ones of our own. It's how we try to understand and relate to other people's emotional reality. *Again, it's how we truly listen.*

The function of INNER OBJECTS is not to use them physically but rather to trigger emotions.

I worked with one particular actress on many episodes of a popular television show about lawyers. Her character had to fight a particular case for a client who had been raped. In the show's storyline, the rape was personal to her character because she had been raped, too, but had never filed a police report. The challenge for this actress was to find the INNER OBJECT for being raped. Fortunately, she had never experienced this form of violation. I explained to her that rape is not just a physical violation—it's an emotional violation, as well. I asked her if there was any event in her life when she felt emotionally violated. She revealed that she was overweight as a child and that her father constantly criticized and humiliated her for it. Even though she is quite svelte and has been so for a long time, her father's ridicule has stayed with her. She looks in the mirror and sees someone who's horribly disfigured and fat. She came to realize that she indeed felt attacked by her father's words and behavior and had been changed forever by it. She decided to try to use it as her INNER OBJECT. In her performance, every time she spoke of the rape that had happened to her client (and to her character), she pictured the worst and most humiliating event from her childhood regarding her father and her weight issues. By using this as an INNER OBJECT event, her uncontrollable emotions surfaced organically.

Make Your INNER OBJECTS Personal

My brother-in-law is an internationally recognized trial lawyer who wins nearly every case he argues. His clients are usually big corporations. Fighting cases on behalf of big business can be challenging. It's an uphill battle because most people—especially those on a jury—are inclined to side with the individual rather than with the big bad corporate machine. So how does he win? He makes each case about himself, his wife, his parents or his children. He finds a way to personalize it, making it about defending his family and values. By doing this, he's not fighting for the depersonalized corporation, but for what he cares about the most. He argues hard and works fanatically. He does this because he knows that no matter how altruistic you are, you'll always do more for yourself and the things that matter to you (e.g., your family) than you'll ever do for others or their ideals.

INNER OBJECT choices are not always linear.

Adam Baldwin, who has starred in films such as *Full Metal Jacket* and *My Bodyguard*, was acting in a play where his character was a newly sober character who was "qualifying" (the point at which an alcoholic tells their story) at an Alcoholics Anonymous meeting. In Adam's character's story, he has to talk about the injustices in his life—particularly, the fact that he sobered up to stop the abuse he was heaping on his loving and patient wife, who then died. Adam's character is devastated and confused. Adam and I searched for appropriate INNER OBJECTS, and it was challenging. Adam is not an alcoholic and his wife is very much alive. We needed to come up with something that, when he talked about this eventful death, would destroy him as much as the untimely death of a loved one.

Adam had been in a series called *Firefly*, which Joss Whedon of *Buffy the Vampire Slayer* fame had created. There were high hopes for the series. It was incredibly well written and Adam had the best character of his career to play. There was also the fact that Whedon, who had a hit series under his belt, was involved, which made it seem that this would be the role that would allow Adam to keep his wife and three children fed, clothed and living with a roof over their heads for a long, long time. Adam also felt that he had finally landed a soul-food kind of role that, as any actor will testify, is a rarity. He loved the other cast members like family, as well. The series was canceled after only one season. Adam was devastated. It was a huge loss, much like losing a family member. As an INNER OBJECT, *Firefly* provided elements similar to those that a good wife offers—security, love, inspiration, nurturing and protection. The death of the series and his resulting moody behavior were perfect to use as nonlinear INNER OBJECTS. They allowed him to stay in the moment and feel feelings that were poignant and pervasive.

INNER OBJECTS are enormously effective when working with material that is rich in jargon, be it political speak, financial lingo, psychobabble or scientific or techno gibberish.

The producers of the show *Star Trek: Deep Space Nine* hired me to help establish and make Terry Farrell's character, Dax, seem real. The producers described what they wanted to see: "Dax is a three-hundred-year-old worm who used to be a man and is now a gorgeous woman. She is wise (because she's so old) and unaffected by sexuality (again, with the old)—too wise, in fact, to have a sense of humor."

I told them, "Okay, no problem . . . makes sense to me . . ." I am not as intrigued by science fiction as so many of those who count themselves among the "Trekkie" population, but I do know that in order for anyone to like a character, they must relate to that character in some fashion. What the producers wanted was for Dax to be a character that the public would love and, at the same time, that would stay true to her science fiction persona. This combination could be achieved only by humanizing Dax, by providing earthly duplications to her alien attributes so that those of us who still reside on planet Earth could understand and connect to her. Using INNER OBJECTS, I was able to give Dax sexuality (a primal force everyone can relate to) and a sense of humor (humor appeals to most people) and to personalize all the technobabble (making words like *wormholes* and *quarks* feel like commonly used words). The producers saw the dailies after the first few days of Terry's work and were thrilled. Apparently, by humanizing the alien they got "exactly what we wanted." It's not that we were intentionally defying the powers in charge. They, too, wanted the best performance that would also accurately portray their vision of the character and inspire a large audience to tune in. Not being trained actors themselves, producers and directors often don't have the right language to describe what they want. It's up to you to translate their words into a great performance by introducing the human element (yourself), making it exciting and relatable to the producers, the director and your audience.

Make the Most Current and High-Stakes INNER OBJECT Choices

Using recent painful circumstances from your life keeps you present and raw because you are still unaware of the ramifications of how they will resolve themselves. The point is not only to concern yourself with finding INNER OBJECTS that make your performance honest, but to find the pictures that are presently the most volatile and risky.

Try different INNER OBJECT choices.

As with all the other tools, don't intellectually decide what should work. By trying different INNER OBJECTS, you'll find the ones that are the most effective. How do you figure out the best INNER OBJECTS? When you are rehearsing and performing, the weaker INNER OBJECT choices will float away—that is, they won't stick in your mind. However, the good INNER OBJECT choices *will* stick. You won't have to think about them—the pictures will emerge, organically and naturally. You'll even find that a strong INNER OBJECT choice will magnify your feelings.

Everyone has a wealth of significant experiences to call upon, and each and every experience has loads of pictures to match up. Most of us have fears to fill several volumes. Just look into your personal Pandora's box and you'll find good, strong INNER OBJECT choices.

Writing INNER OBJECT Choices on the Page: The Practical Application

To establish your INNER OBJECT choices, write in pencil so that you can erase if you change your mind (and you frequently will). Handwrite each IN-NER OBJECT choice directly beneath the word(s) that it's attached to.

To demonstrate how one applies INNER OBJECTS, let's look at how one of my students, Michael, personally utilized them in playing the role of Jack in Oscar Wilde's *The Importance of Being Earnest*. Here we have a story about two young men, Jack Worthing and Algernon Moncrieff. Jack and Algernon feel that their lives are dull, so they invent an imaginary brother, Ernest, as a way to escape the mundane and pursue excitement and romance. Jack uses the phantom "Ernest" as an excuse to leave his boring home in the country, which allows him to cavort in the city and spend time with his ladylove, Gwendolen. Because all lies tend to backfire, Jack's and Algernon's deceptions cross paths, threatening Jack's relationship with Gwendolen.

THE IMPORTANCE OF BEING EARNEST
by Oscar Wilde
(Act I, Scene 1)

[Morning-room in Algernon's flat in Half-Moon Street. The room is luxuriously and artistically furnished. The sound of a piano is heard in the adjoining room.]

[ALGERNON enters]

ALGERNON
How are you, my dear Ernest? What brings you up to town?

JACK
Oh, pleasure, pleasure! What else should bring one anywhere? Eating as usual, I see, Algy!

ALGERNON
[Stiffly]
I believe it is customary in good society to take some slight refreshment at five o'clock. Where have you been since last Thursday?

JACK
In the country.

ALGERNON
What on earth do you do there?

JACK
When one is in town one amuses oneself. When
one is in the country one amuses other people. It is
excessively boring.

ALGERNON
And who are the people you amuse?

JACK
[Airily]
Oh, neighbors, neighbors.

ALGERNON
Got nice neighbors in your part of Shropshire?

JACK
Perfectly horrid! Never speak to one of them.

ALGERNON
How immensely you must amuse them! By the
way, Shropshire is your county, is it not?

[ALGERNON takes a sandwich]

JACK
Eh? Shropshire? Yes, of course. Hallo! Why all
these cups? Why cucumber sandwiches? Why
such reckless extravagance in one so young? Who
is coming to tea?

ALGERNON
Oh! Merely Aunt Augusta and Gwendolen.

JACK
How perfectly delightful!

ALGERNON
Yes, that is all very well; but I am afraid Aunt
Augusta won't quite approve of your being here.

JACK
May I ask why?

ALGERNON
My dear fellow, the way you flirt with Gwendolen
is perfectly disgraceful. It is almost as bad as the
way Gwendolen flirts with you.

> JACK
> I am in love with Gwendolen. I have come up to town expressly to propose to her.
>
> ALGERNON
> I thought you had come up for pleasure? . . . I call that business.
>
> JACK
> How utterly unromantic you are!

(and the scene continues)

As Jack, Michael's OVERALL OBJECTIVE was *"to win in love."* The SCENE OBJECTIVE was *"to get you* (Algernon) *to help me get Gwendolen to fall in love with me."* Michael used as his SUBSTITUTION for Algernon his friend Tom, who was the one who initially introduced him to his INNER OBJECT for Gwendolen (Samantha, the girl that Michael has an unrequited passion for). Now, let's take this scene and write in Michael's personal INNER OBJECTS under the words that require INNER OBJECTS, which will be underlined. They will be handwritten exactly how and where you would write in the specific and personal INNER OBJECT choices. Remember: INNER OBJECTS include the mental images of a person, place, thing or event that you talk about or that you hear the other person talk about.

THE IMPORTANCE OF BEING EARNEST
by Oscar Wilde
(Act I, Scene 1)

[Morning-room in Algernon's flat in Half-Moon Street. The room is luxuriously and artistically furnished. The sound of a piano is heard in the adjoining room.]

[ALGERNON enters]

> ALGERNON
> How are you, my dear <u>Ernest</u>? What brings you up
> to <u>town</u>?

Hollywood

Microstick (Michael's nickname, one he wishes to remain private and between friends)

JACK

Oh, <u>pleasure, pleasure</u>! What else should bring
uncontrollable partying
one anywhere? <u>Eating</u> as usual, I see, Algy!
drinking whiskey

ALGERNON
[Stiffly]
I believe it is customary in <u>good society</u> to
good friends
take some <u>slight refreshment at five o'clock</u>.
drink alcohol at 5 p.m.
Where have you been since last Thursday?

JACK

In the <u>country</u>.
Van Nuys (the Valley)

ALGERNON
What on earth do you do there?

JACK
When one is in <u>town</u> one amuses oneself.
Hollywood
When one is in the country one amuses
<u>other people</u>. It is <u>excessively boring</u>.
suburbanites   *bowling and eating at Denny's*

ALGERNON
And who are the <u>people you amuse</u>?
suburbanites

JACK

[Airily]
Oh, <u>neighbors, neighbors</u>.
boring families, no single people

ALGERNON
Got nice <u>neighbors</u> in your part of <u>Shropshire</u>?
families   *the Valley*

JACK
Perfectly horrid! Never speak to one of them.

ALGERNON
How immensely you must amuse them!
By the way, Shropshire is your county, is it not?
the valley

[ALGERNON takes a sandwich]

JACK
Eh? Shropshire? Yes, of course. Hallo! Why
the valley
all these cups? Why cucumber sandwiches? Why
crystal glasses   expensive Chivas Regal
such reckless extravagance in one so young?
Who is coming to tea?
for drinks

ALGERNON
Oh! Merely Aunt Augusta and Gwendolen.
Kim (Samantha's best friend)   Samantha

JACK
How perfectly delightful!

ALGERNON
Yes, that is all very well; but I am afraid Aunt
Augusta won't quite approve of your being here.
Kim (who hates Michael)

JACK
May I ask why?

ALGERNON
My dear fellow, the way you flirt with Gwendolen
Samantha
is perfectly disgraceful. It is almost as bad as the
way Gwendolen flirts with you.

JACK
I am in love with Gwendolen. I have come up to
town   *Samantha*
Hollywood, where Samantha is.
expressly to propose to her.
ask Samantha to be girlfriend

ALGERNON
I thought you had come up for pleasure? . . . I call
random sex
that business.
stupid

JACK
How utterly <u>unromantic</u> you are!
dull

(and the scene continues)

As Michael was working on the scene for class, he found that some INNER OBJECTS were effective and some were less effective. After each rehearsal with his scene partner, he changed the less effective ones to try ones that he thought might work better. Your work isn't done until either you're finished shooting or the theatrical run is over. There are always new places you can go that will change and improve your work. Acting is an infinite experience; there's always something more to learn and more to experiment with. It's not over 'til the fat lady sings, and in art, the fat lady has laryngitis.

CHAPTER 6

Tool #6:
BEATS and ACTIONS

A BEAT is a thought. Every time there's a change in thought, there's a BEAT change. ACTIONS are the mini-OBJECTIVES attached to each BEAT that support the SCENE OBJECTIVE and therefore the OVERALL OBJECTIVE. An ACTION is phrased as trying to get the other person to do or feel something so that you can accurately respond to whether or not you are getting it. BEATS and ACTIONS provide different tactics in getting what you want.

Whenever a Thought Changes in the Script, a BEAT Changes

Put a bracket around each [BEAT] to indicate when one BEAT ends and the next BEAT begins. How many BEATS are there in this dialogue?

> "Why did you hurt me the way you did? No, don't answer that. . . . I know. Because you don't care, ya never did. And you know what? I don't care either. I don't care twice as much as you! So there!"

There are three BEATS:

> ["Why did you hurt me the way you did?] [No, don't answer that. . . . I know. Because you don't care, ya never did.] [And you know what? I don't care either. I don't care twice as much as you! So there!"]

A BEAT can be one word, one line or even as much as a page of dialogue. The criterion for a BEAT change is when the dialogue indicates a new thought. As with all of these acting tools, there are no absolutes. What will seem like a BEAT (thought) change in your initial script analysis might change when you are saying the words out loud. And the BEAT change might differ depending upon how the other actor(s) is responding to you. Always be open to the possibility of changing up the BEATS (thought changes). Staying open and being available to other choices will keep you present and raw. Think of BEAT analysis as an outline for you to draw from, a foundation you can use as a solid base to make the natural, in-the-moment adjustments that will arise in the heat of live action.

> *ACTIONS are mini-OBJECTIVES, the different approaches you take to most effectively achieve your SCENE OBJECTIVE. ACTIONS are accomplished both verbally and behaviorally.*

BEATS and ACTIONS produce a distinction between the various tactics you take to accomplish your SCENE OBJECTIVE. In other words, BEATS and ACTIONS are mini-OBJECTIVES. They are more precisely worded than your SCENE OBJECTIVE and must support the forward motion necessary *to win* your SCENE OBJECTIVE.

If my SCENE OBJECTIVE is *"to get you to give me a job,"* there are many ways I can go about getting you to want to do that. With words and behavior, the ACTION for a first BEAT may be *"to make you laugh."* With words and behavior, the ACTION for a second BEAT could be *"to impress you with my résumé."* With words and behavior, the ACTION for a third BEAT might be *"to amaze you with my intelligence."* With words and behavior, the ACTION for a fourth BEAT could be *"to get you to trust me."*

BEATS and ACTIONS provide a variety of tactics for getting what you want, supplying more colors to your work.

Working with BEATS and ACTIONS allows you to go after your SCENE OBJECTIVE with specificity and a range of behaviors. BEATS and ACTIONS give the scene variation and diversity, not only affecting how you say the words, but also how you behave. As you go after a BEAT and ACTION verbally, you'll find that your body feels compelled to join in the pursuit. Thus behavior is formed.

Like the SCENE OBJECTIVE, BEATS and ACTIONS have to be worded to elicit a reaction, to affect the other person, not just to talk at them.

Using BEATS and ACTIONS to affect the other person allows you to work moment to moment. Without the need to change or affect another person, it's easy to fall into the trap of memorizing a way of being. This is not particularly human. You want to duplicate the part of your life that is unconscious, unintentional and unplanned, because this will produce unpredictable, spontaneous results.

BEATS and ACTIONS allow you to be present and authentic.

When you are going after a BEAT and ACTION to get a reaction, it can't be planned. You not only have no way of knowing how you're going to say it (because you are focused on the other person rather than on yourself), but you also have no idea how the other person is going to react or how *you* are going to react to that person's reaction and then their reaction to your reaction. As a result, life—rather than a simulation of life—is allowed to take place.

Your need for a reaction from the other person
(BEAT and ACTION) empowers that person, because it
makes the other person feel necessary and important.

If you don't require a reaction from the other actor(s), you diminish them and weaken your ability to win your SCENE OBJECTIVE. Almost everyone has had the experience of being at a party where someone comes up to you and says, "Hey, how ya doin'?" but they don't really look at you or wait for your answer. Instead, they continue on their way or glance around the room, looking for other party guests who might be more important/sexy/interesting than you to talk to. How does this make you feel? Bad, inconsequential, almost like you're not really there, right? This is exactly how you cause another actor (or a casting director in an audition) to feel when you throw a line at them and don't really care how they respond.

Using the same speech we broke down into BEATS, let's play with a few associated ACTION possibilities:

["Why did you hurt me the way you did?]

[No, don't answer that. . . . I know. Because you don't care, ya never did.]

[And you know what? I don't care either. I don't care twice as much as you! So there!"]

Here are some possible BEAT and ACTION choices, staying true to the needs of the SCENE OBJECTIVE of *to get you to stay with me*:

• FIRST BEAT: "Why did you hurt me the way you did?"
   -ACTION: to get you to help me understand
   -Or: to get you to comfort me
   -Or: to make you feel guilty

• SECOND BEAT: "No, don't answer that. . . . I know. Because you don't care, ya never did."
   -ACTION: to get you to calm me down
   -Or: to get you to admit that I'm right
   -Or: to get you to tell me it's not true

• THIRD BEAT: "And you know what? I don't care either. I don't care twice as much as you! So there!"
   -ACTION: to make you feel my pain
   -Or: to challenge you to one-up me
   -Or: to scare you into thinking it's "over"

These BEAT and ACTION choices are all worded to get a reaction so that you can establish interaction with the other person and, thus, a relationship. The wording gives you a way to make the other person your focal point and keeps you from being self-conscious and self-indulgent.

Read the above lines again, but this time recite them out loud, trying each BEAT and ACTION choice for the dialogue.

See how much the way you say the line and your behavior changes upon each BEAT and ACTION choice? And the above choices are just a few possibilities. There are many different ways that you could specifically accomplish the SCENE OBJECTIVE of *"to get you to stay with me."*

The following examples express the same sentiments, but do not demand a response. These are passive and therefore far less effective.

- FIRST BEAT: "Why did you hurt me the way you did?"
  - ACTION: I want to understand.
  - Or: I feel sad.
  - Or: I think you're guilty.

- SECOND BEAT: "No, don't answer that. . . . I know. Because you don't care, ya never did."
  - ACTION: to be calm
  - Or: I believe I'm right.
  - Or: I don't want to believe this.

- THIRD BEAT: "And you know what? I don't care either. I don't care twice as much as you! So there!"
  - ACTION: to feel pain
  - Or: I feel challenged.
  - Or: It's over!

These are feelings, not BEATS and ACTIONS. Feelings do not provoke a reaction. With this phrasing, you don't need another person to interact with. You can have these feelings by yourself. Phrasing your ACTIONS as inactive feelings causes an introspective result as well as a reality that has no goal, need or desire for human interaction. Consequently, there is no movement, and no relationship is being established.

ACTIONS Have the Power to Change Meaning and Intention

This gives you the freedom to discover more interesting and unique ways of being and of speaking the dialogue. Without BEATS and ACTIONS, you are likely to make an obvious, literal reading. Take the sentence "I hate you" and use it as dialogue. On its own, the intention seems clear enough. But let's look at what happens when we switch the BEAT and ACTION up. Try saying "I hate you"

"To make you laugh."

Different from what you originally thought? Now say it

"To get you to admit guilt."

It has an entirely alternate meaning now. Okay, now say it

"To get you to comfort me."

You get the idea. The BEAT and ACTION you choose will determine what you're trying to communicate, regardless of the actual words. The BEAT and ACTION make the meaning of the words change drastically. Have you ever said "I love you" when what you really wanted to do (BEAT and AC-TION) was to get that person to have sex with you? Compare that line reading to the time you said "I love you" and what you wanted to accomplish (BEAT and ACTION) was to get the other person to say "I love you" back. Or the time when "I love you" meant you wanted the other person "to laugh at the absurdity of it all" (BEAT and ACTION). You can see why, if an actor plays "I hate you" or "I love you" using obvious, black-and-white ideas of "I hate you" or "I love you," they miss out on and lose all the other possibilities—the shades of gray—that exist between the black and white. The gray area is literally and figuratively blank and begs for interpretation that is inspired by specific BEAT and ACTION choices.

Ask yourself, "What do I want to win (SCENE OBJECTIVE)?
And what is the best, most effective way (both verbally
and behaviorally) to achieve it (BEATS and ACTIONS)?"

The ACTIONS must support the SCENE OBJECTIVE to create a focused thread that weaves throughout the entire scene. The more you go after trying to win your SCENE OBJECTIVE, BEAT by BEAT, ACTION to ACTION (using different approaches and tactics in both speech and physicalizing), and the more you find that you are *not* winning your SCENE OBJECTIVE, the more you'll be driven to try harder. This causes a crescendo to the arc you're creating in the scene. You also have to make the other character *want* to give you your SCENE OBJECTIVE by making the most effective choices for BEATS and ACTIONS.

Jennifer Beals kept this in mind and got compelling results when we worked on one particular scene in an episode of the Showtime series *The L Word*. *The L Word* is a series about lesbian women and all the inevitable trials and traumas they face in a world filled with homophobia and intolerance. In one scene, Jennifer's character, Bette, is a guest on a talk show, and she's engaged in a heated debate with Faye Buckley, this episode's nemesis. Faye abusively argues that Bette's art exhibition is pornographic. At the end of the scene, the character of Faye takes it too far and hits below the belt by using personal information about Bette, exclaiming,

> *"The Bible condemns homosexuality, Bette. That's why God took your lesbian lover's unborn child. The baby will be spared all the degradation he would have been subject to if he had been born into your deviant lifestyle. That baby is lucky he was never born."*

Bette retaliates by calling Faye a "monster" and by exposing a video of Faye's teenage daughter performing in an adult film, a film that Faye has done everything to keep under wraps. The ACTION for the BEAT when Bette says "monster" and reveals the video on camera could be vindictive. But Bette's SCENE OBJECTIVE is *"to make you* (the viewing audience, as the camera in a talk show is the third person in the scene) *take my side over Faye."* If Bette were to act maliciously and spitefully, she would seem cruel. The most effective way for her to win her SCENE OBJECTIVE was to rise above Faye's caustic words. We used the ACTION for this BEAT, *"to help you* (Faye) *understand your cruelty,"* as Bette gently said "monster" (instead of the obvious, on-the-nose and very ineffectual explosion of anger), and then compassionately slid the video across the table for Faye to see. If Bette were to respond vindictively, she would not be sympathetic to the talk show's audience. By using this BEAT and AC-TION, Jennifer made her character of Bette empathetic, a person whose side we, as the television-viewing audience, would gladly take.

Apply BEATS and ACTIONS to Nonverbal Moments

In an argument with your lover, you might stomp angrily out the door, slamming it behind you. Even though no words are spoken, you are still going after a BEAT and ACTION: *"to get you to stop me from leaving."* More often than not, the harder and more violently you slam the door, the more you want the other person to follow you out the door and stop you, which would prove that the other person loves you. This makes the BEAT and ACTION *"to get you to stop me from leaving"* support the bigger picture of the SCENE OBJECTIVE: *"to get you to prove you love me."*

Or the stage directions say that you are getting ready for bed with irritation and annoyance . . . within the framework of a SCENE OBJECTIVE of *"to make you take the blame so I don't have to."* The BEAT and ACTION could be *"to make you admit you feel guilty"* or *"to make you feel my pain"* or *"to get you to calm me down."*

There's a lot we can attempt to win through using BEATS and ACTIONS. Even when the other actor is speaking, your BEATS and ACTIONS should never stop.

When you are listening, you still need to make sense of what you want from the other character—*with or without words.* When you stop talking and the other person is speaking, you must continue to attempt to get the desired reACTION with behavior. Your needs don't stop just because your words do!

There are no right or wrong choices, just more effective or less effective ones.

You Must Consider Your Character's Modus Operandi, the Who-Am-I

Keep in mind the who-am-I of your character, the specific M.O. (modus operandi) of how your character would be most effective in winning the SCENE OBJECTIVE. A seductress or player generally wins a goal (SCENE OBJECTIVE) by using his or her sexuality. An intellectual generally wins a goal (SCENE OBJECTIVE) by using mind games and his or her intelligence. A class-clown type is going to use humor as his M.O. to win. A mobster, fighter, or gang-member type would use violence and aggression to get his way. In other words, always keep in mind *who* the character is and *how* they generally operate in life when making specific BEAT and ACTION choices.

I worked with Jon Voight on the movie *A Dog of Flanders*, where he played a father figure to a boy who believed he was an orphan. Until the end of the film, Jon's character does not know that he is the boy's biological father. The boy's mother died before she had a chance to tell him. To help the audience accept the story's ending, Jon used every opportunity to show the audience that he was and could be paternal with the boy. Within the spoken dialogue, he used BEATS and ACTIONS like *"to make you feel safe," "to get you to believe in yourself," "to make you feel protected," "to impress you with my loyalty"* and *"to make you feel loved."* These BEATS and ACTIONS helped serve as a kind of bookend for the movie. When he and the audience finally discover his character's paternity, they can accept it. Due to his BEATS and ACTIONS, his being the biological father made sense.

You Must Consider the Other Character's Modus Operandi, the Who-Are-They

You also have to consider the type of person the other character is, which will help you determine *how* to get what you want. The other character might be someone who uses their intellect to get what they want in life. You have to attempt to appeal to that person on their playing field, because they're more likely to give you what you want if they're getting what *they* want.

Your BEAT and ACTION Choices Should Be Focused and Driven

All your ACTION choices should come from the feeling of having a proverbial gun to your head. Because you're taking risks with your OVERALL OBJEC-TIVE, SCENE OBJECTIVE, OBSTACLES, SUBSTITUTION and INNER OBJECTS, the stakes should be personally very high for you. And when the stakes are high, as you know, every little thing that you do or say is important. Nothing is ever a throwaway. Every *how, why* or *what* means something. Imagine making a throwaway comment while someone is holding a gun to your head. It wouldn't happen. Every remark, every move counts when you're trying to save your life. Every scene should be about trying to resolve, overcome and accomplish something that is extremely valuable or meaningful to you, too. Your BEATS and ACTIONS must complement and further the realization of an extremely important goal (SCENE OBJECTIVE). This infuses your work with the power of a life-and-death struggle. That means you can't discount any moment or call anything irrelevant. Everything you say or do should advance the accomplishment of your goal, making the use of BEATS and ACTIONS imperative for the entire script.

Respond to the reaction of your BEAT and ACTION.

For instance, say you're telling a joke and, obviously, your ACTION for that BEAT would clearly be *"to make you laugh."* Think of all the possible reactions that can happen to the BEAT and ACTION of *"to make you laugh"*—a patronizing laugh, a forced laugh, a smirk, a voiced "Ha-ha, that's so funny I forgot to laugh," etc. You will have a different emotional reaction depending upon *how the other person responds* to your BEAT and ACTION. If the other person laughs, you'll feel great inside; if the other person doesn't, then you might feel terrible. It's important to go after your BEAT and ACTION and then see what kind of reaction you're getting, feel it (the good, the bad and all the in-between) and then respond accordingly.

Working to get a reACTION keeps you
out of your head and in the moment.

When you are deeply focused on getting a reACTION from the other person, it's difficult to watch yourself and set or preplan a way of saying and performing the dialogue. This creates spontaneity. Just think about those really high-stakes moments in your life, a situation when you wanted something so badly that you could just taste it. Remember how concentrated you were on the response of the other person (the person who could give you what you wanted). Diction, body language and every blink, sideways glance and inflection were interpreted, reinterpreted and retold to be interpreted yet again by your friends. You were hyperaware of everything they said or did. You need to be in the same state when you are acting.

You can repeat a BEAT and ACTION in the scene.

What you repeat depends on what's most effective given the circumstances of the material and the M.O. motivation of the character.

Try different BEATS and ACTIONS in rehearsal to identify the best ones.

As with many of the tools, do not intellectually determine your BEATS and ACTIONS. Let me repeat: Acting is a physical art form that requires you to experiment out loud and on your feet. You will not know what the most effective BEATS and ACTIONS are until you test-drive them and discover whether or not they effectively propel your SCENE OBJECTIVE forward.

BEATS and ACTIONS Realize the Words

When we first began working together on *The Larry Sanders Show*, one of my first notes to Garry Shandling was that he had to make his work more physical. Garry rose up the Hollywood ranks as a stand-up comedian. This means that, as a performer, he was used to relying on the words to be funny. But I pointed out to him, as I do to all of my clients, that what usually makes us laugh is not what someone says, but what someone *does*. BEATS and ACTIONS not only serve the dialogue, but also create behavior that goes along with it. When we walk out of the movies or the theater, we usually say, "I love the way the actor *did* something." It's rare when we comment, "I love the way the actor *said* a line."

One of the first exercises I did with him was to teach him how to physically realize a script's words. I did this by utilizing BEATS and ACTIONS. We would pick a scene, and then we'd figure out what the ACTION was to each BEAT. Next, I would read the cue line in the script and then he would behave the BEAT and ACTION rather than saying the lines. Let's look at a scene from an episode of *Larry Sanders* called "Adolf Hankler." Larry (Garry Shandling) is talking to his producer, Arthur (Rip Torn), about his brother, Stan, who's coming to visit. Larry is leaving his network talk show, and Jon Stewart (ironically played by Jon Stewart) is supposed to take over. For a long time, Larry's show has been his obsession—he has worked sixteen-hour days, and even his social life is geared around the show. Larry is panicked; he has no idea what he's going to do with his time after the show is over for him. He reaches out to family, to his brother, Stan, hoping he can get the love and support he so desperately needs now that he feels so displaced. Stan is an entrepreneur—well, he thinks he is. He's actually one of those pie-in-the-sky types whose moniker would be "the One Who Always Has a Stupid Plan That's Supposed to Make Me Rich but Actually Puts Me in the Poorhouse." Arthur is not only Larry's producer but his best friend. He knows that Stan is up to no good, because he's always up to no good. In the following scene, Arthur tries to warn Larry to stay away from Stan, no matter how much he might need him emotionally.

Now, let's take this scene and break it down into BEATS, indicated by brackets, and ACTIONS (mini-OBJECTIVES or tactics), which are always handwritten (in pencil) on the side to the right. This is so they will not be confused with the other tools that you'll also be writing on the page. These are possible ideas for BEATS and ACTIONS from Larry Sanders' point of view. These BEATS and ACTIONS are not etched in stone. Like all the tools, they can change upon your personal interpretation.

These particular BEATS and ACTIONS are geared toward driving the SCENE OBJECTIVE of *"to get you to help me feel better."*

Larry Sanders has just finished the show and is walking offstage when his producer, Arthur, stops to compliment him. These are BEATS and ACTIONS from the point of view of Larry.

THE LARRY SANDERS SHOW
EPISODE "Adolf Hankler"

ARTHUR
[Ahoy, Captain Sanders! The U.S.S. Hilarity is now
safely in her berth.

make you laugh

LARRY
Has anyone ever told you you should wear a
sailor's cap?

ARTHUR
Yeah, the late Rock Hudson.

LARRY
That's another conversation.]

ARTHUR
[So your brother Stan's coming to town?

get you to feel how desperate I am

LARRY
He's staying with me.]

ARTHUR
[Ah.

get you to stop judging me

LARRY
What's that supposed to mean?

ARTHUR
Oh nothing. Just practicing my Chinese.
(BEAT)
Just mail him a check?]

LARRY
[Because I can use the company.

make you feel my pain

ARTHUR
My advice? If you want expensive companionship,
buy yourself a shar-pei.]

LARRY
[Then there'll be two of us drinking out of the toilet.]

make you laugh

When Garry and I rehearsed this scene, I cued him using Arthur's dialogue; then Garry would wordlessly, physically express the BEAT and ACTION, using the INNER OBJECTS we had previously selected. Notice that Larry Sanders' M.O. is to be a funny guy, so the ACTION of *"to make you laugh"* is repeated. Garry's physicalized version produced some very funny comic behavior. Once he successfully realized the BEATS and ACTIONS through physicalizing, we went back and ran the scene using BEATS and ACTIONS this time with voiced dialogue. The behavior underlined the dialogue, making it twice as effective. BEATS and ACTIONS inspire an actor to physicalize the dialogue, making the experience more three-dimensional and relationship focused. The test for any good performance is to be able to cut the sound and still be able to laugh, cry and feel because the BEATS and ACTIONS reveal and drive the character's intentions.

Commit to Your BEATS and ACTIONS

Go after your ACTIONS boldly and without fear. Push the envelope. And don't be afraid to boldly realize your BEATS and ACTIONS. The more risks you take and the more fearless you are, the more exciting the end result will be.

Don't censor yourself.

Try anything that might seem even vaguely appropriate. You'll be surprised at the choices that work the best. Try different BEATS and ACTIONS in rehearsal to identify the best ones. As I've said many times thus far—you can't know unless you try it.

> *Consider what the character is really trying to do in accomplishing the SCENE OBJECTIVE. Read between the lines.*

You could be doing a scene where an angry couple is discussing a divorce. Just because your lines say you want to split up doesn't mean that's what your character really wants. As we saw earlier with the slamming door, more often than not, when we threaten to leave, we're really trying to get the other person to make us stay or prove in some way that they love us. Or you may be doing a scene in which your character is talking about how much they loved and respected some piece of literature. The truth is, they may have never read the book or they did read it and thought it was boring, but they're saying they liked it because they want to impress the other person with their brilliance or they simply want to make the other person like them.

Elisabeth Shue's critically acclaimed work for an off-Broadway production of Lanford Wilson's *Burn This* is a great example of how to read between the lines in which she supports her character's SCENE OBJECTIVE of *"to make you prove that you can love me without hurting me."* Here's a small excerpt of the script along with our notes, which will show you how we broke the scene down into BEATS and ACTIONS.

Remember: Bracket your BEATS and write your ACTIONS to the right side of the BEAT so you know exactly the words they connect to. There is not just one way of going after your SCENE OBJECTIVE. As long as you are being true to your SCENE OBJECTIVE, the who-am-I of your character and the who-are-they of the other character, you can use any of the hundreds of possible BEAT and ACTION choices. The choices below are the ones we initially made. Depending upon how her costar Peter Sarsgaard responded, she would change her BEATS and ACTIONS accordingly.

BURN THIS

by Lanford Wilson
(Excerpt from Act II)

(Anna's living room. It's late at night.)

ANNA
[Pale, I have never had a personal life. I wasn't scared of it, I just had no place for it, it wasn't important. And all that is different now and I'm very vulnerable,

impress you with my vulnerability

I'm not going to be prey to something I don't want. I'm too easy. Go someplace else.]

PALE
[I come to you.

make you beg to stay with me

                    ANNA
No, I said no. I don't want this. I'm not strong
enough to kick you out physically.]
[Why are you being so damned truculent? I said I
don't like you. I don't want to know you. I don't
want
                              make you sexually "want" me
to see you again. There is no reason for you to
come here. I have nothing for you. I don't like you
and I'm frightened of you.]

Even though the words *say* that Anna wants him to leave, the truth is that she wants Pale to stay. Too fragile and damaged by a tragedy that takes place earlier in the script, Anna needs to test Pale by pushing him away. If he stays no matter how abusive she is, then that is proof that he really loves her. If Elisabeth were to just play these lines using a literal, black-and-white interpretation of the script, then she actually would be trying to get rid of this man. But Elisabeth knew that her character needed love as well as a way to earn the right to get to the end of the script, where Anna and Pale profess intense love for each other.

> **Look at BEATS and ACTIONS as a subset of SCENE OBJECTIVE, and**
> **SCENE OBJECTIVE as a subset of your OVERALL OBJECTIVE.**

Seeing them this way, you can see how they make sense and fit together. They must drive an overall journey for the entire story.

Now that you have found the best way to put forward motion to the story in the scene, you have to understand how and why you got there in the first place. This is taken care of by using the MOMENT BEFORE.

CHAPTER 7

Tool #7:
MOMENT BEFORE

The event that happens right before you begin the scene, which gives you a place to move from, both physically and emotionally. It provides the how and why, triggering with great urgency and desperation the need to get your SCENE OBJECTIVE. You choose an event that emanates from information based in the script, but you use your real life in executing the MOMENT BEFORE. It should support and make sense to the personalizations you've made in your inner work.

The right MOMENT BEFORE will drive your SCENE OBJECTIVE, inspiring great need and urgency. There are three questions you must ask yourself when looking for your MOMENT BEFORE:

1. **What do I want?** SCENE OBJECTIVE.
2. **Why do I want it so badly?** Your OBSTACLES, SUBSTITUTION, and INNER OBJECTS provide you with a need to win your SCENE OBJECTIVE.
3. **Why do I want it so badly right now?** The MOMENT BEFORE increases your need to win your SCENE OBJECTIVE by giving it *urgency* and *immediacy*. In other words, the MOMENT BEFORE provides the scene with the idea and pressures of *time*.

The MOMENT BEFORE ramps up your need to win your SCENE OB-JECTIVE immediately. Whether you are playing a heated love scene or having a verbal or physical battle, the MOMENT BEFORE is the tool that moves you into the appropriate urgent mental, physical and emotional space for the scene. Additionally, the MOMENT BEFORE gives you a place to begin because, like life, a scene never starts from ground zero. The MOMENT BEFORE helps you know *why* and *where* you're coming from and *how* badly you presently need your SCENE OBJECTIVE.

It's important to know that a scene doesn't begin where it begins in a script. There is an assumed or implied event that has occurred to motivate the text. The practice of using a MOMENT BEFORE makes the on-the-page scene become a continuation of an ongoing interaction rather than the beginning of one. The MOMENT BEFORE allows you to treat every scene as if you are already in the thick of it.

In a play, an actor will use the MOMENT BEFORE directly before the curtain goes up, an act changes, and at the points where he leaves the stage for a time and then returns.

The MOMENT BEFORE is an even more crucial tool for actors working in film and television, because more often than not, scenes are shot out of order and as separate entities. For instance, the last scene of the movie—the one where the wife dies in her husband's arms—may be the first scene you have to shoot. The MOMENT BEFORE, in conjunction with the other work you've done—OVERALL OBJECTIVE, SCENE OBJECTIVE, OBSTACLES, SUBSTITUTION, INNER OBJECTS, BEATS and ACTIONS—will make it possible for you to have the heightened emotions and behaviors required for the scene.

Using the MOMENT BEFORE is also essential for film and television scenes because they're generally quite short. You simply don't have the time to start from nothing and build to a crescendo with less than three pages of dialogue. To keep the tension high with material connected by many short scenes, you must start each scene from an emotionally charged place.

Furthermore, due to the slow physical process of filmmaking, there are frequent delays. The MOMENT BEFORE is an essential tool for film work because it enables you to get back into character whenever you need to. The MOMENT BEFORE is the key to effectively and efficiently reestablish the needs of your character and their predicament.

APPLYING THE MOMENT BEFORE

1. Determine what personal event will produce a high-stakes need. (We'll discuss how to determine and choose the best event next.)

2. Just before the director says "Action!" or right before you walk onstage, give yourself about a minute to relive the personal event you've chosen. Think about it as if the event has just happened.

3. To relive the event, remember every detail. Think about the space—visualize what it looked, felt and smelled like and what the other person looked, felt and smelled like; hear the actual words you and he/she used; and feel your actions and reactions viscerally. Essentially, refeel it with all your senses. Let this reliving put you in a heightened emotional and physical state.

Applying the MOMENT BEFORE should never take more than a minute.

If it does, then you've picked the wrong event as your MOMENT BEFORE. Your personal event choice for a MOMENT BEFORE must affect you easily and immediately. Many actors will spend hours trying to pump up the appropriate emotions to keep themselves in the proper headspace for the scene. If it is a highly charged emotional scene, the actor may spend those hours trying to work up the memories of "the day their dog died." This way of working is not only draining for an actor, but also generates a huge mushroom cloud of feelings when the director finally calls "Action!" or the curtain goes up. And just like an explosion, it erupts quickly and then dissipates just as quickly. The resulting performance is vague for two reasons. First, a performance fueled by unrelated emotions will not be script motivated. This is problematic because when the feelings are unrelated to the story and the needs of your character there's no through line or direction for the emotions to go. Second, pumped-up emotions don't last very long—particularly if they are not grounded by what's happening in the script. Unless we human beings have the gravity of an event pressing on us, pinning us to our pain, our bodies instinctively move away or shut down when there is pain. A story-driven MOMENT BEFORE event will keep the appropriate feelings going throughout the scene because it's related to the material and makes logical sense to the story being told. Also, artificially inflated feelings don't allow for the emotions to naturally build and evolve the way they do in life. If you use the first six tools and choose an effective MOMENT BEFORE, it allows for all the details, subtleties and layers of emotion that real people display.

Always use personal events for your MOMENT BEFORE that are recent or based on past events where the issues remain unresolved—the lack of resolution keeps your feelings percolating in your heart and your mind.

Don't use an event that has been resolved. Knowing the outcome to an event, being aware of exactly how it's all going to turn out, doesn't inspire movement. It only creates regurgitated feelings. When choosing your MOMENT BEFORE event, it's important to think about what's going to motivate you to win. Using an event that you have anything less than a burning need to resolve undermines your fight to win your OVERALL and SCENE OBJECTIVES. If you use issues that are current, you won't need to emotionally stew for long periods of time, because you'll be trying to overcome a problem that you are living with every day and that is therefore emotionally available to you. Likewise, there may be an experience you had a long time ago but have not had closure or resolution on. This event, for all intents and purposes, can be considered a present event because it remains unresolved in your heart and mind. The repercussions of the event and your burning need for its resolution make the event a viable and powerful MOMENT BEFORE choice. Using something that deals with a current life issue as your MOMENT BEFORE wipes away the need to play mind games with yourself or to arbitrarily dig deep to get to that place that you ceased to care about long ago.

The only way to know if the feelings for an event are resolved is to try it using the MOMENT BEFORE.

Sometimes we think we have resolved an issue when in fact, lurking around in the dark corners of our mind, it continues to reside in a land I like to call *denial*, which is essentially the subconscious working overtime so that we don't have to deal with something that our brains and hearts deem too painful. Sometimes we'd like to think we're over someone or something because we need to feel that we are. In my experience, I've found that, more often than not, the emotional residue of painful events lingers in our subconscious for decades. You'll know if a MOMENT BEFORE event is unresolved and usable only by trying it.

Often we are unaware which personal events or relationships are unresolved. This became clear when I was trying to find a triggering MOMENT BEFORE for Gina, a student who needed to personalize the funeral scene of a loved one. Most of the time I explore my own life alongside my students to help them discover the most effective inner work choices. Revealing my own traumas, painful events, insecurities, fears, can help remind my students of their own experiences. We all suffer similarly. Allowing my own secret inner world to be exposed gives permission to my students to embrace their pain. We are all in this together.

Gina had never experienced the death of anyone close to her, so I opened up about the death of my father. He had died many years earlier and I believed that with therapy, soul-searching and time taking its course I had moved on and was over it. As we were going over the dialogue, images of my father on his deathbed kept emerging in my head. Although my conscious mind kept telling me I had found closure, I clearly had not, because the more we discussed the scene on her behalf, the more I started to cry on my own behalf. Why? I truly had resolved so many feelings about my father's death, but what I hadn't resolved, and probably never will, is that my father had never told me that he loved me—which made me wonder if he ever really did.

Telling my story reminded Gina that she had similar issues with her ex-fiancé, who had never said the words *I love you* to her. And although her ex-fiancé was very much alive, we could use the fact that he was unlikely to ever say those words to her because they had broken up. The death of a relationship that was supposed to establish a family and last a lifetime was an effective duplication of an actual death. So, as her MOMENT BEFORE, we used the event when he broke it off and the appropriate reactions and feelings were there to organically emerge as she performed the funeral scene.

As with all the tools, don't be afraid to change your MOMENT BEFORE choices. In the arts, change is inherent because interpretation is infinite.

You'll often come up with a great and powerful MOMENT BEFORE, but then something extreme occurs—someone unexpectedly dies, you have a car accident, you get dumped by your mate of ten years, you find out that your girlfriend's pregnant, you get fired and so on. Extreme changes in your life will be what is on your mind. The poignancy of the MOMENT BEFORE choice you've already made is weakened by the present, more pressing event. If this happens, change your MOMENT BEFORE to the tumultuous event that's just occurred.

One of my students, Susan, was doing a scene in class from Woody Allen's *Hannah and Her Sisters*. The scene opens with Hannah's sister Holly running into Hannah's ex-husband, Mickey, at a record store. Holly, an ex-actress turned screenwriter, asks Mickey, a television writer, if he will help her with her script. After many gibes at her expense, he agrees.

Susan performed the scene for the class. Her first run was lifeless because her MOMENT BEFORE event wasn't motivating her needs and feelings for the scene. The other problem was that her version of the scene—a Woody Allen scene—wasn't funny. And that's not good. I asked Susan what she was using, and she related to me a light event, because she had assumed that one should use light choices in humorous material. That's when I knew she was really on the wrong track. The truth of comedy is that the inner choices an actor makes must be more desperate, painful, angry and darker than drama! So I asked Susan what was going on in her life that would drive her to be more desperate and angry. She tearfully confessed that she had been violently carjacked a few nights before. She was mildly bruised, but her husband was critically injured. This event was so traumatizing that they were considering moving away from Los Angeles to safer shores. But the decision to leave L.A. meant that she would have to give up her dreams of pursuing an acting career. Her pressing dilemma was that she needed help to make the decision whether she should stay in Los Angeles, continue to follow her dreams and live in a constant state of fear, or leave, give up and feel safe.

The carjacking as a MOMENT BEFORE was a great choice because it was unresolved and wrought with repercussions that could conceivably be life-changing. This MOMENT BEFORE also allowed Susan to use her need to get help about whether she should move or not as her INNER OBJECT for Holly's need to get help on her screenplay. We had to also change her SUBSTITUTION for the character of Mickey to a friend who was a V.I.P. in the film business.

All of this work heightened the personal stakes for Susan and her character. She ran the scene again. This time, when Holly asked Mickey for help with her writing, Susan felt like she was asking for help with her decision to stay or go from someone whom she trusted and who would know the best answer. Changing the MOMENT BEFORE event to one that was more currently significant—which changed her INNER OBJECTS and SUBSTITUTION—allowed Susan to tell a linear story for both her inner and outer work. Her new MOMENT BEFORE choice also provided an edge and urgency to the scene and drove Susan to go after her SCENE OBJECTIVE of *"to get you to love and help me"* as if her life depended on it, because it did. And the laughs that were so sorely missing in the first run of the scene were plentiful in the rework.

Using WHAT IF Circumstances

If your life is pretty steady—if there's nothing particularly pressing happening—and you can't come up with an unresolved past event that appropriately affects you, don't try to make more out of a present event than there is or try to use some past event that you've ceased to care about. Instead, use a WHAT IF event based on a real fear. A WHAT IF event is what it sounds like: an imagined experience born out of a deep-seated, well-founded personal fear. To use a WHAT IF event as your MOMENT BEFORE, you imagine all the details of an event that *could* happen as if it *has* happened. For instance, if a loved one is terminally ill, then you could use your feelings—the fear, anger, sadness—to imagine and picture what it will be like when they actually die. Or if you feel your job is in jeopardy but you haven't yet been fired, you can still imagine the event—the boss calling you into her office and sitting you down, and you getting cold sweats, not having a way to pay your bills, becoming homeless, etc.

When using a WHAT IF circumstance as your MOMENT BEFORE, it must be based on a real, plausible fear that is personal to you.

If you don't fear your mother's death because she's in good health, then you can't use her death as a WHAT IF event because it's too implausible for you to suspend disbelief. This is not an effective WHAT IF fear. It's too far-fetched for your psyche and imagination to latch on to. Although, if a fear is well-founded, the possibility of the event manifesting itself is often more intimidating and powerful than actual events, because we have no idea how they are going to turn out. And as you know, we always imagine the worst. It's part of being human. People are paranoid creatures and we gravitate toward the negative. But ironically, our negative tendencies and fears often produce a positive result in acting by providing us with weightier and more powerful MOMENT BEFORE events. The MOMENT BEFORE event must have a germ of possibility and, even better, the odds of probability.

Amy Smart had a particularly difficult role in the movie *The Butterfly Effect*. The film tells the story of Evan Treborn (played by Ashton Kutcher), who tries to recover his memory by traveling to his past. But every time he changes something about his past, it changes his present reality. Amy plays the character of Kayleigh Miller, Evan's childhood friend and love interest. As a result, each time Evan changes something in his past, it affects Kayleigh's life, too—who she is as a person, her life events, her memories. As the result of one of his trips into his past—in which Evan abandons young Kayleigh after he discovers that she was being molested by her father—Kayleigh becomes a prostitute and a heroin addict. In one particular scene that explores this prostitute-addict scenario, an older Evan runs into the older Kayleigh and sees how destroyed her life is. Evan knows it's his fault and tries to fix it. Amy and I came up with the SCENE OBJECTIVE of *"to make you take the blame so I don't have to,"* not only so her character doesn't have to take responsibility for her predicament, but because it is, after all, his fault.

We needed a good MOMENT BEFORE for this scene. Something that would not only duplicate Kayleigh's damaged persona, but that would include the pain and abandonment caused by someone she once loved very much. We had to find something in Amy's life that would parallel this kind of pain so she could become Kayleigh.

Needless to say, Amy is not a prostitute or a drug addict. Primal abandonment issues were not available to her because Amy has a terrific relationship with her happily married parents. The only painful thing we could identify was that Amy and her longtime boyfriend had split up right before the movie began to shoot. But it wasn't anything huge that had happened; in fact, they got back together soon after the film wrapped. So we needed to use a WHAT IF as her MOMENT BEFORE.

It's natural in any split-up to fear that you are dispensable and easily replaced. Most people fear that their estranged mate is bound to find someone else and that sex is likely to happen. Even though there was no real proof of Amy's boyfriend having sexual liaisons with anyone else, the fear that he might have been was real. It *could* have been happening. As a result of this organic fear that she was feeling, we came up with her MOMENT BEFORE: WHAT IF she found out that her boyfriend was with someone else and falling in love with that person? Amy then made the fear real to her by picturing it happening—actually visualizing her boyfriend in sexual congress with a girl and saying "I love you" to her. She became upset and angry and felt betrayed and abandoned. Her MOMENT BEFORE made her feel inordinately ugly, replaceable, hurt beyond repair and needy for relief from the pain (giving her the reality of a heroin addict). With this WHAT IF MOMENT BEFORE, sweet, even-tempered Amy became a foulmouthed, in-your-face, drug-addled prostitute.

Or you can take a real event from the past—a rape, abuse, violence or abandonment event—but instead of trying to re-create the past event, imagine the same event happening again right now.

In other words, WHAT IF it were to happen again? Imagining a traumatic event happening yet again is an effective choice to use for your MOMENT BEFORE. It works on two levels. First, as we saw with my student Susan, who was carjacked, traumatic events cause us to live with a profound fear of the event happening again. Traumatic events will always live in our minds in vivid detail, along with the constant apprehension that they could come to pass once again. Working with this ever-present fear makes this WHAT IF MOMENT BEFORE event accessible and intense. Second, imagining WHAT IF an event happens again *now* makes the MOMENT BEFORE present. You know how it turned out last time, but a second time leaves you with other possible repercussions. Why? Essentially, the second time becomes an entirely new event, because you're a different person now, and the differences are informed by the original trauma—you may be more leery and less naive now. This gives you great OBSTACLES to overcome, because if the event happens again, it might just be your fault for being a magnet to your personal trauma, a self-saboteur. This kind of MOMENT BEFORE drives you to especially need to accomplish your SCENE OBJECTIVE because there's so much at stake.

Always Make a MOMENT BEFORE Event Choice Come from an Emotional, Relationship Point of View

Rather than an event that is exclusively script inspired, your MOMENT BE-FORE event should come from an emotional, relationship point of view. Your interpretation should be motivated by your unique, individual life story. This creates a more compelling, one-of-a-kind performance because there's only one you. In one episode of the critically acclaimed series *Once and Again*, Susanna Thompson's character of Karen Sammler is having a nervous breakdown and then has a horrible accident—she's hit hard by a speeding car while out walking—that forces her to reassess her life. At the time, Susanna was going through a similarly disruptive time in her personal life. After living in the same house for eight years, she was told that she had to move within a month. It was Christmastime and the cast and crew were in the midst of a heavy shooting schedule (working days). For Susanna, this home was her base, her sanity. We talked about how displaced she felt. That her whole orientation—the ease of knowing where she shopped, ate, did her dry cleaning, not to mention where she kept her personal effects—was off. The situation caused her to feel discom-bobulated, alone and terribly insecure about her future. Therapists and studies alike say that moving is one of the most stress-inducing experiences there is. I'm sure if you've suddenly had to move from a safe haven to an unknown fu-ture abode, you know what an anxiety-ridden experience it is. And to add to her stress, it was December, the holiday season, a very difficult time to find new digs in L.A., which gave rise to the not-so-unreasonable fear of being to-tally homeless. So duplicating a true nervous breakdown via thinking about a move isn't so far-fetched. I told Susanna to picture being homeless and horribly displaced in midwinter as her MOMENT BEFORE event for the car accident scene. An accident that the audience has to believe might have been no acci-dent at all but a suicide attempt. By imagining her own personal horror of being homeless, she was allowed to feel the shock, upset and disorientation that one feels when having a nervous breakdown. This helped her create an eerily accurate representation of how a real nervous breakdown looks and feels. Why? Because she was really feeling it.

Sometimes using a straw-that-broke-the-camel's-back event from your life as your MOMENT BEFORE choice can be very effective.

Although a particular event might not be so terrible when viewed in and of itself, when it is compounded by previous other bad events, it can turn an otherwise unpleasant event into something excruciating. What if you were to just find out that you've lost your job and soon after your mate told you that they were leaving you? The previous event makes the present event that much more bleak.

When David Spade was in my class (before he was on *SNL*), he did a scene from the movie *Broadcast News*. In the scene, his character of Aaron Altman is home alone lamenting how badly he's screwed up his first opportunity to be a news anchor. Aaron was so nervous and sweating so profusely on the air that audience members had called in because they were afraid he was having a heart attack. Needless to say, Aaron wasn't going to get another chance at his dream. But who should pop by unexpectedly but Jane Craig, the girl he's in love with. For a moment, it seems like things are looking up. But unfortunately, Jane has stopped by to tell Aaron she's in love with his archrival, Tom. Not Aaron's day. As Aaron, David needed a strong MOMENT BEFORE to make Jane's news feel lethal. As his MOMENT BEFORE, David chose to use a dire event of his own—he had recently blown a showcase for *The Tonight Show*, which is considered a career maker for stand-up comics. When it happened, David was at his wit's end and feeling completely distraught about his career, which made for a potent MOMENT BEFORE.

Common MOMENT BEFORE Examples

Remember: The MOMENT BEFORE is an event that takes place before the scene begins and one that makes you *need* the SCENE OBJECTIVE with urgency and desperation. Your MOMENT BEFORE must make sense to your SCENE OBJECTIVE and correlate to your inner work choices.

The following MOMENT BEFORE suggestions are set up without your personalizations, but are common options to give you ideas of what you can use from your own life (whether they are real or WHAT IF events). Always consider the weightiest event that would most likely motivate an urgent need to accomplish your SCENE OBJECTIVE. And relive the event in the most visceral way (sounds, smells, visuals, what was said, etc.). Even if it's a WHAT IF event, experience it as if it actually has happened, and imagine it in the most emotionally dire ways.

If the SCENE OBJECTIVE is *"make you fall in love with me,"* then an appropriate MOMENT BEFORE is something that has happened to you recently or a worst-fear event (a WHAT IF event) that makes you shamelessly and desperately need to be loved *right now*. Some possible events include:

- Your mate has broken up with you—the event when it happened.
- You find out your mate is cheating on you—the event when you caught them in the act.
- You told your friend that you have deeper feelings beyond a friendship connection and they revealed they don't feel the same way.
- Your best friend likes another friend better than you, and you overhear that person saying so.
- Your sibling has expressed they no longer want a relationship with you.

If the SCENE OBJECTIVE is *"to get you to give me my power back,"* then an appropriate MOMENT BEFORE is something that has happened to you recently or a worst-fear event (a WHAT IF event) that makes you urgently need to get your power back *right now*. Some possible events include:

- You've just been made to feel very stupid by your lover, a family member or a friend.
- You've just been unreasonably fired in front of everyone and you feel compelled to seek revenge.
- You've gotten into a violent fight with someone and lost the battle.

- You've been mugged, robbed or carjacked or you have experienced some sort of physical violation that made you feel powerless.
- A person has emasculated or diminished you in a horrible, life-changing way.
- You've been lied about or to, and it has caused irreparable damage.

If your SCENE OBJECTIVE is *"to get you to worship me"* or *"to get you to look up to me,"* then you must have a MOMENT BEFORE that makes you feel so small and diminished that it becomes essential that you achieve your SCENE OBJECTIVE, because it's the only way to feel confident again. Some possible events include:

- You've just been fired from your job.
- Your mate just dumped you for not being good enough for them.
- A director/producer/casting person just told you you should give up acting.
- You've asked someone for a date and that person says no and acts like you're a bad smell that won't go away.
- You've been criticized by your mother, who implied you were a loser.
- You've been cruelly blamed for something you didn't do.

MOMENT BEFORE for First-Time Sexual Scenes

Many feel there's nothing more uncomfortable than doing a scene that includes some form of intimacy. A good MOMENT BEFORE takes away the inherent discomfort of these scenes by playing into the problem, instead of avoiding it (which only makes you more uncomfortable). The following MOMENT BEFORE suggestions tap into our deepest insecurities, neuroses and desires. For example:

Before first-time sex (for both men and women):

MOMENT BEFORE: First, think about your deepest insecurities in this area: what you fear *might* occur or sexual issues that *might* emerge during the sex act.

Imagine a time when the worst of your sexual issues/fears were realized or use WHAT IF it happens again. Then vividly fantasize sexually about the person/actor in front of you and hope (and pray) that your sexual issues won't be revealed.

- *If you're a man*, think about size issues, sexual dysfunction, performance anxiety, weird sexual predilections that could be misunderstood and rejected, talking too much during the sex act, etc.
- *If you're a woman*, think about breast-size issues, fat or cellulite in places that only the act of sex can reveal, a propensity for being too vocal or too quiet, weird sexual predilections that might make you look like a slut or a prude, etc.

Directly after first-time sex (for both men and women):

MOMENT BEFORE: Think about your deepest insecurities in this area and deal with your worst sexual fears or issues having *just occurred* in their full glory during the sex act and now you have to suffer the torturous consequences of the aftermath. As a MOMENT BEFORE, viscerally relive an event when the worst of your sexual issues were revealed. Imagine your sex partner thinking the worst thoughts about your issue.

- *If you're a man*, think about size issues, sexual dysfunction, performance anxiety, weird sexual predilections that are misunderstood and rejected, talking too much during the sex act, etc.
- *If you're a woman*, think about breast-size issues, fat or cellulite that can and has been discovered during the act, your propensity to be too loud or too quiet, weird sexual predilections that might make you look like a slut or a prude, etc.

MOMENT BEFORE for Fight Scenes

There's always a reason for a fight, be it physical or verbal. Consider your SCENE OBJECTIVE, which in a fight scene is usually *"to make you wrong so I can be right"* or *"to get my power back from you."*

MOMENT BEFORE: You must first look at your SUBSTITU-
TION choice and the inner story that reflects this SUBSTITU-
TION, because whom you picture will establish the subject of
the fight and the event you'll use as your MOMENT BEFORE.
The MOMENT BEFORE event should be one that will trigger
the fight. So when the scene begins with the verbal and/or
physical dispute in its full glory, you have a heightened reason
and purpose to fight.

In the film *In the Bedroom*, there's a verbal war between a husband (played
by Tom Wilkinson) and wife (played by Sissy Spacek) over which of them is to
blame for their son's death. The SCENE OBJECTIVE for each character is *"to
get you to take the blame so I don't have to."* Both characters were simultaneously
taking responsibility *and* blaming each other for his death, which is a very realistic depiction of this kind of trauma. To play either character in this scene,
a MOMENT BEFORE could be to remember a tragic event that's happened to
you and that you feel very guilty about (or imagine a WHAT IF tragic event
that you fear could happen to you and that you would feel guilty about). Your
SUBSTITUTION choice would be the person who you want to believe caused
the tragedy. By using a tragic event that you feel guilty about as your MO-
MENT BEFORE, it propels you to try to assuage your guilt by winning the
SCENE OBJECTIVE of *"to get you to take the blame."*

Another classic fight scene is in Noël Coward's play *Private Lives*. In the
second act, ex-lovers Amanda and Elyot are holed up in Amanda's apartment,
trying to piece their relationship back together. Both characters have the
SCENE OBJECTIVE of *"to make you be the bad guy so I can be the good guy."* It's
late at night, they're drinking and, of course, the subject of their breakup
comes up. They each have their own perspective about what happened and
who is responsible, and each blames the other. Both Amanda and Elyot feel
like they're the victim of the other's abuse. They begin to verbally spar and end
up in a physical brawl. For this scene, your MOMENT BEFORE would be to
recall the most abusive event that was caused by your SUBSTITUTION.

MOMENT BEFORE for a Make-Up Scene

The SCENE OBJECTIVE for a make-up scene is usually *"to get you to love me in spite of what I did"* or *"to get you to absolve me of my guilt."*

> MOMENT BEFORE: Think of an event that makes you feel that you were wrong, something that instills great guilt in you. This makes you feel like you must fix the problem because it's your fault. Pick events that are applicable to your SUBSTITUTION and the inner story you've created. Some possible MOMENT BEFORE events include:
>
> • A specific time when you cheated on your mate.
> • A specific time when you were caught doing something illegal.
> • A specific time when you lied about substance-abuse problems.
> • A specific time when you were caught lying to or slandering your SUBSTITUTION.
> • A specific time when you were verbally/physically abusive to your SUBSTITUTION.
> • A specific time when you were caught stealing from your SUB-STITUTION.

The MOMENT BEFORE is a real or WHAT IF event that takes place before the scene begins and that makes you need your SCENE OBJECTIVE to happen A.S.A.P. You take this event and you imagine it happening, in its vivid entirety, right before the scene begins. You recall or imagine the space, the smells, what was said or could have been said, and the high-stakes emotions that accompanied or would accompany the event, and you feel them viscerally happening in the present. I know I'm being hyper-repetitive here, but with this particular tool, the repetition is warranted.

You've got to rehearse with your MOMENT BEFORE to find out if the MOMENT BEFORE event you've chosen—real or WHAT IF—is going to affect you and best instill an urgent need to win your SCENE OBJECTIVE. A powerful MOMENT BEFORE choice will push your buttons immediately. If it doesn't affect you within a minute, then continue to try other MOMENT BEFORE choices until you find one that really drives your SCENE OBJECTIVE.

CHAPTER 8

Tool #8:
PLACE and FOURTH WALL

> Using PLACE and FOURTH WALL means that you endow
> the physical environment with attributes from a PLACE
> from your real life to create privacy, intimacy, history, mean-
> ing and reality. The PLACE and FOURTH WALL you choose
> must support and make sense with your personalizations.

The PLACE and FOURTH WALL must support and make sense to the choices you've made for the other tools to be able to bring an additional layer of the real human experience to your work. Applying information from the inner story you have created, ask yourself the question "What PLACE from my life will inform my choices and make the ones I've already made have even higher stakes?" In life, different places motivate different emotional responses.

Say your SCENE OBJECTIVE is *"to get you to admit you're wrong and apologize,"* and you're using your mother as your SUBSTITUTION. You need a PLACE that heightens your reality—something that really magnifies the feeling of betrayal and propels your need to accomplish your goal (SCENE OBJECTIVE). To find your PLACE, you must first identify where the scene in the script takes place. Inside or outside? Is the inside or outside space private or public?

Once you have identified what kind of space the scene is in, you then correlate the script's space with a PLACE from your life. In this case—getting someone to admit they are wrong and apologize and using your mother as your SUBSTITUTION—you would need to think of a PLACE where your mother deceived you or let you down. This PLACE from your life should be either the PLACE in your MOMENT BEFORE or a PLACE where a similar event of betrayal happened with your SUBSTITUTION (in this example, your mother) that makes sense to the scripted scene. If the scene is in a public inside space, like a restaurant, think of a PLACE where your family always dined and where your mother always belittled you—perhaps the place where she berated you for being too fat. If the scene is an inside private PLACE, an effective PLACE could be your childhood bedroom, where your mother frequently physically or verbally abused you. If the scene is an outside public space, you could use the elementary school steps that you waited on for three hours when she forgot to pick you up from school when you were eight.

No matter what kind of space a scene is in—inside and public, inside and private, outside and public, outside and private—the process of identifying the type of space and then identifying your personalized PLACE will help round out the inner personal story you've built with the first seven tools, which all support and reflect your character's feelings and goals.

The best way to understand how using PLACE can support an actor's work is by looking at a specific scene and breaking it down. At one point in the film *Titanic*, the character of Jack Dawson sketches the character of Rose DeWitt in her stateroom. Except for a priceless necklace, Rose is completely nude. Rose, a society girl, is engaged to Cal, a manipulative and wealthy young man. Jack is young, without a family, and poor. He won his steerage seat on the ship in a card game. Rose's SCENE OBJECTIVE is *"to get you* (Jack) *to fall in love with me."* Obviously, the scene's space is inside and private, although there is the chance that Rose's mother or fiancé, Cal, could burst in and surprise them at any time. This is just one of the many OBSTACLES that you would need to keep in mind for this scene. You must always consider the scene's inherent OBSTACLES in making a choice for PLACE.

Rose's OBSTACLES are:

1. Possible rejection.
2. I'm nude and I'm not comfortable with my body (be specific—hips, stomach, breasts, cellulite, etc.).
3. WHAT IF he thinks I'm too easy?
4. My fiancé could burst in at any time and kill Jack or me or both of us.

5. My mother could burst in at any time and have a fit.
6. The disparity of social standing between us.

If you were playing the character of Rose, the PLACE you find from your life would not be the one that most replicates a ship's luxurious, walnut-paneled stateroom. Instead, you would have to think of a PLACE from your life that invites these six OBSTACLES and works with your SUBSTITUTION for the character of Jack.

As with all the tools: Always reproduce the physical aspects of the script from an emotional point of view.

PLACES that might work for the *Titanic* stateroom scene include:

- If you're using your ex-mate as your SUBSTITUTION for Jack because you still have feelings for him, then:
  - PLACE: Your ex-mate's living room.
  - This choice naturally infuses the stakes of history with your ex-mate, as well as the danger of being hurt again. The risky person who can burst in on you could be your present mate or the friend and/or relative who always disliked that person.

- If as your SUBSTITUTION for Jack, you're using a crush or someone you have a crush on who is in some way related to your present mate by friendship, family or work association, then:
  - PLACE: Your present bedroom, where you live with your mate.
  - This PLACE is dangerous by the very nature of the constant reminder that you are being unfaithful. Furthermore, your mate could show up at any moment.

- If you're using a platonic friend (for whom you have feelings that go beyond friendship) as your SUBSTITUTION for Jack, then:
  - PLACE: Your friend's apartment.
  - This choice incorporates the danger of the loss of friendship. If the affair doesn't work out, it's unlikely you'll ever be able to

get back to being friends again. The person that could burst in on you could be another friend who is a part of your group who would be alarmed at your state of undress and bound to tell everyone else.

- If you're using your boss as your SUBSTITUTION for Jack, then:
  - PLACE: Your boss' office.
  - This place will remind you of the impropriety of the situation, as well as include the danger that a coworker, secretary, spouse, etc. can abruptly enter uninvited. Also, if an affair doesn't work out with someone you're employed by, you might lose your job.

Of course, these are just four suggestions drawn from the infinite list of possibilities. If you were really playing the character of Rose, then in your rehearsal time, you would try as many SUBSTITUTION-related options for PLACE that came to mind to see which one felt the most powerful and fueled your SCENE OBJECTIVE.

Once you've identified a few locations that you might use as your PLACE, based on your SCENE OBJECTIVE and SUBSTITUTION, you must create it. Creating PLACE means that you endow the location—set, stage, classroom—with attributes from your personal PLACE. Let's look at how you would create PLACE with the first example for the *Titanic* scenario, your ex-mate's living room.

APPLYING PLACE

Remember notable parts about your ex-mate's living room. This includes thinking about the furniture, the flooring, the color of the walls, the posters or art on the walls, the windows and doors, the smells, the sounds, the temperature. Once you have conjured up as accurate an image as possible, match the shapes on the set with similar shapes that exist in your ex-mate's living room. For instance, match the couch on the set with the couch from your ex-mate's living room—see the colors, the fabric. Endow the side table on the set with the stereo system from your ex's living room. The paintings on the wall of the set are windows. The wood floor becomes the blue carpeting. The smells are his personal brand of cologne. The sounds are of the traffic that was constantly flowing by. Feel a chill in the air because your ex always kept the thermostat on low because he hated to sweat. As you endow each significant part of the PLACE, think about events—both traumatic and wonderful—that have taken place in that space. Remember the first time you made love on the couch. And then recall that this was the same couch where you discovered the flowered thong underwear that didn't belong to you. See the poster that you bought for him. Hear the CD he used to play ad nauseam. Picture the door that you slammed as you exited for the last time. Do this until you feel like you have transported yourself from the soundstage, acting class or theater to the actual PLACE you've chosen.

BOTTOM LINE: Once you choose the best PLACE, spatially endow the existing set with the reality of what's in the room of the personal PLACE you've selected.

If you're doing stage work, endow PLACE before every rehearsal. If you're doing film or television work, spend some time on the set of the scene you're about to shoot. Create your PLACE, get comfortable in your PLACE and make it real to you by remembering emotionally appropriate events and experiences that happened in that PLACE.

My late husband, Lyndon Chubbuck, and I produced and he directed a movie called *Kiss Toledo Goodbye* starring Christopher Walken. With each new set and on every new location, Walken would walk around on the set before it was lit, touching and generally using the furniture—sitting in a chair, touching items on the coffee table, perusing the books on the bookshelf—until the space was real to him and contained the appropriate history and feelings. He was invoking his PLACE. So when it was time to actually film the scene, there was no distinction—Walken's world and the set were one.

The choice you use for PLACE should have *inherent* obstacles.

If the PLACE you choose is too easy to be in, you won't be compelled to win your SCENE OBJECTIVE. Let's say you're doing a scene in which your character is on a job interview and the SCENE OBJECTIVE is *"to get you to love me so you'll give me the job."* If you use a PLACE where you were once easily hired, there are no stakes. This is because that PLACE doesn't give you the nervous feeling that you get when you are on an interview and really want the job. A more effective PLACE choice would be a PLACE where you once blew an incredibly important audition. This PLACE feeds your SCENE OBJECTIVE, infusing your work with a desperate need and desire to make the audition go well because you don't want to screw up the way you did last time.

It's amazing how substantially PLACE affects us. Think about a restaurant that you used to frequent with a past mate. Now think about how it would feel to eat at this restaurant with a new person just weeks after you broke up with your former partner. The feeling changes, right? What was once a cozy second home becomes a PLACE that produces anxiety and discomfort. You'd fear your ex showing up (after all, it was your special place), you'd remember the horrible arguments that occurred there and that could happen again if your date turns out to be a long-term partner and you'd think that you might never have a mate again because the PLACE is a constant reminder that you failed so miserably with your ex. Where we are affects our feelings and needs.

David Hare calls attention to the importance of PLACE in *The Blue Room*, his play freely adapted from *La Ronde* by Arthur Schnitzler. Just by naming his play *The Blue Room*, Hare calls attention to the integral role that PLACE plays in every story. The play chronicles a series of sexual encounters. In one scene, a senator is having an affair with a very young intern. I asked Bill Moses, star of *Melrose Place*, *Falcon Crest* and numerous television movies, to do this scene for me in class. Bill knew that his character's central OBSTACLES were that he was married and a senator. The senator would worry that his wife, the press and his constituents would discover his indiscretion. As we've seen so many times in my country's illustrious political past, this kind of discovery is a shortcut to the unemployment line. Additionally, there was the age OBSTACLE—the intern's inappropriately young age would not be good for the ol' résumé. Bill and I talked about what PLACE would summon this kind of sexual heat and the danger of discovery. Bill had already gone through one divorce with a child involved. If he were to get caught having an affair, he would have to go through the whole ugly mess again—a trauma he would have gladly forgone. So, Bill used his bedroom with the WHAT IF of he was having an affair and his wife and child were out of the house. Having sex on the bed (he had endowed it with his own bed, which he shared with his wife and where their child had been conceived) took on dangerous heat when he imagined sharing it (in the biblical sense) with his SUBSTITUTION. Bill endowed PLACE using shapes and memories: picturing the furniture he'd bought with his wife, sniffing smells of his wife's clothes and perfume and being aware of the bed's idiosyncrasies. This magnified Bill's feelings of guilt and fear (his wife could show up at any time) and he became sexually charged (it's always more erotic when there's danger involved). It was a powerful performance that was fueled by a strong, effective PLACE.

> **PLACE is an essential tool, even if it's supposed to**
> **be a PLACE your character has never been in before.**

A lot of actors will try to play a trick on themselves: They won't go on a set until it's time to shoot if it's supposed to be a new PLACE to the character or a PLACE they're entering for the first time. This works well for the first take, but what about the second or the fourteenth? How about all the setups for each scene? You'll be using the set again and again for the master shots, two-shots, close-ups, etc. What do they do then? This is why making a conscious choice to use a personal PLACE is always important. You need a PLACE that you can rely on that will supply the appropriate feelings over and over. And believe it or not, there are many PLACES in your life that can duplicate the anxiety of being in a space for the first time.

For instance, if you're doing a horror film and the direction in the script is for your character to walk into a haunted house for the first time, a very effective PLACE choice could be the home you grew up in but haven't been in for years. And to make this first-time experience scary—it is a haunted house, after all—remember and picture unpleasant memories (INNER OBJECTS) from your childhood as you look around the PLACE. This will give you the same eerie feeling that one has when walking into a haunted house. Note that when you work this way, the PLACE also informs your SCENE OBJECTIVE by giving you even more OBSTACLES (the bad memories) to overcome.

Use PLACE to Create a Feeling of Privacy

PLACE helps you feel like you are unwatched and alone. We as the audience should feel like flies on the wall watching something so intimate and private that we feel like we're observing events that we shouldn't be privy to.

Using a PLACE that originates from your childhood can be extremely powerful because it's so primal.

The memories that emanate from our childhood are potent because so much of who we are today stems from those past experiences. No matter how old we get, we always seem to vividly remember important childhood events. This includes not only *what* happened, but *where* it happened. And the *where* seems to instill very strong pictures and feelings. If you've ever revisited your old elementary school or driven through the old neighborhood or even gone to that Burger King where you and your friends used to hang out—the memories of experiences, good and bad, come flooding into your head.

Use PLACE to enhance your feelings.

Every PLACE from your life has an emotional base. It doesn't matter how innocuous a PLACE seems to be, an event has occurred there that has some form of an emotional attachment. You must choose a PLACE that has the most powerful emotional connections to produce the highest dramatic intent.

For many years I've worked with Emmy Award–winning actress Michelle Stafford on her character of Phyllis on the daytime drama *The Young and the Restless*. In one of her storylines, Phyllis is framed for setting fire to her husband Jack's guesthouse. Phyllis is thrown in jail. Feeling alone, betrayed and defeated, she goes crazy. We talked about what we could use for PLACE that would be rich with the sense of being imprisoned. I told her that prison can be any PLACE that motivates a sense of being physically and/or emotionally caged. So Michelle used a PLACE where a traumatic childhood event occurred. All childhood traumas color and affect our feelings and behavior as an adult. They also cause the ever-vigilant need to protect ourselves from similar emotional injuries. Michelle's PLACE choice gave her the general sense that she had no way out and no one to turn to, the same feeling she had when she was a child experiencing her trauma for the first time—in other words, the feeling of being imprisoned.

FOURTH WALL

The FOURTH WALL is the dimension of the PLACE that makes the space you're working in (a stage, set, classroom, location, etc.) private, separating the actors and the stage or set from the audience or camera crew.

The FOURTH WALL is the edge of the stage or set. The FOURTH WALL encloses your PLACE, establishing a sense of intimacy and privacy. When you are personalizing the floors, walls and furniture of the set from your PLACE choice, you have to personally endow what's on the FOURTH WALL, as well. In your personal PLACE choice, the real FOURTH WALL could consist of a chest of drawers, a sculpture and a window, even though on the set there are a camera and lights in the actual area where the FOURTH WALL would be.

APPLYING THE FOURTH WALL

When you are looking at the FOURTH WALL area of soundstage, imagine seeing the camera as the chest of drawers or a key light as the sculpture and a light diffuser as the window. In other words, even though the set lacks a literal FOURTH WALL, you must fill out your entire PLACE, spatially duplicating and completing what would be on that wall in your PLACE choice. Pick big items from your PLACE choice—a window, television, painting, art object, chest of drawers, armoire, etc. Because these things are similar in shape to the actual items on the set, it's easy to spatially endow your personal FOURTH WALL.

PLACE coupled with the FOURTH WALL also enables you to take away the intimidating force that the camera and the audience always has on an actor. PLACE and the FOURTH WALL establish a feeling of privacy—they take away the feeling that we are watching actors acting and instead make us feel that we are watching human beings truly interact. The best acting you can do should make your audience feel like they're Peeping Toms catching real live people going through truly intimate moments. It's always important to create privacy in your work, but particularly crucial when doing a highly charged emotional or sexual scene.

Accurately assimilate the FOURTH WALL of the PLACE you have chosen and endow it accordingly.

Take what's on your personal FOURTH WALL and endow it on what's actually there—the actual wall dressings, furniture, camera or whatever. Endow the space with choices that are easy to imagine; otherwise you'll have to play mind games that make doing so complicated and confusing. If there's clear space with an audience, as in a theater, just pick some of the more obtrusive items on your FOURTH WALL and imagine them there. Or if it's a small theater space, see the wall that is beyond the audience. Then take the actual shapes that exist there and endow the imaginary wall with them.

When endowing PLACE and the FOURTH WALL, you don't have to imagine each and every item in that PLACE and on that FOURTH WALL.

Just picture the key pieces that define your personal PLACE and FOURTH WALL—particularly the items that hold some history or special meaning. Picturing these few specific and key pieces will transport you to the PLACE and FOURTH WALL, because the items are significant enough to conjure them up. And if you've picked the correct emotionally charged objects to project, they will often inadvertently call up less charged objects that will flesh out the space you're endowing.

APPLYING AN OUTSIDE FOURTH WALL

In an outdoor PLACE, the FOURTH WALL is what would be on the horizon. On a beach, you'd see the surroundings of that special beach that you've picked as your PLACE, and the FOURTH WALL would be the view of that specific body of water—the color, the sounds, the movement of the waves. If you were outside in the city, your FOURTH WALL would be the specific buildings that face you in that familiar and poignant street from your life.

When making PLACE and FOURTH WALL choices, you have to keep in mind whether it's an inside/private PLACE, an inside/ public PLACE, an outside/private PLACE, or an outside/public PLACE.

Different PLACE and FOURTH WALL(s) naturally create different feelings. When you're inside and alone, you don't feel you have to be secretive because you're not encumbered by peering eyes and ears. On the other hand, when you're outside in public, there's always the possibility that you can be overheard or seen by the wrong people.

Inside/private PLACE and FOURTH WALL.
- Your home (including the bedroom, living room, study, kitchen, etc.)
- Your office
- A hospital room
- A hotel/motel room

In an inside/private PLACE and FOURTH WALL, you are alone with only one or two other people. In this kind of PLACE, anything can be said and done because there's no one else there to spy, reveal, judge or change the tone of your activity. You can still be aware of the possibility of interruption or being discovered, yet without the other invading person(s) actually being in the room, you are left to feel that in private anything can and will happen. This includes the privacy of sex, secrets told or experienced, violence or death.

Inside/public (or populated) PLACE and FOURTH WALL.

- A restaurant
- A hospital waiting room
- A doctor's waiting room
- A courtroom
- Your home with a party going on
- A movie or stage theater
- A bar
- A police interrogation room (there's the possibility that others may be spying through a two-way mirror)
- An airplane
- A train
- A store
- A mall

PLACES that are inside but public change the tone of the scene because you can possibly be overheard and/or seen. In inside/public PLACE and FOURTH WALL(s), you always have the OBSTACLE of other people in the scene discovering something and then disclosing what they've seen or heard to that person or persons that your character wishes not to know—their mate, the police, their boss, their friend that they're disparaging, their parent, their child.

Personalizing a nonspeaking person around you in an
INSIDE/ PUBLIC PLACE will enhance your behavior—especially
if the specific person threatens you either emotionally
and/or physically—because it amplifies the scene's OBSTACLES.

When you're thinking about an inside/public PLACE and FOURTH WALL, it's helpful to identify exactly who it is that is lurking around your public place in order to up the stakes. Imagine a first-date scene that takes PLACE and FOURTH WALL in a restaurant. Take one of the actors/extras at one of the other tables in the restaurant, and for your SUBSTITUTION for that actor/extra, use your ex-mate (who'll judge your present date as unattractive, stupid, weird or perverted and make you feel that you have substantially lowered your standards); or use a parent who is obsessed with your marital status changing from being single to being married with children (this fixation makes you feel compelled to make this date work out, no matter how wrong this person is for you); or use a friend who always finds a way to ridicule you (making you overcritical in watching your date, which will taint your interaction); or use a friend of your ex who will be happy to gossip to your ex about how you've lowered your standards. Whoever you select for your SUBSTITUTION will absolutely vary and enhance your behavior.

Another instance of endowing an actor/extra in an inside/public PLACE and FOURTH WALL is a scene in a bar where your character is relating their life's troubles to a stranger. Using a SUBSTITUTION—someone who really matters to you—for the idle patron sitting nearby or the nonspeaking bartender can deepen the conflict and the drama of the scene. The inconsequential observer is now your mother, who has issues with your drinking, or an enemy (or friend of your nemesis) who would gain pleasure in knowing your secrets and sharing your flaws and failures with others.

Or perhaps your character is the defendant in a court case. If you use SUBSTITUTION, by imagining that one member of the jury (an extra) is a person from your life who would love to see harm done to you (an ex, a longtime enemy, someone whom *you've* hurt in the past, etc.), you will deepen your desire to win your SCENE OBJECTIVE, *"to make you believe in my innocence."* Because there's someone in a position to control the decision-making process who has a vendetta against you and who's going to be negatively subjective when looking at the facts of the case, you will work harder to win. Again, this adds to the drama in your work and in the scene.

Outside/private PLACE and FOURTH WALL.
- A secluded beach or a beach at night
- A park at night
- A secluded parking lot
- A dark alley
- A pool in your backyard
- A backyard
- A street or road in the middle of the night
- The woods

The difference between outside/private PLACE and FOURTH WALL(s) and inside/private PLACE and FOURTH WALL(s) is that when you are outdoors, there's an even greater possibility that you can be discovered or caught. There are no walls to keep a person out. In an outside/private PLACE, the FOURTH WALL is the horizon. Always use what would truly exist in your personal FOURTH WALL of the PLACE you've chosen.

- A beach: The FOURTH WALL would be the shore and the waves crashing against the shore.
- A park: The FOURTH WALL would be the specific trees, park benches and park signs that are in the PLACE you've chosen.
- A secluded parking lot: The FOURTH WALL would be the specific buildings that you know surround the parking lot—or, in the case of an underground parking lot, the walls that line the structure.
- A dark alley: The FOURTH WALL would be the buildings that you know exist outside the entrance of the alley.
- A backyard: The FOURTH WALL would be the specific house that the backyard is a part of.
- A street or road in the middle of the night: The FOURTH WALL would be the buildings and/or homes or foliage (trees, etc.) that line the street or road.

Outside/public PLACE and FOURTH WALL.

- A crowded beach
- A populated park in the day
- A parking lot with lots of cars and people in the daytime
- An alley close to a heavily trafficked street in the middle of the day
- A pool with other people swimming and lounging about
- A backyard where other people are or that they can enter from the house at any time
- A crowded street
- A sidewalk on a street that has lots of cars buzzing by

Obviously, an outside/public PLACE and FOURTH WALL will offer the greatest risk of being exposed. You must not only endow the PLACE and

FOURTH WALL you're actually in with a familiar, emotionally duplicated PLACE and FOURTH WALL from your life, but, as with an inside/public space, you must also use SUBSTITUTION to endow one of the nonspeaking people who are located around you with someone who would emotionally affect you in some way. Say you're doing a scene where your character is in a park buying heroin from a shady drug dealer. Choose a PLACE and FOURTH WALL where you did something illegal or immoral. Then choose one of the innocuous characters—perhaps the woman walking by with a poodle—and SUBSTITUTE a parent, a critical friend, a teacher, a policeman, a child, someone who will make "drug shopping" a truly nerve-racking experience.

In an automobile.

Cars are different because generally you're not stationary—cars move, and as a result, the FOURTH WALL is always changing. Plus, you're confined inside while also being outside. You'll find a car scene in just about every movie or television show, so listen up.

APPLYING PLACE AND FOURTH WALL IN CAR SCENES

First, endow the inside of the car with a car you're familiar with, one that brings up the appropriate history to the script. For instance, if the scene is a happy joyride, use the car your family had when you were a child and your entire family drove cross-country; or if the scene is a sex scene, use the car you had unbridled sex in for the first time; or if the scene is about freedom and excitement, use the first brand-new car you ever bought; or if the scene is traumatic, use the car that you drove your child around in before they were taken away from you in a custody battle. You get the idea.

Once you've identified the car, then you must personalize the scenery, making sure that what you're passing makes logical sense with the script. For example, your character is driving through a dark, scary wooded area. You can picture an area where something frightening occurred, or imagine an area filled with creatures that terrify you—spiders, rats, snakes, roaches. This creates additional imagery from the thought: "What if my car breaks down and I have to actually face down those spiders, rats, snakes or roaches?" Or perhaps your character is driving home. Then you would endow the neighborhood they're driving through with your route home, including the neighborhoods you drive through, or a childhood neighborhood that brings up the proper emotions for the script. Or maybe your character is driving through a city they've never been in. Here you would endow the city with a specific town in which you've experienced awful events. This will give you feelings of being displaced, uncomfortable and needing to assimilate and fit in.

Make a choice for your car and the contiguous area that you see outside it, double-checking to see if these choices follow and make sense to the linear inner work you've already done.

PLACE and FOURTH WALL also infuse history into
your work, making not only the event of the script real
but where it is happening real, too. It acclimates you.
And...
PLACE and FOURTH WALL are necessary acting tools—
don't ignore or forget to use them.

In my many years as a teacher, getting actors to use PLACE and FOURTH WALL has been like pulling teeth. The rationale for using the other tools is more obvious because they clearly allow the emotions to flow, and actors like emotion—a lot. Though the power of PLACE and FOURTH WALL is less obvious, it is essential for maintaining and intensifying the emotions that the other tools induce. But more important, PLACE and FOURTH WALL lessen the feeling of being watched and judged, which is often what prevents actors from being able to stay present and in a scene. In many cases, the self-consciousness created by a live audience or a running camera actually nullifies an actor's feelings. PLACE and FOURTH WALL will serve to strengthen your emotional reality and the sense of privacy, which helps foster even more feeling.

CHAPTER 9

Tool #9: DOINGS

> The handling of props, which produces behavior that allows for us to regroup, find safety, make a statement, expose or hide what we are really thinking, reveal a character's weaknesses and vices, etc. DOINGS also add weight to the scene, because when we are in high-stakes circumstances, it's hard to be still.

DOINGS are the physicalization of our intentions through the use of props. All the things that people do in life are DOINGS—brushing your hair while speaking, washing the dishes, getting ready for bed, setting the table for company, cooking, primping and cleaning, just to name a few.

DOINGS also tell us more about the who-am-I of a character. Imagine a kitchen-argument scene in which your character uses food as a way to deal with rising tension. The simple act of getting a gallon of ice cream out of the freezer, grabbing a spoon, slamming the silverware drawer shut, forgoing a bowl and ravenously shoveling spoonfuls of ice cream down your throat while the other person is yelling at you speaks volumes to the other actor(s), as well as to the audience. Or envision a therapy scene where you, the patient, make intricate origami paper sculptures out of Kleenex. Without hearing the words of the script—simply through the behavior created by your making origami sculptures out of the facial tissue (which, given the delicate nature of facial tissue, requires a lot of skill and extreme focus)—the audience understands that the character is anal-retentive, obsessive and incapable of exposing his feelings.

Words can lie. Behavior always tells the truth.

In conversation we often say what we think the other person wants to hear. We use words to conceal our true feelings. They enable us to lie, deceive and sometimes protect others from the truth. Even when you think you're telling the truth, whether you like it or not, your most honest reactions are going to emerge through your behavior. You may be saying one thing, but your behavior betrays your true feelings. This is because most of our behaviors are subconsciously motivated, which makes them impossible to consciously control. No matter how much personal inner work you've infused into your character, your feelings—expressed solely through dialogue—will produce minimal behavior. The handling of props allows you to behave naturally, and the inner work will inform *how* you handle them.

Only actors think standing around, staring intensely at another person and emoting is a powerful and true depiction of life. However, the reality is that when human beings are faced with hyper-dramatic situations, we do things. And more often than not, we do them fervently.

When the Stakes Are High, We *Do* a Lot

Think about the time you were in the apartment of someone you really liked, alone together for the first time. The sexual tension was high. What did you do to ease your nerves? You might have moseyed over to the person's bookshelf and attempted to casually peruse their collection. Or you might have anxiously eaten some jelly beans out of a bowl on the coffee table as a way to deal with the tension. In your discomfort, you might've even handled something fragile as you cruised the joint. Did you break something or see something you weren't supposed to see? Probably. Coping with your nerves produced spontaneous behavior. These unplanned moments cannot happen without DOINGS.

Or picture being in a scene where your character, who is preparing a salad for dinner, is in the middle of an argument with a loved one. You could stop and just stand there and yell at the other person, but it's much more effective and realistic to simply continue making the salad. It allows the other character, as well as the audience, to understand what you're really feeling when you forcefully and with vengeance cut that cucumber as if it is humanly attached to the subject of your wrath. You could viciously tear at a head of lettuce as a threat, showing the other person what's to come if they continue to be so damn critical and derogatory. In this context, making a salad, usually a fairly benign activity, becomes a menacing one. With these DOINGS, there would be no need to yell. The use of DOINGS is so powerful that it allows you to convey your rage even if you're speaking softly.

DOINGS also give the actor an alternative place to go. When the stakes are high, it's simply impossible to look that person straight in the eye *all the time*. DOINGS give you a legitimate reason not to have to face the other person. It's so much easier to "lie" while you are busy stirring a pot, rolling a cigarette, preparing a drink, dressing or fixing a pipe under the sink—legitimate activities that prevent you from ever having to look that person directly in the eyes, which, if you were forced to do, would reveal that you were being dishonest or uncomfortable.

The next time you're in a highly charged situation of any kind, just watch how physical you become. It's surprising how much activity takes place when you're excited or upset about something. Jim, one of my students, challenged this idea. He insisted that any time he was involved in a heated argument, he stood there and yelled. Nothing more. He maintained this theory until he had a fight with his estranged father, whom he had not seen in years. They were standing on the lawn in front of Jim's house and the old look-what-*you*-did-to-*me* blame game evolved into a heated confrontation. As things grew more intense, Jim's father unconsciously began ripping dandelions out of the lawn and tearing them apart. Jim saw this DOING and smiled because he realized that I was right. Unfortunately, Jim's father thought the smile was for him and that his son was being condescending, which, of course, infuriated him even more. The lawn suffered, but Jim got the point: When we get scared, upset, angry or excited, we DO.

The choices you make for your DOINGS flesh out your character's neurosis, social background, educational background, financial status and *real* feelings about the other character. Your choice of props/activities should be appropriate to the character's life (psyche, economic background, present job status, history, sexual predilection, geographical location, time period, etc.).

DOINGS for a low-rent character on a date at a fancy restaurant with someone who is making them feel hostile could be:

- You might find yourself playing with your food in an aggressive way—stabbing the lettuce with your fork, hacking your meat or stuffing food in your mouth to avoid blurting out, "You're such a boring moron," which is what you really want to say.
- You might clean the silverware with your cloth napkin by spitting on it and then wiping it down with ferocity.
- You might play with your food, perhaps rudely sucking the pimento out of an olive and then making hand puppets by slipping the empty olives onto your fingers.
- You might drink too much wine, swigging it down and filling and refilling your glass as the conversation gets more painful and uncomfortable.

Whatever you choose to do, hiding your animosity with DOINGS gives us more information about *what* you're really feeling and *how* you deal with those feelings.

DOINGS can create a sense of unpredictability.

Let's explore a character who would be considered a bad guy, someone who is attempting to scare their intended victim in a gangster scene. Some standard approaches might be to stand and yell and/or grab and/or physically pin down the other actor. A DOINGS-driven approach might be to eat Girl Scout cookies (a seemingly innocent act) while you threaten the other character with heinous, unspeakable acts of torture. His munching on cookies that he's acquired from some innocent Girl Scout makes the fear inspired by the bad guy more palpable, because it makes him look like he hurts, mutilates and kills casually—as if it's something he does every day. He can kill you just as easily as he idly consumes a sugar wafer. When someone is violently yelling and pushing you up against a wall, it's pretty obvious that pain and death are bound to follow. DOINGS allow for other possibilities, which disarm the victim and confuse them about what's going to happen next. Not knowing what your predator is going to do moment to moment is much more frightening.

DOINGS are essential because we see before we hear.

A picture is worth a thousand words. A cliché? Yes. But it's a cliché for a reason. We should be able to take the sound out of a scene and still know precisely what's going on from the behavior.

DOINGS Must Further Your SCENE OBJECTIVE

DOINGS are not random handlings of props. You must consider your SCENE OBJECTIVE. If your SCENE OBJECTIVE is *"to get you to fall in love with me,"* then throwing sharp items at the object of your affection is hardly going to help you accomplish this goal.

A great illustration of considering a character's life circumstances, the who-am-I of the character and the SCENE OBJECTIVE is Brad Pitt's very first scene for class. Brad had just arrived in Hollywood and hadn't taken any professional-acting classes. (Yes, there was a time when Brad Pitt was a young man with dreams and no money. He started out like everyone else, taking three menial jobs as a way to support himself and pay for his acting classes.) I assigned him a scene from a play called *Tribute*. In the scene, Brad's character, Jud, is having an indoor picnic with a girl hired by his gregarious and charismatic father to seduce him. Jud is unaware that his father has arranged this. Jud's father feels justified—Jud is painfully shy, a presumed virgin and someone who's spent his childhood having to live in his father's shadow. Brad's SCENE OBJECTIVE was *"to get you to love me in spite of my lack of experience."* His OBSTACLES were sexual tension and a lack of knowledge of how one plays "the game." It's not written in the script that Jud serves the girl wine, but Brad brought two long-stemmed wineglasses along with a bottle of wine (a facsimile, not real alcohol—*never* use real alcohol when you are acting) to class for the scene. Brad began the scene by emerging from the kitchen with the bottle and the glasses. Although the dialogue consisted of I'm-just-getting-to-know-you babble, the scene implies seduction. Eating the food for the picnic—the DOINGS written in the script (the handling and eating of food can be very sexy)—along with using the wine and glasses created an unspoken sexual tension between Brad and his scene partner. Brad's apparent inner thoughts made him unconsciously place the glasses on his chest and seductively twist the stems of the glasses. Although the dialogue was some nebulous discussion of the girl's high school days, it was clear by Brad's DOINGS and the resulting behavior that school was not on his mind. We saw what Brad (as Jud) was *really* thinking about through his behavior. When you are going after your SCENE OBJECTIVE and really need reactions from the other person, it creates unconscious behavior. By going after his SCENE OBJECTIVE so strongly, Brad wasn't, as the actor, self-conscious or self-aware—his behavior was allowed to happen the way it does in life, without premeditation. It allowed Brad to become, *as the character*, self-conscious and self-aware, because it became so real to him. When I asked Brad, "Did you know you had the wineglasses on your chest and were twisting the stems like one would do to nipples?" He looked at me truly surprised and blushed a deep purple. Apparently not.

Brad knows the benefits of using DOINGS, and he continues to explore them in his career. In the movie *Ocean's Eleven*, he plays Rusty Ryan, a character in the midst of a complex Las Vegas casino heist. Las Vegas is infamous for its cheap food, which is designed to lure the unsuspecting bargain hunter into a casino to gamble. Brad's character, Rusty, is a con man, and all con games involve aspects of wanting and needing to feel powerful. Keeping in mind Rusty's OVERALL OBJECTIVE of *"to be empowered,"* Brad figured that Rusty would beat the system and get the food without being tempted into the glitz of possible riches via slots and blackjack. He told the director, Steven Soderbergh, that he felt his character would always be indulging in Las Vegas food, like the ninety-nine-cent shrimp cocktail. Soderbergh was all for it, and with the use of DOINGS, Brad turned a typical and slick con-man role into a quirky, flawed and unique character.

DOINGS spark mannerisms, unique affectations and quirky behavior.

Directors often workshop their scripts in class before they go off to shoot or stage their productions. Screenwriter David Marconi, who has written blockbuster movies such as *Enemy of the State*, brought a scene from a feature that he was about to direct. The scene he put up in class was a necessary expository scene to establish the backstory. The character of Iverson, a handsome and sexy FBI agent, tries to convince Tulsa, a young, gorgeous, drug-addled model, to go undercover to help him discover which wrongdoer killed her best friend. In order to do this, Iverson must explain the case's history, including who he is and why she would be the right person for the job. The scene takes place after Iverson has spent the night at Tulsa's place—she was so drunk and stoned and in trouble with the cops that he chivalrously brought her home and tucked her in (it doesn't go *there* yet—he slept on the couch). The first time the scene was performed in class, it was static. Basically, we watched two people sitting on a couch talking. I told the actor playing Iverson, Rod, to take off his socks (his character had been wearing them for a good twenty-four hours) to get more comfortable. Rod did this as he relayed the details of the case. As soon as he had his socks off, he noticed a smell, as did Sarah, the actress playing Tulsa. Rod's socks stank. Embarrassed, he teasingly put them in front of her face. Sarah's face soured and then she giggled. Then, still talking about the case, Rod put one foot to his nose and realized that his socks weren't the only things that reeked. Sarah laughed. These simple DOINGS bonded Rod and Sarah, along with their characters. They now shared a private joke, and the humanity and trueness of the moment made a dry expository scene absorbing. And it helped earn the right of getting to the end of the script, where they end up together.

DOINGS give your character a safe place to go.

Whether we're lying or sexually attracted or simply in danger, we have a tendency to need someplace to go and do something that's familiar. DOINGS help provide a safe haven. Remember my student Jim's father pulling the dandelions out of the lawn? The DOING of pulling the dandelions out was a safe place for him as his son berated him for not being a good dad. And this wasn't acting—it was a scene that happened in real life.

Obviously, if DOINGS help provide us with a sense of safety in the real world, then they are just as valuable (if not more valuable) in the world an actor creates. When Barry Pepper played the sharpshooter Private Daniel Jackson in *Saving Private Ryan*, his character was in the midst of war (terrifying to even the strongest of veterans) and needed something that would give him a sense of well-being. Because Barry is a religious man, we came up with the idea of using a cross that he would always wear around his neck, and whenever the war got too scary, he would touch it and look at it, gathering strength and peace from it. This DOING was not written in the script, but it ended up giving the audience deep insight into this character—that God and religion are his resources when he is frightened.

DOINGS bring out a script's humor.

I often assign the same scene over and over again so that my students can see how using the tools and doing the inner work from their own personal events and feelings allows their unique mannerisms and quirks to emerge, thereby making the scene a different and distinct experience for the actor and the audience. For instance, I asked Matthew Perry to do the same scene from *Broadcast News* that I also gave to David Spade, which we discussed for MOMENT BEFORE (tool #7). To recap, this is the scene in which the character of Aaron Altman (played in the movie by Albert Brooks) is at home, ruing his poor performance as a news anchor. He knows that he's blown his shot at his dream. Aaron is momentarily elated because Jane Craig (played by Holly Hunter), the love of his life, has come by to see him. He thinks she's there to comfort him after his horrible day. But Jane has stopped by to tell Aaron she's in love with his rival, Tom, a successful news anchor.

The first time Matthew Perry did the scene, he had no props. Matthew, being an inherently funny guy, made the scene mildly amusing. I told him that the scene could be much funnier. We discussed the who-am-I of the character, which is essential in making DOINGS choices. The character of Aaron is a guy who uses humor as his defense and as his way to win. Through working with people like Jim Carrey, Garry Shandling, Aubrey Plaza, Craig Robinson, Damon Wayans, David Spade, Chloe Fineman, Matthew Perry and Ryan Gosling I have found that really funny people seem to collect and own a lot of toys. So I asked Matthew if his home resembled a mini Toys"R"Us. He gave me a surprised yes. Then I asked him to bring a large sampling of his toy collection to use as DOINGS for the rework of the scene. He didn't think this was such a great idea. "What newscaster wannabe has toys?" he asked. He also challenged me by saying, "I'm going to bring so much and do so much that you're going to hate it." I said, "Do it anyway. The worst that can happen is that I'm wrong. And I'm okay with that."

The following week, Matthew brought in a huge suitcase filled with the kind of toys only Matthew Perry would own. Throughout the scene, he played vigorously with his toys. Through the activity of his playing and his choices of specific toys, we as the audience were better able to understand Aaron's angst, his love for Jane and his personality. We saw Aaron's humanity—his frustration, insecurities and failed history with women. These DOINGS gave Aaron a three-dimensionality that made him more accessible and that turned him into a person whom we as an audience could relate to. An audience will feel much more compelled to laugh if they're relating to the way a character handles an extremely uncomfortable situation, and they can say to themselves, "Been there, done that." Matthew, fully expecting to prove me wrong, used the DOINGS with a vengeance. Yet the more DOINGS he did, the bigger the laughs he got. In fact, he had to stop speaking several times because the class' laughter was so strong. Matthew learned a valuable lesson, and this scene turned out to be his breakthrough scene. Soon afterward, he began to book just about everything that came his way, including his heralded and iconic performance on the long-running series *Friends*.

You can change the DOINGS.

The writer may have put particular DOINGS in the script, but these are often just suggestions. If the DOING doesn't rely on the scripted dialogue, then it's up to you, the actor, to use your imagination—always considering the who-am-I of the character, the time period and the character's SCENE OBJECTIVE. Don't just use DOINGS where they're indicated in the script. The more DOINGS you have, the more behavior can emerge.

Personalize Your DOINGS by Infusing Information About Your SUBSTITUTION and INNER OBJECTS

You must personalize your DOINGS so they mean something special to you. If you are at a future lover's home and happen to pick up one of the photographs displayed on a counter, you need to use your SUBSTITUTION and endow what's pictured in the photo with a person that makes emotional sense to the scene and you. Let's look at the first date scene in Neil Simon's *Chapter Two*, when the character of George picks up a photo of Jennie's ex-husband. George's wife of ten years has recently died, and this is his first time out. Because it's been so long since he's dated and he's still mourning the death of someone he loved, he's extremely awkward. In the dialogue, George asks Jennie who the man is in the photo. Jennie tells him that it is her ex-husband. If you were playing the character of George, you might endow the picture with someone from your personal life who is a competitor, a nemesis or someone that could put a damper on having a future relationship with your SUBSTITUTION for Jennie.

You might be playing an alcoholic whose DOING is—surprise, surprise—drinking alcohol. If you actually have a propensity toward alcoholism, you would endow the liquid in front of you with your alcohol of choice. If not, then you'd endow the drink in front of you with the vice you do have (most people have at least one): drugs, sex, gambling, food, shopping, social media—you name it. Anything done in profound excess with detrimental results can be considered a vice.

A scene might require your character to play some music, so you'd then endow the particular music playing with that special song that you shared with your SUBSTITUTION for the scene. Or you might endow the music with music that reminds you of emotionally charged past events that match up to the feelings you're supposed to have, as supplied by the script's text.

Charmed is a television series that brings the supernatural to three women's lives, which means the DOINGS often don't make sense for those of us who are not witches or warlocks. In a number of scenes in one episode, the character of Chris, played by Drew Fuller, has a ring that he holds, touches, muses over and gives to his one true love, who then returns it. It's not just a ring that signifies love—there's a mysticism attached to it. The ring originally came from the future and now resides in the past, which, by the way, equals today. Confusing, yes, but it doesn't have to be. By endowing this magical ring with something real from Drew's love life, Drew could make the ring into something that inspired great significance. As we were trying to figure out what he would use for this ring, I happened to notice a leather band on his wrist. I asked about it and he told me that his girlfriend and he wear matching leather bands to symbolize their love for each other. They never take them off. In fact, their agreement is that if either one of them does take the band off, it means the relationship is over. Eureka—the perfect solution! I told Drew to endow the ring (his DOING throughout a good part of this episode) with his leather band, infusing all of its personal implications. Endowing the ring in this way made it easy to elicit the proper emotions that he needed the ring to represent—love and the eventual loss of love that were supposed to come from the scripted DOING.

When Identifying Your Character's DOINGS, Consider Their Neurosis, Career Path and Modus Operandi

DOINGS visually expose a character's neurosis.

Most characters have a defining phobia or neurosis. If not, then it's up to the actor to come up with something that makes the character stand out. In *Scarface*, Al Pacino's character of Tony Montana wouldn't have been as rich without his extreme paranoia. *Othello* would not be *Othello* without Othello's obsessive jealousy. Lady Macbeth would be just another nagging wife if she didn't have her fanatical ambition. Joe Pesci needed his Napoleon complex to justify the character of Nicky Santoro in *Casino*. The character of Virginia Woolf would have been just any morose writer if she hadn't had suicidal tendencies in *The Hours*. Brick in *Cat on a Hot Tin Roof* would be a bore without his alcoholism and his unresolved father issues. And Oedipus would merely be a mama's boy without his mother obsession. DOINGS help to create a deep, visual understanding of how and why a character's neurosis or psychosis exists.

Under the same category of neurosis are those characters that have serious substance-abuse problems. The following are examples of how some of my students and I realized their characters' particular addictions by the use of DOINGS.

Overeating

In class, Robin McDonald put up a scene from the play *Pizza Man*. She played the character of Alice, an overeater who has lost weight for her married boyfriend. In the scene, Alice comes home after she discovers that her boyfriend has gone back to his wife. This is a great excuse for her to do some major consuming. She quickly notices that her alcoholic roommate and friend has spent all their money on liquor. Most people with substance-abuse problems will have secret stashes hidden for binge crises. For this scene, Robin put a Kit Kat in a flowerpot, Twinkies behind the curtains, potato chips under the couch and beef jerky underneath the couch's cushions. This setup gave Robin the motivation to move around the room, surreptitiously finding each item and trying to find a way to eat it without the roommate noticing. Most addicts don't display their addiction; they imbibe secretly. Alice's words were underlined by behavior that was created by her on-the-sly munching.

Alcoholism

Leticia in *Monster's Ball* is a woman in denial. Who wouldn't be, after your husband is executed, your child dies in a car accident and you lose your job? Halle and I decided that Leticia would make her alcohol abuse seem like less of a problem by having her only drink out of little airplane bottles of whiskey. This way, Leticia could drink ten bottles in one sitting but rationalize her behavior by thinking, "I don't have a drinking problem. I mean, how much could I *really* be drinking if the bottles are so small?" The small containers made her feel like she was drinking a whole lot less. When she offered Hank a drink, Leticia could feel as though she were entertaining in style—daintily screwing off the tiny metal cap and handing Hank the mini bottle—without revealing that she might have a drinking problem. In the film, the characters sit together, talking about her dead son and sipping from these doll-size whiskey bottles, which provides the film with a great visual that also indicates her social, financial and emotional status.

Drug Abuse

An integral part of drug use and abuse is the ritual of getting high or stoned. For instance, as part of their ceremony, potheads will pull the marijuana from the baggie, smell it, flake the weed onto the papers, roll the joint and then lick the paper so as to seal it and make it compact. Cokeheads will chop, cut and snort cocaine with their preferred devices on their preferred surfaces. These DOINGS create anticipation and are an integral part of the intoxicating experience.

Eriq La Salle directed and starred in the HBO movie *Rebound,* which is about Diego, a die-hard junkie and basketball player who pulls his life together to become a basketball coach and mentor to young people who've felt the magnetic yet destructive pull of heroin. Eriq played Diego, yet Eriq had never done any drugs of any kind. He had no idea what it felt like to do heroin and was oblivious to the heroin-using rituals. We talked about how there's a sexual quality to "entering" a needle in a vein and releasing a feel-good substance into it. The cooking of the liquid in the spoon and the needle sucking the heated liquid into the needle's cylinder are like sexual foreplay. And that sex, when it gets to a certain point, becomes a must-have event, a necessity, the same way heroin is to an addict. When he fully understood this DOING, Eriq could feel the gritty reality of the why, the how and the desperation of his heroin-addicted character.

Sexaholism

Sexaholics use sex as their way to feel powerful. Sex, too, is such a strong, primal force that often it makes people do things they wouldn't ordinarily do. Using sexuality is a great way to win what you want. A sexaholic is aware of the power that sex has over people. Deborah Kara Unger understood the power of using sex when she put up a scene in class from Shakespeare's *The Taming of the Shrew.* As the character of Kate, Deborah needed to find a way to have power over her worthy adversary and future mate, Petruchio. Considering the day and the age of the play, Deborah knew that Kate's sexuality was her most valuable commodity. She came up with the DOING of cutting an orange and then forcefully squeezing the pulpy juice so that it poured into her mouth and then dripped sensually down her lips, chin, neck and chest (she was wearing a low-cut top with plenty of cleavage). She then wiped her lips with the back of her hand and luxuriously rubbed the juice and pulp into her chest. The actor (I don't remember who he was—frankly, I was so entranced by her DOING that I can't remember much else) became putty in her hands, and Deborah won the scene.

No matter what your character is addicted to, addicts take huge risks—robbing banks, killing, having multiple affairs and being willing to lose a friend, family or a job just to get their drug. If you're playing an addict, your DOINGS should consider and reflect these extreme behaviors.

DOINGS reveal your character's modus operandi.

Neuroses and psychoses are different from one's modus operandi. Mental and chemical imbalances are not in our control. They are usually OBSTACLES, additional hurdles to jump over in attaining and winning the SCENE OBJECTIVE. A modus operandi (how we operate) is a set of behaviors that we use to *help* us to achieve and win our goals.

All of us have an M.O. we use to get our way and win. When in doubt, we use what we know has successfully worked for us in the past. Some of us use sex, some use violence, some use humor, some use intellect, some use physical prowess and some use their authority or power position in life. The following are examples of possible DOINGS for these M.O.s. Don't be limited by these suggestions. Be creative.

M.O. for People Who Use Violence

Films and plays featuring this type of character: *In the Boom Boom Room, Goodfellas, American Psycho, Streamers, Reservoir Dogs, A Clockwork Orange, Danny and the Deep Blue Sea, Edmond, Secretary, Cape Fear.*

- Playing with a gun or knife or practicing moves with it; cleaning your gun or knife; whittling with a switchblade; hitting a punching bag or some facsimile; using hand-exercise equipment; throwing or breaking something; violently squeezing clay to mold an object; eating the kind of food that makes hard sounds; making a salad by wielding a large knife and viciously cutting into the carrot, cucumber, lettuce, etc.; building something that requires a hammer or a saw; doing drugs like smoking a joint, snorting coke; using sharp scissors to clean and cut your fingernails; etc.

M.O. for People Who Use Humor

Films and plays featuring this type of character: *Annie Hall, The Gingerbread Lady, Lost in Translation, Animal House, Chapter Two, Bringing Up Baby, Life Is Beautiful, Frankie and Johnny, When Harry Met Sally . . ., A Thousand Clowns.*

- Playing with funny toys like windup dolls; mini figurines; paddle sticks; toy army men; a doll that speaks, burps or passes gas, etc.; trying on weird hats or clothes; playing with food like sucking up spaghetti or trying to eat peanuts by throwing them up in the air and catching them in your mouth or making a puppet show out of carrot sticks; crumpling up paper and trying to make baskets into any circular object; picking up and playing with items that belong to the other person, maybe even intimate things; drinking wine by gargling with it first; drinking anything that allows for a spit take; putting underwear on your head; etc.

M.O. for People Who Use Their Intellect

Films and plays featuring this type of character: *Geniuses, The Real Thing, Speed-the-Plow, Uncommon Women and Others, My Dinner with Andre, Brideshead Revisited, Reversal of Fortune, Dead Poets Society, True West, Equus.*

- Using a computer; reading something scholarly, doing Sunday's *New York Times* crossword puzzle; writing; taking photographs; always pulling out a writing pad and jotting down your thoughts; eating food that is exotic; drinking brandy or fine wine; fixing or installing something that is technically difficult; sketching or painting; cooking something that's complicated; playing with a pen or pencil; etc.

M.O. for People Who Use Sex

Films and plays featuring this type of character: *The Misfits; The Last Seduction; Sexual Perversity in Chicago; American Gigolo; Body Heat; Last Tango in Paris; The Unbearable Lightness of Being; Summer and Smoke; Sex, Lies, and Videotape; Fool for Love; Desire Under the Elms.*

- *Women:* Eating a juicy peach; shooting whipped cream directly into the mouth; drinking and letting some of the liquid drip down your chin and chest; bending over to choose a CD to put in the stereo; dancing and swaying to music as you play with a CD cover; eating something phallic; putting lotion on chest and arms; sensuously removing sweat with a tissue above your breasts; fixing your nylons; drinking alcohol and playing with the ice in the glass or the stem of a wineglass; etc.

- *Men:* Chugging down a beer; cracking nuts with your bare hands; seductively fixing something mechanical with a screwdriver; lasciviously eating a mango or kiwi; using any excuse for legitimate contact with the person who is the object of your desire, like picking lint off her sweater, etc.; creating an excuse to take off your shirt and taking it off; wiping sweat off chest or brow; etc.

M.O. for People Who Use Power/Authority

Films and plays featuring this type of character: *Wall Street, Nixon, Angels in America, Working Girl, Hamlet, The Great Santini, A Few Good Men, Speed-the-Plow, Sweet Bird of Youth, Hedda Gabler, Mary of Scotland, Faustus.*

- Balancing your checkbook or writing a check; using a tape recorder or videotape recorder; entering data into your cell phone or iPad; cleaning off your utensils before you eat; writing in a notebook in a way that says, "I'm writing something 'telling' or 'secretive' about you. . . ."; dressing or undressing in an impeccable manner; going through your billfold and counting a large amount of money; smoking a cigar; shining your shoes fastidiously; drinking fine brandy; eating exotic and expensive foods like oysters, quail or pâté; etc.

M.O. for People Who Use Athletic Prowess

Films and plays featuring this type of character: *The Wager, Raging Bull, Bull Durham, The Hustler, The Color of Money, Rocky, The Great White Hope.*

• Playing basketball, golf, football, etc.; using mini exercise
equipment like barbells, travel-size foot bikes, a StairMaster, a
mini trampoline, etc.; dressing or undressing in a manner that
allows you to show off your physique; constantly throwing a ball
into the air and catching it; waxing down a baseball glove; picking up anything heavy and using it as a barbell; drinking Gato-
rade; lifting and/or moving heavy objects; hitting a punching
bag; making and drinking a protein shake; practicing your sport
in some way; etc.

DOINGS define the career of the character.

Here are some examples of classic jobs that are represented again and again in
movies, television and theater and the DOINGS that can be used with them.
These are just a few of the thousands that can be done. Use your imagination
to come up with DOINGS choices that are career appropriate. Remember to
also consider the neurosis and the M.O. of the character when making your
decisions for DOINGS.

• **Police Officer**
  Cleaning or unholstering or holstering your gun; playing with your
  handcuffs; fiddling with the police radio; using a tape recorder; writing
  on a pad; smoking; drinking, spilling, cleaning up coffee; eating on-
  the-run junk food like doughnuts, Slim Jims or PowerBars; putting on
  makeup; using Handi Wipes (for those anal-retentive cops who have to
  touch filthy things in a crime investigation); etc.

• **Doctor**
  Writing out a prescription; organizing or giving out pill samples;
  putting on or taking off surgical gloves; sterilizing medical instruments;
  washing hands; playing around with medical instruments; buttoning a
  white lab coat; perusing medical records; looking at X-rays; looking
  something up in a medical manual or on a computer; etc.

• **Psychiatrist**
  Writing on a pad; using a tissue dispenser; making coffee or tea;
  drinking coffee or tea; playing with worry beads; writing on or perus-

ing a patient's records or session notes; knitting; doing a crossword puzzle; raking a mini Zen garden; etc.

• **Nurse**

Writing into or examining a patient's records; preparing medical instruments; putting paper on an examining table; rearranging a patient's personal items; eating junk food; eating off a patient's food tray; sterilizing medical tools; preparing for a patient to come in or cleaning up after a patient; taking a patient's temperature or blood pressure; adjusting an IV; preparing a syringe and hating the sight of blood; emptying bedpans and being grossed out; making a bed military style; etc.

• **Painter**

Painting or sketching; cleaning paintbrushes; arranging a model or things that are to be painted; drinking or doing drugs; preparing unique and colorful food; organizing studio space; taking pictures; munching on jelly beans; etc.

• **Housekeeper**

Sweeping; polishing tables, silverware, etc.; mopping; dusting; plumping pillows; sponging off dirty areas; using cleaning products; washing or drying dishes; cooking; eating; doing laundry; going through an owner's personal effects; etc.

• **Bartender/Waiter**

Cleaning or polishing drinking glasses; cleaning a counter or table; organizing a bar; counting tip money; arranging a cash register; drinking; preparing a bill; refilling peanut bowls, ketchup or mustard bottles; restocking drink condiments or preparing drink condiments (like cutting orange or lime slices and maybe eating them at the same time); etc.

• **Prostitute/Stripper**

Putting on or taking off sexy clothing; putting on makeup; preparing and/or drinking alcohol; smoking marijuana; preparing and snorting cocaine; taking pills; cleaning off body parts like the neck, arms, upper chest or legs; putting on body cream; eating something phallic shaped, like a lollipop, licorice stick or baguette; spooning out something like ice cream or oatmeal and licking the spoon; smoothing your nylons while wearing them; putting on or taking off nail polish; styling hair; etc.

- **Politician**

    Going through your briefcase; reading your own press coverage in the paper; highlighting items in a newspaper or magazine; shaving; putting on cologne or aftershave; jotting down notes; checking yourself in a mirror; talking into a tape recorder; eating mints; using hand-exercise machines; applying hair products; etc.

- **Receptionist/Secretary/Assistant**

    Filing; organizing papers; eating a brown-bag lunch; preparing or drinking coffee; using the computer; taking notes; filing nails or putting on nail polish; putting on makeup; putting on hand cream; massaging one's hands or feet; sharpening pencils; paper-clipping papers; brushing hair; filing; sharpening pencils; perusing files; using scissors or a paper cutter; looking for appropriate items in desk drawers; playing video games on an office computer; etc.

- **Housewife/Mother**

    Cutting out coupons; folding laundry; cleaning; picking up the kids' toys; making a bed; putting away groceries; making lists; putting on various antiaging products; doing yoga; flipping through magazines; dusting; taking pills; obsessing over social media; etc.

- **Construction Worker**

    Eating fast food or a sandwich; drinking beer, soda or water; going through or organizing your tools; chewing on breath mints; adjusting safety goggles; sandpapering calluses off fingers; cleaning tools; etc.

- **Actor**

    Primping by using hair products like gels and hair spray; looking into a hand mirror; eating low-cal snacks; putting on showy accessories; putting on makeup; perusing a script; playing with toys, props or awards from previous acting jobs; drinking designer water; trying new facial expressions or moves; etc.

- **Lab Technician**

    Using, fixing, cleaning or storing appropriate scientific tools; making a sandwich with tools; eating in a precise way; experimenting; etc.

Eric Szmanda plays Greg Sanders, a lab technician, on the hit television series *CSI*. The key to playing this role is to use as many DOINGS as possible.

In fact, Eric got the role by miming the use of macabre DOINGS in his audition. A medical examiner's lab is filled with devices ranging from the norm—swabs, sutures, scalpels—to the gruesome—morbid tools that perform all sorts of ghastly tasks on the dead. Eric's audition scene was about Greg Sanders reporting to the M.E. what he had done to determine the cause of death of a victim. The dialogue included a lot of medi-speak. I instructed Eric to physically illustrate everything his character discussed. For instance, in one of his monologues, Greg had to discuss his findings, which he gathered from "an anal swab." In the audition, Eric (playing Greg) mimed what his character had done with an anal swab and then unconsciously brought the swab to his nose and smelled it. As a result, Eric realized a character who was distinctive and unique from all the other actors who auditioned. He also made his character easy to write for. This is key, because more often than not television writers are also producers, the very ones making casting decisions. Eric inspired the show's writers/producers so much that his role, which was originally supposed to recur occasionally, was expanded. Because of his DOINGS, which were so compelling and quirky, Eric's character eventually became a regular starring role.

Outside PLACE DOINGS

In addition to considering your character's neuroses, M.O. and career, you should always consider the space you are in. The possibilities for outside DOINGS can be slim, because there are often not as many legitimate props available. This does not mean that this is an excuse not to have DOINGS. Here are some suggestions for outside PLACE DOINGS:

- **In a Car**

    Going through your purse; playing with the radio; tapping the steering wheel; rolling a window up or down; eating candy or fast food; drinking coffee or soda; spilling coffee or soda or food; cleaning a mess up; putting on makeup; etc.

- **In a Park or at a Bus Stop**

    Drinking soda; drinking coffee; eating candy or fast food; playing with leaves on the ground; playing with a tree twig; whittling; listening to music; people watching; playing with buttons or a zipper on a sweater or jacket; using a toothpick; throwing breadcrumbs to birds; drinking out of a flask; reading; writing; going through a purse or wallet; taking photos; looking at photos; drawing; etc.

- **On a Beach**

  Putting on suntan lotion; making a sandcastle; drinking beer; pulling food out of a cooler; eating; rocking out to music; putting on colored sun blockers; flipping through a magazine; people watching using binoculars; reading a book; taking photos; drawing; eating fast food; cleaning sand off your body; etc.

- **Walking and Talking**

  Using a toothpick; playing with change in your pockets; playing with a rubber band; putting on a scarf or gloves; sipping coffee; drinking designer water; playing with buttons or a zipper on your shirt or jacket; eating candy or fast food; applying ChapStick; kicking a rock; tossing a rock; etc.

Inside PLACE DOINGS

Inside PLACE DOINGS will be determined by the space itself and what props and furniture might naturally exist within that environment. Don't be afraid to use what already exists in the space. Here are some suggestions for inside PLACE DOINGS:

- **In an Office**

  Scanning copies; getting a cup of water from a watercooler; making yourself some coffee in the office coffeepot; working on a computer; using a calculator; going to a file cabinet and rearranging files; etc.

- **In a Restaurant**

  Occupying yourself with utensils, napkins, bread and butter, crudités, water, wine and wineglasses, sugar packets, condiments like mustard or ketchup, saltshakers and pepper shakers, etc.

- **In a Hotel/Motel Room**

Perusing the inevitable Bible; unpacking or packing your suitcases; looking through a local guidebook; raiding the minibar; stealing towels; playing with the shampoo, conditioner, body cream, sewing kit and shower cap; playing with the blackout curtains; etc.

- **In a Garage**

Fooling around with tools; playing with a parked car; dusting off stored furniture; investigating what's in the stored boxes; using the out-of-commission exercise equipment; etc.

Sometimes a great prop person will fill the space with the right props to help an actor with their DOINGS, but don't necessarily leave it up to someone else. It's up to you, the actor, to make sure that you're not left with nothing to do, becoming a boring, uninteresting "talking head." You can bring personal props or talk to the prop master and director about providing the props you need. Don't worry about offending the director or production designer. As long as everyone sees that it's in the best interest of telling the story, most directors and designers will welcome your input. If you have a good idea, it only makes the director and designer look better because it enhances the production, which is good for everyone.

By now you should have a pretty good sense of how to think about a character's DOINGS—by considering your character's SCENE OBJECTIVE, neurosis, career, M.O. and locale. Finding the appropriate DOINGS is a game of mix and match. There are no right or wrong DOINGS choices; let your personality and imagination be your guide.

. . . .

DOINGS further intensify a scene's arc as well as support and strengthen a character's (and actor's) journey, which is initiated by the SCENE OBJECTIVE. And DOINGS are important because behavior rarely happens by just standing there and saying words.

CHAPTER 10

Tool #10:
INNER MONOLOGUE

The dialogue that's going on inside your head that you don't—and in most cases shouldn't—speak out loud. Essentially anything you can't say out loud without some version of consequences. The INNER MONOLOGUE must be voiced in your head with detail and in full sentences and generally is informed by your INNER OBJECT choices.

While INNER OBJECTS are the pictures and images in our minds that are attached to the words in the script, INNER MONOLOGUE is actual *dialogue*— words and sentences going on inside our head. Although INNER MONOLOGUE and INNER OBJECTS are separate tools, they are inextricably linked, because they must work together to create a linear and comprehensive inner story. For instance, in the movie *The Wizard of Oz*, Dorothy often speaks about wanting to go home. The INNER OBJECT would be the visual of the home the actor would want to return to and the INNER MONOLOGUE would be the inner dialogue regarding going home that she can't speak aloud. So, as the actress playing Dorothy is visualizing the picture of the home she's using, she might be saying as her INNER MONOLOGUE, *"I'm never gonna get home with you losers helping me out. I mean, you, Scarecrow, don't even have a brain, and you, Cowardly Lion, well, I think your name says it all. And your pal the Tin Man is a heartless shell of a man. I am so screwed."* These would be her real thoughts, even though she's expressing in the scripted dialogue that these weird creatures are her friends. Just working with INNER OBJECTS is not enough. You need dialogue around them. The tools complement each other, providing your brain with pictures (INNER OBJECTS) and words (INNER MONOLOGUE) that make your character's thinking truly human. Using INNER MONOLOGUE in conjunction with INNER OBJECTS serves to accurately duplicate the way a real person's thought process works.

The spoken words are available to the actor in the script, but it's up to the actor to fill in the inner conversation. Generally speaking, INNER MONO-LOGUE is defined paranoia: all the things you can't say because they will make you seem wrong, vulgar, mean, insecure, crazy, stupid or prejudiced.

INNER MONOLOGUE includes:

- Thoughts and ideas of what you're going to say next.
- Second-guessing what you've already said or done as inane, inap-propriate, too forward, not forward enough, stupid, trying too hard, scary, not scary enough, etc.
- Interpreting what the other person is really saying and doing: *"Are you covering? Do you like me? Do you hate me? Are you trying to get away from me? Do you think I'm stupid? Do you think I'm ugly?"* Anything that makes you question the other person's feel-ings and perception of you.
- Thoughts of past history with that person, or past history that occurred in a similar circumstance.
- Your slanted and paranoid interpretation of what the other per-son is trying to say to you while the other person is saying it (oth-erwise known as *listening*).
- Anything you would censor if you were to say it aloud. Dialogue that remains in your head can be smutty, not politically correct, inappropriate, evil, judgmental, paranoid and ignorant. After all, you're the only one who knows what you're *really* thinking.

Using the word *you* enables interactive behavior as a result of the INNER MONOLOGUE.

The INNER MONOLOGUE is always stated in a way that connects with the other person. INNER MONOLOGUE is not talking to yourself. INNER

MONOLOGUE is the unspoken communication between people. It creates an unspoken interaction. Write your INNER MONOLOGUE in a way that establishes intercommunication between you and the other character(s). To do this, use the word *you* when addressing your thoughts to the other person, instead of expressing your thoughts to yourself by using *he* or *she*.

For example, it is *not*:

- *"Why is* she *looking at me so weirdly?* She *must think I'm crazy. . . ."*

Using *she* creates introspection, which means the actor is acting in a vacuum.

Instead, it *is*:

- *"Why are* you *looking at me so weirdly?* You *must think I'm crazy. . . ."*

This interactive INNER MONOLOGUE will help to produce behavior, as well. Just think about the physical actions and facial expressions you might instinctively make if you're thinking, *"I'm so not qualified for this job. In fact, you'd be making a mistake if you hired me. . . ."* while you are saying aloud, "I really think I'm the best person for the job, and I feel I will be an asset to your company."

> **In the same way we all use spoken dialogue to generate**
> **a response from another person, INNER MONOLOGUE**
> **is also used to create a reaction from your fellow actors.**

INNER MONOLOGUE helps you work to create a relationship even when you are not speaking. We as an audience will pick up on an actor's INNER MONOLOGUE. The truth of what you're thinking versus what you're saying will make us relate and respond. We identify with it because we rarely say what's *really* going on in our minds. Saying what's really on our minds is often contrary to achieving our goal. We couch what we really want to say to elicit the response we desire. If you want someone to have sex with you, you can't very well say, "Hey, you, I really want to have sex with you." Instead, you tell the person they're attractive; you wine and dine them; you're sympathetic, understanding and charming; you pretend that you're actually listening when that person is aimlessly babbling; and you generally spend too much time talking about a lot of things you don't care about. When Jack Nicholson's character of Melvin Udall in *As Good as It Gets* visits Carol Connelly (Helen Hunt) at the restaurant where she is a waitress, they discuss Carol's asthmatic son's health. While she talks about her son's critically bad health problems, Jack, as Melvin, clearly has an INNER MONOLOGUE that has nothing to do with her son's health. When you watch Jack listening to Carol, you see in his behavior that he's thinking about something a lot more risqué. Of course, Melvin can't say anything that would remotely touch the romantic arena—it would be insensitive and inappropriate—but he *can* and *does* think it. This INNER MONOLOGUE not only establishes Melvin as a flawed and human man but also generates chemistry between the two characters.

Another example of a common INNER MONOLOGUE that you may have experienced is when you ask someone, "Do I look like I've gained weight? I feel like I might have put on a few pounds." But your INNER MONOLOGUE is actually driven toward trying to provoke the other person to tell you that you look like you have *lost* weight. You're thinking, "Please, just say I look thinner. . . . I've spent so much time and money on frozen, minuscule, preprepared, cardboard-tasting meals. . . ."

Your INNER MONOLOGUE should be written out the way your mind really thinks.

This means that even if you are a Rhodes scholar, your thoughts are simple, unrefined, rudimentary, uncomplicated and just plain base. Sometimes our inner dialogue is so simplistic that it can seem akin to childlike non sequitur ramblings. Most of our intellectualizations and rationalizations take place when we're speaking out loud. What we say and what we think are dissimilar and often even contradictory. INNER MONOLOGUE is the script attached to the ever-present movie (INNER OBJECTS) that plays behind our eyes at all times. By having an INNER MONOLOGUE, an actor can realize their character's actual inner life and truths, which add layers that could not otherwise be achieved.

INNER MONOLOGUE makes you work harder to win your SCENE OBJECTIVE.

This is because your spoken words are frequently so different from what you're really thinking that your thoughts force you to overcompensate as a way to make the other person believe that what you're saying is true. You always know the two people at a party who hate each other the most. They are the two who, when they meet, squeal with mutual delight about their reunion. They say things like "It's been too long! It's so good to see you! You look amazing! We really have to get together. Let's do lunch!" When what they are really thinking is "It hasn't been long enough! Seeing you reminds me of all the wretched things you've done to me! You are repulsive! If we do have lunch, I'll probably vomit on your ugly face!" The equation goes something like this: the bigger the greeting glee, the bigger the hatred.

INNER MONOLOGUE is what you can't say out loud because it will be antithetical to winning your SCENE OBJECTIVE.

Envision a scene where your character, a journalist, is being denigrated by their boss, the newspaper's editor.

Sample dialogue:

EDITOR
This piece you wrote is awful—a ten-year-old
could have done better.

YOUR CHARACTER
Thank you, sir. I'll work on it.

EDITOR
Great. If you need help, my assistant, Edna, will
work with you.

YOUR CHARACTER
Edna's good. That's an excellent suggestion.

EDITOR
Now, get out of here and get on it.

Your INNER MONOLOGUE (I.M.) might go something like this:

> **EDITOR**
> This piece you wrote is awful—a ten-year-old
> could have done better.
>
> I.M.: *"You no-talent ass, what would you know about writing?
> You spend more time with the bottle than the page. . . ."*

> **YOUR CHARACTER**
> Thank you, sir. I'll work on it.
>
> I.M.: *"Yeah, thank you for sleepless nights. Thank you for
> making me loathe myself. And thank you for making me want
> to kill myself. . . ."*

> **EDITOR**
> Great. If you need help, my assistant, Edna, will
> work with you.
>
> I.M.: *"Edna the slut. Yeah, she's gonna be a lot of help. . . ."*

> **YOUR CHARACTER**
> Edna's good. That's an excellent suggestion.
>
> I.M.: *"Edna's good, all right. She's got the scuffed-up knees to
> prove it. . . ."*

> **EDITOR**
> Now, get out of here and get on it.
>
> I.M.: *"You should die a slow and horrible death. . . ."*

Obviously, your character can't say what they really think or they'll face repercussions, like losing their job.

> *Our INNER MONOLOGUE can spice things up*
> *when we're having banal, boring conversations.*

Having inappropriate, vulgar, illicit thoughts makes these conversations a whole lot more exciting. Whenever you're spending time with a member of the opposite sex (or the sex you're attracted to), there's always an opportunity and an inclination to think about them sexually. We wonder what it might be like to kiss them, what they are like in bed, etc. Even when there's no chemistry between you and the other actor, it's up to you to create it. Sexuality is a primal force that everyone can relate to, making boring dialogue and a boring scene captivating.

When I was an actress, I had an actor friend who had a bit part on *Archie Bunker's Place*, the spin-off of *All in the Family*. Ordering from an attractive waitress, his dialogue was "I'd like the steak, please." My friend, not being aware of the adage "There are no small parts, just small actors," gave a reading of the line that he felt it deserved, about five words' worth. Award-winning actor Carroll O'Connor, the star of the show, walked up to my friend and whispered in his ear, "Hey, do you think the girl who plays the waitress is pretty?"

"Heck, yeah!" my friend responded.

"Would you like to sleep with her?" O'Connor asked.

"Oh, yeah!!" my friend said with all the testosterone he could muster.

"So, when you say your line, 'I'd like the steak, please' . . ."

"Yeah?"

My friend waited for O'Connor to continue.

"Use it!"

> INNER MONOLOGUE *provides information that the*
> *actual dialogue does not—helping you earn the right of*
> *future events in the script, which are often not in the written*
> *word because doing so would reveal too much too soon.*

One of the early scenes of the Neil LaBute film *Your Friends & Neighbors* is a dinner party given by the characters of Mary and Barry, who have just moved to the country because they've had enough of city life. In the scene, Mary extols the virtues of country living—how glad she is that they've moved, how improved her life is and how much better her relationship with Barry is. She says all of this despite the fact that she's completely miserable. She feels isolated from her friends and her former work life. Mary has also discovered that spending more time with Barry, one of the main reasons for moving out of the city, is *too much* time.

In the film, Mary's unrest ultimately leads her to have an affair with the handsome and slick Cary (Jason Patric). When looking for inspiration for the character of Mary's INNER MONOLOGUE in this scene, I told Amy Brenneman, who plays Mary, that she needed to feel an earlier pull and yearning for Cary that would support her affair with him in later scenes. We decided that when Mary is talking about her terrific decision to move to the country, her INNER MONOLOGUE would be something like this: *"I hate being here. No,* hate *is too weak a word. I loathe and detest being here. Barry has become country boring."* This line of thinking would be interrupted by Mary (Amy) looking over at Cary (Jason) and thinking, *"You are so hot. I'd like to* [**_fill in the blank_** *with Amy's personal desires*]. . . ." Even though the dialogue for Mary had nothing to do in any way with her relationship—past, present or future—with Cary, Amy's use of INNER MONOLOGUE made Mary's feelings and intentions loud and clear to Cary and the audience. Using INNER MONOLOGUE for this scene achieved two things. First, by using the INNER MONOLOGUE, Mary (Amy) is subliminally telling Cary (Jason) that she wants him. This gives him subconscious permission to pursue her, which he wouldn't have done otherwise because she's married and seemingly unavailable. People don't generally put the moves on someone unless they feel there's a good shot that they won't be rejected and that they are wanted. Second, by establishing that the heat is rising between these two characters, the INNER MONOLOGUE helps to foreshadow events to come, which creates audience anticipation.

INNER MONOLOGUE gives you something to say when there is no dialogue.

In theater and especially in film, there are scenes where there is no dialogue or the other character is reciting a long monologue and you're the listener. Instead of you merely standing around feeling and looking like a sounding board, INNER MONOLOGUE keeps the listening active. While I was working with Travis Fimmel as Ragnar Lothbrok on *Vikings,* we came to a scene where Ragnar sits on a mountain cliff overlooking the village he lives in. Even though the scene had no dialogue and was only around a minute of screen time, Travis and I still explored it with depth and layers using all the tools. INNER MONOLOGUE was especially helpful so the audience could still go on a journey with him and not rely on dialogue to do so. With personalization, we used INNER MONOLOGUE that included Ragnar's turbulent internal debate whether he should give up his life exploring new worlds and lead the peaceful life of a farmer and family man or continue his path of adventure. He also had to consider the great cost of this choice: If he continued to explore and conquer new lands, he was putting his own people in jeopardy (because people who are being conquered tend to not give up that easily). We personalized not only the inner verbiage in Ragnar's tortured contemplation but made what he was looking at a personal PLACE that would inform Travis' INNER MONO-LOGUE, making his decision more momentous and life-changing.

The audiences felt included in Ragnar's secret world because when the IN-NER MONOLOGUE is strong and specific, an audience feels that they can read the character's mind. It was such a strong device to use in creating a committed audience reaction that the scene became a fan favorite, and the writers kept writing different versions of the on-the-cliff-overlooking-something scene even after Ragnar died. Bjorn, Ragnar's firstborn played by Alexander Ludwig, inherited the cliff-overlooking-something scene. Since I worked with Alexander, too, we filled in those scenes with deep and provocative INNER MONOLOGUE, creating a kind of funny legacy: like father like son on the mountaintop.

I remember talking to a critic who was doing an article on me for a newspaper. When we were done, she said, "I cover the show *Vikings* for my newspaper. Would you like to know what my favorite scenes with Travis are?" "Of course, go on . . ." I said, awaiting her reply eagerly. The first scene she brought up was the cliff scene. All the other scenes she loved were mostly those with no or very little dialogue. She then began to tell me what she believed Ragnar was thinking, not in generic terms but with certainty: "And then he was thinking . . ." she said many times regarding the scenes she particularly liked. Her take was pretty accurate to what Travis/Ragnar had been thinking, and I was not surprised by how spot-on she was! The point is, people can read your mind, and they like doing it. INNER MONOLOGUE is a very important tool on so many levels.

INNER MONOLOGUE can give purpose and magnitude to scripted moments that seem mundane or insignificant.

In script analysis, there should not be a moment in time or a piece of dialogue that can be considered unimportant. When the stakes are high, even a sigh has significance: a step away, a sense of emotional urgency. Nothing should ever be thought of as throwaway, because when *you* throw something away, your audience does, too.

For example, in many scripts you'll find a character singing along with a group. This might seem innocuous enough: a group of people singing, say,

"Happy Birthday" or drunkenly belting out show tunes around a piano in a party scene. It is up to you to find more personal and noteworthy meaning in the event itself and in the words of the song. In *Their Eyes Were Watching God*, an ABC movie based on the novel by Zora Neale Hurston and executive-produced by Oprah Winfrey and Quincy Jones, there is a scene where the townspeople sing as a group. The movie tells the story of Janie (played by Halle Berry), a young woman in the early 1900s who has spent most of her life being subjugated, controlled and criticized. She meets Joe Starks, who offers her a new life, a great life filled with the freedom to explore and discover. Joe proposes to take her to Eatonville, the first city in America run by, as Joe tells her, "colored folks that's got together. They've made their very own town." She leaves with him, and when they get to Eatonville, they find it needs Joe's moxie and know-how to create a true and real city. Joe becomes the official mayor and Janie the first lady. The first streetlamp is delivered to Eatonville by a Sears, Roebuck and Company truck. To celebrate the auspiciousness of the occasion, there is a lamp-lighting ceremony to mark that Eatonville is now considered "the first incorporated colored township in all America!" as Joe expresses in his speech to the townsfolk. When a character named Amos requests a few words from Mrs. Mayor Starks (Janie), Joe quickly shuts him down, saying, "Mrs. Mayor Starks don't know nothing about speechmaking. I didn't marry her for that." This devastates Janie. Joe promised her the world but instead does what everyone else has done in her life: squelched her spirit by making her feel stupid, powerless and inconsequential. She isn't allowed to speak. Joe finishes his rousing speech to his constituents and gets them all singing. There are looks of hope on the townspeople's faces in direct contrast to Janie's look. Joe was her only hope for a different life and future, and clearly that was a lie.

As Halle and I broke this scene down, we could've easily infused it with the truth of a woman who felt the pain and disappointment of a life gone terribly wrong. But solely providing the reality of hurt and betrayal would have implied that she had given up and has been defeated. There's no win in admitting and giving in to defeat. Doing so creates hopelessness, not only for the character but also for the actor and the audience. You as an actor should never make the choice of becoming helpless and victimized by life's traumas. The journey stops when you cease to try to change even the most untenable of situations.

To accomplish a winning scenario, as opposed to Halle becoming a victim to defeat, we first infused the scene with Halle's personal issues that required hope and change, issues that at the time of shooting this scene seemed to weigh in on the doomed-to-fail end of the scale. Then we provided INNER MONO-LOGUE that would create a sense of hopeful expectation. As she closed her eyes, she sang the words to the song:

This little light of mine, I'm gonna let it shine.

This light of mine, I'm gonna let it shine. This little light of mine, I'm gonna let it shine. Let it shine, let it shine, let it shine. . . .

And at the same time, we infused the scene with hopeful possibilities by having Halle think an INNER MONOLOGUE that went something like this:

"I hate him and he lied to me just like everyone else in my life, but I won't give in to hating myself. I won't be a victim! Not anymore. I'll find a way, there's gotta be a way, there's hope for me, there's light for me, I'm not giving up. I can't—if I do, I'll die. This light is mine, I'm not gonna let anyone take that away from me again, I'm gonna let my hopes and dreams shine. I won't give up. I don't know how and when it's gonna change, but I'm gonna expose the light of who I am, and I'm gonna let it shine, let it shine, let it shine!"

This INNER MONOLOGUE enabled Halle and her character to gather strength to carry on and fight the inevitable battles that she was going to face—as a woman as well as a woman of color. In a scene that was written to express Janie's downfall, INNER MONOLOGUE gave the scene purpose, hope and possibility.

When you personalize your INNER MONOLOGUE, make sure it makes sense with your SCENE OBJECTIVE, SUBSTITUTION, personalized OBSTACLES and INNER OBJECTS.

Because of the nature of INNER MONOLOGUE and of my work—an acting coach is ethically bound by a rule that is similar to a psychiatrist's promise of client/patient confidentiality—it's impossible for me to discuss someone else's personal INNER MONOLOGUE work. An actor must trust that I'll never re-veal their secrets so that they'll feel comfortable telling me intimate information they often don't share even with their family or therapists. I use these secrets for the inspiration, dimension, shadings and hues of an actor's work. The use of secrets in an actor's work is essential for producing a dynamic performance. Because I cannot reveal anyone else's secrets, I will use a case from my own life using a miscreant cad of an ex-mate (if you're wondering if it's *you*, it probably is) to show you how to personalize your INNER MONOLOGUE. In the play *Boys' Life*, there is a scene where the character of Lisa finds another girl's panties in her bed as she begins to make love to her boyfriend, Don. Don has indeed been fooling around and feels he must cover his misdeed in order to keep Lisa around because, despite his indiscretion, he loves her. Lisa loves him, too, but letting him off the hook too easily would make Don feel he could do it again—so she must put him through his paces before she takes him back.

- **OVERALL OBJECTIVE:** *"love without pain"*
- **SCENE OBJECTIVE:** *"to make you say or do something that will fix it"* (so we can stay together)
- **The script's OBSTACLES:**
  1. Don is likely to do it again.
  2. Don's lack of remorse.
  3. Don's charm and humor mean that he's used to getting away with his bad behavior.
  4. Lisa's history with "bad boys."
  5. If Lisa becomes too aggressively antagonistic, she just might lose Don.
- **SUBSTITUTION:** My ex. A man who cheated on me with not just one but several nubile beauties, as well as one gay man named Alan.
- **Personalized OBSTACLES:**
  1. My ex seemed to be a sex addict, which would have been that much harder to change or fix.
  2. My ex wasn't particularly remorseful when he was caught, unless I threatened to leave.
  3. My ex said he was sorry so many times yet committed his unfaithful acts again and again anyway.
  4. My belief quotient because I'd been lied to so many times in the past.

5. My history with dishonest men.

6. My ex's history of cheating with prior girlfriends.

7. And what the heck was his sexual preference anyway?!

- **MOMENT BEFORE:** The time when we were hosting a party and I found him in our bedroom with Connie in the "middle" of breaking one of God's commandments. As I stood there in disbelief, wondering if my presence (or cold water) would stop them, he said, "Leave. Can't you see I'm busy?!" (I'm not making this up; he really said this—a vivid memory that will, no doubt, stay with me forever.)

- **PLACE and FOURTH WALL:** The bedroom we shared when we were going together and the sight of the above crime.

Following is an excerpt from *Boys' Life*. My character's OVERALL OBJECTIVE and SCENE OBJECTIVE, my SUBSTITUTION for Don and my personal OBSTACLES, MOMENT BEFORE, PLACE and FOURTH WALL and INNER OBJECTS will become obvious because of my INNER MONOLOGUE.

In the scene, Lisa carefully lifts the offending underwear and begins to confront Don, who is silently staring at the incriminating panties.

BOYS' LIFE

I.M.: *"So whose stinky, cheapo panties are these? Slutty Jillanne? Skanky Connie? Or how-did-he-get-in-the-mix Alan? Huh? Huh?!"*

LISA
Is that all you have to say about it?
I.M.: *"You always put me down, calling me stupid all the time. Well, who looks like an idiot now, you jerk!"*

DON
What else do you want me to say?
I.M.: *"You think you're such a big-time writer, yet you have nothing to say. . . . All those big words that you use—incorrectly, I might add—can't help you now! . . ."*

LISA
How about *sorry*?
I.M.: *"Hey, pea brain, has it ever occurred to you to say 'I'm sorry' and actually mean it?! Perhaps, Mr. Writer-man, you don't know*

the meaning and derivation of the word. God, I'm such an idiot for always taking you back. . . ."

Now, looking at the scene from the P.O.V. of Don or Lisa, go through it and try using your own INNER MONOLOGUE (based on doing the prior tools). See what behavior comes of doing so. Notice how the INNER MONOLOGUE provides another dimension of behavior, allowing you to speak and think at the same time—just like real people do.

INNER MONOLOGUE is not to be memorized, but the thoughts and ideas behind the monologue are.

An INNER MONOLOGUE will vary every time a scene is run, but the general concepts of what was written down will be retained. Think of the INNER MONOLOGUE you've written down on the page as an extensive outline; then let your imagination run from there.

INNER MONOLOGUE regarding science fiction, fantasy, horror with monsters, the paranormal and superheroes (and the like) must be humanized.

As popular as these topics are, what makes them appealing is the human aspect. There's always something relatable and truthful to our own world in fantasy-based plotlines. To make for a performance the audience can connect with, the INNER MONOLOGUE must be even more down and dirty in its humanized verbiage. We aren't trying to believe that monsters and the like really exist; we are attempting to become the character in an unlikely environment by making choices and having feelings that we've actually experienced in the real world. This is the most effective way to be truly invested so the other actors we are playing opposite are invested in us and our audiences are more engrossed in watching us.

Take for example my work with Christina Chong, who plays the character of La'an Noonien-Singh in *Star Trek: Strange New Worlds*. La'an is from a planet that is not Earth, but she is at least part human, albeit an augmented one, because her ancestor is the infamous Khan Noonien-Singh, a notorious augmented human in the *Trek* universe. All that being said, the most important part of La'an's backstory is her severely traumatic childhood. The spectacularly cruel Gorn ate her family while they were still alive, and five-year-old La'an somehow survived. This is the short version of someone whose childhood innocence was hideously cut short and her sole focus became survival. As a result, her adult demeanor is cold and standoffish. Her INNER MONOLOGUE could be something like *"Do the job. Do it well and get on with it."* But that is not adding to the three-dimensionality of the character, just paraphrasing her surface attributes. The depth comes from discovering the reason she is this way and then supplying that information via her INNER MONOLOGUE. We can assume that the horror La'an witnessed and survived makes her leery and self-protective and saddles her with the belief that if she loves or is loved by anyone, they will die. She's still a child in an adult body, and she believes that the Gorn (or anyone that mildly resembles their evil behaviors) could emerge at any moment. The INNER MONOLOGUE that Christina and I crafted reflected a child's vulnerability, not the emotionally detached persona La'an puts forward in her pursuit of self-preservation.

The science fiction plot, which was often filled with sci-fi jargon, was informed with INNER MONOLOGUE that detailed and mirrored Christina's own personal dramas and emotional-pain scenarios. Each episode and its major plotline were personalized, too. In this way, Christina accessed the hurt and pain that caused La'an to need to solve the mystery of the week from a heartfelt place while never losing her protective layer of cool remove. The aliens were personalized with specific INNER MONOLOGUE that exhibited the connection that Christina (as La'an) had to her pain (antagonist alien) or the one that she had to her feelings and experiences that involved love (protagonist alien). This brought to Christina's work richness as well as subliminal reasoning for the audience to understand and feel empathy and a special attachment to La'an.

In another episode, La'an and young Captain James T. Kirk (played by Paul Wesley) are in an alternate reality and in a past timeline (which happens to be our present). They fall in love, but in the normal reality, they've never met. When the normal reality returns to, well, normal, La'an remembers they've met and fallen in love, but Kirk does not. There's a sci-fi explanation for this, which I've never understood, but it wasn't necessary for Christina to comprehend the logic to give a great performance. It's the actor's job to simplify via the inner work. And humanizing this plotline to become a basic love-gained-and-lost arc with the sci-fi aspect functioning as a backdrop makes the episode more fascinating and intricate.

I worked with Ian Somerhalder on the audition that booked him the lead role in *The Vampire Diaries*, Damon Salvatore. Damon is a vampire, and his brother, Stefan, yes, is a vampire, too. Both audition scenes were contentious brother exchanges. Ian and I never even considered his vampire-sucking ways in our script analysis, but rather filled his INNER MONOLOGUE with normal sibling rivalry, using personalizations that would accurately depict for Ian a combative familial relationship and the thinking that goes along with it. This booked him the job.

The INNER MONOLOGUE provides a basic human reality even if the world of the story is surreal or fantastical. The bottom line is that the true human experience includes fundamental inner thoughts and feelings that are going to be relatable and stand the test of time, making whatever you are working on relevant.

Continue the INNER MONOLOGUE until you've made a clean exit or the director has said "Cut."

Just because you are heading offstage or walking out the door or the spoken dialogue is finished, it doesn't mean the scene is over. INNER MONOLOGUE is an essential tool.

Your mind continues to think even when you're not speaking.

Great actors always have a strong INNER MONOLOGUE playing behind their eyes at all times. Watch a scene with one of the legendary actors and notice how much time the camera stays on him or her. Why did the film editors cut back to him or her even when they were not speaking and the other actor was delivering an impassioned speech? More often than not, it's because the nonspeaking actor or actress is using INNER MONOLOGUE. Their INNER MONOLOGUE plays out on their face, in their eyes, in the way they hold their bodies, their hands. Frequently, the actor who is using INNER MONOLOGUE displays more need and passion than the actor who is speaking. INNER MONOLOGUE is one of the most powerful tools an actor can use.

Have a LAST THOUGHT

Just because the dialogue is over doesn't mean the scene is. The LAST THOUGHT is INNER MONOLOGUE that continues the need based on your SCENE OBJECTIVE after the dialogue is over. The LAST THOUGHT must be substantiated by the personal work you did in the scene. The LAST THOUGHT should make you and all who are viewing your work, whether it's a booked job or an audition, think there's so much more to look forward to regarding your character.

The LAST THOUGHT also includes how the character plans on not letting the OBSTACLES in the scene get in the way of achieving the goal posed in the SCENE OBJECTIVE. We don't want to end our experience of you in the scene with a feeling of defeat. Instead, we want to be left with the impression that you/your character will find a way to overcome the problem and win no matter how discouraging the outcome appears to be. This helps the viewer see you as a winner. We want you to win; we don't want to feel sorry for you. When you/your character wins, a viewer wants to see what you'll do next.

For example, after Will's first session with the psychiatrist in *Good Will Hunting*, he exits the doctor's office. Based on the SCENE OBJECTIVE *"I need you to prove you are up to the task (of being my doctor),"* the LAST THOUGHT could be *"Okay, you passed this test, but can you pass the next one, which I will make so much harder?"* (You'd relate this to your SUBSTITUTION.) Or if it's a scene from *Room* where the kidnapped mother must deal with the kidnapper, her LAST THOUGHT could be *"You believed me when I told you I cared about you, but you will get yours. I don't know how, I don't know when, but I will destroy you."* (Again, personalizing the words based on your SUBSTITUTION.) Or if it's the scene in the diner in *When Harry Met Sally . . .* that Sally ends with her version of a fake orgasm to prove that even Harry, as good as he might be in bed, can be fooled, Harry's SCENE OBJECTIVE could be *"I need you to love me in spite of and because of who I am,"* and his LAST THOUGHT could be *"If I ever get the chance, I am so going to prove to you that your orgasm will be real, because, damn, that was a really believable orgasm."* (That LAST THOUGHT INNER MONOLOGUE could create funny behavior, too.) A LAST THOUGHT makes the viewer feel more invested in you winning your OVERALL OBJECTIVE.

CHAPTER 11

Tool #11:
PREVIOUS
CIRCUMSTANCES

A person's history. The accumulation of life experiences that determines who they are—*why* and *how* they operate in the world. First, you do this for the character; then you personalize the character's PREVIOUS CIRCUMSTANCES with what makes sense to your life, thus comprehending more fully—and without judgment—the layers of what makes a human being do what they do.

Who we are today is an accumulation of past events, our reactions to these events and other people's reactions to us. This is also true for any character you are playing. When you are playing a thirty-year-old character, you must give your character the details of thirty years of existence. In every script the character has PREVIOUS CIRCUMSTANCES that define *who* they are, *how* they move in the world, and *what* they feel they must do to survive, both emotionally and physically. You have to look at the character's who-am-I today by investigating the information provided in the script and making assumptions based on the dialogue and your character's past and present activities. This will tell you *why* your character embodies a specific nature. The next step is to consider your character's history and the kind of psyche and behavior that result from that particular history—in other words, *how* the PREVIOUS

CIRCUMSTANCES have manifested themselves in present word and deed. Finally, you must personalize by identifying how your character's history relates to yours. So, to recap, here is the formula for:

APPLYING PREVIOUS CIRCUMSTANCES

1. You look at the PREVIOUS CIRCUMSTANCES of the character by reading and investigating the character's behaviors and dialogue, as well as how your character is discussed in other dialogue (whether or not your character is in the scene).

2. You consider how your character deals with life physically by examining the activities, past and present, that your character chooses and relies on to exist and survive in their world.

3. You look at why the character makes the choices they do—both socially and career-wise. This information is derived from your exploration of the character's PREVIOUS CIRCUMSTANCES, in which you consider the actual information written into the script, as well as anything you might be able to assume based on the written information.

4. Personalization. You look at how this information relates to you and your own personal PREVIOUS CIRCUMSTANCES.

Let's look at how this works with a character who is a killer. First, you look at the character's dialogue and what others say about the killer for the first layer of understanding of why your character kills. You consider how they speak, what language they use, how they relate to others, what behavioral traits they have and how others see them. Next, you look at why, how and whom your character chooses to kill. Then you examine the PREVIOUS CIRCUMSTANCES that are described in the script, and you speculate on and explore what kind of temperament the character's particular history would establish. Generally speaking, a murderer kills because of some need to assert the ultimate power. After all, for such a character, there is no greater power trip than taking someone's life. More often than not, a person who feels the need to go to this extreme has, in some way, had their power cruelly and heinously taken away (and it's usually by a primal somebody, often from your childhood)—either through physical and/or mental abuse. The act of killing allows the killer to feel like they are getting their power back. Usually, killers subconsciously make their victims a symbolic version of the abuser. When they are killing, they feel that they are asserting their dominance over the original offender. The killer is acting out as a way to *heal* their past. As you can see, thinking about a killer in this light takes the act of murder out of the one-dimensional evil realm and humanizes the behavior.

If you were playing the role of a killer, you must relate this desire to assert the ultimate power over someone to your own life. You might be asking, "What does this have to do with me? I have no massive trauma like this in my history nor do I have a desire to assert this kind of power." But the fact is that everyone has, at some point in their life, thought about killing someone. For most of us, it's a brief and momentary fantasy to murder as a way to resolve a relationship that has become ruthlessly intolerable, but nevertheless, the killing instinct is there. It's up to you to figure out when and what triggered these feelings so that you can use them to fuel your character's words, feelings and actions. This is a way to look at the PREVIOUS CIRCUMSTANCES of the character and then identify how they are duplicated in your own personal PREVIOUS CIRCUM-STANCES.

Let's look at the movie *The Silence of the Lambs* again but this time from the point of view of how one might personalize the PREVIOUS CIRCUM-STANCES of the character Clarice Starling (played by Jodie Foster). Based on the script, we know that Clarice Starling is an FBI agent who grew up on a "backward" sheep farm. Through her dialogue with the character Hannibal Lecter, we learn that Clarice's family never paid much attention to her and was emotionally abusive. We can also assume from their conversations and her behavior that she became an FBI agent in order to find a way to "silence the screaming lambs" in her head and her heart. We can also presuppose that Clarice is using saving the life of a senator's kidnapped daughter as a salve for her own emotional disquiet and pain. To play this role, you would have to find corresponding history (PREVIOUS CIRCUMSTANCES) of your own to make Clarice's needs and issues yours. It's not very likely that you have ever been an FBI agent or the daughter of a sheep farmer or that as a child you ran off with a screaming lamb cuddled in your arms. However, you probably do have "emotional disquiet and pain" that emanates from another source. For example:

- You may have become an actor (likened to becoming an FBI agent) as a way to deal with an abusive stepmother ("screaming lambs in your head"), and grew up wanting to run away (running off with the lamb in your arms). Or . . .
- You seek great success as a way to overcome that bully you grew up with who always made you feel diminished, small and inconsequential, and you seek comeuppance with the same type of people that are currently in your life. Or . . .
- You have (or had) an abusive boyfriend or girlfriend whose demoralizing, terrorizing remarks and attitude plague you with self-loathing, and you seek to estrange yourself from this person but don't have the courage.

Creating these kinds of parallel similarities between the written character's history and your own will help you become the character.

What if you have to play someone whose PREVIOUS CIRCUMSTANCES are all about growing up as an orphan, and you are not one? Here you would find something in your history that would duplicate the feelings of growing up as an orphan. For instance, maybe at a critical moment in your life, one or both of your parents were not emotionally there for you, which left you feeling lost and alone like an orphan.

All of this is to show you that you don't have to experience the hard realities of the character you're playing to bring realism to the role. While being homicidal and being orphaned are singular experiences, the feelings of being powerless or abandoned are things that we can all relate to, at least at some point in our lives. You have a lifetime of experiences and a myriad of feelings attached to them that you can call upon to give you a history that corresponds to the character on the page, which will enable you to embody that character heart and soul.

PREVIOUS CIRCUMSTANCES are applicable in all genres, as is doing the deep work to go along with them. I worked with the rappers Redman and

Method Man on the comedy *How High*, which was about a couple of stoners who smoke a magical blend of weed that helps them do extraordinarily well on their college entrance exams and they wind up at Harvard. These characters believe that the only way they can be considered substantial and special in the world is if they smoke the marijuana that was fertilized (by accident) by their dead friend's ashes. They surprise most of the Ivy League people (students and professors alike) by how smart and successful they are in such a rigorous and difficult academic environment. When they run out of the magic weed, though, they stop doing well. They go from the best students to the worst. In time, they realize, they never needed the magic marijuana at all, and in the end, they ace everything using their own natural intelligence.

Now, this is a silly comedy, generally termed a physical comedy. Most actors think that comedy is lighter than drama. But the truth is that in the name of emotional pain and desperation, we do many crazy things that actuate comic behaviors. When breaking down a comedy, remember it's deeper and more desperate than drama. Thus, you need to break comedy down the same way as you would a drama. In using the OVERALL OBJECTIVE of *"self-worth"* for both characters that Red and Meth were playing, we needed to dig into their own issues of self-worth and the PREVIOUS CIRCUMSTANCES of their lives that would make them feel worthless. Because of this, the movie doesn't just appeal to people who have a special connection with marijuana, but to all those who suffer from self-worth issues—which is about everyone on the planet. By using their true PREVIOUS CIRCUMSTANCES to substantiate their characters, their performances ended up helping *How High* transcend the stoner-movie genre and become a cult classic.

Redman's using what we worked on regarding digging deep is how my name ended up in a rap song.

Red bravely revealed through the poetry of his rap lyrics in "Self-Medication" a painfully dysfunctional childhood environment, and referred to sexual abuse that came from a babysitter. He ended the thought about our work together by expressing how much he learned from using his troubled past in his art and life, and giving the credit to: "Twelve steps, Ivana Chubbuck."

What he is saying is that he is proud of the man he's become because he's empowered by his pain. Thank you for the shout-out, Red, and let every artist understand through your words, we can't change the past regarding our pain, but a true artist uses it to overcome and win.

Using PREVIOUS CIRCUMSTANCES gives you substantial reasons from past events to have to win your OVERALL OBJECTIVE.

Doing so becomes a way to heal the past, creating an opportunity for catharsis. Everyone has had painful events in their past (PREVIOUS CIRCUMSTANCES), but how artists deal with these experiences shows how they are different from everyone else. Simply put, there's a fork in the road of life—to the left are those who take past traumas and *destruct* with them. It's a road well traveled, because it's the path of least resistance. Then there are the few who choose to take those same past traumas and *construct* with the information. That less-traveled road is more like a dirt path riddled with all sorts of hazardous obstacles and gruesome creatures—it makes the journey difficult, but ultimately it's a far more satisfying journey. Constructors, in other words, take adversarial situations rather than make the safe choice. Instead of accepting life's horrors and becoming self-pitying, they use the conflict and pain to fuel their passion to win. These are the true winners and artists.

By using your painful PREVIOUS CIRCUMSTANCES as a way to fortify your need to win your OVERALL OBJECTIVE in the script, you are establishing a dynamic journey that will be cathartic to play and will create hope in your audience, because if you can win despite all your past conflicts, perhaps they can, too.

Never Ignore Who *You* Are When You're Getting into Character.

The actors that are the most celebrated for their talent are those who never lose sight of who they are as people when they perform. Robert De Niro, Jack Nicholson, Meryl Streep, Cate Blanchett and Al Pacino have each played a variety of characters, but you can always see traces of their true selves in their work.

This comes from infusing their personal PREVIOUS CIRCUMSTANCES in their work. They know that who we are today is shaped by our histories. Besides, all you've got is *you*. You aren't De Niro, Nicholson, Streep, Blanchett or Pacino, which is good because that makes you distinctive and unique and therefore special.

When Jim Carrey first came to me, it was at a time in his life when he couldn't get arrested. He had done three movies that had failed miserably, along with a series called *The Duck Factory*, which was also considered a colossal bomb. Jim was blamed for the failures and was having trouble even getting in the door for auditions. He realized that if something's broken, you've got to at least make some effort to fix it, especially if it's your livelihood. So he came to me to see if he could change what looked, at this point in his life, like a bleak future.

In true Jim Carrey fashion, he would arrive at my door fully animated, saying and doing things that invariably caused a nonstop laugh fest. But as soon as we began working with a script, he would become soft-spoken, still and, well, boring. I asked him why he wasn't bringing himself to the work. He said he was afraid it would be considered overacting. Over the years, I've found that most actors' biggest fear is that they'll be told they are overacting. This causes them to censor their natural impulses and prevents them from taking risks—and as you should know by now, risk-taking is essential to being a great actor. I told Jim what I tell all my students: "What's the worst that can happen if you overact? The overacting police will come and arrest you and put you in overacting jail? The overacting police don't exist, so you're pretty safe to go balls to the wall." I assured him that as long as his work was honest and he had strong OBJECTIVES and a heightened need to win them, he couldn't ever go too far. That in fact he should risk going too far. When we humans are faced with urgent needs and the necessity for survival, we have a tendency to do strange and outrageous acts. Think about that date with that special person where you blurted out inanities and behaved absurdly. Or that important job interview where you expressed yourself too boldly, perhaps even fudging the truth in insane proportions. In his acting, Jim needed to communicate and relate the way he did in his day-to-day life. I told him not to pull back. I explained that when the stakes are high, we're always a hyper version of ourselves, and that to truly reflect real behavior, he must be himself.

We found that by using his daughter, Jane, as a frequent SUBSTITUTION in his SCENE OBJECTIVE statements, he was motivated to win. His love for her connected him to the work and inspired him to work hard to overcome the script conflicts, because he was doing it for her. Relating himself and his life to his work gave all the crazy Jim Carrey behavior a context and made his acting work make sense, because he was doing it for his little girl. Once we figured this out, anytime Jim would perform a scene, I'd say, "You can do more!" He'd say, "Really?" And I'd respond by saying, "Yes, *you* can do more, because who you really are as a person *is more*." And, well, we all know how this story ends.

Your past constructs your present and future, thereby making you a three-dimensional human being.

When you are personalizing PREVIOUS CIRCUMSTANCES, it might be helpful to make a list of important, emotionally triggering events that have happened in your life so you can pick and choose which ones make most sense for your character's OVERALL OBJECTIVE. I will give some examples from my life to help spark ideas for you. These are simply sluglines, but when you choose yours, you need to remember them in a visceral, more complicated way—with detailed images of all that happened around the chosen events. This will trigger feelings from the reexperiencing of them to establish a strong underbelly to the character's journey.

PREVIOUS CIRCUMSTANCES event list examples from my life:

- I was four years old and hiding in the closet, trying to get away from my mother, who I believed was going to hurt me. She almost found me. I was terrorized. She was capable of violence, and I never knew what would cause her to go there. I now believe she suffered from mental illness but was never diagnosed. But from my child point of view, that didn't really matter.
- A rare (maybe the only) moment of nurturing from my mother: I was three years old and cradled in her arms as my family rode in our station wagon during the long drive home from New York City, where

she was from, to Detroit, where we lived. I was vomiting a lot, and she continued to just hold me and make me feel loved.

- On my sixteenth birthday, my first experience having sex was so painful that I told the guy to stop. He wouldn't, said it wouldn't hurt so much the next time and just kept going. I felt alone, scared, confused and angry.

- I caught my first husband having sex with another woman in our bedroom at a party we were hosting. He told me to get out, as he wasn't finished yet.

- When I was about nine years old, my mother told me that I was the only one of her children that was planned (I have six brothers and sisters), but now she wished I had never been born.

- Standing by my father's bedside in the hospital and waiting to hear, for the first time, the words "I love you" before he died, I had a moment alone where I talked to him, hoping what I was saying would elicit these most precious words. He was semiconscious. I wasn't sure what he was hearing and taking in, but he had tears in his eyes, so I had hope he understood what I was saying. But he died never having said the words "I love you."

- I was thirteen and crying about something, and my mother said I was a crybaby and needed to stop crying all the time. I dared to talk back to her with words that apparently triggered her to choke me. I made a vow at that time that I would never cry again, and stared at her— daring her to go all the way and kill me. That stopped her. But I maintained the vow; I didn't cry again until I moved to Hollywood and sought help from a hypnotherapist to be able to cry, because at the time, I was an actor and not having that facility was problematic.

- During my second pregnancy, I got a phone call from the doctor telling me that I had a severely damaged fetus. I'd already named the baby Walker and I still keep the picture of the ultrasound.

- Feeling powerless and afraid while I was watching TV and a relative suffering from alcoholism was violently screaming at me, I thought he was going to kill me. I didn't know how to stop him as I hadn't done anything to provoke him in the first place.

- Discovering my second husband's body after he died of a prolonged illness, I felt a confusing mix of relief and sadness, and then I felt an enormous amount of guilt about that reaction.

Create your own list and keep adding to it as you remember events or as new, instigating events take place. ALSO, you might find this list useful when coming up with a triggering event for a MOMENT BEFORE.

• • • • • • • •

PREVIOUS CIRCUMSTANCES will stop the playacting and help you *become* the character from within by supplying you with the history of *why* your character is who they are and behaves the way they do.

CHAPTER 12

Tool #12:
LET IT GO

> Once you've completed all the steps, you have to trust the work you've done and then ... LET IT GO. This will allow for organic impulses and surprise thoughts and behaviors that give you the freedom to truly embody, in full glory, the character. And this is where the fun begins.

Once you've analyzed the script using the previous eleven tools, you will have comprehensively established a strong and detailed foundation for living the role. Now you must take all of the work you've done and trust that it will be there and LET IT GO. The focus as you LET IT GO should be only on your MOMENT BEFORE, which will propel you and the action of the story forward. When you trust all of the other work you've done, letting it go helps recreate the way we act in life.

For spontaneous and original behaviors to emerge, you need to be and feel free. You must LET IT GO and try not to retain all the detailed thoughts that your script analysis inspired. You don't want to be stuck in your head. You must *trust* that all the preparation you've done with the first eleven tools will come up naturally. This will happen because, by the time you've applied the first eleven tools to a script, you've built a powerful muscle structure and foundation that will activate and respond to true human impulses. The trigger to activate these tools is to LET IT GO. This is crucial, because without letting it go, you can't help but be in control, trying to duplicate something you did in rehearsal and overintellectualizing.

To reproduce real life, you have to feel like anything can happen and anything's possible.

You can't successfully LET IT GO unless you trust that all the work you've done won't disappear *when* you LET IT GO. Yes, I know you feel it's difficult to trust that if you don't constantly concentrate on the choices you've made, it will all just float away. But if the choices are weighty and have high stakes, it will not only stay, but the act of letting it go will *magnify* your feelings and needs. This is because your rational, thinking head isn't involved and therefore is unable to stop the flow with cerebral rationalizations. If you haven't made strong enough choices, it will be apparent very quickly, because those will be the choices that will not emerge when you LET IT GO. This is good, not bad, because it tells you what you need to revisit and work on, providing you with the opportunity to go back and find a more effective choice. Even in performance, you can change the less effective choices to better ones in your next take or setup, or during the next night onstage.

How Do You LET IT GO?

Don't think about the work. Don't try to remember the choices you've made. Trust and allow the information you derived from your script analysis and rehearsals to permeate and inspire your feelings and needs and to help them organically surface. This will also provide space for you to truly listen to the other person (people) in the scene, because you won't be in your head thinking about all the work that you've done. Watching an actor's wheels turning makes the work visible and less compelling to an audience. In life, who we are—how we speak and behave—is seamless. Letting it go allows the actor to organically move from each action and reaction, creating a natural flow of life. New responses will come up spontaneously because of the detailed and layered foundation you've established. This means that if you don't do all of your work, not much will happen when you LET IT GO. So . . .

Don't be lazy!

You can't LET IT GO unless you've created a strong enough base via the previous eleven tools. You must do the work. The formula goes like this:

If there's nothing to LET GO of, nothing is what you'll get.

Exactly how much work you accomplish will be exactly the amount of work that will remain when you LET IT GO. That is to say: Do a little work, and a little is what you'll get. Do deep work and deep is what you'll get. The more work you've put in, the more substantial the results you'll get when you LET IT GO, which brings us to . . .

Work Ethic and Rehearsal Time

Every time you rehearse, you'll find more nuance and detail about the human being you're trying to become. Every rehearsal gives you more information about the choices you've made—what's effective and what isn't as effective. Remember: There are no right or wrong choices, just more effective and less effective ones. Any choice is a good choice, because no matter what, it always provides you with more information about your character. Making no choice makes the moment empty. So take a stab at coming up with something. It just may work! And if it isn't very effective, it will still inspire more thoughts that will eventually lead you to that ideal choice. Extensive rehearsal time, where you can continue to try new ideas and choices for each tool, is what leads you to the most powerful choices, because it provides the space for you to find the subtleties, textures and layers of a scene. The more you work out, the more your skills as an actor will grow.

And to answer a question my students ask *all* the time:

No, you cannot rehearse too much!

All actors of note know this. When I was working with Charlize Theron on the film *The Devil's Advocate*, I discovered that Al Pacino is an actor who is enormously committed to the rehearsal process. In one scene that was only three pages long, Pacino stopped and started for each BEAT of the scene, altering choices that didn't work, refining the ones that did. He moved on to the next BEAT only when the BEAT he was working on felt right. This rehearsal process, for a tiny three-page scene, lasted for a few days!

Your rehearsals should include lots of starts and stops so that you can make sure:

- You're being true to your OVERALL OBJECTIVE.
- You're going after your SCENE OBJECTIVE.
- There are OBSTACLES getting in your way.
- The SUBSTITUTION is the most compelling choice.
- The INNER OBJECTS are emotionally loaded.
- The BEATS and ACTIONS are the most effective.
- You're using a MOMENT BEFORE that creates a pinnacle of urgency.
- You're using a PLACE and FOURTH WALL that is full and informed.
- You're utilizing DOINGS that are appropriate and helpful to promoting the reality and SCENE OBJECTIVE.
- You're employing INNER MONOLOGUE that is free-flowing.
- You're being substantiated by PREVIOUS CIRCUMSTANCES.
- And each rehearsal provides you with enough of a foundation so that you can LET IT GO in performance.

The Rehearsal Process for Class

1. Read the script at least once.
2. Do some of the rudimentary, broad-stroke script analysis as homework before you meet with your scene partner. (Write in pencil so you can erase, because you will be constantly experimenting with alternative choices.)
3. Get together with your scene partner, and by running the scene several times, figure out which choices work for you and which choices need to be changed.
4. At home, based on your experience in rehearsal, reconfigure the choices you've made. Identify new possibilities for your next rehearsal.
5. Rehearse again with your scene partner. Stop when you feel the choices you've made aren't working and redo that section of the script over and over until you find choices that do work.
6. After rehearsal, go home and find alternative choices for the ones that didn't work in the last rehearsal . . . and bring the new choices to the next rehearsal.

7. Repeat until you feel you've gone as far as you can or until it's time for the performance.

The more you study and work out, the more likely you are to succeed.

In the many years that I've been teaching, I've found that among the many prominent and successful actors that I've been instrumental in establishing, there's one common dominator for success as an actor. No, it's not being pretty or handsome or even talented. Especially in Hollywood, pretty and handsome actors are a dime a dozen. Unnurtured talent is around every corner. What's the secret?

Be open to learning.

Know that there's always more. Jon Voight once told me that a great actor never stops training and learning.

Take risks.

Fear stops the creative process. Never be satisfied; don't rely on safe choices. In doing your script analysis, always make the deepest, darkest, boldest, don't-be-afraid-to-look-foolish choices. And most important . . .

Work hard.

The more ardently an actor (writer, director, etc.) works, the higher the success rate. Charlize Theron was open to learning; she is a risk-taker in her choices and one of the hardest workers I've ever seen. The years when she was in class, she rehearsed all the time, often asking to be assigned double the work and to do two scenes at a time. She also always asked for challenging scenes and in her scene work would make the boldest and riskiest choices. Her fellow students watched her with great anticipation, waiting for another unpredictable original move. When she was working on one of her movies, which happened to be shooting at a studio half a mile away from my school, she would come to my class during her lunch hour. When she was on the final days of a movie shoot, she'd call me to ask for a scene partner so she could start working on a scene for class. And to back up her bets, she would call one of her friends from class and ask if they wanted to do a scene during her two or three weeks of downtime—just in case I didn't come through with someone. That was how dedicated she was to learning her craft. It wasn't a surprise to me or to her fellow students that she reached the spectacular heights of respectability and award-worthy performances. She worked hard and prospered. Sure, she's gorgeous. But the fact that her role as the unseemly and very unattractive Aileen Wuornos in *Monster* won her an Academy Award is a testament to her dedication to her craft and the work, not to her beauty. You can do the same, so let this story inspire you. Charlize is just one actor's success story. I could go on and on about actors who walked through my door, never having acted a day in their lives, but through openness to learning, making fearless, risky choices and doing dedicated hard work on the craft became renowned, award-winning actors.

. . . .

Now you have the tools. It's up to you. The more time and effort you put toward exercising them, the better you'll become. You can't be expected to win an Olympic gold medal if you don't practice, practice, practice. Reward will follow if you . . .

STAY OPEN, TAKE RISKS AND WORK HARD.

PART II

·······

EMOTIONAL DIARIES

CHAPTER 13

EMOTIONAL DIARIES

As an artist, you need to understand your emotions and your own real triggers so that you can create an authentic character with depth. An EMOTIONAL DIARY is a quick way to get to the subconscious where all those emotions and triggers reside—the true feelings, pain, traumatic events, and deeply heart-rending issues.

Our conscious mind acts as a safeguard, protecting us from what is hidden in the subconscious so that we can deal with life without suffering. The conscious mind is there to rationalize, forget, negate, deny, and change the narrative. It exists for good purpose—it shelters us from the volatility of the past, enabling us to make life manageable. The subconscious experiences past pain, no matter how long ago it happened, in vivid detail, as if you are experiencing it today. Thus, the conscious mind is necessary to keep us from the havoc of what lies within our subconscious.

Artists need to be able to easily access our subconscious because that is where the truth in all its gritty glory lies. It is like striking gold in a search for who and what really triggers us so we can quickly and effectively substantiate the "personalizations" for the inner work. Inner work stemming from information accessed from the usually inaccessible subconscious is the most profound, rich, layered, and primal. Using the information that lives in our subconscious makes for a more dynamic end result whether you are using it to act, write or direct.

But how do we get into that part of our psyche? After all, the conscious mind is stubbornly strong and is dedicated to keeping us from exploring the depths of the subconscious. This is the function of the EMOTIONAL DIARY. I developed it based on the concept of automatic writing—something therapists use to open up a patient to memories that have been lost or hidden. Automatic writing is a means to help find resolution—a way to unlock the truth and enable a patient to heal more productively.

Of course, acting isn't therapy; it's storytelling. And in telling a story we need to have a beginning, middle and end—creating a dramatic arc. So while automatic writing is free-flowing and unconscious and allows a person to produce written words without trying to control what comes out and without hesitation, the EMOTIONAL DIARY is automatic writing that starts with a specific prompt. The prompt is either the OVERALL OBJECTIVE or SCENE OBJECTIVE. Doing an EMOTIONAL DIARY will facilitate a complex arc and a more provocative story.

Written like a journal (not a list), the EMOTIONAL DIARY allows you to explore your inner-most private thoughts, and you can use what comes from it to establish more need, urgency and desperation in telling your story in your script analysis. In this way you are being proactive with your emotions, not just feeling your emotions for emotions' sake. Being proactive is key in telling a more effective story—we never want to watch people just sit in their emotions.

See your emotions as fuel for your OBJECTIVES.

Emotions by themselves are ineffectual. Without an OBJECTIVE, they just sit there. We always have to remember, art is a journey that provides growth, resolution and catharsis. And all our choices regarding all the tools should provide that.

Formula for Doing the EMOTIONAL DIARY

You need only four things for an EMOTIONAL DIARY:

1. A pen. It flows better than a pencil, which makes it harder to control the content.
2. A pad of paper (preferably lined). Never use technology (a phone, tablet, computer, etc.), as the very essence of technology is to desensitize you. What we want to do is the opposite. When trying to get into our true selves, we want to make it easy not difficult. Pen and paper are tactile, allowing for much better results.

3. A prompt, which is your OVERALL or SCENE OBJECTIVE.
4. An open mind.

About that last one:

- Remember: You are trying to open your subconscious and keep your conscious mind from taking over and writing what is safe and unexciting, which is antithetical to the artistic process. You DO NOT want to plan in any way what will come up, or you will not be able to conjure up the "good stuff."
- **<u>Once you start to write, do not stop to think. Let your pen feel like it is magical and has a mind of its own.</u>** Trust that it will write something that surprises you: events you've forgotten about, feelings you didn't think you had about someone or something, issues that you thought you'd resolved and so much more.
- However old you are, there are that many years of feelings stored in your subconscious, a literal gold mine for the artistic mind.

To be able to not pre-think your results, it helps to "empty out the vessel" by imagining emptying all your thoughts, then seeing white light for two seconds. And then begin to write. Once you've begun, continue to free flow write without stopping to think for at least a full page if you are writing on a large legal pad or two to three pages if you are writing on the size of a steno pad. Don't use a small pad as the size of it tends to contain and limit your free flow experience. Don't worry about spelling or grammar. Don't even worry if your handwriting is legible. Allow yourself to write whatever comes up, knowing that there's a good chance you'll want to burn it after you write it. Some of my students can be considered control freaks, so I tell them not to even look at the page that they are writing on so as to avoid the "control command" in their brains being initiated.

You will end with some sort of "Death Resolution." Death takes many forms. In art it is just a final ending. For example, at the end of the diary, ". . . if I don't get this . . . I will be alone forever, or I will never have children, or my relationship with [SUBSTITUTION] will be severed forever, or I will go to prison, or I will give up on my dreams, or I will die spiritually" or whatever makes sense with what's coming up as you write.

If you are not surprised by what comes up, you should do another, because the reasons behind why we are the people we are and why we do the things we do are infinite, and an exercise like this should lead to surprising results. I assure you, it really is an exciting exploration into ourselves. And the better we know ourselves and the intricacies of our motivating sources, the better artists we will be. Greatness is in the details!

Let's say your SCENE OBJECTIVE is *"I need you to love me"* and your SUBSTITUTION is your mother; the prompt to begin your EMOTIONAL DIARY would be: *"I need you to love me, Mother, because . . ."* The "because" part of the prompt is crucial because it supplies the "why"—the chunky substance that informs your INNER OBJECTS, INNER MONOLOGUE, MOMENT BEFORE, PREVIOUS CIRCUMSTANCES—essentially the details of your inner work. Why we need whatever is in the prompt is as important, if not *more* important, than the "who" (in this case, your mother).

SCENE OBJECTIVE EMOTIONAL DIARY

On the opposite page there is part of an example of an EMOTIONAL DIARY I did using the SCENE OBJECTIVE prompt *"I need you to love me, Mom, because . . ."* (Of course, first, I emptied out the vessel and saw two seconds of white light before I put pen to paper and wrote without stopping to think. And I ended in some sort of Death Resolution [to create the urgency to accomplish my OBJECTIVE].)

This is the first of my two-page EMOTIONAL DIARY. I'm including an image so you can see how it is hard to read—sometimes EMOTIONAL DIARIES are just random thoughts or disjointed ideas, because pure emotions (the kinds that reside in the subconscious) are total chaos; it is up to the artist to find a unilateral journey to all one's inner-emotional mayhem to create a story.

With that in mind, let's look at the takeaway bullet points of what I discovered from my EMOTIONAL DIARY. First, let's see what came up that surprised me. I find the parts that are surprises or forgotten events are the best to examine first.

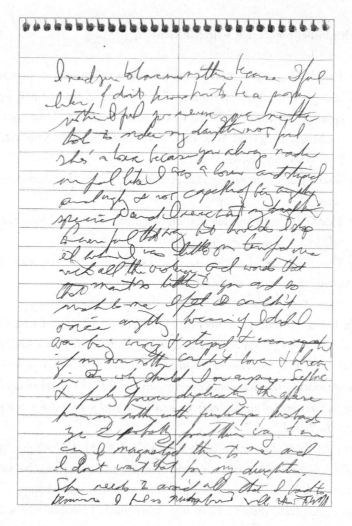

Surprise takeaways:

- That I remember the time when I was five years old and hiding from my mother in a closet so she wouldn't hit me.
- That I think I am responsible for attracting abuse.
- That I feel like a loser, and I'm confused about that.
- That I think that accomplishment didn't fix me or give me the ability to be a good mother.
- That my daughter might feel like a loser, and if she does it's because of me. (As I always attributed that she felt that way to my husband, this is a biggie!)

Other bullet points that I already knew:

- That because my mother didn't give me a role model so I could be a good mother, I feel like I failed my daughter and it is my fault whenever she feels anxious and self-doubting. How could she be anything else? After all, children mirror their parents. And I was mirroring mine.
- That I feel like anything that goes wrong for my daughter is my fault.
- That if my own mother couldn't love me, why should anyone? Self-love is in question here, too.
- That no matter how old I get, I still suffer from the very visceral memory of my mother's abuse.

The Death Resolution to this EMOTIONAL DIARY for SCENE OBJEC-TIVE is *"If I don't get my mother to love me, then my daughter will have to suffer the way I suffer because I won't be able to stop her from doing so. So, if I get my mother to love me* (accomplish my OBJECTIVE)*, then my daughter can feel as special as she truly is, and I can feel my purpose as a mother has been fulfilled."*

Let's use this information from my EMOTIONAL DIARY (my subconscious) to bring more specific life to the famous last scene from the movie *Titanic*, in which Rose floats on wood paneling from the sunken ship.

Dialogue: "Jack, there's a boat. Jack, come back. Come back! I will never let go, I promise."

My mother is the SUBSTITUTION for Jack, and the hurt child in me, who will be there forever, will never give up on hoping my mother will become the mother I always wanted. "I will never let go" means that I will never let go of believing that there's hope in her becoming that nurturing mother, and that I will overcome my anger and hurt to become the mother my daughter needs me to be, thereby taking the pain of my EMOTIONAL DIARY and finding something positive in the pain. (My mother passed away years ago, but even when an important person has passed, our needs remain. It doesn't matter if your SUBSTITUTION is alive or dead for it to be effective.)

OVERALL OBJECTIVE EMOTIONAL DIARY

Now let's look at doing an EMOTIONAL DIARY for an OVERALL OBJECTIVE to help us understand the script as a whole. An EMOTIONAL DIARY with the prompt that includes the OVERALL OBJECTIVE is necessary to fill in the details that will inform the other tools more specifically. An EMOTIONAL DIARY for an OVERALL OBJECTIVE is useful in understanding the overall journey of a character throughout the script. Exploring larger issues may be helpful when digging deeper in an overall analysis of an entire script.

Let's look at the OVERALL OBJECTIVE for Daniel Plainview in *There Will Be Blood* (played by Daniel Day-Lewis). The character is a ruthless businessman who, among other things, viciously kills a preacher and physically punishes his "child" for losing his hearing, which of course wasn't the child's fault. His OVERALL OBJECTIVE is *"to get my power back."* The prompt for this OVERALL OBJECTIVE EMOTIONAL DIARY, then, would be **"I need to get my power back because . . ."**

(As always, I emptied the vessel, saw the white light, put pen to paper and wrote without stopping to think. . . .)

Here are my takeaway bullet points from doing this EMOTIONAL DIARY. First, the surprising ones:

- I say "I'm sorry" all the time, if not aloud, then in my head.
- The memory of a friend named Joan, who used to belittle me, diminish me and make me feel bad about myself. She exploited her powerful industry job to bully me, yet I considered her one of my best friends. (She hasn't been in my life for many years, and I rarely think of her at all. Yet she came up as a really important trigger of my issues with powerlessness.)
- My first husband—someone who I haven't seen in thirty-plus years and who I thought I'd resolved my issues with—came up, as well. It was weird, because in all the EMOTIONAL DIARIES I've done over the years, Joan or my ex-husband have rarely come up. (Again, this is how the subconscious works, and these two people are gems to use in my script analysis of playing Daniel in *There Will Be Blood*.)

Not-surprising-but-important bullet points:

- I always espouse in my philosophy that we need to extricate the victim in us, even when we are being victimized. Yet I continue to let people abuse me again and again.
- I attract and am attracted to those who might make me feel powerless.
- I attract them because I feel like I deserve to be powerless, because my mother abused me and my father didn't do anything to protect me.
- Even though I have six brothers and sisters and we all experienced some form of abuse, I've always felt I had to handle the ramifications of my abuse alone.

The Death Resolution to the EMOTIONAL DIARY for this OVERALL OBJECTIVE is *"If I don't get my power back immediately, I will continue to give away my power and never have a satisfying life. And that has to stop NOW, because I can die at any time without truly being a role model who empowers the world through the arts."*

Using the information gathered from this EMOTIONAL DIARY for the OVERALL OBJECTIVE *"to get my power back"* for playing Daniel in *There Will Be Blood*, I can apply my takeaways to all the other tools in my script analysis.

- **PREVIOUS CIRCUMSTANCES:** I can use my childhood abuse and my feeling of being alone when I experienced it to give me righteous reasons to be cruel as Daniel. The things I would have to do to exact revenge or get my power back are justified by my childhood need to survive in contrary circumstances.
- **SUBSTITUTIONS:** These would be the people in my life who were the abusers; using them would make untoward behaviors in me (as Daniel) defensible.
- **INNER OBJECTS and INNER MONOLOGUE:** As opposed to being vague about my abuse and my need for retribution, I can use the specifics revealed via my EMOTIONAL DIARY to cre-

ate a more visceral experience with my choices of INNER OBJECTS and more detailed verbiage for my INNER MONO-LOGUE.

- **OBSTACLES:** What could be preventing me from getting my power back? A lot of things . . . like: I don't know what to do with my empowered self, as it is so foreign to me. I don't feel like I'm worthy of healthy love, so why shouldn't I accept someone's cruel behavior? And so on. Using the details of the OBSTACLES helps me to overcome them with more urgency and momentum in my attempt to overcome my issues and achieve my OVERALL OBJECTIVE.

All this came from doing an EMOTIONAL DIARY that elicited information I wouldn't have had otherwise. And it took only a couple minutes to do.

INFORMATIONAL EMOTIONAL DIARIES

INFORMATIONAL EMOTIONAL DIARIES are just that: informational. This is based on the same concept as EMOTIONAL DIARIES (using automatic writing to get to the truth—not the safe choice but the most compelling choice that creates inspired artistry), except with this it's just to get information that isn't easily accessible or to figure out something that triggers you for more effective inner work. These are shorter and don't require a Death Resolution. INFORMATIONAL EMOTIONAL DIARIES enable you to more easily figure out the most effective choice to use for your inner work when it isn't obvious. Always remember that in writing the INFORMATIONAL EMOTIONAL DIARIES, the "because" part of the prompt is just as important to fill in, as it provides the "why"—and supplies the details of why it is the most effective choice.

In the same way we start EMOTIONAL DIARIES with a prompt derived from OBJECTIVES, the INFORMATIONAL EMOTIONAL DIARY starts with a prompt—one that precisely gives you the answers that you seek. The same concept applies as in EMOTIONAL DIARIES. You're still doing "unconscious writing," and if you stop to think at any point that you are writing, you'll be in control, which means the conscious mind will take over and the result will be safe and not particularly meaningful. There's no drama in safety. Control also takes away the surprise of the truth.

The INFORMATIONAL EMOTIONAL DIARIES are often used to figure out a name for a SUBSTITUTION choice.

Example

Actor LC was doing a scene from *The Fisher King* and had determined that her OVERALL OBJECTIVE was *"love without pain."* Her SCENE OBJECTIVE in this particular scene was *"I need you to prove that you can love me without hurting me."* But she had a few choices for who might fit the need of that prompt— from ex-boyfriends, to friends, to parents. In order to get the most triggering SUBSTITUTION that would affect her most deeply in her performance, she did an INFORMATIONAL EMOTIONAL DIARY with the prompt *"I need you to prove you can love me without hurting me, **name**, because . . ."* Letting the pen free flow directly from the prompt without stopping to think and allowing the name to "magically" emerge from the pen, her father's name came up. Then continuing to write "because" without stopping to think, so as to allow the subconscious thoughts of *"why"* it is her father that she needs most to prove he can love her without hurting her. Writing with abandon until many issues and events come up.

What came up for LC in her INFORMATIONAL EMOTIONAL DIARY: The takeaways LC already knew and needed to be reminded of:

- No matter what she does, she shouldn't let her father affect her life choices.
- She hates and loves him simultaneously.
- He pushes people away, making her wonder if he sees her like he sees everyone else—and does not see her as special, like a father should feel about his daughter.

Her surprise takeaways that came up from doing the exercise and accessing her subconscious:

- She has much more anger than she thought she had.
- Her father treats her like he does his own mother.
- She worries that she will end up with a guy like her father, which makes her feel apprehensive about her future.

. . . .

By using this specific knowledge, she was able to provoke the other character (using her father as her SUBSTITUTION) to pass her test so she could feel safe in love. She used her issues to inform her inner work so that she could more accurately and proactively play a character who needs to find love and requires safety to do so.

Here are some other common INFORMATIONAL EMOTIONAL DIARY prompts that will help to find the best SUBSTITUTION.

*"I need you to fall in love with me, **name**, because . . ."*

*"I need you to take the blame so I don't have to, **name**, because . . ."*

*"I need you to believe in me, **name**, because . . ."*

*"I need to get my power back from you, **name**, because . . ."*

*"I need you to take responsibility for what you did to me, **name**, because . . ."*

*"I need you to admit I am the winner and you are the loser, **name**, because . . ."*

*"I need you to worship me, **name**, because . . ."*

*"I need you to protect me, **name**, because . . ."*

*"I need you to love me without abandoning me, **name**, because . . ."*

*"I need you to love me without judgment, **name**, because . . ."*

*"Before I die I need to resolve my relationship with you, **name**, because . . ."*

*"I need you to be the bad person so I can be the good person, **name**, because . . ."*

*"I need you to fall in love with me to get my power back from you, **name**, because . . ."*

*"I need you to give me hope, **name**, because . . ."*

Etc.

INFORMATIONAL EMOTIONAL DIARIES are also useful in getting other information.

Although often INFORMATIONAL DIARIES are trying to find the most effective name of a person to use, they are also fruitful in getting more specific inner work regarding elusive issues and disturbing events applicable to the script, such as guilt issues, button pushers, dire secrets, specific insecurities, addictions, uncomfortable thoughts, unhealthy priorities, most traumatic events and, and, and . . . just about anything that is on the page that requires a specific and triggering thought.

Example

Actor AP was doing a scene in class from the series *Succession*, playing the role of Kendall, the eldest brother of the three main siblings. AP was using the OVERALL OBJECTIVE of *"to be the chosen one."* And the SCENE OBJECTIVE was *"I need you to admit that I am the winner over you. . . ."* in a scene where the three siblings were hashing out who would take over temporarily after their father died. We needed to find what made this personal and necessary for AP, so we did an INFORMATIONAL EMOTIONAL DIARY using the prompt of *"I need to be the winner in __fill in the blank__ because . . ."*

What came up for AP was *"I need to be the winner in __having a healthy relationship__ because . . ."* The takeaways of what came up in his INFORMATIONAL EMOTIONAL DIARY that he could use in his inner work were:

- He needed to break the cycle of his parents' highly dysfunctional relationship.
- He had to stop blaming himself for everything and feeling great self-hatred when things went wrong.
- He wanted to duplicate his grandfather and grandmother's soulmate relationship. But he was confused by his grandfather's suicide after his grandmother's death. Does love mean destruction in severe ways?
- He didn't feel worthy of a healthy relationship because he overwhelmingly felt like he was a bad guy. Because his father regularly cheated on his mother and gave AP love and pride only when he duplicated his father's ways, validation from his father came only when AP did to other people the same kind of hurtful things his father had done.
- If he had a healthy relationship, he would just screw it up, recreating his parents' reality.

Surprising takeaway information that came up:

- His grandfather's suicide affecting him as much as it did.

All this substantiates a powerful need to be the winner of the sibling rivalry—the chosen one. This EMOTIONAL DIARY helped AP strengthen his inner work so that AP as Kendall fought among "his siblings" with new-found vigor.

Example

Another example is when actor SD was doing a scene from the movie *In Bruges*. Her character, Chloe, falls in love with Ray, who is filled with massive guilt over accidentally killing a child. Chloe is also guilt ridden, but in the script, it's not entirely clear why. Her behaviors and many of the things she says indicate that she shares an overwhelming sense of guilt, which establishes the commonality of pain to create a deep love story. (Refer to chapter 14, Creating Chemistry, for more information on this.) Sometimes the details for the motivations of your character are not in the script and it's up to you create something. In this case, SD had to fill in something that in some way matches the enormity of Ray's guilt.

This is another way that doing an INFORMATIONAL EMOTIONAL DIARY can be used to find something that hugely affects you, even when the script doesn't supply any specifics. If it's not written, infuse it with exploratory inner work anyway. Nothing should stop a true artist from their exploration of depth and layers. You don't need to be told precisely what's going on and why. You can expand on what information *is* in the script with inner choices (often derived from INFORMATIONAL EMOTIONAL DIARIES) to create great work. We had to figure out what SD's personal guilt was. She wasn't sure what she could use from her life that would give her this level of guilt.

SD did an INFORMATIONAL EMOTIONAL DIARY using the prompt: *"I feel so guilty about **fill in the blank** because . . ."*

What came up for SD was *"I feel so guilty about **wondering if I married the right person** because . . ."*

The takeaways she could use in her inner work were:

- At thirty-two years old, she was an entirely different person from who she was when she got married at twenty-one because big changes had taken place in her life.
- At one time, she needed her husband to take care of her as she had never been taken care of. Even when she was growing up, she had wrongly been deemed the caretaker. Her husband was someone who took great pride in doing everything for her—fixing, providing, nurturing to such an extent that she was swept away. She had finally gotten what she needed, but she didn't need it anymore, and she found herself emasculating her husband and diminishing the very thing that had made her love and need him in the first place.
- She had a child and didn't want to be the reason for a split family. Having come from one, she knew how detrimental it could be for a child.

Surprise takeaway information that came up:

- It shocked her how weighty this was to her and how deep the guilt ran.
- Maybe getting married was a choice she had made out of fear and weakness.
- At the time, her husband was in a dark depression. What if she pushed him over the edge? He didn't deserve that.

SD could use her guilt to inform Chloe's guilt (which is the foundation for the love story between Ray and Chloe) with specificity and need.

Example

Actor VL was doing a scene from the movie *Magnolia* where she was playing Claudia, a young woman who had a problem with cocaine and abusive relationships. She falls in love with Jim, a police officer who she is afraid cannot love her because of her drug addiction and propensity to seek out bad men. This police officer isn't aware of any of this. A police officer's goal is usually to protect and serve, which is precisely what she needs. But a police officer is bound to judge her and decide she is either a criminal (a cocaine addict) or a victim (her past with abusive men), so he will probably see her as weak and certainly not very "sexy" or worthy of love. In this particular scene, it is their first date, and she wants to let him know her secret before she becomes too attached. But Claudia is also terrified that the one person who can solve her problems and love her might judge her and not want to even begin a relationship. The OVERALL OBJECTIVE that VL used was *"love without judgment,"* and her SCENE OBJECTIVE was *"to make you love me in spite of my secret."* But VL didn't know what she could use as the secret that would elicit the most impact. VL suspected a few things, but when she said them aloud to the class, she wasn't emotionally triggered, which was a sign that there was probably something much better hiding in her subconscious. It was time to do an INFORMATIONAL EMOTIONAL DIARY to find out what secret would create the most powerful performance.

We used the prompt *"I never want anyone to know the secret of **fill in the blank** because . . ."*

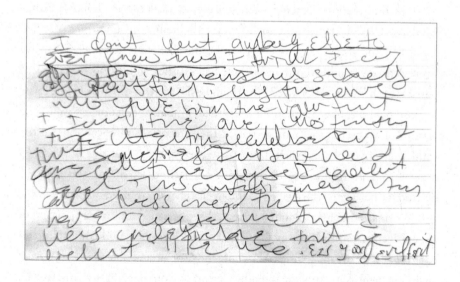

I've included a portion of VL's diary so you can see that it's barely legible, which illustrates that EMOTIONAL DIARIES come out differently for everyone. All EMOTIONAL DIARIES are unique to the individuals writing them. As long as you know what you are writing, your EMOTIONAL

DIARY doesn't have to make sense to anyone else. What came up for VL was "*I never want anyone to know the secret of __my being molested as a child__*."

Takeaway information that she knew:

- She thought it was her fault that the abuse had happened because she believed she deserved it, thus the shame factor.
- Even as an adult, she always went overboard to please because of this.
- She was very afraid of relationships because she thought she would get hurt again and be too vulnerable.

Surprise takeaway information that arose:

- Because of the abuse, she felt ugly and unworthy of ever being loved in a healthy manner.
- She had a lot of shame.

This information gathered from writing an INFORMATIONAL EMOTIONAL DIARY turned out to be very enlightening to questions VL had about why she always felt gross, ugly and unlovable. This extremely beautiful twenty-three-year-old who many people had crushes on never believed it was possible for her to be truly loved. She thought she was just too awful to be loved because of the abuse. She had an inordinate amount of shame, as well. The victims of all events that can be put in the category of physical abuse often think they are to blame, when it is clear to everyone else that this is not so. In order for VL to find a way to overcome her feelings of shame and her self-destructive behaviors, she needed to imbue her characterization of Claudia with this information to help Claudia ultimately see herself as an innocent victim of an abusive person. In this way Claudia (and VL herself) could truly acknowledge that "It wasn't my fault" so she could move on and be able to love and trust again. By identifying this, we took the victimhood out of being a victim in VL's portrayal of Claudia. Because VL found empowerment in her pain through her personalization, Claudia became more attractive to Jim, setting up the conclusion of their story, where they end up together. The information garnered from doing the INFORMATIONAL EMOTIONAL DIARY allowed VL through her portrayal of Claudia to find resolution and closure for both herself and her character, thereby creating an emotional hero for the audience, as well, especially for those that might have suffered the same.

We can't change the past, but we can choose to use pain as a powerful fuel to find prosperity of heart and spirit.

We can self-destruct with our pain, or we can construct. It's a choice. By giving voice to our pain through using the information found by doing INFORMATIONAL EMOTIONAL DIARIES, we can find freedom and cleansing, and playing the character with this information can be fun and revelatory.

With the Chubbuck Technique, we are NEVER trying to bring emotions up to sit in them, be miserable or feel defeated and hopeless, but rather to find how to take trauma/pain/insecurities/fears and turn them into a solution, evolvement and catharsis. The choices you make should drive you to that. When you are breaking down a script with deep inner work, the clue is that if you are not having fun, you've made the wrong choices.

Here are some other examples of INFORMATIONAL EMOTIONAL DIARIES:

> *"I need to find the answers to __fill in the blank__ because . . ."*
> *"My worst fear is __fill in the blank__ because . . ."*
> *"I feel shame when __fill in the blank__ because . . ."*

Your character is in prison but you have never been imprisoned. The concepts of being confined and captive can take many forms. In what way do you feel an emotional version of prison?

> *"I feel like I'm in prison when __fill in the blank__ because . . ."*

You're going to play an addict, and you don't have an obvious addiction.

> *"I feel so addicted to __fill in the blank__ because . . ."*

You're playing someone who's lonely, but in your own life, you don't feel loneliness.

> *"I feel so alone when __fill in the blank__ because . . ."*

Essentially, anything that requires further and more accurate personal information can be found by doing an INFORMATIONAL EMOTIONAL

DIARY. Make sure that you end prompts with the "because" part of the sentence, as that allows for more specific reasons why you feel that way. And don't scrimp on the "because." Write with abandon, as getting to know the details of who we are and why we do what we do is fascinating. Human nature, and the exploration of such through EMOTIONAL DIARIES, is exciting. Remember: We do these not only to be more authentic but to better understand who we are in order to make for a more dynamic end result. It bears repeating that this technique is about solving, evolving, informing and achieving catharsis. The EMOTIONAL DIARIES are to help in our further investigation in doing so.

EMOTIONAL DIARIES for the Writer and/or Director

Writers and directors can also benefit from doing EMOTIONAL DIARIES. As part of their creative processes, it can help to establish a more uniform message and theme for the script—one that has not only a story but also a theme that will best "solve, evolve, inform and achieve catharsis" for the writer and/or director. To do so, one has to understand what the message is and why it's so meaningful.

The prompt:

"I need to write this script because . . ."
"I need to direct this script because . . ."

IMPORTANT POINT

Always write all versions of EMOTIONAL DIARIES in your primary language—the first language you learned. This lends itself to more powerful choices to emerge from your subconscious because you are coming from a primal and pure place—one that is ultimately more accurate, too, as your conscious mind will try to control it and change the truth if possible, but it is easier and more fluid to get what really affects you when you are emanating from a primal reality.

AN EVEN *MORE* IMPORTANT POINT!

When you are writing an EMOTIONAL DIARY, if you say, "But nothing came up," then you are doing it wrong. The concept of automatic writing is to write without consciousness. If you let the pen write whatever it is going to write, like it's a "magic" pen, it will write something. Even if the answer that came up surprises you (and it is likely it will), don't stop to ponder the result. Keep writing. The "because" part will give you even more to consider. There will be revelations and epiphanies that are useful to your character and to yourself. The better you know yourself, the better artist you will be. Truly understanding yourself also enables you to lighten the load of your pain, as you're creating something beautiful with it. Don't be afraid, as the knowledge will set you free to create and ultimately find resolution and achieve catharsis with whatever presently ails the character (and yourself).

Using EMOTIONAL DIARIES is just more material that allows for growth. Knowledge is power. The power of the actor . . . ya know?

PART III

· · · · · · ·

Other Acting Tools and Exercises

* The following acting tools are not to be confused with the twelve-step system. It's important to do the work using the twelve tools first and to consider any of the other acting tools as icing on the cake to be utilized *only* after you've accomplished the twelve steps using the twelve tools.

Certain scenes require very specific states of being, such as being high (from alcohol or drugs), being afraid, dying, feeling the death of a loved one, being pregnant, being a parent, being physically impaired or injured, experiencing sexual chemistry and having the psyche of a serial killer.

These particular states of being affect us physiologically as well as emotionally.

These states of being affect our body chemistry. For instance, if we're afraid, our fight-or-flight instincts kick in and our bodies react. Our pupils contract, our hearts beat faster and adrenaline surges through our systems. These are involuntary muscle reactions. While you cannot make your pupils contract, you can provoke these states of being, which will compel your involuntary eye muscles to respond.

I have developed a system of formulas to help the actors I coach access and organically feel these primal states, even if they have never felt them before.

Because these reactions are so scientifically predictable, they can each be assessed, calculated and broken down into a kind of mathematical equation.

I've found that the best way to truly feel one of these states is to first understand *why* a particular state of being works for our human condition. Therefore, the following will first explain *why*, from a psychological base, our bodies respond to these states of being. And second, I will explain how to provoke the biological and physiological responses. In short, I'll show you why the formula works and then how to use it so you can truly and organically feel the responses.

CHAPTER 14

Creating Chemistry
An essential part of the performance.

Watching two actors who are supposed to love each other but have no natural heat between them can be a tedious and unsatisfying experience. An audience only gets what you feed them. If there's no chemistry between the actors, nobody will care about the story, as stories are based on relationships. On the other hand, if there's a palpable connection between the actors, then the audience will be riveted by the story.

From the actor's point of view, it's always more engaging to work with someone who excites you, someone you have a spark with. The chemistry factor can often determine the success or failure of a film, play or television show. It isn't the plot that keeps us hooked—it's the connection the audience has with the characters and their relationship. The plot facilitates the growth of a relationship. Chemistry gives the relationship more weight and makes it more captivating.

You know that feeling when you see a person across a crowded room and you may never actually speak to them, but you feel a special connection. Or when you see someone on the other side of the street walking in the opposite direction, and you can't help but give a more meaningful glance in that person's direction. Or when the person serving you at a restaurant elicits a flirty conversation instead of the usual mundane communication involved in ordering food. Or, or, or. . . Even though the connection may be fleeting, it makes you feel something special. Chemistry is everywhere but not always when you need it.

As an actor, you must create chemistry in ALL relationships—with family members, work colleagues and friends (same sex and opposite sex) as well as with the grocery clerk, your lawyer, your doctor and anyone you interact with no matter if they have one line or they are the main player in the script. Even if someone is the enemy, you must've loved them once to hate them so much now. You should also create chemistry with the crew. In this way the director will direct you lovingly, the director of photography will shoot you lovingly, the gaffer will light you lovingly and on and on. Everyone wants to feel attractive, which is what you are doing when you do the CHEMISTRY EXERCISE. And it's always more invigorating to do something when you have a crush on someone.

The CHEMISTRY EXERCISE creates the organic reality of feeling the chemical sparks between two people even when there were none before. Frankly, as you well know, it's rare to feel truly connected to someone. The CHEMISTRY EXERCISE allows us to bypass the rarity and create connection pretty much every time. The CHEMISTRY EXERCISE is a win-win for all.

About two-thirds of the average human body is made up of water, mostly within the cells. Water is a strong conductor of electricity. According to this thought process, when electrical impulses emanate from our psyches, they turn into actual physical and electrical connections in our bodies, much like light bulbs and filaments create light. To establish a true chemical connection between two people, we must think in terms of what would spark their psyches to create organic chemical connections in their bodies. In other words, we create chemistry.

THERE ARE TWO PARTS TO THE CHEMISTRY EXERCISE:

The Commonality of Pain Exercise
The Sexual Fantasy Exercise

By connecting these two exercises, we are joining the heart with the body to create an all-encompassing chemistry experience.

Creating COMMONALITY OF PAIN

The COMMONALITY OF PAIN exercise establishes the heart part of chemistry. Essentially, the COMMONALITY OF PAIN is the profound emotional connection that bonds people together—the personal and emotional issues that come from trauma, fears, insecurities and neurotic issues that you share with that other person. The energy of this connecting resource is powerful, and it can bypass logic and intellect. Bonding isn't about both people liking to ski or loving the color red. The COMMONALITY OF PAIN exercise comes from both people having gone through similar emotionally painful experiences and from both having reacted to them in similar primal ways. It's a feeling that this person gets you in a way that no one else in the world gets you, because they've experienced comparable traumas/pain/fears and feel the same way as you do—the COMMONALITY OF PAIN.

In the CHEMISTRY EXERCISE, you never use a SUBSTITUTION. You always use the actual person you are establishing chemistry with. Using SUBSTITUTION would introduce a degree of separation and prevent true connection. Use the very person with whom you want to create that special chemical bond.

COMMONALITY OF PAIN Exercise

To do the COMMONALITY OF PAIN exercise, look at that person (they don't have to be looking at you) and think (don't say aloud), *"You, too, know what it feels like to **fill in the blank with trauma, fears, insecurities or whatever your issues are that define your most extreme pain**."* Then think (don't say aloud), **_"Thank you for getting me in a way no one else gets me. I love you."_**

EXAMPLES OF WHAT YOU COULD USE TO FILL IN THE BLANK

You, too, know what it feels like to . . .

- . . . need to make your father proud and love you because you never heard the words "I love you" from him and you put him on a pedestal like I do. (my inner work)
- . . . experience loss through death and have the belief that maybe that person who died didn't love you enough to stay alive, which makes you feel lonely even when you're not alone. (mine, too)

- ... endure physical and emotional abuse from your mother, making you feel that if your own mother can't love you, why should anyone else? (mine, as well)
- ... feel abandoned by everyone and always be afraid that every person you love is going to leave you.
- ... have addictions that you have no control over and that make you do self-destructive things that you can't take back or change.
- ... be cheated on, which makes you believe that you aren't worth anything and that there's always going to be someone out there who will be better than you.
- ... have or have had a life-threatening disease and always live in fear and worry the end is near.
- ... feel not smart or good-looking enough or weak and constantly victimized by life and the world.
- ... suffer from an alcoholic's abusive words and actions, which make you believe that you deserve to be beaten up emotionally and that you aren't worth love. (mine, as well)
- ... experience the death of a loved one at an early age in life.
- ... become an addict because of an abusive childhood.
- ... suffer from cheating mates in your life.
- ... experience the fallout of loving an addict.
- ... be beholden to a parent for your happiness and well-being.
- ... believe that you are responsible for a mother's (father's, mate's, sibling's, etc.) happiness and that your duty in life is to parent and love them at your own expense. (okay, true for me, too)
- ... feel like a fraud because to the world, it seems that you are confident and empowered, but truly, even in a crowd, you feel that you are alone and overwhelmed by loneliness.
- ... be filled with so much anger that you have no control over your emotions and you find yourself instigating problems where there are none.

There are so many things that can make you feel small, useless, misunderstood, unlovable, invisible, etc. This list is just to give you some ideas of what to use in this exercise. As you can see through the ones I've labeled as mine, we aren't just defined by one issue. Use what you are particularly feeling in the moment and also try being intuitive about the other person's issues, as you are bound to have some of the same ones.

After completing that thought, end with *"Thank you for getting me in a way that no one else gets me. I love you."* "I love you" is the most powerful thing you can feel and say to someone. Even saying "I love you" only in your head creates a strong energy that radiates on film and onstage. Once you energetically communicate via your thoughts, your common pain will establish a special bond, a profound link to the other actor's delicate, fragile inner self. You are privy to the part of their soul that they struggle to hide and protect. This connection— your ability to understand, protect and relate to the other actor from a similar pain source—will draw the two of you closer together than you can imagine. In fact, these are the tenets of love. You can achieve chemistry with authenticity because you identify with and possess an intimate empathy for the other person. In other words, *you really get each other.*

Creating Sexual Fantasy

Emotional connection between two people is heightened and infused with a much more intriguing complexity when combined with a physical connection. Adding a physical component to the equation is essential in producing chemistry between people. This is obviously true in lover relationships but is also true in all important relationships. Freud, the father of psychoanalysis, maintains that there is an innate innocent sexuality between a son and a mother, between a daughter and a father, and between siblings. The sexual feelings are not meant to ever be acted upon; they remain in the subconscious, but they do exist. There is sexuality in friendships and with enemies. Pretty much any relationship that is an essential part of your day-to-day has some physical component alongside the heart/feelings part, making for a more comprehensive connection.

Why is using the sexual/body element so essential? Because sex creates life, and there is no bigger or more significant energy than the energy that creates a living, breathing human being. Also, it is considered one of the most important energy chakras, even more important than the third eye (enlightenment) or the heart chakra. There's a reason why athletes often abstain from having sex before a big game—they want to keep the preciousness of the sex energy (the energy of creation) to help them win.

It is also essential to add the body energy to the heart/feelings energy in making the chemistry more tantalizing. I always like to ask the question: Who would you rather spend time with for three hours?

1. A person who is a scintillating conversationalist but with whom you have zero desire for intimate contact.
2. A person you have insane sexual desire for but with whom you have nothing much to talk about.

I have posed this question when doing masterclasses all over the world, and no matter what the students' countries, cultures, religious beliefs or political affiliations are, the answer has always been the second one. The energy of creating life can be mighty compelling! Also, when we are sexually connected to someone, we imbue them with intelligence and humor. Isn't it funny how when you stop being sexually attracted to someone, you say to yourself, "That's weird, he/she got so stupid, and they used to be so smart and humorous." That's why pairing the COMMONALITY OF PAIN with SEXUAL FANTASY is the one-two punch of tangible chemistry. Without the primal connection created by combining the sexuality/body and the heart, you are overlooking a very basic human need—one that is not to be judged but used to complete your character and your character's important relationships.

SEXUAL FANTASY Exercise

Begin by sexually fantasizing about the other person, imagining your silliest sexual fantasy as you include that person in whatever sexual activities you've visualized.

We use the silliest, craziest sexual fantasy to create the fun part of the body connection. You always know that two people are attracted to each other when they giggle too much together and they always seem to be sharing private jokes. It doesn't matter whether you are straight or gay when doing the SEX-UAL FANTASY exercise, as there is always a fraction in all of us that is intrigued by being intimate with someone who is not our usual sexual gender preference.

Formula for Doing the CHEMISTRY EXERCISE

1. Identify the trauma/pain/insecurity/fear issues that most define you at this moment.
2. Think, *"You, too, know what it feels like to __fill in the blank__ (with the commonality of pain issue)."*
3. Then think, *"Thank you for getting me in a way that no one else gets me. I love you."*
4. Then do the Sexual Fantasy Exercise.
5. LET IT GO.

You don't have to look directly at the other person when doing this exercise. You can also do this exercise when talking to the other person about something entirely different. We do it all the time. We can be speaking about one thing but thinking about another, especially when our feelings are involved. The other person will respond to you differently, as they are feeling this new bond subliminally. They'll feel this inexplicable sense of closeness—otherwise known as chemistry.

I coached an Academy Award–winning actress on a movie where she met her love-interest costar and had an immediate dislike for him (and him for her). The CHEMISTRY EXERCISE was so effective that not only did they develop real-life crushes on each other, but the tabloids published that they were embroiled in a torrid affair, which, by the way, they were not.

Another story that proves the power of the CHEMISTRY EXERCISE took place when an actor had a charity audition (meaning that the casting director didn't like her and in fact had not seen her for an audition for three years and saw her for the audition as a favor to her agent). This actor knew how this female casting director felt about her and decided to do the CHEMISTRY

EXERCISE during the part of the audition where they were just talking. During their conversation, the casting director went from being somewhat hostile to being really interested in this actor's life. The actor then did her reading and booked the part.

It's not just with the acting world that the CHEMISTRY EXERCISE works. Try it with anyone you might come across: a cashier at a market, a person driving next to you, a waiter, an ex-friend, anyone. You'll find an immediate chemistry with that person, and they will feel the same way about you. It takes only a few seconds to do and you'll see an instant change come over the other person. The fun part is that it's so subtle that they'll feel connected to you by an indefinable something and they won't know why. Take Kian, one of my friends and students, who went to Las Vegas to see Adele sing in a four-thousand-seat venue. He thought, "Well, what the heck? I am seated in the middle of four thousand people. Let's see if the energy of connection via the CHEMISTRY EXERCISE is that strong." He did the CHEMISTRY EXERCISE toward Adele while she was onstage singing. A few moments later, Adele came off the stage, went straight to Kian and asked him a personal question, which he answered truthfully in front of those four thousand people. Adele gave him a big hug, and everyone took pictures of them. Coincidence or not? I prefer to think that the CHEMISTRY EXERCISE works. I have so many stories for proof that they could fill an entire book. But even so, say this was just one lucky moment. It's okay to believe you have the power to make people like you. It feels good that you don't always have to wait for someone to feel something for you, that you have the power of change, because frankly you do, no matter how it finds its way. Know that.

Creating Chemistry in an Audition

You can do the CHEMISTRY EXERCISE in the audition situation, as well. Creating a crush on someone, making them like you and feel chemistry with you, also means they'll want to have you around. And that essentially means wanting to cast you. Obviously, you must add a good reading to the equation, which means you must do the work described in the twelve steps. But if they have a choice between two actors who are somewhat equal in their abilities, they will cast the one they are more attracted to. People might not want to admit it, but it does make a work environment more fun when we are around a person we have a crush on. This is human, and there is nothing wrong with it. Just put yourself in their shoes—wouldn't you do the same? Most people would in any work situation.

Even when doing audition self-tapes, do the CHEMISTRY EXERCISE with the person who is reading the other lines. The casting team, as they watch your tape, will feel the special chemistry through the film and not only will they be excited by the reading, but they will see you as a better actor because of an added layer of charisma.

Basically:

The CHEMISTRY EXERCISE is a combination of
COMMONALITY OF PAIN and SEXUAL FANTASY.

The effort in doing the CHEMISTRY EXERCISE is small. But it's fun to do, and the rewards are great.

CHAPTER 15

Playing an Addict

When you are playing an addict, the first thing you must consider is what the character is addicted to and why. This will help you dig deeper into the character's need to use their addiction to emotionally survive and overcome what ails them. Each addiction cures different emotional ills.

Addictions take many forms; they are not just to substances. The essence of an addiction is that it is believed by the addict it will solve a problem. Addicts feel their addictions are the only ways to overcome specific issues that plague them. The circle of addiction begins when someone has troubles that seem unsolvable by anything other than using this substance, thought process or behavior. The issue occurs, they go to whatever they are addicted to in order to deal with it and they have a fairly short period of time when all feels fixed and right with the world. Then they come down. The depression begins. Depression turns to self-loathing and shame about the addiction itself. Then the need to turn to their addiction becomes uncontrollable. And they indulge in the addiction to have that feeling that they seek that makes them feel that their problem is solved. The slice of the addiction pie where the addict feels good is small. But it feels so good, even though the high doesn't last long, that they find themselves "chasing the high."

In playing an addict, you need to know what problem the character's addiction is solving. Then, and only then, can you personalize it, duplicating the character's feelings with your own. Unless the character's addiction happens to coincide with your own, you would take the fraction of your similar needs and add it to the character's addiction to make the need for the character's particular addiction more potent to you.

• • • • • • •

First, let's look at the more clear and obvious addictions:

ALCOHOL inspires courage and fearlessness. For those who feel fearful all the time, this becomes the solution.

STIMULANTS (INCLUDES COCAINE, CRACK, ADDER-ALL, SPEED, ETC.) inspire feelings of being powerful. Stimulants help those who feel powerless and inadequate.

OPIATES (INCLUDES HEROIN, MORPHINE, PAIN MEDI-CATIONS, OPIUM, ETC.) inspire the feeling of being emotionally pain-free or of euphoria. For those that experience untenable pain, this helps to numb it.

FOOD AND EATING DISORDERS OF ALL KINDS inspire feelings of being nurtured. People who feel neglected and starved for nurturing love can have a dysfunctional relationship with food.

SEX ADDICTION inspires love without pain, as having many partners without emotional investment allows one protection from loving and the pain that often comes with it. This addiction indicates a person who connects love with pain because that has been their experience with it.

GAMBLING ADDICTION inspires a feeling of being in control in those who feel that their existence is out of their control.

MARIJUANA inspires a feeling of total freedom for those who feel that they have been inordinately repressed.

CUTTING AND OTHER SELF-INJURIES are ways to cope with or make manageable one's self-anger and guilt. They are ways to punish and thus attempt to alleviate guilt.

SPEED AND OPIATES TOGETHER (OFTEN CALLED A SPEEDBALL) allow the user of both these substances to feel simultaneously powerful and pain-free. This is not an unusual combination.

BENZODIAZEPINES (VALIUM, XANAX, ETC.) inspire a feeling of emotional safety for those who suffer from severe anxiety and panic disorders.

HALLUCINOGENS (LSD, MUSHROOMS, MESCALINE, ETC.) inspire insights and revelations that users feel they cannot experience any other way. They are confused and hurt by what life has given them and feel that the only way to understand why they've been hurt without cause is through the ensuing intense revelations that often aren't logical but are soothing in offering them reasons and the lack of culpability.

SHOPPING inspires a sense of self-worth and value. Shopping addicts spend money they generally don't have. Adding to the shoppers' possessions (often things that they don't need at all) gives the illusion of wealth and value that they don't feel they have without those worldly goods.

These next addictions are not so obvious but can be regarded as such because they solve problems for addicts.

MISERY/DEPRESSION: Some people find comfort in their misery. When something good happens, they assume it's bound to sour eventually. Going straight to depression instead of joy allows the depression addict not to be disappointed.

PHYSICAL PAIN AND HYPOCHONDRIA: Pain and sickness give people reasons to be nurtured and taken care of. Otherwise, there'd be no excuse for someone to make the effort.

SELF-SABOTAGE: This inspires control in one's life regarding experiencing bad events. If a bad event happens out of our sphere of control, it hurts a lot more than when we cause such an event and injure ourselves.

BEING A VICTIM: For the I-am-a-victim addict, this one inspires others to feel your pain and feel sorry for you and (you hope) come to your aid. This strategy rarely works, but when it does, it is massively fulfilling for the victim addict. But because the general response to people who play the victim card is to avoid them, the victim addict will continue to chase the high when playing the victim card does work.

MEMBERSHIP IN A CULT: There are two different types of needs that are being met being a cult member. First, a cult leader gives cult addicts a sense of belonging to a family that really cares—something they never felt in their real life. Second, some cult addicts feel lost, and cult leaders can give them a sense of being "found" by providing them with answers to questions about their ultimate value and purpose. Cult addicts can include people who are attracted to those who have cult-leader-type qualities.

Now that you understand why your character has a particular addiction, find a way to use your own circumstances in life to personalize why you would need this addiction. Determine the catalyst that might cause you to need to take your character's substance of choice. In other words, find your trigger. For instance:

> If you're playing a cocaine addict and something tumultuous is happening in the scene or someone just said something demeaning to you, you would go to use cocaine to feel powerful again.

> Or if your character's circumstances remind you of a time when you experienced trauma or loss, then your character might shoot heroin or take a few opiate pills to eradicate the rush of emotions that overtake you.

The occasions in a script when addicts go to their addictions are when they need to fix or solve a particular problem. Even when you are playing a recovered addict, if your addiction is being offered to you in some way, you must respond to it as if it still has a hold on you. As any recovering addict knows, you may be presently sober, but that doesn't remove the extreme desire and pull that your addiction still has on you, which could last a lifetime. But no matter what you are playing—a recovering addict or an active one—if you are in a scene where your character's addiction of choice is readily available, use the pull of it. Talk to it in your INNER MONOLOGUE about how it is benefiting you—in a way humanizing the addiction.

Behavioral Formulas

Once you've completed the twelve steps and have a deeper comprehension of *what* and *why* your character uses (alongside your personal reasons), then you can use the following behavioral formulas to generate the organic feelings associated with the drug.

- **Note #1:** With these formulas, you never have to have actually used a particular substance to truly feel the effects of it. *And* more important, you NEVER have to use or experiment with the substance to create a more realistic performance. The following formulas will take you there. Using them is cheaper and there's no hangover or health risks.

- **Note #2:** Before you do any exercise to feel inebriated or stoned, it's key that you do your script analysis first. Otherwise the scene will be only about intoxication and will lack your character's OBJECTIVES and the intricacies of your inner work. So remember: First, complete emotional and active script analysis, and then do the substance exercise.

- **Note #3:** DO NOT DRIVE OR OPERATE MACHINERY AFTER DOING THESE EXERCISES. I'm not kidding. These exercises really do alter the way you think and behave and can seriously impair your ability to react and act. The effects can last for up to about ten to fifteen minutes.

Feeling Drunk

When drunk, one loses control of one's faculties, which prompts our survival instinct to try to appear sober to other people as well as to ourselves. Our mind attempts to compensate for our faulty vision, slurred speech and poor coordination, and it overcompensates so that it can feel sober and in control again. In essence, *it's our need to overcome our loss of faculties in order to feel and appear sober that creates drunken behavior.*

The specific body part—eyes, tongue or legs—that is affected most by alcohol depends upon the individual. If you are visually inclined and if your eyes are not working properly, you will naturally focus on attempting to correct your off-kilter vision. If you are verbally inclined and if your speech is slurred, you will be driven to overcome your lack of cohesive speech. If you are physically inclined, then not being in total control of your legs will cause you to attempt to override and overcompensate for your sloppy movements.

Often my students don't know what kind of person they are, so I have them try all three of the following exercises. Even though you're using only one element of your body, if it's the right choice, it will make your whole body feel inebriated. You'll know which one works for you after you try all three. One will make you feel drunk while the others will not. I have found that most people are visually inclined, so I ask my students to try the *eye* formula first. After that, the *tongue* seems to be the second most effective exercise. People who rely on their physical ability are less common, and they should therefore try *legs* last.

Formula for Feeling Drunk

Eyes

1. Without focusing on anything in particular, fog up your vision. Don't cross your eyes; just randomly cloud your vision.

2. Put the concept of focusing at the backs of your eyeballs, then take the idea of "Focus" from the backs of the eyeballs and around the actual balls of the eyes (not through the eyeballs, because you will actually focus). Again, place the concept of "Focus" at the backs of your eyeballs, and then take your attempt to focus *around* the balls of the eyes until it gets to the front of the eyeballs, then try to focus through the fog. Do this at least three times.

3. Now walk around for a few moments and LET IT GO. If the eye element works for you, it should stick and you'll feel drunk without thinking.

Tongue

1. Let your tongue rest in your mouth and feel like all its muscles are useless and gelatin-like. Don't stick your tongue out; just let it rest idly in your mouth without being able to use it; let it become just a mush of tissue.

2. Then use your lips and overpronounce your speech to compensate for your useless, mushy tongue. In other words, isolate the lip muscles around the unusable tongue and try to speak.

3. Do it for a few moments and then LET IT GO.

Legs

1. Stand and feel like all the muscles in *one* knee have become entirely useless, formless, gelatin-like. You should barely be able to stand because those muscles have melted away in the one knee.
2. Next, use the muscles around the knee to walk in a way that overcompensates for the liquidity of your knee muscles. Keep walking, with the knee muscles feeling like oozy pulp and the other muscles in your legs working overtime, overcompensating around the mushy knee muscles.
3. Walk around for a few moments; then LET IT GO.

(Don't do all three drunk exercises at the same time. The specificity of using one physical trait will be more powerful in producing a true feeling of being drunk.)

No matter which body part works for you, the goal is to effectively affect one body part so that it does not function properly and you must overcompensate for its failure. Once you pinpoint which body part affects you the most, you will have found your impetus for feeling drunk in the rest of your body. You should feel really drunk and act drunk, because for all intents and purposes, you *are* drunk.

Once you set these feelings of being drunk in motion, which should take a few moments, always LET IT GO. This enables you to color the scene with the drunken behavior, as opposed to making the scene *all about* being drunk.

Formula for Creating a Marijuana High

1. To feel a marijuana high, begin by thinking that your brain has been replaced by a large glob of pink cotton candy and you're looking at it under a microscope. Think of the fluff, think of the pinkness and the sweetness and see how the air hits the cotton candy and how it becomes tiny, yummy, sparkly sugar icicles. . . .
2. Now imagine a glob of pink cotton candy in front of your eyes and attempt to *think* and *see through* the fluff, the pinkness and

the drippy warmed sugar. . . . Your brain no longer exists—*think* and *see through* those pink, pink, fluffy, sugary, hairy filaments, a whipped-up, sugary, cottony mass. . . .

3. Now LET IT GO and begin the scene.

Feeling High on Heroin

A heroin high makes you feel euphoric to the extent that when you're faced with a problem or obstacle, the problem or obstacle ceases to exist—a heroin high seems to make life's encumbrances and difficulties disappear. Life feels good when you're at the peak part of the high, and you feel you can overcome anything. This is probably one of the reasons that heroin addiction is one of the hardest addictions to overcome.

Formula for Feeling High on Heroin

1. Begin by thinking that your brain has been replaced by a large glob of pink cotton candy and you're looking at it under a microscope. Think of the fluff, think of the pinkness and the sweetness and see how the air hits the cotton candy and how it becomes tiny sugar icicles. . . .

2. Now imagine a glob of pink cotton candy in front of your eyes and attempt to *think* and *see through* the fluff, the pinkness and the drippy warmed sugar. . . . Your brain no longer exists—*think* and *see through* those pink, pink, fluffy, sugary, hairy filaments, a whipped-up, sugary, cottony mass. . . .

3. Then give yourself a feeling of nausea in your stomach by thinking about big chunks of the food you most recently ate and feeling them churning around and around in your stomach.

4. Feel your stomach acid trying to break down the big food chunks. Then pick a point of entry (where the hypodermic needle would go to inject the heroin)—a good place is in the crook of your arm where you're used to getting blood tests taken—and begin there.

5. Then think, *"Liquid warmth, peace, love, power,"* and imagine it going into your veins, starting from your point of entry. Feel the *liquid warmth, peace, love, power* slowly course through your veins and up your arms . . . across your shoulders. . . . Feel the comforting, exquisite *liquid warmth, peace, love, power* travel through your veins and up to your neck . . . to your chin . . . to your lips, and then let *liquid warmth, peace, love, power* settle and engorge the fullness of your lips. Feel that for a moment. . . . Feel the sensuality, the tingle as *liquid warmth, peace, love, power* fill your lips. Then feel the *liquid warmth, peace, love, power* go up to your face, your nose and your eyes, and feel the *liquid warmth, peace, love, power* engorge your eyes and lids. Feel that for a moment; let the heated pleasure linger as it fills your eyeballs and lids. Then take the *liquid warmth, peace, love, power* down your face, neck, chest until you get to your nipples, and let the *liquid warmth, peace, love, power* engorge your nipples. Feel them swell with the sensual heat of the *liquid warmth, peace, love, power.* Feel that for a moment. Then take the *liquid warmth, peace, love, power* and bring it down your torso, then to your stomach until it gets to your sexual zone, and then let the *liquid warmth, peace, love, power* engorge that area. . . . Feel the tingly warmth swelling that area with sensuality. Feel that for a moment. Then take the *liquid warmth, peace, love, power* and let it travel through your veins down your legs, your knees and your feet and out through your toes.

6. Then attempt to open your eyes by slowly lifting your eyelids (this will organically create the junkie nod).

7. LET IT GO.

Experiencing Organic Heroin Withdrawals

Before you can "jones" (have withdrawal symptoms) on heroin, you must first experience the high of heroin. This is so when the high starts to dissipate and the sickness begins to permeate your system, you'll truly need a fix to feel good again. Begin with the heroin exercise and continue from there.

Formula for Organic Withdrawal Symptoms for Heroin

1. Do the high-on-heroin exercise detailed above.
2. Now take thousands of tiny spiders . . . with the pinpricks of their spindly spider legs crawling en masse all over your neck and the backs of your hands and arms.
3. Add to the nausea you've already created and make yourself really feel like you're going to vomit. Feel the semi-digested pieces of your last meal surging and swirling, attacking the lining of your stomach. Feel a sour taste coming up your throat and lying putridly on your tongue.
4. LET IT GO.

Feeling High on Cocaine or Crystal Methamphetamine

Cocaine gives the user a feeling that every thought is a revelation, that every thought is effusive, unrestrained and irrepressible. And furthermore, the thought must be spoken aloud. The revelations can be extraordinary in the positive and extremely intense in the negative, causing profound paranoia. There is no subtlety to a cocaine user—the discovery is monumental, the rage like a volcano, the self-loathing enormous, the feeling of power Herculean. There's a lot of INNER MONOLOGUE when you're on cocaine. Every move, every word the other person is saying is worthy of several interpretations—after all, that's the basis of paranoia, and paranoia is an integral part of the cocaine or crystal meth experience.

Formula for an Organic Cocaine or Crystal Methamphetamine High

1. Begin by thinking that your brain has been replaced by a large glob of pink cotton candy and you're looking at it under a microscope. Think of the fluff, think of the pinkness and the sweetness

and see how the air hits the cotton candy and how it becomes tiny sugar icicles. . . .

2. Now imagine a glob of pink cotton candy in front of your eyes and attempt to *think* and *see through* the fluff, the pinkness and the drippy warmed sugar. . . . Your brain no longer exists—*think* and *see through* those pink, pink, fluffy, sugary, hairy filaments, a whipped-up, sugary, cottony mass. . . . Your brain is gone, and that feels so good. . . . Continue to *think* and find a way to *see through* all that pink, pink, fluffy, whipped-up, sugary-sweet, cottony mass. . . .

3. Then put thousands of tiny spiders on the back of your neck and hands, and feel the little spider legs piercing like little needles, dancing, frolicking on the back of your neck and the backs of your hands and up your arms to your elbows. Don't scratch the feeling off. This way you create an organic tweaking experience.

4. Acknowledge everything you say aloud as a revelation.

5. LET IT GO.

Heroin-and-Cocaine Combination (A.K.A.: "Speedball")

A person that uses both heroin and cocaine at the same time is someone who requires both an emotional pain reliever and a feeling of power. In replicating this behavior, you must first follow the formula for a heroin high, then do the formula for a cocaine buzz. This will reflect the way both highs physiologically affect your body.

Formula for an Organic Heroin-Cocaine High (A.K.A.: "Speedball")

1. Do the high-on-heroin exercise detailed above.

2. Do the cocaine exercise detailed above.

3. LET IT GO.

LSD, Peyote, Mescaline and Other Psychedelics

Because people who are into psychedelics are feeling creatively and intellectually repressed, you must establish a personal and present need to be creative. Look at the part of your life that is staid, uneventful and uninspiring. "Tripping" will be the right prescription to fix your sense of being trapped within the norm and the mundane by bringing you color, light and inspiring revelations.

Formula for a Psychedelic High

1. Begin by thinking that your brain has been replaced by a large glob of pink cotton candy and you're looking at it under a microscope. Think of the fluff, think of the pinkness and the sweetness and see how the air hits the cotton candy and how it becomes tiny sugar icicles. . . .

2. Now imagine a glob of pink cotton candy in front of your eyes and attempt to *think* and *see through* the fluff, the pinkness and the drippy warmed sugar. . . . Your brain no longer exists—*think* and *see through* those pink, pink, fluffy, sugary, hairy filaments, a whipped-up, sugary, cottony mass. . . .

3. Now look at the underside of your hand. Notice closely and carefully all the wrinkles and various colors that you see there. Explore the pink, blue and green of the veins; the yellow, brown and red pigments of your skin; the purple where the stronger indentations are. Marvel at the intricacies and details of something as seemingly simple as your hand.

4. Now lift your head from your hand and notice the infinite details of a particular item around you. See the object's textures, its various colors, the quality of its surface and marvel at its incredible capacity and its earth-shattering purpose. Example: See a toaster's silver-and-black veneer. See how it shines in some spots and is tarnished in others. Look at the inside and notice the crevices and intricate wirework, and revel in the fact that those wires turn cold to hot, gray to red in just a few seconds. As you're staring

at the toaster, marvel that this amazing contraption can actually change something white to brown and sometimes even black in a matter of moments. How does it know how to do that?!

5. LET IT GO. Start the scene, and as you do the scene, continue to pinpoint specific things around you to examine and explore in extreme detail and fascination. This includes the other actor's face as you are speaking to him or her.

Substance-Abuser Ritual

Along with the feeling of being high, substance abusers get off on the ritual of imbibing. It's the foreplay before the orgasm. And just as foreplay is an integral part of sex, the user's ritual is key to an addiction. Let's look at some sample substance-abuser rituals.

- **Cocaine:** Calling the dealer. Pouring the cocaine onto a shiny surface. Tasting it. Cutting it into fine lines with a credit card or razor blade. Snorting it with a particular device—a dollar bill, the right knuckle, a spoon.
- **Heroin:** Measuring the heroin. Loading a spoon. Pouring the precise amount of water onto the spoon. Cooking the heroin with a favorite lighter. Putting a piece of cotton in the heroin. Filling the syringe. Tying off with a belt. Finding a good vein. Slapping and pumping the vein. Injecting.
- **Alcohol:** First, identifying the alcohol of choice: beer, wine, vodka, gin, whiskey because most alcoholics stick with one type of alcohol. Going to that special place: a bar, the den, the hall closet or somewhere you keep or hide your alcohol of choice. Ordering a drink in a specific way or checking to see how much alcohol is left in a bottle. Analyzing how many future drinks are possible. Using the proper glassware. Making the drink or asking for it the way it is *always* prepared and with the usual ingredients: for instance, with exactly three ice cubes, two olives, a splash of water, one large cocktail onion, a quarter wedge of lime, sugar-

free orange juice or a pink umbrella. Filling the glass to a specific level. Drinking.

- **Marijuana:** Opening the plastic bag. Burying your nose inside the bag and smelling and breathing in the woody, spicy scent with anticipation. Taking the marijuana out of the bag. Rolling it around with your fingers. Selecting your favorite pipe or bong or rolling papers. Rolling the joint or loading the bong. Putting your mouth to the stem. Lighting up with your favorite lighter. Inhaling.

- **Pills:** Going to your favorite secure hiding place. Taking the lid off a pill container and counting how many pills you have left to figure out how many more times you can get high with the contents. Putting the pill in your mouth and swallowing it.

Drugs and alcohol allow the user to feel pain-free and powerful, at least while the drugs are at their peak potency. When the good feelings start to go away, the user chases the high in order to feel good again. An actor who plays a substance abuser should keep this in mind—when the bad feelings emerge, you fix it by snorting, injecting, drinking, ingesting or smoking some more. This need, along with the ritual, should become part of your DOINGS throughout the scene/story.

Creating an Addictive Personality

Beyond the emotional need to use addictive substances and the love of the ritual, addicts find a deep sense of safety and security in the actual handling of whatever they are addicted to. This is because they know, absolutely, that the substance they are handling gives them power and strength when they need it the most. People are unreliable, events are unpredictable, but the one thing an addict can count on again and again is their substance (or behavior) of choice, which gives them the sense of well-being they so desperately need.

Formula for Creating an Addictive Personality

1. Take the alcohol bottle or glass (or pill container, bag with powder, binge food, whatever your character is addicted to) and press it against your face as you close your eyes.

2. Now feel a sense of *peace, power, warmth, well-being and love* emanating from the container and pouring into your heart and soul.

3. Take the addictive substance SUBSTITUTE (for example: tea or water substituting for alcohol) and pour it out of the container and into your mouth, letting the liquid settle on your tongue for a while as you feel a sense of *peace, power, warmth, well-being and love*. Then swallow.

- If it's food, chew slowly and feel a sense of *peace, power, warmth, well-being and love* as you taste and savor your character's binge food. Then swallow.

- If it's pills (substitutes like candy, vitamins, mints, etc., will work), shake a pill into your mouth and let it sit there, feeling a sense of *peace, power, warmth, well-being and love*. Then swallow.

- If it's cocaine (use a substitute like powdered milk, etc.), snort it up and feel a sense of *peace, power, warmth, well-being and love* as the substance SUBSTITUTE drains down your throat.

- If it's marijuana (use tobacco or herbal-cigarette filling), take a hit and feel a sense of *peace, power, warmth, well-being and love* from the smoke that's filling your mouth and lungs.

Like an addict, you'll find after doing this exercise that you'll want to ingest the substance whenever you're triggered by anxiety, angst, turmoil, confrontation or any uncomfortable situation. You will organically feel the need to go to your addiction as a way to cope, responding to specific emotional triggers that come from the scripted material. This is the way it happens with real addictive personalities, not the way so many actors portray addicts by randomly ingesting their substances as scenes progress.

CHAPTER 16

Playing a Killer or Someone Who Is Killed

No matter how cruel someone is, there's always a reason.

In keeping with the philosophy of the Chubbuck Technique—that our actions and behaviors are a way to solve, learn, evolve and achieve catharsis—even the act of killing or being killed can be seen as positive. Since we are not actually killing anyone or being killed, we can view doing either as integral to telling a compelling, relatable story. Instead of in-the-ground death, think of killing or being killed as an energy resource that needs to "die" for us to prosper. I call this an ENERGY KILL.

ENERGY KILLS

Playing the killer.

To be able to understand what is generally deemed horrific and evil behavior, look at killing as a metaphor. That's what great storytellers do. Think about Herman Melville's *Moby-Dick*: Captain Ahab isn't killing an actual whale; he is killing his demons, which take the form of a whale. These demons must be destroyed or else Captain Ahab will emotionally perish. An ENERGY KILL of that whale becomes necessary for Captain Ahab to find resolution so that the demons cannot control his life anymore.

Judging instead of trying to understand the killer creates a two-dimensional analysis. We want a three-dimensional, rich and layered portrayal. Think of the person you're killing as an energy resource that causes you destruction and pain. Then "killing" the person attached to that energy becomes a necessary and positive act.

To be clear, here are some personalizations for playing a killer using the concept of ENERGY KILLS as a way to find a solution and growth.

- You are obsessed with a person, and that person does not return this affection, making you feel creepy and unlovable. If you ENERGY KILL that person (who is your SUBSTITUTION), then you will no longer have someone to be obsessive about. This will free you and enable you to move on to healthier relationships.

- Your mother always told you that you were stupid and ugly and would never amount to anything and you have internalized this (okay, that was what my mother did to me . . . but anyway . . .). If you ENERGY KILL her, you are actually "killing" the voice that continues to lead you to make decisions that are self-destructive and hurtful. The ENERGY KILL allows you to move on.

- Your ex has custody of your children and isn't very good at allowing your court-mandated days with them. You ENERGY KILL your ex so you can spend time with your children.

- Your father is slowly and painfully dying from a terminal disease. You ENERGY KILL your father so he doesn't have to be in pain anymore. It's important to note that this is self-serving, as well, because watching your father being in pain is also excruciating for you by virtue of your powerlessness to do anything to help.

- Your friend betrayed you and stole your half of the business. You ENERGY KILL your thieving friend so you can move on to something else that isn't about the negative energy of revenge, allowing you to find new success.

- Your sibling always makes life choices from anger and past hurts, and you find you are doing the same in mirroring that sibling. You ENERGY KILL the offending sibling so that you can live life from a more effective place and avoid more hurtful situations of your own making.

- You've been molested, and although it happened a long time ago, the residual reality of being sexually abused stays with you. You

ENERGY KILL the molester so that person no longer affects your ability to have trusting relationships.

- Your mother abandoned you when you were young. You EN-ERGY KILL her to eliminate the belief that she left because you weren't worth staying for. This will allow you to feel worth loving and be able to stop manifesting what you fear—that love equals abandonment.

These are just a few examples of effective personal ENERGY KILLS you can use in your work. Killing negative energy allows you to do something positive. It creates a path for your character (and ultimately yourself) to have more constructive behaviors. While you're playing a killer (or writing one), the most effective way to find what your ENERGY KILL needs to be is to do an INFORMATIONAL EMOTIONAL DIARY. (Reminder: This is automatic writing, writing without conscious control. Refer back to chapter 13, EMOTIONAL DIARIES.) Use this prompt:

"I need to ENERGY KILL you, __name__, because . . ."

You will get a name, and what information follows the "because . . ." will be the energy substance that needs "killing" for you and your character to be able to survive emotionally, move on and have a more prosperous life. The more you write, the more information you have to fill in your INNER OBJECTS and INNER MONOLOGUE with—specific, detailed triggers to create the most extraordinary end result (whether from the point of view of acting, writing or directing). Try it right now and you will see how liberating it is. It's often surprising what comes up. Remember: You are destroying an ENERGY KILL that is stopping you from overcoming a crucial obstacle in your life.

Playing the person being killed.

To take the victim out of being a victim, we have to see the character's death as something that is desired, keeping in mind it is an ENERGY KILL, not actual death. What's being killed off is energy that is destructive to our well-being. To avoid being a victim and to "die" with purpose and dignity, we have to see it as an energy suicide. What's fascinating about human nature is that the impulses to kill and to die by suicide come from the same place—two opposing sides of the same coin. What we are trying to kill in ourselves is the part of us that makes us fail, hurt, self-destruct and self-sabotage. So when we are being killed in a script, the SUBSTITUTION is the person responsible for the part of us that needs to be ENERGY KILLED so that we can move on and thrive in life. For example, if you operate from a place of fear, what needs to be killed (EN-ERGY KILLED) are the illogical and self-destructive beliefs that cause the fear. Therefore, the most effective SUBSTITUTION you will be making for the killer is the person who instilled that thinking in you in the first place. Say your mother stayed with your abusive father because she was weak and fearful, thereby causing you to make similar decisions in your own life. Then the person/SUBSTITUTION that needs to ENERGY KILL your palpable fear would be your mother.

Other examples of being killed via ENERGY KILLS:

- Your spouse is holding you as an emotional hostage, making you feel guilty for having a life outside of them. The offending spouse/SUBSTITUTION would ENERGY KILL your guilt so you can free yourself of the emotional bondage.
- Your father has always called you a loser, which has caused you to make decisions that will ultimately lead to failure. Your father/SUBSTITUTION would then ENERGY KILL the part of you that feels like a loser so that you can move on to succeed and feel good about yourself.
- Your ex has moved on with your best friend. You would have the ex be your SUBSTITUTION to ENERGY KILL your need for revenge, as that is an all-consuming energy that keeps you from moving on to a healthier relationship.
- Your father abandoned you, and because of that abandonment, you expect all people are going to do the same. You would use your father/SUBSTITUTION to ENERGY KILL your abandonment issues so that you can trust again.
- If you were abused growing up (sexually or emotionally), you would have the abuser/SUBSTITUTION ENERGY KILL in you the constant need to attract and be attracted to abusive people in your life.

You get the idea. Even what is considered a terrible act can be "spun" as a means for resolution and growth in the fantasy world of art. The best way to find what makes sense for who you choose as your SUBSTITUTION to kill the destructive energy in you is to do an INFORMATIONAL EMOTIONAL DIARY.

The prompt:

"I need you, **_name_**, to ENERGY KILL me because . . ."

The information that follows "because . . ." will include what the energy resource is and why it needs to be killed by that particular person. The more you write, the more details you will uncover for your inner work.

Playing a serial killer.

When a person becomes a serial killer, it is usually a response to heinous physical, emotional and/or sexual abuse they endured as a child. A child is powerless to respond to the abuse because of size, authority control and reliance on the abuser for money, shelter and sustenance. However, when the child becomes an adult, the serial killer then has the power to get revenge against the abuser. There is no greater power that a human being can have than to have the power over whether someone lives or dies. A serial killer's victims almost always symbolize their original abuser. When a killer murders his victim, he feels he is finally winning his power back from the person who took it away. Because the person being killed is not the actual perpetrator of the abuse, the acquired power is momentary. And because the relief is fleeting, the serial killer, like a drug addict, chases this high by killing again. His (or her) killing becomes essential in maintaining his sense of control and power. Thus, a series of murders is committed, and a serial killer is produced.

Case in point is the infamous serial killer Ed Kemper. Growing up, Ed was tormented by his mother. She accused him of molesting his sister and of wanting to rape the coeds on a college campus. She verbally abused him and locked him in a suffocating, windowless, dark and damp cellar filled with vermin so that he wouldn't harm anyone. All this for crimes he hadn't committed. When Ed was old enough to fend for himself, guess what he did. He raped and killed. Who? Yup, those very coeds his mother had unfairly imprisoned and chastised him over. One of his last victims? His mother. Ed beat her to death with a claw hammer, cut off her head and carefully extracted her larynx—the part of the body that gave his mother the capacity to shower Ed with her brutal accusations and hateful admonishments. And then Ed had sexual intercourse with the detached head. He was punishing *her* sexually, the equivalent of being punished for crimes that he had been accused of as a boy but hadn't committed then.

> *You have to be aware of the manner in which your*
> *character kills, because it is always fraught with*
> *symbolism—symbolism that makes sense and matches*
> *the childhood abuse that was inflicted upon the killer.*

More often than not, sexuality plays a key role in a serial killer's M.O. Why? Because both killing and sex involve power. For a killer, murder is an aphrodisiac. For most murderers, even if there is no actual sex, the act of killing is sexually stimulating. So arousing, in fact, that the killer often reaches the point of orgasm.

> *When you are playing a serial killer, the act of killing can be*
> *compared to a seduction and should be performed that way.*

Another aspect of being a serial killer is that they don't just kill upon contact with their victim. Like a cat with a mouse, there's the joy of the hunt—playing with his food—before the murder is committed. This gives the killer additional power in watching the victim squirm and beg. The ritual of the lead-up to murdering will match in some way the abuse that was suffered in the serial killer's childhood.

A serial killer will say and do things that push the buttons of the victim until the victim retaliates with behavior similar to that of the original abuser. This enables the killer to justify his murder. In the killer's mind, the victim actually deserves to die.

> *There's stunted emotional growth and a*
> *childlike quality to a serial killer.*

Their traumas are often so severe that their development is arrested and they remain emotionally very immature. Mature adults rationalize their history so that they can emotionally survive life's dilemmas. A serial killer doesn't understand this and, like a child, acts out, immaturely striking back without thought to the act or its repercussions.

How does that relate to you, someone who is a rational adult?

All acting is taking a fraction of who you are and turning it into a whole so you can become and live the character on the page.

Everyone has homicidal urges at one time or another in their life, but few actually act upon them. You have to look at your life and the times you've felt homicidal urges. Who caused them? In the fantasy land of acting, you get to have the upper hand for a change by taking someone from your life that you feel has abused you horribly, preferably someone from your childhood but it could be an abuser from your present life, and ENERGY KILL them in your performance. The symbolic SUBSTITUTION for your victim may be someone who:

- Abandoned you when you were a child
- Sexually molested or raped you
- Beat you up emotionally and/or physically
- Didn't protect you from someone who abused you—emotionally, sexually or physically
- Humiliated you in vast proportions

All these deeds deserve to be punished. And as an actor playing a serial killer, you can get payback over and over again!

Symbolically killing this person within the confines of acting should give you great joy because of your newfound power over someone who, in the past, used it cruelly against you.

Reminder: Don't ever judge your characters. Even serial killers feel their behavior is justified.

The ENTRAILS EXERCISE

Creating the visceral experience of killing.

The ENTRAILS EXERCISE gives you a practical way to create a visceral response to the act of killing when you are playing a killer. Whether your role involves a crime of passion, a serial killer's murders, an act of self-defense or a vampire's or werewolf's slayings, etc., an actor needs to trigger the primal, animal need "to kill" that allows the actor to feel what we all inherently are—the human animal. We may be at the top of the food chain, have a better ability to think and have opposable thumbs, but nonetheless we have animal instincts. After we explore the psychological reasons for the crime, we need to add the physiological response. We do that by using visuals. We want to avoid coming from an intellectual thought process; the kill needs to be raw, gritty and instinctive.

I have created an exercise that produces the killer instinct organically. You can even use this exercise if you are just thinking about killing a character and your character never makes the actual move, as the thought to do so precedes the act. This could happen if someone stops you, or the other person gets to you first, or you decide that you don't want to kill that person after all. It doesn't mean you didn't think about it in the most visually vivid way. The exercise doesn't take long to do, so you can do it on the fly midscene. The truth is, it takes longer to read the instructions than it does to follow them.

The ENTRAILS EXERCISE.

The below is not to be physically acted upon or said out loud. It is a visual exercise to perform in your head.

1. Picture the person you've determined is your SUBSTITUTION. Look at them and remember the worst of what that person did to you. Let it enrage you.

2. Imagine violently breaking open their chest cavity with your bare hands, brutally separating the ribs upward from the body.

3. Imagine inserting your hand into the opened chest, pushing through all the slimy organs—the liver, the stomach, the spleen—

and roughly sliding your hand through all the slime and the guts until you get to the heart.

4. Imagine pulling the heart out of the chest but keeping it attached to the inside of the body.

5. Imagine lifting your arm and squeezing the heart until all you have left is flattened heart tissue in your fist. Feel the blood, pulp and goo of the heart's insides slowly drip down your arm like molasses.

6. Let the feeling go and find its own way into your system without thought or control.

*NOTE: The steps all take place in your imagination, but the effects of the ENTRAILS EXERCISE will elicit a bodily response. I have done this exercise with so many different people from different cultures, and the many extremely different responses people have to it are fascinating. The reactions range from crying to steely resolve, to fear, to laughter, to physical pain, to elation, and more. Don't predetermine what you are going to feel and how it's going to look. Be surprised; let the exercise happen in a way that is real to you. The result will be more authentic this way, both for you and the audience's experience. As in all your choices, don't judge your reaction with whether it is good or bad (whether morally or artistically), but let the response breathe, creating its own unique and therefore special energy.

Whether you are the killer or being killed, don't judge it. As an overall note, you should never judge your characters anyway.

CHAPTER 17

Creating Organic Fear

Fear Is the Most Difficult Feeling for an Actor to Re-create

This is because most of the telltale physical responses that indicate fear are involuntary to your system. Such responses include:

- Pupils contracting
- Heart beating fast
- Adrenaline pumping into your system
- Skin blanching
- Body and mind exhibiting unusual levels of courage and strength

In order to make these physical reactions really happen in your body, you have to investigate what actually causes fear. Fear is our body's way of protecting ourselves when we suspect that we might be or truly are in danger. Fear emanates from the need to stay alive—it's part of our innate survival instinct. Because fear motivates the parts of your body that control action—and gets blood and adrenaline flowing in greater amounts through your system—it creates faster movement, a quicker thought process, and physical prowess that we wouldn't ordinarily have.

It's a common misconception that fear comes from a rush of information. Actually, thinking about *one* aspect of our lives when we're afraid makes us want and need to survive. For example, if someone has a gun to your head, you might think about the fact that you are the only person around who can take care of an ailing parent. You have to survive to keep that parent from being left alone to fend for him- or herself.

Creating Organic Fear

To establish your specific personal issue in creating fear, make a list of all the regret possibilities. **The list should include any and all issues that if you were to die today you'd never be able to accomplish, resolve or take care of.**

List at least ten to fifteen ideas. Don't stop at five. The issues that emerge after number five are often the most affecting because they stem from your subconscious—the material that is deepest and darkest and that you don't necessarily want to admit to yourself. Logically, the issues we hide even from ourselves are always going to be more deeply felt.

The following is an example of a fear list (which you'd handwrite on lined paper):

Fear List

Think, "If I die today . . ."

1. I'll never have a child.
2. (Or if you do have a child) I'll never be able to watch my child grow up and they'll never know me as their mother (or father).
3. I'll never find true love.
4. I'll never know what it feels like to be truly loved.
5. I'll never be married.
6. I'll never know if my mother (or father) ever really loved me.
7. I'll never make my father (mother, child, sibling, mate, etc.) proud of me.
8. My mate (parent, sibling, friend, etc.) will believe I died a loser.
9. I won't be there to take care of my financially bereft (or ailing) mother (father, sibling, mate, child, etc.), who was always there for me.

10. I'll never resolve or have closure in my relationship with my father (mother, child, sibling, mate, ex-mate, best friend, etc.).

11. I'll never hear the words "I love you" from my father (mother, sibling, child, mate, etc.).

12. I'll never be able to say, "I love you" and "I'll miss you" to my mother (father, sibling, mate, ex-mate, friend, child, etc.).

13. I'll never hear the words "I'm sorry" from my father (mother, mate, ex-mate, sibling, friend, uncle, etc.) for their abuse (molestation, abandonment, cheating, etc.).

14. I'll never prove to my child (father, mother, mate, etc.) I could be successful.

15. (If you were adopted or abandoned) I'll never know my real mother (or father).

Before you can do the fear formula for performance, you have to first determine which regret issue from your fear list would affect you the most. You must pinpoint precisely the regret issue from your fear list before your actual performance. This will enable you, during your performance, to realize organic fear within a minute of using the fear formula.

Finding Which Regret Issue from Your Fear List Will Be the Most Effective

Once you're done with your list, read each item aloud (alone, you'll feel more available and less judged). There will be one particular regret on your fear list that will pull at you more emotionally than the others. If two or three seem to speak to you equally, then try the following exercise with each one and see which creates the most tangible fear response.

After you've picked the one (or two or three) from your fear list that inspires the largest emotional reaction in you, close your eyes and picture what it would feel like to accomplish or fix the regret in the best possible way. Enjoy picturing your success. Then open your eyes and visualize your achievement or resolution being taken from you in an abrupt and tragic manner. Then say over and over again in your head, "I have to survive to keep this from happening. I have to survive to keep this from happening. . . ."

You repeat a survival mantra because it's the need to survive that actually creates fear, not the fearful situation itself.

Applying the Fear List

Using regret issue #1, "If I die today, I'll never have a child" (which, by the way, is frequently a highly effective regret issue because procreation is such a strong, primal need):

1. *If you're a woman:* Picture a baby that looks just as you did when you were an infant and imagine baby-you floating in your womb.

   If you're a man: Picture holding a baby that looks just as you did when you were an infant, and in your mind's eye, see it placed gently in your arms. (The reason you see the baby as yourself as a child is because parents see offspring as little versions of themselves—a second chance, if you will, at fixing the woes and devastations that happened in the parents' childhoods. That's why pride and letdowns are so intensified with regard to your own child, because basically it's just "little you" having to deal, yet again, with life's trials and tribulations.)

2. Look into your baby's eyes and see your baby's unconditional love, the kind of love you've never received before, and feel it wash all over you. Then look down at your baby and silently speak to your child, vowing to protect and love him (or her) and keep all the bad things that have happened to you from happening to your baby. Be specific in remembering personal traumatic events and personal insecurities that you're going to shield your baby from. This should take only a few moments. Now see the baby look at you with unconditional love, thanking you for protecting him (or her) from all the bad things that happened to you and allowing him (or her) to stay safe, hopeful and innocent. Feel the love wash over you again.

3. Feel the baby pulled from your womb (or arms). Forever. Feel the profound emptiness of the loss—and the idea that you will never feel unconditional love. Then quickly open your eyes and realize that the last image is going to happen if you die today.

4. Then say in your head like a mantra, "I have to survive to keep this from happening. I have to survive to keep this from happening. I have to survive to keep this from happening. . . ."

5. LET IT GO and begin the scene. The fear should stay with you, driving you to survive.

Let's look at another example so that you really get the idea. We'll use #7 from the sample list: "If I die today, I'll never make my father proud of me."

1. Get comfortable. Relax. Close your eyes and picture a close-up of your father's face beaming with pride at your future accomplishments—the kind of look you've never seen from him but have always hoped you would see one day. Hear him say the words "I'm so very proud of you" with great feeling and emotion. Take a few seconds to let the feeling of your father's pride wash over you, the feeling that "I've finally gotten what I've always wanted from him."

2. Abruptly change the image to your father looking at your tombstone, shaking his head in disappointment, thinking what a loser and screwup you were and how much you let him down. Watch him cry because you were such a failure and a mistake. Let that feeling make you sick.

3. Quickly open your eyes and realize that the last image is going to happen if you die today, and say in your head like a mantra, "I have to survive to keep this from happening. I have to survive to keep this from happening. I have to survive to keep this from happening. . . ."

4. LET IT GO and begin the scene. The fear should stay with you, driving you to survive.

After you've figured out your most effective regret issue from your fear list, you can go ahead and use the formula for creating fear.

Formula for Creating Organic Fear

1. Close your eyes. Take the regret issue that you've previously chosen from your fear list and see the upside of what you want to accomplish, resolve or take care of happening in the most wonderful and vivid way—exactly the way you've always wanted it to be and imagined it would be. Thoroughly enjoy it.

2. Then imagine the worst that can happen if you were to die today without having a chance to fulfill your need. Picture it in all of its horrible details. Let the image fill you with anxiety.

3. Open your eyes. Then, with great angst, acknowledge that the worst image is definitely going to happen if you die today and internally repeat the survival mantra "I have to survive to keep this from happening. I have to survive to keep this from happening. I have to survive to keep this from happening. . . ."

4. LET IT GO and let the fear happen organically.

This whole process should take only a minute, which will allow you to be in fear mode quickly when the director says "Action!" or when the curtain goes up.

Remember: Always do the fear list as part of the homework you do *before* you arrive on the set or onstage so you'll know in advance which regret issue will be the most effective—it takes time to make the list and figure out which item will work best for you. In this way, when it's time to shoot or make your entrance onstage, it will take less than a minute to take the choice you've already made from your list and do the fear exercise.

It's also important to note that just because the choices you make to create fear work for you today, it doesn't mean that they're going to work forever. Priorities change, needs change and circumstances change as your life progresses and so will the issue that will be most crucial to motivate a need to survive. For every new script you analyze in which a need for fear comes into play, do an entirely new list because as life happens, your priorities can change.

Place-Motivated Fear

If the fear is place motivated—such as in a haunted house or in a scene in which some unknown entity is chasing you—there's another technique available to you.

Formula for Place-Motivated Fear

1. Figure out which vermin or creatures give you the creeps: spiders, rats, roaches, snakes, worms, maggots, pit bulls, possums, etc.

2. In the space in which you're acting, imagine that every dark corner, light fixture and drawer is grotesquely swarming with whatever you've selected. Now think, "If I can't escape, I will be covered by them—in my hair and my mouth, up my nose, up my sleeves and pants legs."

3. Let the creatures of choice get to you viscerally by imagining them biting, sliming and crawling all over you in masses.

4. LET IT GO.

CHAPTER 18

Creating Organic Feelings of Death and Dying

Experience Dying from the P.O.V. of the Dying

Many actors see dying and death as a final giving up on life. The truth is that when someone is dying, that person grasps onto life like never before. Even the breath that a dying person takes is an attempt to desperately take in more air. Physiologically, our organs shut down when we are dying, and the intensive struggle to get breath—which brings life-building oxygen—becomes impossible. It's sort of like trying to put gas into a broken engine—no matter how much fuel you attempt to get in, the engine still won't get the motor running, and for all intents and purposes, the car dies.

Because breath brings oxygen, which feeds the body and keeps it alive, physicalizing the obstruction of breathing is where you want to begin when you are playing someone who is dying. After you truly feel that you are aching with the need for life-giving oxygen, then you would do the formula for creating organic fear found in the previous chapter.

You use the formula for creating organic fear when you're playing someone who is dying because dying and fear are inextricably connected. In the same way that we struggle for physical lives (via the need to breathe), we also struggle to keep our emotional lives. In other words, when we are dying, we don't want to give in to death because we don't want to lose our emotional connections, so we fight voraciously to stay alive. There's usually one climactic emotional reason that will make you feel like you have to stay alive. Therefore, just like with the fear list, you make up **a dying list of regret issues that you'd never be able to accomplish, resolve or take care of** if your death were about to happen. In the same way you dealt with the fear list, you discover and explore the particular regret issue from your dying list in *advance* of performance.

Once you've figured out the best, most effective regret issue from your fear list, then you can do the following exercise to duplicate the terrifying feelings experienced by someone who is dying imminently.

Formula for Dying from the P.O.V of the Person Dying

1. Close your eyes. Create labored breathing by imagining a large rock on your chest and throat and attempting to breathe around the pressure of the excessive weight. Grapple to gain breath around the weight on your chest, throat and esophagus. Your breathing will sound gravelly and make you cough. Then struggle to gain back the air that the coughing let escape.

2. Fight to breathe as you would fight for life.

3. Once you really feel that you're desperately and agonizingly trying to get some air in your lungs to survive, do the formula for creating organic fear. Take the regret issue that you've previously chosen from your fear list and see the upside of what you want to accomplish, resolve or take care of happening in the most wonderful and vivid way—exactly the way you've always wanted it to be and imagined it would be. Thoroughly enjoy it.

4. Then imagine the worst that can happen if you were to die immediately and never get a chance to fulfill your need. Picture it in all its horrible details. Let the image fill you with anxiety. Open your eyes.

5. Then, with great angst, acknowledge the worst image is definitely going to happen if you die today and internally repeat the survival mantra "I have to survive to keep this from happening. I have to survive to keep this from happening. I have to survive to keep this from happening. . . .")

6. Continue the fight for breath and life, because so much depends on it.
7. LET IT GO.

Why does it work? Fighting to live instead of surrendering to death makes your work active and eventful and eventually cathartic. Fighting to live makes the dying feel real because this is what we do—our inherent survival instinct doesn't allow us to give in and give up. This formula infuses the dying process with passion and the human will to live. If you give up and let death take you, the audience will give up, as well. Your specific needs, which will be revealed by your fight for life, will engage your audience. They will identify and root for you to overcome death. And when you don't, your audience will be moved.

Experiencing Death When a Loved One Is Dying

Whenever someone we love is dying, our natural instinct is to deny their impending death and to try to keep them alive. We usually have unfinished business that needs closure or that requires more time with this person. This is why you'd use the SCENE OBJECTIVE *"I need to keep you alive"* when you are playing a character who is experiencing the imminent death of a loved one. This drives you to fight for their life, thereby substantiating the goal that needs to be achieved with the SCENE OBJECTIVE—*"I need to keep you alive."* If you were to just accept the loved one's death, there would be nothing to do and nowhere to go.

Next, identify a SUBSTITUTION. Ask yourself, "Who is it that I need to keep alive?" If someone that you are close to is very sick or dying or has recently passed away, then it's easy. Use that person. However, if you are fortunate enough not to be dealing with sickness, dying or death in your present life, then ask yourself the question "The death of which person in my life would devastate me if he or she were to die today because important issues would remain painfully unresolved?"

Choosing a relationship-fraught SUBSTITUTION adds a higher charge to your hypothetical situation. If a loved one you feel is safe dies, it will leave you feeling sad, but you won't have the extra inner turmoil that comes from using a SUBSTITUTION with inherent unresolved issues. This choice raises the stakes because if that person dies today, your specific issue will be unresolved forever. This possibility intensifies your passion to win your SCENE OBJECTIVE of *"I need to keep you alive,"* because if you fail, you'll be left with permanent emotional scars. If you need to, do an INFORMATIONAL EMOTIONAL DIARY with the prompt, *"I need you to stay alive, **name**, because . . ."*

Once you select your SUBSTITUTION, you must identify precisely what it is you will lose if that particular loved one dies. As with the fear and dying lists, what you lose, regret and will not resolve must be significant and specific to your own life and relevant to your issues with your SUBSTITUTION choice. This possible regret gives you a very personal and emotionally charged reason to fight to keep that person alive. Generalities are hard for our brains and hearts to latch on to. Specific intimate information always makes us think and feel. The truth is that when someone you love is dying, there's usually a momentous reason why you feel that person must stay alive.

As with the fear list, identify the specific issue that needs to be accomplished, resolved or taken care of before your choice of SUBSTITUTION dies. Make a list. In your handwritten list, state at least ten regret issues that are relevant to your SUBSTITUTION.

Sample Loved-One-Is-Dying List

(Think, "If you die today . . .")

1. I'll never know what you could have become or achieved.
2. You'll never know what I could have become or achieved.
3. I'll never know if you were ever proud of me.
4. I'll never know if you loved me.
5. I'll never resolve and understand why you abandoned me.
6. I'll never resolve and understand why you abused me.
7. I'll never know if you forgave me for what I did to you.

8. You'll never see me happy and in love.
9. (If you're using a parent as a SUBSTITUTION) You'll never meet your grandchild.
10. You'll go to your grave thinking I'm a loser.
11. You won't be there to love and take care of me.
12. I'll be all alone.
13. I'll never hear you say the words "I love you."
14. You'll never know how much I love you.
15. I'll never know if you're sorry for what you did to me.
16. (If you're using your child as a SUBSTITUTION) I'll never know if you forgive me for not being able to protect and save you.

As with the fear list, evaluate which regret is the strongest by reading each one aloud and feeling which one emotionally pulls at you the most. If more than one feels viable, try all your final contenders and evaluate which one affects you the most.

Always identify in advance which SUBSTITUTION as well as which issue from your loved-one-is-dying list you'll be using to exemplify your need to keep your SUBSTITUTION alive.

Formula for Organically Feeling a Loved One's Impending Death

1. Think of your SUBSTITUTION as dying; then use the issue from your list that will never be resolved, accomplished or taken care of if the person were to die right now. Now close your eyes and picture the accomplishment or resolution as you would most like to see it come to pass if that person were to stay alive. (For example, if "I need you to say 'I love you' before you die" is your regret issue, see and hear in your mind's eye the dying loved one saying "I love you" with great emotion, precisely the way you've always wanted it to happen.)

2. See your SUBSTITUTION die before you can get what you want (as per the example: death before the loved one can say "I love you").

Then imagine the grave site of the loved one and feel the finality of never hearing "I love you" and knowing that your regret will affect you forever. Open your eyes.

3. Then recite this mantra over and over in your head, "I have to keep you alive to keep that from happening, I have to keep you alive to keep that from happening. . . ."

4. LET IT GO.

You'll be surprised by the emotions that surge out of you. They will not necessarily be what you expect. How we really respond to a loved one when they are dying is always different from how we imagine it will happen. And the only way to have real, spontaneous and present feelings is to put yourself in a similar predicament by using the formula.

Experiencing the Dying of a Loved One That Is Highly Unexpected and Happens Quickly

While you are driving, you hit black ice, spin out of control and hit a telephone pole. Your best friend, who is in the passenger seat, gets thrown through the windshield, and you get pinned to the steering wheel and must watch her die. You witness your child being shot in a drive-by shooting. While you are working at the local convenience store, you see your friend and coworker get stabbed. Your home is invaded and you're forced to watch your wife be raped and stabbed. These are examples of unexpected, out-of-the-blue circumstances of dying. Because your brain doesn't have time to react and your emotions don't have time to percolate, these particular life-and-death situations provoke different instinctual internal reactions.

Here is an exercise that will trigger the feelings that arise during unexpected dying/death moments.

Formula for Doing the COFFIN EXERCISE

The COFFIN EXERCISE allows an actor to organically feel those moments when dying or death is unexpected or startling, or to authentically portray those times when one experiences an unsettling intuition that a loved one is going die. This is a brief exercise that you can use at the start of a scene; it also works effectively midscene if the dying/death moment happens to take place then.

1. See your SUBSTITUTION in an open coffin.
2. Look at the lifeless face and think, "I must memorize your face— your eyes, your lips, your nose, your eyebrows—because this is the last time I'm ever going to see it in person. I'm sorry I couldn't keep you alive. I will miss you. I love you." As you say these words, feel the shadow fall over the SUBSTITUTION'S face and head as the casket's lid slams shut, enveloping your loved one's body in ultimate darkness forever.
3. See the coffin dropped into a six-foot hole.
4. Watch some shovels full of dirt being tossed on top of the coffin.
5. See the coffin with your loved one in it surrounded horrifically by what seems like infinite amounts of earth. Experience the stark finality of the scene, and accept the knowledge that even if that person were still alive somehow, they would suffocate to death.
6. The need to keep that person alive will emerge as you repeat the mantra "I've got to keep you alive to keep that from happening. I've got to keep you alive to keep that from happening. . . ."

It is the last part—the mantra of keeping someone alive even if in the scene that person doesn't have a chance to stay alive or has been pronounced dead— that makes for a true organic human response. Just as our survival instinct is such an important element to our day-to-day existence, so is the need to believe that a loved one cannot die. It often takes years to accept the passing of someone close to us, and in some cases, one may never find resolution. That's why the last part of the exercise is essential, as it makes it so dramatically accurate.

For those whose cultures do cremation instead of burials, here is a variation on the Coffin Exercise.

Formula for the COFFIN EXERCISE (Cremation)

1. See your SUBSTITUTION on a viewing slab, the one that a body is placed upon before it goes into a cremation oven.

2. Look at the lifeless face of your loved one and say to yourself in your head, "I must memorize your face—your eyes, your lips, your nose, your eyebrows—because this is the last time I'm ever going to see it in person. I'm sorry I couldn't keep you alive. I will miss you. I love you." As you say these words, feel the slab inching toward the inferno-like blaze that lies within the cremation oven.

3. See the entirety of the body in the cremation oven.

4. Watch the flaming body lose human form and become a mass of ashes.

5. The need to keep that person alive will emerge as you repeat the mantra "I've got to keep you alive to keep that from happening. I've got to keep you alive to keep that from happening. . . ."

You can use the Coffin Exercise for funerals, too. Although, as most funerals are long, ritualistic events, you can use the fear list from the previous chapter (what you will never resolve, take care of, or accomplish if a person were to die today) alongside the Coffin Exercise.

CHAPTER 19

Losing or Regaining Consciousness

Going into or just coming out of consciousness—this includes being anesthetized, being knocked out, fainting, and physically dying—gives you a feeling of discombobulation. Your vision is distorted and your mind feels hazy; you have the sense of being off-balance, with no equilibrium. To truly feel this sensory experience, follow these steps.

The GRAY COTTON BALL Exercise

1. Picture a big clump of gray cotton as if it were under a microscope. See the dense gray fibers and the intertwining hairy, cottony fluff. The dull grayness of it all.

2. Imagine replacing your brain with this image, and put a big clump of the gray cotton in front of your eyes.

3. Attempt to see and think through the heavy, cottony, gnarled gray threads. You have no brain, just a big hunk of dense dark gray cotton that extends through every inch of your skull. Try to think and see through the clump of the gray cotton in front of your eyes. Very little light filters through the hairy lead gray fibers. Continue to try to see and think through the fluffy, fibrous gray mass.

4. As you lose consciousness, make the gray cotton more and more dense until you can't see through it, which will cause the feeling of passing out.

FOR GAINING CONSCIOUSNESS: Do the same exercise but start with a very dense gray cotton mass and then make it more and more easy to see through. Let the light find its way through the fibrous, wiry cloud until you feel a sense of the world coming back into your sight.

CHAPTER 20

Experiencing Feeling Pregnant (from the Male and Female P.O.V.)

Pregnancy—There Is No SUBSTITUTION

When you are pregnant or someone is carrying your child, there is no SUBSTI-TUTION that can correlate to the baby in you or to the mother of your child. Some actors believe that thinking about a pet or a niece or nephew will elicit a similar feeling of love. But unfortunately, as much as you love Fluffy your dog, or Amy your godchild, or even Adam, your beloved sister's son, how you feel about your own flesh-and-blood child is inherently different.

The best way to describe how we feel about our children is to say that we see them as little versions of ourselves. That's why when someone compliments your child by saying things like "Your child is gorgeous" or "Your child is so smart," you respond with "Thank you!" as if the compliment was meant for you. That's because your child is little-you, giving you a second chance to cure the insecurities that have arisen from your bad experiences. That's why a parent sees red when they observe anyone dealing with their child in a way that is similar to the manner an abuser behaved in their own history. They're not seeing the actual person in front of them but rather a symbolic version of their own abuser, motivating them to change what happens *this time* because they couldn't do so the *first time*. This is where the strong, innate urge to protect and nurture your child comes from—it's the same urge that comes from one's own need to survive. And thus the following formula was—excuse the expression—born.

Formula for Feeling Pregnant (from the Male and Female P.O.V.)

1. Sit. Get comfortable. Close your eyes.
2. If you are a female, take your hand and rest it on your lower abdomen where your womb is. If you are a man, with permission put your hand on the lower abdomen of the woman playing your pregnant partner, or imagine yourself as a baby in your own arms.
3. Think about a picture that was taken of you when you were an infant and imagine yourself as that infant floating in your womb, or being cradled in your own arms if you are male.
4. Zero in on the eyes of yourself as a baby and see the innocence, purity and hopefulness (the kind of hope where anything is possible)—the innocence, purity and hopefulness that can only exist before any of your painful experiences have taken place.
5. Then, in your head, talk to yourself as a baby, and tell him or her that you vow to keep any of those painful events and bad self-images that you've personally experienced from happening to him or her. And vow to protect baby-you from experiencing the awful moments that you were forced to endure, because you know how bad they felt and know all too well the aftermath of those terrible events: how insecure, self-sabotaging and self-loathing you became as a result; how you made stupid decisions in choosing a mate, how you allowed people to take advantage and abuse you, how you made harmful life choices all because of those horrible experiences. Continue to speak, in your mind, to baby-you and profusely assure him or her that you are bound and determined to keep your baby, your child, from ever having to suffer what you had to suffer. Be extremely specific about the events and feelings that you don't want baby-you to go through. (Examples: "I will never abandon you like my father did to me when I was seven,

only coming to see me when it was convenient for him. I will always be there for you." Or "I won't let anyone make you feel ugly, stupid and worthless like my mother did to me." Or "I won't ever hit or abuse you like my brother did to me. I'll make sure no one ever hurts you the way I was hurt.") Talk to baby-you for about thirty seconds.

6. Now look at baby-you smiling that gummy, toothless, innocent grin, looking back at you with pure unconditional love, thanking you for your love and protection. Let the unconditional love wash over you. You've never before experienced that kind of love . . . a love without conditions.

7. Now protectively and nurturingly rub the abdomen and say in your head, "I won't ever let you feel the pain that I felt growing up. You will always feel cherished and loved, taken care of. I'll always be there for you because I'm your mommy (or your daddy) and I love you." (Or as a man, say it to baby-you in your arms.)

8. Feel the eyes of baby-you look back at you again with unconditional love, thanking you and feeling safe in your love and protection. You've given your child feelings that were not given to you so purely and completely. Continue to feel your child's love wash over you, making you feel special and cherished. Let it feel really good.

9. LET IT GO.

Procreation is such an inherently human drive that even if you're someone who has no desire to have children, this exercise will trigger feelings that you didn't know you had.

CHAPTER 21

Experiencing Parenthood

Creating an Organic Connection Between a Parent and a Child

First of all, remember that when playing a parent, you use the younger version of yourself as your SUBSTITION. Think of this as your second chance to fix something unresolved from your childhood. Also, you need to create a connection with the actor who's playing your child. No matter how good an actor you are, it's easy to tell when an actor is pretending to be a parent. When I worked with Anna Friel on the movie *The War Bride* (directed by a brilliant director who also happened to be my late husband, Lyndon Chubbuck), she had to play a mother of an infant. At twenty-three, Anna wasn't a mother, nor did she have any concept of being one. Yet she had to deal with a screaming three-month-old infant. The baby scene was about to be shot, so I told her to do the following exercise as she held the unruly baby in her arms. The baby was hollering and screeching (in decibels that only a baby can reach) and pulling away from Anna, desperately trying to get back to his real mother. She began to do the exercise, and within moments, the baby had quieted down and begun to lovingly snuggle into Anna, his pudgy little hand reaching for her little finger and grabbing on. This was the behavior of a baby who felt he was with someone who loved him like a parent. A baby can't be directed nor can a baby take acting classes (well, he can, but I don't know how much good it would do), but this easy exercise made the parent-child connection real and organic for both the actress and the child.

Formula for Organically Feeling like a Parent

1. Look directly into the eyes of the baby, child or teenager that is playing your child and see the same exact pain, insecurities, anger, paranoia, traumas and emotional issues that you possess. These might include:
   - Issues of abandonment
   - Self-loathing
   - Self-consciousness and/or hatred of some physical trait
   - Fear of rejection
   - Trust issues
   - A history of abuse or being the victim of violence
   - Inordinate insecurity and fearfulness
   - People-pleasing tendencies
   - Suicidal tendencies

2. As you continue to look into the child's eyes, think about the specific events that caused these problems and visualize the child in front of you experiencing the same traumas in exactly the same way you did. (Essentially doing the COMMONALITY OF PAIN exercise.) By doing this, you are creating a kindred spirit—someone you will feel you need to protect and nurture, because for all intents and purposes, this is little-you.
3. LET IT GO.

By utilizing this formula, you are essentially turning a virtual stranger into the child version of yourself. This exercise works because that is precisely how we see our own children.

CHAPTER 22

Playing a Paraplegic or Quadriplegic

Organically Replicating Extreme Physical Handicaps

There's often a traumatic event that has occurred that has created this condition. It's important not only to supply the reality of the physical condition to your characterization, but to add the constant reminder of the emotional trauma that was involved in *causing* the crippled state. The following formula will combine both these elements into a truthful and organic duplication of someone who's lost the use of their limbs.

> ### Formula for Organically Feeling like a Paraplegic or Quadriplegic
>
> 1. Sit down. Take the afflicted areas (paraplegic—the lower part of your body; quadriplegic—everything below the neck) and relax all of the muscles in those areas until they no longer feel like muscles but like warm gelatin melting into the ground. There's no form or substance, just a mass of warm gelatin melting into the ground. Sit still and feel this until you feel like you truly can't move.
>
> 2. Then place your hands on the tops of your legs and relive a painful emotional event using real traumatic events, fears and emo-

tions from your life that make sense to your established inner work. Then, with your hands, press those feelings and images into your legs. If you're playing a quadriplegic, press them into your torso and arms, as well.

3. LET IT GO.

Your OVERALL OBJECTIVE in the script will include finding other ways to physically and emotionally survive despite your character's predicament. Also, use the handicap as an emotional and physical OBSTACLE in your script analysis. Being a paraplegic or a quadriplegic is a powerful OBSTACLE to overcome in surviving any OBJECTIVE and will produce a dynamic result.

CHAPTER 23

Creating Emotional Realities for Scars and Bruises

Organically Realizing Physical Traumas

In drama, a character's bruise or scar is usually a result of abuse—self-inflicted or otherwise—or a consequence of some form of a traumatic event. The following formula will help make the scar or bruise real to you.

Formula for Organically Feeling Your Character's Scars and Bruises

1. Find an event from your life that emotionally duplicates the event in the script that caused the bruise or scar. For example:
   - If the character has a scar from a parent's abuse, think of the strongest, most profound time when you felt physically and emotionally destroyed, decimated by an authority figure (it doesn't have to be a parent if there is a severe emotional scar that was caused by a teacher, older sibling, uncle, grandparent, employer, etc.).
   - If your character's bruises are caused by a mate punching them in the face, recall an event where you loved someone so much and they rewarded you with blame for their failures and decimated you with words of discouragement, making you feel dejected and

heartbroken. Or use an actual violent event committed against you by someone you cared about.
- If the bruises and lacerations are the result of a terrible car accident or a violent crime, recall an event where you felt emotionally helpless and all alone, or use an actual event of violence.

2. Press two fingers onto the area where the bruise or scar is supposed to be.
3. As you press down, picture the event you've chosen to emotionally duplicate the story's event, remembering the space, words and deeds and feeling again the painful emotions as if they were happening today. Be very specific and detailed as you viscerally relive the horrible event, infusing the pictures and emotions into the appropriate area with the pressure of your two fingers.
4. Remove your fingers and LET IT GO.

When referring to the bruise or scar or touching it, it will feel tender and the wound will feel real.

CHAPTER 24

Organically Realizing the Character's Occupation, Profession or Career

Career Defines You

Too often actors play the obvious characteristics of their character's profession without regard to how and why that character chose his or her career. Our careers are how we spend most of our time. It's what defines us. And there's always a reason why someone picks his or her chosen profession. Whether the occupation is something that the character aspires to do or the character has accomplished a great degree of success in that profession, there is always a purpose and an incentive for picking that particular career. More often than not, the character made the choice to resolve and accomplish something that is essential for emotional survival.

In your analysis of your character, you must not only understand what your character does, but also why the character does it. I've analyzed a few common occupations to give you an idea of how to think about why someone chooses the career path that they do, which will provide you with a more comprehensive understanding of your character.

Police Officer

A person often chooses police work as a career because that person has been deeply affected by crime in one form or another. They have family members who are cops, or they have witnessed tragic crimes (like murder, sexual assault, victimization at the hands of a con man, arson and rape) that involved them or loved ones or seen the results of the crimes. Children who are victims of or witnesses to crimes feel helpless, and rightfully so because there's not much that young people can do. When they become adults, they are capable of choosing a career that can empower them or the victims that they couldn't save as a child. Becoming a police officer enables the young victim/witness to effect a change in a troubled area of the past.

In this way, you can consider that playing a character who is a police officer is a means to solve something that happened in your childhood. The cases that your character is involved with are symbolic of the crimes that you dealt with or witnessed as a child. As a cop, you are finally in the position and have the power to make a difference. Your painful past will fuel the interrogation or investigation because the need to solve the scripted crime is part of your and your character's healing. The antagonist in the script then becomes the symbolic perpetrator of the original childhood crime experience and an effective SUBSTITUTION. This creates an arena that allows possible closure to a childhood trauma that will ultimately lead to more effective resolution. Thus, with every criminal you arrest and prosecute in performance, you are doing something that is much deeper than just doing a job—you are healing past wounds. And making it necessary "to protect and serve."

Thief/Crime Career

A good many people who have chosen a life of crime grew up in financial poverty. They grew up noticing that the few who managed to escape from their poor circumstances easily and with panache were those that chose life in the underworld. In a place like the ghetto, it's the criminals that are living large, wearing fancy duds and carrying ready cash. Enviable, sure, but more important, it's those with money that have position, dignity and power.

This kind of character's backstory might include a father who was a working stiff providing for his family, living a hand-to-mouth existence and suffering under an abusive boss, all to ensure that food was on the table and a roof was over his family's head. As a child, this future underworld character would have grown up hating the fact that those with money held the power, whereas the people whom he loved and who deserved better were made to kowtow. By becoming a thief (or any kind of underworld character), they would not only provide more money than the family is used to but also create a sense of empowerment and superiority in being successful at mocking authority and the law.

When playing someone of this ilk, you want to get power back from whoever you feel symbolizes the person (SUBSTITUTION) who made you and/or your loved ones feel diminished and insignificant. A lower station in life foisted upon you through the social system—whether by issues of race, money, gender or familial roots—was absolutely inequitable and unfair. Therefore, you wouldn't view the criminal activity your character is engaged in as wrongdoing, but rather righting the wrongs of your personal circumstances, which justifies any illegal actions as righteously motivated.

Psychiatrist/Psychologist

A person usually chooses psychiatry or psychology as a profession due to some unresolved childhood emotional trauma. Being a psychiatrist or psychologist allows that person, as an adult, to attempt to resolve the problem. There are many different fields that a therapist can focus on. A specialist in sex crimes might have been a victim of a sexual assault or molestation when they were a child or might come from a family where this was an issue. A couples' therapist might come from a broken home or have parents who came from one. A child psychiatrist might have trouble with the responsibilities of adulthood or with relating to adults.

When you are playing a therapist, realize that the patient is that part of your character that needs fixing in the therapist's area of expertise. Essentially, the patient symbolizes you. (For this reason, it can be very effective to use yourself as a SUBSTITUTION for the patient.) Playing a therapist with this understanding and focus creates a more critical need to heal the patient's mental illness, because you're doing it to heal yourself. This humanizes your role as a psychiatrist. This is important, because too often actors play doctors, lawyers, teachers or any authority figure as one-dimensionally officious—acting out authoritative behavior without concerning themselves that there is actually an individual human being behind the official trappings.

Once you've figured out the character's focus in his or her practice, you must relate that to a specific emotional issue of your own. See the patient in front of you as your chance to rectify the dire emotional issue that has been plaguing you.

Doctor

It takes years of premed studies, then several more years of medical school and another couple of years of residency to launch a career in medicine. It is not a career path you choose or follow on a whim. Becoming a doctor is a life mission to heal.

Think of a childhood or current event in which you were or are powerless to heal someone you loved and that person died, became handicapped or suffered a downward quality-of-life change. Becoming a doctor gives you a second chance to cure the loved one that, in life, you were helpless to make well.

Prostitute/Stripper

Although prostitutes and strippers work in professions that are ostensibly sexually oriented, being a sex worker actually has very little to do with sex. It is, conversely, an act of retribution and power that stems from a child or young adult who has been raped or sexually abused. A prostitute's johns or a stripper's audience are symbols for the person who raped or abused her or him. The sexual power over a john or audience is an attempt to reclaim the power that was taken away as a young girl or woman. Sex workers use the same venue that was used to take away their power—sex—to turn helplessness into empowerment.

If you've been raped or abused, you can use the person responsible for the assault as the SUBSTITUTION for your character's clients. Fortunately, not everyone has been a victim of a sexual crime. However, rape takes many forms. If you feel you have been violated emotionally, you can use the person who mistreated you as your SUBSTITUTION in your power plays enacted with your john or lap-dance partner.

Lawyer

Good lawyers personalize their cases, making them about an issue that he or she needs to rectify. Yes, there are those cases that a lawyer might be less interested in and that he or she might simply go through the legal motions to win, but detached commitment is not what we want to see on the stage or screen. With nothing personal at stake, the fight will be removed and dispassionate for you and the audience. A great lawyer personalizes the crime or damage that has been done in the case at hand as if it happened to him (or her) or to someone they love, like a family member, because they will fight harder and more ardently to win the case if it becomes a personal vendetta. Drama isn't re-creating a slice of life; drama is dramatizing life, taking life to its extreme. So infusing your own heightened personalizations with the scripted material is a necessity.

In order to do this, you have to take some current altercation, crime or mystery that presents itself in your life today and that is affecting you or someone dear to you (you can also use an unresolved problem that comes from your past history). In your role as a lawyer, you must attempt to solve a problem, affix blame or get payback, depending on what the best resolution would be to the personal crime with which you've endowed the one in the script. In some instances, trying to achieve all three resolutions may seem fitting. As inner work, you must personalize the bad guys (meaning those detrimental to you— they don't have to actually be bad people) in the script with the bad guys that make sense to your personalized legal scenario. Personalize the good guys (meaning those important to you—they don't actually have to be good people but the ones whom you want to protect or who have been victimized in the script) with the appropriate good guys from your personalized legal scenario. There are often many players involved in legal battles. Personalizing the players involved in the legal case you're working on in the script provides you with a more impassioned drive to win.

Armed Forces/Military

A person who is determined to join the military is someone seeking order, stringent rules and regulations and a chain of command. Perhaps that person's childhood was out of control and lacked an effective authority figure. Children require guidance through rules and boundaries. It helps them understand how to deal with life as an adult. If a child doesn't get enough of this, he or she will grow up seeking it. What better way to get the feeling of order that comes from following many stringent rules and regulations than by being a member of the military?

From an Enlisted Person/Low-Ranked Enlisted Person P.O.V.

To play an enlisted person, you have to look at your feelings about a particular parent, teacher, aunt, uncle or some other authority figure who wasn't there to guide you as you grew up—someone who made you feel that you simply were not worth the effort. In this way, the officer who is in charge of your character's unit, platoon, etc., will serve as a SUBSTITUTION for the offending childhood authority figure. Your relationship with your presiding officer becomes more like the one with the parent or another authority figure you felt you never had but needed. This personalizes the relationship beyond the plot, making you need to affect and be more affected by the officer in charge. This also makes the relationship that develops throughout the script more remarkable, deeper and more emotionally urgent than a simple and undeveloped interplay between an officer and someone of a lower rank.

From an Officer P.O.V.

An officer in the military is in a position of life-and-death power. Being an officer in the military is one of the few legal occupations with such a huge power base. Someone who requires such a power-infused job is usually someone who was made to feel powerless while growing up. This could have happened because the child was emotionally or physically beaten up by a parent, neighborhood kids, a babysitter, etc., or horribly ridiculed by the same. A child is powerless to do anything about abuse, but an adult has choices—ways to turn around the power positions.

Being an officer in the military gives that person the power of life and death over a group of people who, given the rules of the military, must obey every order.

When you are playing an officer, think of a person or a group of people (a group that makes sense together like your siblings, the members of a club you belong to, your classmates, your coworkers, the popular group, etc.) that you feel has abused you in some way and against whom some form of retribution would be especially sweet. Endow that person or group as SUBSTITUTIONS for those who are playing your subordinates. In this way, harshly giving orders and humiliating the man or men who are below you in your chain of command will be righteous and satisfying. This takes away the cruelty factor, and we as an audience will support you because your motivation isn't to be malicious, but to get your power back from the person or persons who symbolically took it away from you.

Actor

The essence of what drives a person to become an actor is the need for attention and to be loved unconditionally by vast numbers of people. That need causes an actor to have a tendency to overdramatize anything that happens in their lives. To be an actor, you must always have your emotions on the surface, available for the roles that you play. Covering or being introspective isn't conducive to a great performance—an actor has to be ready to bring up whatever charged emotion is called for. Because of this, actors enjoy their emotions—the more painful the better. They view them as fodder for performance, whether onstage or not. And like it or not, there's very little disparity between an actor's onstage and offstage behavior.

This is why when playing the role of an actor, you have permission to be a drama queen or king. The fun of playing an actor is that nothing is too much. You can do anything in the name of getting attention and love, because anyone and everyone who is in an actor's general vicinity becomes an instant audience for their award-winning performance of life. The trap of playing an actor is to do a caricature, a cartoon version. You must keep in mind that the OVERALL OBJECTIVE and passion that drive the inner work to get the SCENE OBJECTIVE must be real—ultra-dramatically real. An actor, on-screen and off-screen, always knows how to find the light, cheats to the audience (real or imagined) and is always trying to win the Oscar.

In terms of the inner work, well, you *are* an actor—identify the issues and events that made you personally want to become an actor in the first place and let that drive you to want to win your OVERALL and SCENE OBJECTIVES with dramatic intention and without restraint.

Wall Street Stockbrokers / Financial Expert / CEO, Etc.

People attracted to these high-powered jobs are people willing to do anything to win. To even get these particular positions of power, you have to be uncompromisingly driven. And you have to have a deep, deep love of money and understand, profoundly, the power of what money can buy.

To play this type of character, you need to find what would motivate you to become aggressive and ruthless and at the same time would make you feel righteous in doing so. Find a person or a group that in some way destroyed your life or that of a loved one. Make the person or group from your personal life the SUBSTITUTIONS for the people you are wreaking havoc on in the script. Then the person or group will deserve your merciless power plays and acts of vengeance.

But no matter what your character does career-wise . . .

Acting gives you the chance to realize a fantasy, something that you'll never be able to do in life. Acting is an opportunity to influence and change events that you are powerless to change in real life.

CHAPTER 25

ACTIVE LISTENING

Listening is such an integral part of communication. ACTIVE LISTENING has its own chapter because actors' inability to really listen is a universal problem. Having relationships with directors, casting directors, writers and producers from all over the world, I know firsthand the biggest complaint they have: Actors do not listen!

Sometimes it's just a matter of actors concentrating only on their dialogue, waiting for their line to be engaged and invested in. But for the most part, actors do try to hear what other characters are saying. Often, whether it's in an audition or an actual role, when actors are asked if they are listening, they will say, "I've heard every word the other person said." And this is true. They might have heard every word the other character said, but they are not listening in the way that people in the real world listen. When real people are listening to a story, they're also thinking about how that story relates to them and their own personal stories. If I tell you details about my abusive ex-husband, what he did and how it affected me, you are not going to try to imagine what my ex-husband looked like or my visuals regarding the event I am speaking about. You will listen while also thinking about an abusive relationship from your own life that mirrors mine. If I talk about my specific insecurities about not being attractive enough to ever find someone to love me, you are not going to listen with sympathy as a sole response. You will relate with your own similar issues and how they have either screwed up an existing relationship or made you feel hopeless about having one in the future. Essentially, we always listen through the lens of our own worlds and stimulate a Commonality-of-Pain connection.

Passively listening can be boring to an audience—and frankly to you and the people you are performing with. To drive a scene, even if you are just listening in that scene, you must upgrade the listening experience to ACTIVE LIS-. TENING.

Formula for ACTIVE LISTENING

1. What you hear defined from your own story / inner work.
2. How you feel about it emotionally.
3. What you want to do about it.

When you are actively listening, the audience can hear you, not in the traditional sense, but they'll pick up on your proactive thought choices. It makes them support your journey, as you aren't being complacent; you're actively going after your SCENE OBJECTIVE even when you aren't speaking. The audience often watches the listener in a scene more than the speaker because they can process many thoughts simultaneously. However, when you are talking, you must think unilaterally in order to speak, so the layered thought process is more difficult to apply. When you are ACTIVELY LISTENING, you can fill a screen and a stage.

When I worked with Judith Light on the Broadway play *Other Desert Cities*, a scene with multiple characters on the stage provided a great example of ACTIVE LISTENING. The play takes place at Christmastime when a dysfunctional family (is there any other kind?) meets up in Palm Springs at Polly and Lyman's home. Judith played Silda, Polly's sister, who just got out of rehab for alcohol addiction. There's a scene where Judith had very few lines, but it was filled with all the other characters doing long monologues. This was not a short scene, as most theater scenes are not, so it was a real exercise in ACTIVE LISTENING for Judith.

In the monologues, the other characters weren't discussing Silda at all. But Judith and I decided this was a perfect opportunity to try ACTIVE LISTENING. Using the plot information that Silda had just checked out of rehab, we could assume she was someone with big enough of a problem to go to rehab in the first place. And as with most people who've just left rehab, she was not equipped to deal with life without her usual medication (alcohol) even though she now was sober. We identified Judith's personalizations, but I will not be giving those away here. Instead, I will go through the ACTIVE LISTENING process from the character's point of view.

What you hear.

Even though the other characters were talking about their issues with other people, Judith as Silda believed that they were really talking about her and that they had disguised their issues with Silda by using other people's names. We came up with this choice because after rehab, you can no longer medicate your pain with the substance that you've relied on for years. And since the alcohol had been dulling all these feelings for so long, the emotions were huge. Because Silda had no alcohol, it was as if the emotional dam had broken and unmanageable feelings were coming out in floods. One common emotion for those that are newly sober is paranoia. So it made sense that Silda thought the other characters were really talking badly about her, not about the people they said they were talking about. "I'm not a fool. I know you're really talking about me!" was her paranoid INNER MONOLOGUE.

How you feel about it.

Silda felt angry and lonely. Her thought process was "Why do they have to lie? Why can't they face me and tell me their real feelings about me? Are they trying to get rid of me, oust me from the family because I'm too screwed up? Will I be left to fend for myself without the help of alcohol? Will I survive without my family? You all hate me!"

What you want to do about it.

This depends on exactly what is being heard and the inner work using the actor's personal life, but in the interest of privacy (again), here are some possible choices from the character's point of view: "I am going to leave you before you can leave me." Or "I will get your daughter to hate you." Or "I will start drinking again and blame you." Or "I will tell that secret of yours so you can see how it feels to be humiliated."

· · · · · · ·

Judith's ACTIVE LISTENING created unique behaviors, one of which was OCD. The repetitive behaviors made for a very visual experience for the audience. ACTIVE LISTENING absolutely creates mannerisms and quirky behaviors that are organic and not preplanned.

Judith won a Tony for this performance, and for the first time in Tony history, she won back-to-back awards when she won again the following year.

Passive listening is fine, but ACTIVE LISTENING is riveting.

CHAPTER 26

Scenes with
Three or More People

In a scene that has more than two people, you must determine who the HOT PERSON is that you want your SCENE OBJECTIVE from, keeping in mind the rules still apply and the SCENE OBJECTIVE must support the OVERALL OBJECTIVE. Not only is it confusing for you if you apply SCENE OBJECTIVES for everyone, but doing so takes away the ability to tell a single story. As in life, we can be in a group, but there's usually one person, the HOT PERSON, who holds more importance than the others, the one you need something from above and beyond anyone else in that group (especially when the stakes are high, which should always be the case for the choices you make regarding your script analysis). The other people serve as WITTING or UNWITTING ALLIES in your getting what you want (SCENE OBJECTIVE) from your HOT PERSON.

Life Examples

UNWITTING ALLY: When you are at a party, there's always that cute guy or girl, or that important producer or director, or that ex-mate, or that person from your past who is a good thing or a bad thing. You might never talk to that HOT PERSON, but everything you do is for the HOT PERSON and to get the HOT PERSON to notice you and give you the special attention you want from them. Say the SCENE OBJECTIVE in regard to the HOT PERSON is *"I want you to fall in love with me to get my power back."* While speaking to your UNWITTING ALLY, whom you are conversing with to get the HOT PERSON's attention, you are being extra sexy, witty, intelligent and generally impressive not for the benefit of the person you are actually talking to, but for the benefit of the HOT PERSON, who you hope is watching from across the room. (Now, there is the instance when you are with your bestie, better known as your wingman, who is privy to your need to affect the HOT PERSON and is there to help. Therefore, this person becomes your WITTING ALLY, as they are helping you get what you want from your HOT PERSON.)

UNWITTING ALLY: Think about the times you've been on a double date (a four-person scene). Who's the HOT PERSON? Your friend's date. The SCENE OBJECTIVE is *"to get you to choose me."* It won't work to use your own date as the HOT PERSON because you've already proven you can get that person to choose you. Getting your friend's date to choose you is more dramatically complex and interesting. First, you can prove to yourself and to your friend that not only can you get your own date to choose you but that you are attractive as well to your friend's date. Second, there's a danger element in going after your friend's date. You can lose your friendship and your date because of your flirtation. It's not that you ever have to take it any further than flirtation. You just want to know that you *can* win this SCENE OBJECTIVE, not that you ever intend to do anything about it. The flirtation itself raises the stakes, making the evening more provocative for you. And it's an ego boost if you accomplish your goal. Your date and your friend have become your UN-WITTING ALLIES in accomplishing your goal. Think about past double dates that you've been on. You'll see how it is generally true that we want what we can't or shouldn't have. It's human nature.

WITTING ALLY: Say the scene consists of you playing a con artist who specializes in the game of three-card monte. The HOT PERSON would be the mark, a.k.a. the person you're trying to scam out of his/her money. The SCENE OBJECTIVE would be *"to get you to love and trust me"* so they'll spend more money on the game. The shill is your WITTING ALLY, who will help gain the mark's trust for you by appearing to be a stranger who's winning money in your game.

WITTING ALLY: You are trying to sell a car to a customer and in order to do that, you can't let them know that is your OBJECTIVE. You must make that customer believe you have their best interests at heart. The sale of the car is incidental to making a new friend, or so you want the future car owner to believe. Your SCENE OBJECTIVE is *"to make you my new best friend."* When making the deal with the customer, you, as the salesperson, always need to go to the manager of the car dealership to confirm the great prices that you've been offering to the customer. The manager comes out and exclaims to the customer, "Wow, my salesman [you] must really like you, because these are wholesale prices. We are barely making any money on this!" Of course, the manager is your WITTING ALLY, helping you make the sale and his/her own percentage.

UNWITTING ALLY: In a similar scenario, you are trying to sell a car to a husband and wife. Again, the SCENE OBJECTIVE is *"to make you my new best friend."* The HOT PERSON would be the person that you glean is the person that makes the decisions in this couple. Say the wife doesn't make the decisions. This means you need to make her your ally and in this case an UNWITTING ALLY. You would find yourself enlisting the wife's allegiance to you by saying things to her like "Jeez, your husband is one great salesman. He's making me give this car away practically for free. You must be proud of your man. I gotta watch out, or he'll own the whole lot!" Then back to the husband (the HOT PERSON): "Your wife is a lucky lady, having you to make sure she's protected." Then to the two of them: "I really like you both. I usually don't do this, but let me give you the car for [an amount of money] and find out if my manager will back me up. I doubt it because he never lets deals like this happen. But you"—to the husband—"are one smart guy!" Then of course you go to the manager and gossip about the weather or some such thing. And then you come back in about fifteen minutes and exclaim with all the surprise you can muster, "That never happens. The manager must like you two as much as I like you. Welcome to your new automobile." Of course, the salesman makes back the money he claims to be giving away by adding to the sale all the bells and whistles like AC and special rims, etc.

In the world of procedurals—scripts that include police, detectives, FBI agents and such—there are often scenes with more than two people. Here's an example of the work I did with Emily Deschanel and David Boreanaz on the hit procedural show *Bones.* Working on a typical interrogation scene, we used the concepts of the HOT PERSON and the WITTING/UNWITTING ALLY to create a lively interaction that could transcend the tedium of listening to legalese and law enforcement terminology and make the scene entertaining.

Remember: There are rarely any new plots, so relationships are what audiences are most interested in. And relationships allow for unique realities, as there is only one you and you and you ad infinitum. Putting two unique realities together and letting them communicate will create an infinite number of possibilities for their exchanges.

Plot *Facilitates* the Growth and Evolvement of a Relationship

With that in mind, in the interrogation of a perp or witness, I often had Emily as Brennan and David as Booth make each other their HOT PERSON. And the perp or witness was the UNWITTING ALLY. I also contend that a good relationship, whether it be between lovers or friends, flourishes more when there's healthy competition. It is stimulating to spend time with that person who makes you raise your game because that person is equal if not better than you at playing the games of life. It's inspiring, as well, because it's energizing to compete with a worthy opponent. With that in mind, their SCENE OBJECTIVES were *"to be the winner over you"* regarding who asked the best questions and who retrieved the best answers in the interrogation du jour. The perp or witness had no idea that they were a part of the contest. Without the perp's or witness' knowledge, they ended up being a sort of (unaware) referee in a game that depended on their responses. It also created a fun and funny environment, as whoever won, Booth or Brennan, often gloated while the loser sulked or had a next-time-I'll-win attitude. Because we didn't follow the obvious formula of a procedural interrogation and made it more about exploring the characters' ever-growing love story, *Bones* lasted twelve years and is one of the most imitated procedurals internationally.

Utilizing the formula of the HOT PERSON and the WITTING/UNWITTING ALLY can also up the stakes and make even a small role with unexciting dialogue compelling. I worked with Eva Mendes when she was in the movie *Training Day*, in which she had only two scenes. One had seven uneventful lines (the niceties of an introduction) in less than two minutes, and the other had no lines at all and was just a quick shot of her running and being afraid. The scene with dialogue was a three-person scene. Eva played Sara,

Denzel Washington played Alonzo (her boyfriend) and Ethan Hawke played Jake. This is the scene:

TRAINING DAY
by David Ayer

SARA (O.S.)
(through the door)
Papi!

ALONZO
Mami.

(Sara opens the door.)

SARA
Hey, Papi.

(They kiss while Jake watches. They stop when it is obvious that Jake is uncomfortable.)

ALONZO
(to Sara, referring to Jake)
New guy Jake.

SARA
Hi, nice to meet you. Welcome to my house.

ALONZO
Get him some food, take care of him.

SARA
Of course. How are you?

(In the living room.)

SARA
(to Jake, handing him a TV remote)
I have cake. Watch whatever you want, okay? This is your house. I will be right back.

(Sara returns with some food on a tray.)

SARA
Now, this is all El Salvadorian food.

JAKE
Thank you, looks great.

> SARA
> I have to go.

(She exits.)

As you can see, it is not evident what makes this scene pop out. This is where the work can make even a small part special—special enough to turn this into a star-making part for Eva.

How we did this was by first making assumptions about Alonzo and Sara's relationship based on the rest of the script (most of which she was not in). Alonzo was often cruel to Jake, pushing things way too far and putting him in compromising positions. He was always testing Jake and often in an adversarial way. So we made the assumption that Alonzo was a difficult man for Sara to live with, as well as the assumption that perhaps his emotional abuse could become physical at times. We also assumed that Sara loved him very much, and this was why she stuck around. But she wanted him to feel that she was special and that he was lucky to have someone like her, or else she would have left. Sara dearly did not want to do that; she wanted her family unit to stay together. This made the stakes high and urgent, because if she couldn't get him to feel grateful to have her, she would have had to break up with him. By doing this kind of work, we made the scene significant. We made Sara's OVERALL OBJECTIVE *"to have value."* The SCENE OBJECTIVE was *"to make you jealous,"* where "you" was Alonzo (the HOT PERSON). We added the heat of the possibility that she could fail in her SCENE OBJECTIVE. The main OBSTACLE was if this didn't work, she'd be forced to leave him or he'd leave her. She loved him and their son and she did not want to split up their family.

Jake was the UNWITTING ALLY, the pawn that she would make fall in love with her to achieve her SCENE OBJECTIVE. She needed Alonzo to recognize that she was very attractive to Jake and that Alonzo was extremely lucky to have her. With the INNER MONOLOGUE *"See, Alonzo, how easy it was for me to get Jake to like me? So watch out. If you don't see how lucky you are to have me, I have options!"* (Of course, Eva also personalized this in her work, but in the interest of keeping her personal life private, the INNER MONOLOGUE you just read is from the character's POV). Making these choices upped this scene to being crucial in understanding Alonzo and the theme of the movie better. Alonzo wasn't the only one training someone; Sara was "training" him to be a better man and partner.

Never say that you don't need to do your script analysis work because you feel the role isn't big enough, meaty enough or well written enough. Do the steps, and you can raise any role to unexpected levels.

Bottom line: In scenes with three or more people, using the HOT PERSON–WITTING/UNWITTING ALLY system allows you to focus on one SCENE OBJECTIVE, which keeps you from the confusion of trying to recall many SCENE OBJECTIVES. The concepts of the HOT PERSON and of WITTING or UNWITTING ALLIES work from scenes with three people up to those with a stadium full of people.

PART IV

The Practical Application of the 12 Tools

Script Analysis
for *Uncle Vanya*
Using the 12 Tools

As with every script you will ever work with, you must first read the entire script. This is so you'll have the story's facts and details, which you'll need to inform the choices you'll make for the twelve acting tools. I know how easy it is to either read those oh-so-available CliffsNotes or quickly skim the material. But a more careful reading will inspire a deeper, more textured and distinct characterization.

An Overview of *Uncle Vanya*

Briefly, *Uncle Vanya* tells the story of Professor Alexander Serebriakov and his beautiful young wife, Yelena, who leave St. Petersburg, Russia, in the mid-1800s to settle on Alexander's late wife's country estate. For years, Sonya, the professor's daughter from his first marriage, and her uncle, Vanya, have lived and labored on the estate, accepting small wages and sending the bulk of their earnings to St. Petersburg to support Alexander and his studies.

Alexander and Yelena's arrival sends the estate into chaos, disrupting the daily routines of country life and sparking passions. Triangles of tension develop as the characters struggle with their frustrated desires and disillusionment. Vanya and his friend Astrov, the local doctor, vie for Yelena's attention, while Sonya and Yelena find themselves irresistibly attracted to Astrov.

The relevant facts surrounding a scene from Act III of *Uncle Vanya*.

The following are the key points that will be necessary for understanding how this scene fits into the arc of the play's story. These points include the actions immediately before and after this particular scene, along with the denouement of the story, which will help you understand where each character needs to go and what they need to win for there to be a resolution to their journeys.

- Uncle Vanya is Professor Alexander Serebriakov's brother-in-law from his first marriage. Since Alexander's wife died, Vanya has taken care of the family estate and Alexander's daughter.

- Astrov is a conscientious doctor whose bachelorhood and personal difficulties have made this once idealistic man cynical. He uses excess amounts of alcohol to numb his pain.

- Sonya, Alexander's daughter, is about the same age as his second wife, Yelena, and has been in love with Astrov for a long time. Astrov, however, has no interest in Sonya—it's Yelena he's after.

- Uncle Vanya and Astrov are both in love with the sexually charismatic Yelena.

- Yelena, who is clearly not in love with Alexander, pits Vanya and Astrov against each other to vie for her attention.

- ***Prior to this scene:*** Pretending to be Sonya's friend, Yelena persuades her stepdaughter to confide in her and trust her. Her mission, she tells Sonya, is to selflessly help Sonya create a relationship with Astrov. It would seem, however, that Yelena has a hidden agenda that is more selfishly motivated than what she's communicated to Sonya.

- ***In the following scene:*** Uncle Vanya catches Yelena and Astrov having a romantic interlude.

- ***After the following scene:*** If that's not enough, Vanya is enraged when Alexander attempts to sell the estate of his former wife, and he tries to kill his former brother-in-law.

• ***In the end:*** Alexander survives Vanya's lame attempt at murder. The entire household is torn asunder by Yelena's manipulations, and Alexander and Yelena move off the estate.

And now the scene to be analyzed . . .

UNCLE VANYA

by Anton Chekhov
(A scene from Act III)

ASTROV
[Enters with drawing]
Hello, I understand you wanted to see
some of my artistry?

YELENA
Yesterday, you assured me you would show
me your drawings. Are you available now?

ASTROV
I'd love to!

[He spreads the drawing on a nearby table and fixes it with tacks. She helps him.]

Where were you born?

YELENA
In Petersburg.

ASTROV
And where did you go to school?

YELENA
At the conservatory.

ASTROV
I doubt very much this will intrigue you in any way.

YELENA
Why not? You're right in assuming I don't
know much about the country, but I'm well-read.

ASTROV
Look here. It's a map of this area as it was
fifty years ago. The green color indicates the

forest. Half of the area was surfaced with
forest. Where you see the red over the green—
deer, wild goats and all sorts of wildlife were
prevalent. Look at the third part and you'll see my
rendition of how it is today. There's green, but it's
sporadic. There is no wildlife.
[Pause]
You might say it's progress and I'd agree if the
destroyed forests were making way for
factories or schools. But, no, there is a lot of
unusable muddied land filled with disease
and people who are destitute.

[He looks at her askance. . . .]

It seems to me that you have little interest
in any of this.

YELENA
No, it's simply that I don't comprehend much
of it.

ASTROV
It doesn't take much to comprehend it. I just
don't think you're all that interested.

YELENA
Please excuse my lack of concentration, as my
mind is someplace else. To be honest I wanted to
ask you something but I don't know how to begin.
[Pause]
It's a question about someone you know.
Like friends, let's talk, being totally open with
each other and then forget we ever had this
conversation. What do you say?

ASTROV
All right.

YELENA
It's about Sonya, my stepdaughter. What do
you think of her? Do you like her?

ASTROV
I can admire her spirit.

YELENA
But do you like her as a woman?

ASTROV
[Pause]
No.

YELENA
[Kissing his hand]
You don't love her. I can see that from your
eyes. You know, she's suffering. Try to
understand that you must stop coming here.
[Pause]
Ouch! I hate this. I feel like I've been carrying
the weight of the world on my shoulders. Anyway,
it's done, thank God, so now we can forget we
ever had this conversation and move on. You're a
smart man. I'm sure you realize why you must . . .
[Pause]
I feel all the blood rushing to my head.

ASTROV
If you had told me about her feelings a month or
two ago, I might have thought about it . . . but if
she is sick at heart because of me, then I guess
there's no other recourse. . . .
[Pause]
But tell me, why is it that *you* had to ask me?

[He looks at her a moment.]

Ohhhh, I get it!

YELENA
What are you talking about?

ASTROV
You know. Sure, Sonya may be in love, but
why is it you're asking the questions? Why do
you look so surprised? You know why I come
every day. You're very well aware of the effect
you have on me, you lovely "bird of prey."

YELENA
Bird of prey! What are you talking about?!

ASTROV
You are a gorgeous, frisky rascal . . . and I am
your victim. Well, you win. You can have me.

[He opens his arms and bows his head like a martyr on a cross.]

I give in. I'm here and ready to be consumed!

YELENA
Have you gone mad?!

ASTROV
Oh, you are so coy.

YELENA
I'm not as cunning or as cruel as you're making me
out to be. Honestly, I'm not.

[She tries to leave. Astrov rushes to block her way.]

ASTROV
I'll leave and I won't return. Just tell me . . .

[He takes her hand and glances about to see if anyone is looking.]

Where should we meet? Hurry, someone may catch
us—please tell me where.
[Whispering lustfully]
Your hair smells wonderful. One little kiss, please
let me kiss you.

YELENA
I beg of you . . .

ASTROV
[Stops her from talking]
No need to beg, I'm yours. You are so beautiful.
And your lovely hands, I need to kiss your hands.

[He kisses her hand.]

YELENA
Stop it, please stop . . . go . . .

[She pulls her hand away.]

ASTROV
You know it's inescapable. We are meant
to be together.

[He kisses her, and at that very moment, Uncle Vanya shows up,
carrying a dozen roses, and stops just inside the door. Neither
Astrov nor Yelena sees him.]

YELENA
Don't. We shouldn't be doing this. . . .

[She lays her head on Astrov's chest.]

ASTROV

At two o'clock meet me at the plantation. Promise
me you'll come.

[Yelena sees Vanya looking at them.]

YELENA

Let go of me!

*[She forcefully pulls away from Astrov. Then she goes to the
window.]*
[Muttering to herself]
This is just awful.

*[Vanya carefully puts the roses on a nearby chair. Yelena continues
to look out the window, trying to figure out what she's going to say
or do next, as Astrov looks painfully guilty and attempts to cover up.]*

Before We Begin Analyzing . . .

The following choices made in using each of the tools are suggestions. Because
acting is an art form, everything is subjective. There are no absolutes. As you
read and work with the twelve tools, use your imagination, your history and
your needs and incorporate your point of view.

AND ALWAYS, ALWAYS, ALWAYS WRITE IN PENCIL
DIRECTLY ON YOUR SCRIPT.

**You will write in pencil so your choices can be easily erased if/when you
change them to others that might be more effective.**

It is *critical* that you write directly on your script, putting the tools precisely
by the words or activities that they relate to. This way, as you memorize the
script and glance down to prompt yourself, you'll see the attached thoughts
and choices right away. As a result, you will be memorizing the words and
thoughts together, creating associations and relating the analysis accurately to
the story. If you put your notes on a different piece of paper, your brain will
compartmentalize them and the script as two separate entities, which would
make it difficult to infuse the inner work into the words on the scripted page.

Memorize your lines only after you've done your work.

If you memorize your lines before you've done your work, the dialogue will become a bunch of meaningless words strung together. When the meaning and intentions of the words are unclear, you can't help but memorize one way of saying the dialogue. You'll be doing a line reading and line readings will sound the same way every time you speak the dialogue. This kind of memorized interpretation is cemented in your mind, and like cement, it is extremely difficult to undo. Obviously, this memorized interpretation spoils any chance of spontaneity and truly living the role. On the other hand, if you apply the twelve acting tools first and then memorize your lines, the words will have associated information that will mean something personal to you, allowing organic impulses to emerge.

Tool #1: OVERALL OBJECTIVE

The character's life goal that is pursued throughout the entire script.

Yelena's OVERALL OBJECTIVE.

After having studied the script and gathering pertinent and specific information about Yelena, you must explore why such a beautiful young woman would marry such a crotchety old man. Perhaps for security? Alexander is old and not in very good health. Yelena stands to inherit money and freedom sooner than later. Maybe she has father issues and Alexander gives her the feeling of being with the father she never had.

You must also ask, "Why does Yelena move from the city where she was born and raised to a place she considers to be tedious and lackluster?" In the script, she often talks about being bored, yet when the others give her suggestions for activities, she has no interest in them. However, the country is a new arena in which she can wreak her own personal brand of havoc. Creating chaos and turmoil makes her feel alive. Taking risks and pushing the envelope make the adrenaline flow, make the blood pump faster and create an emotional roller coaster for her and those around her. Now, *that* is exciting! And they're also Yelena's ways of validating her existence. How?

She cruelly leads Uncle Vanya on with no intention whatsoever of making good on her "promises." She makes Sonya act on her feelings for Dr. Astrov, knowing full well that doing so is a fool's errand and Sonya is going to get hurt. Meanwhile, she competes with the naive Sonya for both Alexander's and Astrov's affections by making Sonya think she's her friend—creating even more chaos. Yelena is the catalyst for the climax of the story, which unhinges everyone's once safe relationships and leaves her husband virtually destroyed by all of her games and subterfuge. Why does Yelena do it?

We must assume that she is not an inherently evil person. So she must be motivated by extreme insecurities. In Russia in the 1890s, women didn't have opportunities to have careers to define themselves. They were defined by *if* they were married and *whom* they were married to. A smart woman had few outlets for her intelligence. For Yelena, domesticity is simply not enough. Moreover, Yelena doesn't have a sense of purpose. She is not a mother, she is in a loveless marriage and she has no job or passion or charity to pour herself into. As a result, she makes a lot of noise to feel like she is doing something. As if she were a bratty child acting out, getting attention—any attention, negative or positive—becomes the goal. Often, children who act out feel like they will disappear if they don't do something shocking or drastic (this is especially true for children with abandonment issues). Likewise, Yelena wreaks emotional destruction to feel a sense of life. She makes people fall in love with her and look up to her. This makes her feel empowered and gives her a sense of purpose and a reason to be alive. So . . .

Yelena's OVERALL OBJECTIVE

- *"Love, to get my power back."*

Astrov's OVERALL OBJECTIVE.

Astrov is a doctor in a rural community. He began his practice as a way to conquer diseases that were rampant there, yet he soon learned that he was helpless and that achieving his goal was hopeless. Since his efforts in medicine were without reward, he tried immersing himself in an effort to save the local ecology. Unfortunately, he also failed in curing the land of its modern ills. In short, the big changes Astrov was going to make for mankind never came to pass. After years of treating rich hypochondriacs, he has grown cynical and lonely and has resorted to alcohol to soothe his wounds.

Before Yelena's arrival, he would come to Vanya's home once a month. This all changes with Yelena's arrival. With her presence in the house, Astrov uses Alexander's frequent and mostly imaginary complaints of pain and disease as excuses for daily visits. Before Yelena, Astrov had all but given up hope that he would ever find love. His pessimism caused him to act in a surly manner and be overly critical and to drink enormous amounts of vodka.

Yelena changes his perspective. Because of his strong feelings for her (which are mostly manipulated by the lovely and calculating lady herself), Astrov feels romantic, hopeful and almost giddy. It also doesn't hurt his ego that Sonya reveals her long-term crush on him. In the end, Astrov is so hurt by Yelena's machinations that he proclaims to Vanya and Sonya (the remaining characters in the household) that he will not return for at least a year. The bottom line is that love has a huge effect on his life. We see how the lack of it causes him to be a cynical drunk, while the possibility of love causes him to feel hopeful and industrious. So . . .

Astrov's OVERALL OBJECTIVE

- *"Love, to find purpose."*

As you look over the elements of your character's life circumstances and goals, always be attentive to how they can be emotionally translated into those of your own.

Tool #2: SCENE OBJECTIVE

The goal that your character would like to achieve over the course of an individual scene. It must support the goal of the OVERALL OBJECTIVE.

Yelena's SCENE OBJECTIVE.

Facts of the scene that affect Yelena:

1. Yelena doesn't have much interest in Astrov's drawings or in his enthusiasm for forestry and ecology.
2. What seems to appeal to Yelena as a prime topic of conversation is anything about and for Yelena. Even when she talks to Astrov about Sonya, it's a way to make him say he doesn't want Sonya but instead yearns for her.
3. Yelena may say no to Astrov's advances, but her behavior goads him and gives him the kind of mixed signals that have plagued men for centuries: "There's 'no, no' in your words but 'yes, yes' in your eyes."
4. Yelena is married to someone she doesn't love.
5. Yelena knows that Vanya is in love with her (as well she should know—after all, she made it happen).

In supporting Yelena's OVERALL OBJECTIVE *"love, to get my power back,"* it would make sense that Yelena's SCENE OBJECTIVE would be *"to get you (Astrov) to fall in love with me."* While this might also be Astrov's SCENE OBJECTIVE, because he is truly in love with her, Yelena would go after Astrov's heart to have power over him, which would make her feel alive and validated. Making Astrov fall in love with her will make Yelena his reason for being as well as someone he's willing to destroy his life for. This enables her to become a person of great consequence. We know she doesn't love him, because when she has the option to leave her much richer husband at the end of the story, she chooses to stay with him and move on in her life's journey to another locale and make more unsuspecting men fall for her. In order for Yelena to give herself a feeling of significance that validates her existence, the following choice would be logical for . . .

Yelena's SCENE OBJECTIVE

- *"To get you to fall in love with me to get my power back."*

Astrov's SCENE OBJECTIVE.

Facts of the scene that affect Astrov:

1. Astrov shows off his drawings and his erudite concerns about ecology as a way for him to impress Yelena.
2. He blurts out, in a moment of weakness, that he comes to the house only to see her. His obvious romantic and sexual intentions for her create awkward, I-like-you-too-much behavior.
3. Astrov wants a love relationship, one that he's never had before.
4. He's lonely and desperate because he feels that Yelena may be his last chance to find love.
5. Yelena is married and Astrov's good friend is in love with her, too, which makes getting her to love him complicated and problematic.

You could look at all the sexuality in the scene and say that Astrov's SCENE OBJECTIVE could be *"to get you to have sex with me,"* but that would undermine his life's intentions as stated in his OVERALL OBJECTIVE of *"love, to find purpose."* If sex were all he desired, he could easily bed Sonya, who has behaved like a lovesick schoolgirl for a long time. Additionally, Astrov mentions throughout the script how much he doesn't want to be alone anymore, but he just can't find the right woman. That is, until . . . Yelena. Being married, Yelena also has the draw of being forbidden fruit, which always makes someone or something more desirable. Thus . . .

Astrov's SCENE OBJECTIVE

- *"To get you to fall in love with me."*

***The SCENE OBJECTIVE must always support the OVERALL
OBJECTIVE and be worded in a way to get a response.***

Tool #3: OBSTACLES

The physical, emotional and mental hurdles and
conflicts that prevent the SCENE OBJECTIVE from being
accomplished, thereby making the quest more exciting and fulfilling.

Yelena's OBSTACLES.

Some of the OBSTACLES getting in the way of Yelena's SCENE OBJECTIVE,
"to get you to fall in love with me to get my power back," are:

1. Possible rejection.
2. Yelena is married.
3. Sonya, Yelena's stepdaughter, is in love with Astrov.
4. Vanya—Yelena's husband's brother-in-law and Astrov's good friend—is in love with her.
5. Yelena has zero interest in ecology, which Astrov loves.
6. She comes from the city. Astrov comes from the country. She has very little in common with Astrov. And she has no interest in what someone from the country has to offer anyway.
7. Yelena has an extremely competitive nature. When it comes to competition, she likes the stakes to be high—in this case, competing with Sonya for Astrov.
8. She might get caught by Alexander, her husband; Sonya, her stepdaughter and professed new best friend; Vanya, Astrov's friend, her husband's brother-in-law and a man who is dangerously enamored of her; or any combination thereof.
9. She does get caught.

Astrov's OBSTACLES.

Some of the OBSTACLES getting in the way of Astrov's SCENE OBJECTIVE,
"to get you to fall in love with me," are:

1. Possible rejection.
2. Astrov is in love with Yelena. (As we all know, being in love has inherent OBSTACLES.)

3. Yelena is married.

4. Astrov has never had a long-term relationship and is naive.

5. Sonya is in love with Astrov and could pose a problem.

6. Astrov's best friend, Vanya, also wants Yelena.

7. His drinking problem.

8. Desperation. (Desperation always creates strange and unwanted behavior.)

9. Social and educational disparity.

10. Astrov's cynical nature.

11. A guilty conscience.

Never, ever give up on going after your SCENE OBJECTIVE,
even if the OBSTACLES seem impossible to overcome.

Tool #4: SUBSTITUTION

**Endowing the other actor/character with someone from your own life that
inspires a personal need to accomplish your character's SCENE OBJECTIVE.**

Keep in mind that when you are making a SUBSTITUTION choice, it must
create a personal desire to win, because the SUBSTITUTION contains the appropriate history and inherent OBSTACLES that relate to your character's predicament. Pick someone necessary and difficult, because if you can get your
SCENE OBJECTIVE too easily from your SUBSTITUTION choice, the journey will be uneventful.

Do not judge or moralize in picking a SUBSTITUTION.

Acting is an arena where you can be evil, immoral and manipulative, because
it's not real. It is your fantasy life having a field day. Don't censor yourself. This
art form is just about the only place where you can legitimately do what you'd
never dare do in your real life. So enjoy it.

The following suggestions are merely a few in an infinite field of possibilities. SUBSTITUTION choices are as varied and numerous as your life experiences. Come up with a few choices that are logical; then think outside the box and come up with some that make less sense.

Yelena's Astrov SUBSTITUTION.

Ask yourself the questions "From whom in my life do I want to win my SCENE OBJECTIVE, *'to get you to fall in love with me to get my power back'*? Who in my life inspires the need to play games and take risks and has inherently charged OBSTACLES?" Also try an INFORMATIONAL EMOTIONAL DIARY using the SCENE OBJECTIVE as a prompt. *"I need you to fall in love with me to get my power back, **name**, because . . ."*

SUBSTITUTION suggestions:

- **Your ex-mate:** There's a reason why this person is no longer in your life. Lying, cheating, constant condescension and abuse are all good reasons to play games as payback for all the games that were originally played on you. The risk is that through all of your manipulations you can very well fall in love with him again, making this strategy a dangerous walk to walk. Think of the people who could walk in on you: your present mate, a disapproving parent or friend, your ex-mate's friend or family member who never liked you, etc.
- **Your friend's mate:** Perhaps you have a friend who has in some way been cruel to you. We've all had a friend (past or present) like this. It may be your masochism, but this person nevertheless deserves some sort of game that gives you some power reversal. Going after your friend's mate and getting him to fall in love with you would do just that. The risk is the loss of that friendship and perhaps the loss of other friends who might learn about your behavior and would no longer trust you. The uninvited guests who might walk in could be the friend, your other friends who would be appalled or your present mate.

- **Your boss, teacher, director, producer (people in positions of authority):** People in positions of authority often abuse them. If this has happened to you, all bets are on. This person deserves some righteous game playing and manipulation of the heart. Possible choices for the dangerous interrupter could be your mate, the authority figure's mate, another student or employee, etc.
- **Your extended-family member (cousin, uncle, stepfather, brother-in-law, etc.):** These are not immediate-family members and using them isn't as reprehensible as, say, using a blood father or brother, but doing so is still considered amoral and a social no-no. Yet if a member of your extended family has in some way hurt you (or the family member that this person is attached to has caused you emotional pain), then all of your calculating manipulation will feel absolutely justified. The intruder could be another family member, the family member that this person is attached to, your present mate, etc.
- **A friend you're attracted to:** You know the friend I'm talking about—the one you've always been attracted to but are afraid to pursue for fear that the friendship will be lost. There are intrinsic power issues in this particular kind of friendship because the friend usually knows and often feels the same attraction. Whether this friend fails to act out of fear or because withholding gives them power doesn't matter—you feel as though they have too much power over you. Those who could walk in and cause heart failure could be another friend who knows both of you, your mate, his mate, etc.

Astrov's Yelena SUBSTITUTION.

Ask yourself the questions "From whom in my life do I want to win my SCENE OBJECTIVE, *'to get you to fall in love with me'*? Who in my life would make a relationship feel forbidden, guilty and full of a sense of unrequited love?" Also try an INFORMATIONAL EMOTIONAL DIARY with the prompt, *"My love for you makes me feel guilty, **name**, because . . ."*

SUBSTITUTION suggestions:

• **Your ex-mate:** Whatever issue caused this person to become an ex is always present. It's unlikely that this person has changed much, and the ugliness of the past is bound to rear its head. We all know this, yet most of us ignore probability for the tiny possibility that they've seen the error of their ways and have changed. The more wrong this relationship seems to be, the more we want it. This makes the ex feel forbidden, which makes you feel stupid for wanting them so badly, which makes you feel guilty and the love unrequited (ah, human nature rearing its ugly head). Those who can come upon you unaware and cause you distress might be your present mate, your family members or friends who never liked this person in your life, etc.

• **Your student, your employee or your stepchild:** When you are in a position of authority, it is considered inappropriate, sometimes even illegal, to take advantage of the person over whom you have power. You can be reviled and ostracized by the people you care about, because they simply don't understand that your love for your student, employee or stepchild is deep and that it transcends convention. This doesn't negate your feelings of guilt or the fact that this kind of love is forbidden. Those who can interrupt . . . Well, just about anyone would be a problem in these circumstances.

• **A man to whom you're attracted:** If you're straight and you find yourself attracted to or even obsessed with a man, your attraction will bring up organic feelings of the forbidden and guilt, and because of societal stigma, it will be unrequited. Bottom line: It would be damn scary to pursue the SCENE OBJECTIVE from this SUBSTITUTION, making it a powerful choice. Problem interceders—anyone.

• **A woman who's financially, socially, intellectually or age-wise "out of your league":** If a woman makes more money, is more attractive, is more educated or is from a substantially higher socioeconomic background than you, she can be extremely intimidating and emasculating. You might wonder if by pursuing her you're silently and secretly being viewed as a buffoon by your friends and family. However, you'll do anything and everything to get this person to fall in love with you—no matter how extreme the disparity—because, on another level, doing so will boost your ego. Those who can enter without invitation who might be problematic: any friend or family member who feels you're reaching too high, your present mate, her friends or family that look down on you, etc.

• **Your friend's mate, your stepmother, your sister-in-law (anyone attached to someone you love):** This choice would fall into the category of "you're not supposed to go there." Your guilt for this forbidden and probably unrequited desire is obvious, but that doesn't stop you from the pursuit—because love might conquer all, as it's supposed to. That is, if she loves you back, which she might not, and then all will be lost because you'll lose her *and* the loved one whom she's attached to. Those whose presence would be risky: the loved one that she is attached to; other family members; your present mate; a friend who would disapprove; your preacher or rabbi, who would call you immoral; etc.

Personalizing OBSTACLES considering your SUBSTITUTION choice.

Once you've selected and tried a few people from your life as possible SUBSTITUTION choices and have found a SUBSTITUTION that works, you must go back through the script and personalize your character's OBSTACLES as they relate to this person. The personalization of OBSTACLES will be innately determined from the SUBSTITUTION you end up using in the scene. This means that if you change your SUBSTITUTION, you must accordingly change your personalizations.

When personalizing your OBSTACLES, make vivid and in-depth choices—be specific and detailed when infusing personal information into your OBSTACLES. This will create an intensified struggle to accomplish your SCENE OBJECTIVE, because you will be hyperaware of precisely what will happen if you don't win.

Tool #5: INNER OBJECTS

**These are the visuals attached to the people, places, things or events
from your own life that you think about when you or
the other character(s) are talking about
the script's people, places, things or events.**

INNER OBJECTS are pictures, not words. Picturing these personal images of people, places, things and events creates *real* associations for the words that you speak and listen to. The inner work you've done thus far will help you define your INNER OBJECT choices. Also, make sure your INNER OBJECTS have inherent OBSTACLES (this is true for all the acting tools). If your INNER OBJECT choices aren't infused with history and a highly charged conflict, then the images you've created will not come forward naturally when it's time for you to perform.

Here are some possible INNER OBJECT choices for *Uncle Vanya*. Again, as with all the tools we've discussed so far, these are merely suggestions to help inspire a deeper understanding of the technique and to guide you to come up with your own ideas. The INNER OBJECTS that most affect you will be unique to who you are as a person. Always make choices based on *your* life experiences.

For the purposes of the book and so that you can fully understand how INNER OBJECTS operate, the *Uncle Vanya* dialogue that needs INNER OB-JECTS will be *underlined*, and my list of possible choices for the INNER OBJECTS will be *handwritten*. While you will see a list here, you will in practice handwrite in pencil only *one* choice directly under the word that needs an INNER OBJECT. If you change your INNER OBJECT during the rehearsal process, erase and replace the original choice with the new choice. Once again, this must be written directly beneath the scripted word that needs an INNER OBJECT (the same way it was illustrated in part I, tool #5, in the scene from *The Importance of Being Earnest*).

INNER OBJECTS from Yelena's P.O.V.

UNCLE VANYA

by Anton Chekhov
(A scene from Act III)

ASTROV
[Enters with drawing]
Hello, I understand you wanted to see some of my
<u>artistry</u>?

"... <u>drawing</u> ... <u>artistry</u>" =
Think about your SUBSTITUTION for Astrov. What subject is he obsessed with?
What topic that utterly bores you does he go on and on about?
• The mayoral campaign in Juneau, Alaska
• The Free the Ferrets Act
• Ecology
• Stock futures

YELENA
Yesterday, you assured me you would show me
your <u>drawings</u>. Are you available now?

"... <u>drawings</u>." =
Same INNER OBJECT as above.

ASTROV
I'd love to!

*[He spreads the drawing on a nearby table and fixes it with
stickpins. She helps him.]*

Where were you born?

YELENA
In Petersburg.

"... <u>Petersburg</u>." =
You have to choose an INNER OBJECT visual of a place that your SUBSTITUTION
for Astrov might be intimidated by. This doesn't have to be a city, state or country
where you actually grew up. It could be where you reside today or a section of the
city you live in that is socially or economically superior to where your
SUBSTITUTION for Astrov lives. You have to also be aware of how your
SUBSTITUTION for Astrov will be distressed when he makes the comparison to his
life.
• Beverly Hills (he lives in "the Valley")
• Manhattan (he's from the Bronx)

• Suburbs (he's from the ghetto)
• A large house (he lives in a one-room apartment with a hot plate)
• No roommates (he has several)

> **ASTROV**
> And where did you go to <u>school</u>?

> **YELENA**
> At the <u>conservatory</u>.

"... <u>school</u> ... <u>conservatory</u>." =
Your INNER OBJECT picture must be something that will make your
SUBSTITUTION for Astrov appear less educated, intelligent or savvy. It's an
additional OBSTACLE for you to overcome, because at the same time you want to
impress Astrov, you certainly don't want to emasculate him. Both "good news and
bad" reside in this answer.

• An Ivy League university (he went to City College, or didn't get a B.A.)
• A private school for the gifted (he went to public school)
• Street smarts from the school of hard knocks (he comes from a naive suburban
  upbringing)
• The same school as SUBSTITUTION for Astrov but getting better grades or
  taking accelerated classes
• A big shot at a big conglomerate (he's got a small position in a small company)

> **ASTROV**
> I doubt very much this will intrigue you in any way.

> **YELENA**
> Why not? You're right in assuming I don't know
> much about <u>the country</u>, but I'm well-read.

"... <u>the country</u> ..." =
The same INNER OBJECT visuals you used for "<u>drawings</u>" and "<u>artistry</u>."

> **ASTROV**
> Look here. It's a <u>map of this area</u> as it was <u>fifty
> years ago</u>. The green color indicates the <u>forest</u>.
> Half of the area was surfaced with <u>forest</u>. Where
> you see the red over the green—<u>deer, wild goats
> and all sorts of wildlife</u> were prevalent. Look at the
> third part and you'll see my rendition of how it is
> today. There's green, but it's sporadic. There is <u>no
> wildlife</u>.
> *[Pause]*
> You might say it's progress and I'd agree if the
> <u>destroyed forests</u> were making way for <u>factories or</u>

schools. But, no, there is a lot of <u>unusable muddied land filled with disease</u> and <u>people who are destitute</u>.

Now you have to fill in the details of the topic you've chosen that motivates your SUBSTITUTION for Astrov's passion and your need to take a nap. Let's use "U.S. politicians" as the subject that you find dull. As you hear the script's words, you'll perceive the meaning as follows:

• "... <u>map of this area</u> ..." =
A diagram of the history of high-powered U.S. politicians, including what their accomplishments and disgraces were.
• "... <u>fifty years ago</u> ..." =
Two hundred fifty years ago, America's beginnings.
• "... <u>forest</u> ... <u>deer, wild goats and all sorts of wildlife</u> ..." =
Freedom of speech, freedom of religion, etc.
• "... <u>no wildlife</u> ..." =
No truth or integrity in politics and politicians.
• "... <u>destroyed forests</u> ..." =
Destructive political scandals.
• "... <u>factories or schools</u> ..." =
Helping poor people.
• "... <u>unusable muddied land filled with disease</u> ..." =
Ghettos and poor areas.
• "... <u>people who are destitute</u>." =
Poor people, drug addicts, the homeless.

    [He looks at her askance. . . .]

ASTROV
It seems to me that you have little interest in any of this.

YELENA
No, it's simply that I don't comprehend much of it.

ASTROV
It doesn't take much to comprehend it. I just don't think you're all that interested.

YELENA
Please excuse my lack of concentration, as my mind is someplace else. To be honest I wanted to <u>ask you something</u> but I don't know how to begin.
    [Pause]

It's <u>a question about someone you know</u>. Like friends, let's talk, being totally open with each other and then forget we ever had this conversation. What do you say?

"... <u>ask you something</u> ... <u>a question about someone you know</u>." =
Although Sonya's name isn't stated in the text, she must be an INNER OBJECT here because she is the subject of Yelena's mysterious question. Obviously, your INNER OBJECT visual for Sonya is the SUBSTITUTION you're using for Sonya.

> ASTROV
> All right.

> YELENA
> It's about <u>Sonya, my stepdaughter</u>. What do you think of her? Do you like her?

"... <u>Sonya, my stepdaughter</u>." =
Same INNER OBJECT for Sonya.

> ASTROV
> I can admire her spirit.

> YELENA
> But do you like her as <u>a woman</u>?

"... <u>a woman</u>" =
Sex.

> ASTROV
> *[Pause]*
> No.

> YELENA
> *[Kissing his hand]*
> You don't love her. I can see that from your eyes. You know, she's suffering. Try to understand that you must stop coming <u>here</u>.

Your SUBSTITUTION for Astrov will determine what your INNER OBJECT will be. According to the circumstances you have created, where are you?

"... <u>here</u>." =
• My home
• My office
• My school
• My family's home
• My boyfriend's home

[Pause]
Ouch! I hate this. I feel like I've been carrying the
weight of the world on my shoulders. Anyway, it's
done, thank God, so now we can forget we ever
had this conversation and move on. You're a smart
man. I'm sure you realize why you must . . .
[Pause]
I feel all the <u>blood rushing to my head</u>.

"*. . . <u>blood rushing to my head</u>.*" =
• *Sexually turned on (picture favorite sex act with Astrov)*
• *Dizzy and feeling faint (and if I faint, I can legitimately fall into his*
  arms. . . .)

ASTROV
If you had told me about her feelings a month or
two ago, I might have thought about it . . . but if
she is sick at heart because of me, then I guess
there's no other recourse. . . .
[Pause]
But tell me, why is it that *you* had to ask me?

[He looks at her a moment.]

Ohhhh, I get it!

YELENA
What are you talking about?

ASTROV
You know. Sure, Sonya may be in love, but why is it
you're asking the questions? Why do you look so
surprised? You know why I come every day. You're
very well aware of the effect you have on me, you
lovely "<u>bird of prey</u>."

YELENA
<u>Bird of prey</u>! What are you talking about?!

"*. . . <u>bird of prey</u>.*" =
Again, Astrov is being ambiguous. Let the paranoid possibilities run wild.
• *Two-faced*
• *Untrustworthy*
• *A liar*
• *Vulturelike*
• *A slut*
• *Weasellike*

ASTROV
You are a gorgeous, frisky rascal . . . and I am your
victim. Well, you win. You can have me.

[He opens his arms and bows his head like a martyr on a cross.]

I give in. I'm here and ready to be consumed!

YELENA
Have you gone mad?!

ASTROV
Oh, you are so <u>coy</u>.

"... <u>coy</u>." =
• A liar
• Sneaky
• Slutty
• Two-faced
• A game player

YELENA
I'm not as cunning or as cruel as you're making me
out to be. Honestly, I'm not.

[She tries to leave. Astrov rushes to block her way.]

ASTROV
I'll leave and I won't return. Just tell me . . .

[He takes her hand and glances about to see if anyone is looking.]

Where should we meet? Hurry, someone may catch
us—please tell me where.
[Whispering lustfully]
Your <u>hair smells wonderful</u>. One little kiss, please
<u>let me kiss you</u>.

"... <u>hair smells wonderful</u>." =
• My perfume
• My natural scent
• My shampoo

"... <u>let me kiss you</u>." =
The INNER OBJECT here is a vivid and specific "sexual" fantasy that would motivate
a heightened sexuality in you—a fantasy visual that is so titillating that part of

the OBSTACLE is not being able to stay in control of your sexual urges. Therefore, there is the possibility of going further than you ever intended to go.

YELENA

I beg of you . . .

ASTROV

[Stops her from talking]
No need to beg, I'm yours. You are so beautiful.
And your lovely <u>hands</u>, I need to <u>kiss your hands</u>.

[He kisses her hands.]

". . . <u>hands</u> . . . <u>kiss your hands</u>. "(and the INNER OBJECT attached to the act of kissing the hands) =
The pictured fantasy has to get more illicit, the hands symbolizing the part of your body that is most sensitive. When he talks about your hands and kisses your hands, you are fantasizing that he's actually doing it to the part of your body that is most easily stimulated.
• Nibbling my neck
• Licking the inside of my knees
• Sucking my fingers or toes
• Nibbling my ears
• Kissing my inner thighs

YELENA

Stop it, please stop . . . go . . .

[She pulls her hand away.]

ASTROV

You know it's inescapable. We are meant to be
together.

*[He kisses her, and at that very moment, Uncle Vanya shows up,
carrying a dozen roses, and stops just inside the door. Neither
Astrov nor Yelena sees him.]*

YELENA

Don't. <u>We shouldn't be doing this</u>. . . .

"<u>We shouldn't be doing this</u>. . . ." =
The INNER OBJECT here is the visual image that expresses the danger of your personal circumstances if you get caught. . . .
• Divorce
• Loss of job

- Death or maiming
- No future job
- Expulsion
- Loss of family
- Loss of children
- Loss of friends
- Alone forever

[She lays her head on Astrov's chest.]

ASTROV
At two o'clock meet me at the plantation.
Promise me you'll come.

"... the plantation." =
Use an INNER OBJECT visual of a place that will make sense for you and your
SUBSTITUTION for Astrov to have a private meeting.

- His home
- A local park
- A friend's home
- His or my office
- A specific hotel or motel room
- An empty classroom

[Yelena sees Vanya looking at them.]

YELENA
Let go of me!

[She forcefully pulls away from Astrov. Then she goes to the window.]

[Muttering to herself]
This is just awful.

[Vanya carefully puts the roses on a nearby chair. Yelena continues to look out the window, trying to figure out what she's going to say or do next, as Astrov looks painfully guilty and attempts to cover up.]

INNER OBJECTS from Astrov's P.O.V.

UNCLE VANYA

by Anton Chekhov
(A scene from Act III)

ASTROV
[Enters with <u>drawing</u>]
Hello, I understand you wanted to see some of my
<u>artistry</u>?

"... <u>drawing</u> ... <u>artistry</u>" =
Choose an INNER OBJECT picture that displays what you are personally
passionate about, because these are drawings to help illustrate Astrov's long-term
passion for ecology.

• The Detroit Red Wings
• Democratic politics
• Government programs for the mentally handicapped
• Born-again Christianity
• PETA

YELENA
Yesterday, you assured me you would show me
your <u>drawings</u>. Are you available now?

"... <u>drawings</u>." =
Same as above.

ASTROV
I'd love to!

[He spreads the drawing on a nearby table and fixes it with
stickpins. She helps him.]

Where were you born?

YELENA
In <u>Petersburg</u>.

"... <u>Petersburg</u>." =
The INNER OBJECT picture here is a place that intimidates you in some way. It
doesn't have to be a place where your SUBSTITUTION for Yelena was born. It can
be where she lives now, or a state-of-mind place that makes you feel less than
confident.

• New York City (versus my coming from Hicksville)
• Her high-powered career (versus my serving fries at McDonald's)

- Upper-class (versus my lower-middle-class upbringing)
- Her wealth (versus my poverty)
- Her fame / famous family (versus my average anonymous self/family)

ASTROV
And where did you go to <u>school</u>?

YELENA
At the <u>conservatory</u>.

"... <u>school</u> ... <u>conservatory</u>." =
Here choose an INNER OBJECT visual that makes you feel less educated,
intelligent or socially equal.
- Harvard (versus my vocational school)
- Graduated magna cum laude (versus my barely passing)
- Coming from a famous family that knows the joys of nepotism (versus my not
  being able to even get a cup of sugar from the trailer parked next door)
- A private school for the gifted (versus my trying to get into the same school and
  their refusing to take me)

ASTROV
I doubt very much this will intrigue you in any way.

YELENA
Why not? You're right in assuming I don't know
much about <u>the country</u>, but I'm well-read.

"... <u>the country</u> ..." =
The same INNER OBJECT images you used for "<u>drawings</u>."

ASTROV
Look here. It's a <u>map of this area as it was fifty</u>
<u>years ago</u>. The green color indicates the <u>forest</u>.
Half of the area was <u>surfaced with forest</u>. Where
you see the red over the green—<u>deer, wild goats</u>
<u>and all sorts of wildlife</u> were <u>prevalent</u>. Look at the
third part and you'll see my rendition of how it is
today. There's green, but it's sporadic. There is <u>no</u>
<u>wildlife</u>.
[Pause]
You might say it's progress and I'd agree if the
<u>destroyed forests</u> were <u>making way for factories or</u>
<u>schools</u>. But, no, there is <u>a lot of unusable muddied</u>
<u>land filled with disease and people who are</u>
<u>destitute</u>.

You have to match the images described in the text to images that correlate to the topic you have chosen. Example: using the issue of the mishandling of the mentally handicapped.

- ... <u>map of this area as it was fifty years ago</u> ... <u>forest</u> ... <u>surfaced with forest</u> ..." =
A diagram of social programming the way it was forty years ago when social programming was fully funded by the government and the mentally handicapped were being taken care of.

- "... <u>deer, wild goats and all sorts of wildlife</u> ... <u>prevalent</u> ..." =
Various government social programs were prevalent.

- "... <u>no wildlife</u> ... <u>destroyed forests</u> ... <u>making way for factories or schools</u> ... <u>a lot of unusable muddied land filled with disease and people who are destitute.</u>" =
No government-subsidized social programs. Large corporations run the world. Social programs have been destroyed. The mentally handicapped are left homeless and destitute.

You can take any topic that you are obsessed with, as you will have many facts and figures at your fingertips to which you can correlate the words in the script with pictures from your personal issue.

[He looks at her askance. . . .]

> ASTROV
> It seems to me that you have little interest in any of this.

> YELENA
> No, it's simply that I don't comprehend much of it.

> ASTROV
> It doesn't take much to comprehend it. I just don't think you're all that interested.

> YELENA
> Please excuse my lack of concentration, as my mind is someplace else. To be honest I wanted to <u>ask you something</u> but I don't know how to begin.
> *[Pause]*
> It's a <u>question about someone you know</u>. Like friends, let's talk, being totally open with each other and then forget we ever had this conversation. What do you say?

"... <u>ask you something</u> ... <u>question about someone you know</u>." =
Think of your SUBSTITUTION for Yelena. What possible question would make
sense as being something that she would ask as well as being something that
would disquiet you? As part of the INNER OBJECT visual, you have to deal
with the great possibility that she might know something about you that is
revealing, humiliating or disparaging (don't forget the human-paranoia
factor). Your "skeleton in the closet" might very well be the topic of the question
that she's taking oh so long to ask. The INNER OBJECT pictures would be of
you engaged in the activity you don't want to expose by answering her
question.

Yelena's question possibilities =

• "(Are you) an alcoholic?"

• "(Do you like to) torture small animals?"

• "(Are you) sexually perverted (specify your perversion of choice)?"

• "(Have you ever) been in prison?"

• "(Do you have a history of) beating up on women?"

ASTROV
All right.

YELENA
It's about <u>Sonya, my stepdaughter</u>. What do you
think of her? Do you like her?

"... <u>Sonya, my stepdaughter</u>." =
Your SUBSTITUTION for Sonya.

ASTROV
I can admire her spirit.

YELENA
But do you like her as <u>a woman</u>?

"... <u>a woman</u>" =
Sex.

ASTROV
[Pause]
No.

YELENA
[Kissing his hand]
You don't love her. I can see that from your eyes.
You know, she's suffering. Try to understand that
you must stop coming <u>here</u>.

"... _here_." =
This INNER OBJECT picture would be the place that you've been visiting too frequently to see your SUBSTITUTION for Yelena; that location contains some kind of risk if you have to stop showing up there.

• Your SUBSTITUTION for Yelena's home (which means you'll never see her again)
• Your SUBSTITUTION for Yelena's relative's home
• Your SUBSTITUTION for Yelena's workplace (and if you work in the same place, that means you have to quit and be jobless)
• The school you both attend (which means you have to drop out of school)
• Your friend's (SUBSTITUTION for Vanya) home (which means you will lose your friend)

> *[Pause]*
> Ouch! I hate this. I feel like I've been carrying the weight of the world on my shoulders. Anyway, it's done, thank God, so now we can forget we ever had this conversation and move on. You're a smart man. I'm sure you realize why you must . . .
> *[Pause]*
> I feel all the blood rushing to my head.

"I _feel all the blood rushing to my head_." =
This could have many meanings. The INNER OBJECT images here are the different possibilities, both wishful and fearful, for what she means by that.

• Sexually turned on
• Uncomfortable
• Needs to vomit

> ASTROV
> If you had told me about her feelings a month or two ago, I might have thought about it . . . but if she is sick at heart because of me, then I guess there's no other recourse. . . .
> *[Pause]*
> But tell me, why is it that *you* had to ask me?

> *[He looks at her a moment.]*

> Ohhhh, I get it!

> YELENA
> What are you talking about?

> ASTROV
> You know. Sure, Sonya may be in love, but why is it you're asking the questions? Why do you look so

surprised? You know why I come every day. You're very well aware of the effect you have on me, you lovely "<u>bird of prey</u>."

"... <u>bird of prey</u>." =
- *An elegant swan*
- *A feral animal*
- *A witch*
- *A heartbreaker*
- *A sexual manipulator*

YELENA
Bird of prey! What are you talking about?!

ASTROV
You are a <u>gorgeous, frisky rascal</u> ... and I am your victim. Well, you win. You can have me.

"... <u>gorgeous, frisky rascal</u> ..." =
Same as above

[*He opens his arms and bows his head like a martyr on a cross.*]

I give in. I'm here and ready to be <u>consumed</u>!

"... <u>consumed</u>" =
- *Kissing*
- *Foreplay*
- *Oral sex*
- *Full-out sex*
- *Deviant sex that is geared toward your predilection*
- *A nonsexual expression of love (e.g., Yelena's loving words, hugging, kiss on the cheek, etc.)*

YELENA
Have you gone mad?!

ASTROV
Oh, you are so coy.

YELENA
I'm not as cunning or as cruel as you're making me out to be. Honestly, I'm not.

[*She tries to leave. Astrov rushes to block her way.*]

ASTROV
I'll leave and I won't return. Just tell me . . .

[He takes her hand and glances about to see if anyone is looking.]

Where should we meet? Hurry, someone may catch
us—please tell me where.
[Whispering lustfully]
Your <u>hair smells wonderful</u>. One little kiss, please
let me kiss you.

"*. . . <u>hair smells wonderful</u>.*" =
• *A strawberry scent*
• *Her natural body smell*
• *A favorite perfume*
• *A sexy musk smell*
• *A favorite food smell*

YELENA
I beg of you . . .

ASTROV
[Stops her from talking]
No need to beg, I'm yours. You are so beautiful.
And <u>your lovely hands, I need to kiss your hands</u>.

"*. . . <u>your lovely hands, I need to kiss your hands</u>.*" =
*Picture your favorite sexual activity that uses your favorite female body part as
your INNER OBJECT when you are looking at Yelena's hands. This way you truly
will need to "kiss" her hands.*

[He kisses her hands.]

YELENA
Stop it, please stop . . . go . . .

[She pulls her hand away.]

ASTROV
Tell me, where do you want to meet tomorrow?
You know it's inescapable. We are meant to be
together.

*[He kisses her, and at that very moment, Uncle Vanya shows up,
carrying a dozen roses, and stops just inside the door. Neither
Astrov nor Yelena sees him.]*

> YELENA
> Don't. We shouldn't be doing this. . . .

[She lays her head on Astrov's chest.]

> ASTROV
> At two o'clock meet me at the plantation. Promise
> me you'll come.

. . . the plantation." =
Consider your SUBSTITUTION for Yelena, and picture a place that would make
sense for you to meet your SUBSTITUTION.

• My home

• A local beach

• My parents' home

• A particular hotel or motel room

• Under the football field's bleachers at our school

[Yelena sees Vanya looking at them.]

> YELENA
> Let go of me!

*[She forcefully pulls away from Astrov. Then she goes to the
window.]*

> *[Muttering to herself]*
> This is just awful.

*[Vanya carefully puts the roses on a nearby chair. Yelena continues to
look out the window, trying to figure out what she's going to say or
do next, as Astrov looks painfully guilty and attempts to cover up.]*

INNER OBJECTS provide more detail, texturing and truth to the inner

story you've established.

Tool #6: BEATS and ACTIONS

Consider each BEAT and ACTION pair as a mini-OBJECTIVE.

A BEAT is a thought change. A BEAT can be one line or a whole page. There
is an ACTION attached to each BEAT. An ACTION is the specific tack or

tactics you use to achieve your SCENE OBJECTIVE. (Don't confuse AC-TIONS with DOINGS.)

Although the explanation for BEATS and ACTIONS in part I was quite thorough, they are such important and integral parts of the technique that it bears repeating. BEATS and ACTIONS bring various facets to the forward motion of getting your SCENE OBJECTIVE. They inform precise ways to achieve the goal stated in the SCENE OBJECTIVE. That's why the BEATS and ACTIONS are phrased the same way you word your SCENE OBJECTIVE: to get a reaction. This is so you are not talking at the other person but eliciting a response.

Never stop going after your BEAT and ACTION when you stop talking and the other person speaks. Continue to pursue the BEAT and ACTION. Look to see if you are getting the desired reaction. Be open to the other actor's response to your BEAT and ACTION, and in turn, let that motivate an emotional reACTION in you. Then, based on what it is that you feel (your reACTION), let that reACTION inspire a reason to go on to the next ACTION.

You will find the BEATS bracketed and the ACTION for each BEAT handwritten (remember to write your ACTIONS in pencil) out to the *right* side (DOINGS are written on the left) of the bracketed area in the analyzed scene that follows. This is exactly how you should write on any and every script when establishing your BEATS and ACTIONS. Once again, there are many choices you can make in determining your BEATS and ACTIONS. The following are only suggestions. It's up to you to find the most effective ACTION for each BEAT—one that will most befit the who-am-I of the character, as well as of your own personality.

BEATS and ACTIONS from Yelena's P.O.V.

Keep in mind Yelena's SCENE OBJECTIVE of *"to get you to fall in love with me to get my power back"* in order to substantiate her shallow existence. It is often the case that when you empower another person, they are more likely to fall in love with you. You become indispensable to his or her personal validation. This is how gurus, cult masters, mentors and leaders of any type inspire fanatically dedicated followers. Most of us are fairly self-involved, our favorite topic being me, myself and I. So, when someone makes it all about us and what makes us feel brilliant and special, it's like we become addicts with drugs—we want more and more, because it feels so damn good. Empowering the object of your desire is an extremely effective way to make someone fall—hard—in your direction.

Yelena's BEATS and ACTIONS suggestions.

UNCLE VANYA
by Anton Chekhov
(A scene from Act III)

ASTROV
[(Enters with drawing)
Hello, I understand you wanted to see
some of my artistry?

YELENA
Yesterday, you assured me you would show
me your drawings. Are you available now?

Make you feel important

ASTROV
I'd love to!

(He spreads the drawing on a nearby table and fixes it with stickpins. She helps him.)]

[Where were you born?

To diminish my higher position in life for your benefit

YELENA
In Petersburg.

ASTROV
And where did you go to school?

YELENA
At the conservatory.]

ASTROV
[I doubt very much this will intrigue you in
any way.

Make you believe I'm intrigued

YELENA
Why not? You're right in assuming I don't know
much about the country, but I'm well-read.]

ASTROV

[Look here. It's a map of this area as it was
fifty years ago. The green color indicates the
forest. Half of the area was surfaced with
forest. Where you see the red over the green—
deer, wild goats and all sorts of wildlife were
prevalent.] [Look at the third part and you'll
see my rendition of how it is today. There's
green, but it's sporadic. There is no wildlife].

*Make you feel
like a genius*

*Make you
believe I am
fascinated*

(Pause)
You might say it's progress and I'd agree if the
destroyed forests were making way for
factories or schools. But, no, there is a lot of
unusable muddied land filled with disease
and people who are destitute.]

*Make you
believe I
sympathize*

[(He looks at her askance. . . .)

It seems to me that you have little interest
in any of this.

*Make you feel
smarter than me*

YELENA

No, it's simply that I don't comprehend much
of it.

ASTROV

It doesn't take much to comprehend it. I just
don't think you're all that interested.]

YELENA

[Please excuse my lack of concentration,
as my mind is someplace else. To be
honest I wanted to ask you something
but I don't know how to begin.]

*Make you feel how
grateful I am that you
deign to speak to me*

[(Pause)
It's a question about someone you know.
Like friends, let's talk, being totally open with
each other and then forget we ever had this
conversation. What do you say?

*Empower you
by sharing a
secret*

ASTROV

All right.]

YELENA

[It's about Sonya, my stepdaughter. What do
you think of her? Do you like her?

ASTROV

I can admire her spirit.

YELENA
But do you like her as a woman?

Make you say you're not attracted to (SUBSTITUTION for) Sonya

ASTROV
(Pause)
No.]

YELENA
[(Kissing his hand)
You don't love her. I can see that from your
eyes. You know, she's suffering.]
[Try to understand that you must stop
coming here.
(Pause)

Make you feel rewarded for giving the right answer

Make you believe what a sacrifice this is for me

Ouch! I hate this. I feel like I've been carrying
the weight of the world on my shoulders. Anyway,
it's done, thank God, so now we can forget we
ever had this conversation and move on. You're a
smart man. I'm sure you realize why you must . . .]
[(Pause)
I feel all the blood rushing to
my head.

Make you rush over and hold me to keep me from fainting

ASTROV
If you had told me about her feelings a month
or two ago, I might have thought about it . . . but
if she is sick at heart because of me, then I guess
there's no other recourse. . . .]
[(Pause)
But tell me, why is it that *you* had to ask me?

(He looks at her a moment.)

Ohhhh, I get it!

YELENA
What are you talking about?

Impress you with my innocence

ASTROV
You know. Sure, Sonya may be in love, but
why is it you're asking the questions? Why do
you look so surprised? You know why I come
every day. You're very well aware of the effect
you have on me, you lovely "bird of prey."

YELENA
Bird of prey! What are you talking about?!

ASTROV
You are a gorgeous, frisky rascal . . . and I am
your victim. Well, you win. You can have me.]

[(He opens his arms and bows his head like a martyr on a cross.)

I give in. I'm here and ready to be consumed!

Make you chase after me

YELENA
Have you gone mad?!

ASTROV
Oh, you are so coy.

YELENA
I'm not as cunning or as cruel as you're making
me out to be. Honestly, I'm not.]

[(She tries to leave. Astrov rushes to block her way.)]

*Make you stop me
from leaving*

ASTROV
[I'll leave and I won't return. Just tell me . . .

Make you seduce me

(He takes her hand and glances about to see if anyone is looking.)

Where should we meet? Hurry, someone may
catch us—please tell me where.
            (Whispering lustfully)
Your hair smells wonderful. One little kiss,
please let me kiss you.]

YELENA
[I beg of you . . .

ASTROV   *Make you beg me to*
(Stops her from talking)   *be with you*
No need to beg, I'm yours. You are so beautiful.
And your lovely hands, I need to kiss your hands.

(He kisses her hands.)

YELENA
Stop it, please stop . . . go . . .

(She pulls her hand away.)]

                    ASTROV
[You know it's inescapable. We are meant to be
together.

*(He kisses her, and at that very moment, Uncle Vanya shows up,
carrying a dozen roses, and stops just inside the door. Neither
Astrov nor Yelena sees him.)*

*Get you to continue to
seduce me (no matter how
much I tell you to stop)*

                    YELENA
Don't. We shouldn't be doing this. . . .

(She lays her head on Astrov's chest.)

                    ASTROV
At two o'clock meet me at the plantation.
Promise me you'll come.]

[*(Yelena sees Vanya looking at them.)*

*Get Vanya to believe that
Astrov forced me
into his arms*

                    YELENA
Let go of me!

*(She forcefully pulls away from Astrov. Then she goes to
the window.)*

                    (Muttering to herself)
This is just awful.

*(Vanya carefully puts the roses on a nearby chair. Yelena continues
to look out the window, trying to figure out what she's going to
say or do next, as Astrov looks painfully guilty and attempts to
cover up.)]*

BEATS and ACTIONS from Astrov's P.O.V.

Consider Astrov's SCENE OBJECTIVE of *"to get you to fall in love with me."*

Astrov's BEATS and ACTIONS suggestions.

UNCLE VANYA

by Anton Chekhov
(A scene from Act III)

ASTROV
[(Enters with drawing)
Hello, I understand you wanted to see
some of my artistry?   *To intrigue you*

YELENA
Yesterday, you assured me you would show
me your drawings. Are you available now?]

ASTROV
[I'd love to!   *Get you excited*

*(He spreads the drawing on a nearby table and fixes it with
stickpins. She helps him.)]*
[Where were you born?

YELENA
In Petersburg.   *Get you to open up to me*

ASTROV
And where did you go to school?

YELENA
At the conservatory.]

ASTROV
[I doubt very much this will intrigue you
in any way.
                                                        Make you beg me
YELENA   *to continue*
Why not? You're right in assuming I don't know
much about the country, but I'm well-read.]

ASTROV
[Look here. It's a map of this area as it was
fifty years ago. The green color indicates the   *Get you to*
forest. Half of the area was surfaced with forest.   *anticipate*
Where you see the red over the green—deer,
wild goats and all sorts of wildlife were
prevalent. Look at the third part and you'll
see my rendition of how it is today. There's green,
but it's sporadic. There is no wildlife.]
                                                        Rile you up

ASTROV
[(Pause)
You might say it's progress
and I'd agree if the destroyed forests were making
way for factories or schools. But, no, there is a
lot of unusable muddied land filled with disease
and people who are destitute.]

*Get you
to agree
with me*

[(He looks at her askance. . . .)

It seems to me that you have little interest
in any of this.

Challenge your honesty

YELENA
No, it's simply that I don't comprehend much
of it.

ASTROV
It doesn't take much to comprehend it. I just
don't think you're all that interested.]

YELENA
[Please excuse my lack of concentration, as my
mind is someplace else. To be honest I wanted to
ask you something but I don't know how to begin.

*Get you to ask me
the question quickly*

(Pause)
It's a question about someone you know. Like
friends, let's talk, being totally open with each
other and then forget we ever had this
conversation. What do you say?

ASTROV
All right.]

YELENA
[It's about Sonya, my stepdaughter. What do
you think of her? Do you like her?

*Make you happy
with my vague answer*

ASTROV
I can admire her spirit.]

YELENA
[But do you like her as a woman?

ASTROV
(Pause)

No.]

Make you aware I am available to you

YELENA
[(*Kissing his hand*)
You don't love her. I can see that from your
eyes. You know, she's suffering. Try to
understand that you must stop coming here.]
[(*Pause*)
Ouch! I hate this. I feel like I've been carrying
the weight of the world on my shoulders. Anyway,
it's done, thank God, so now we can forget we
ever had this conversation and move on. You're a
smart man. I'm sure you realize why you must . . .
(*Pause*)
I feel all the blood rushing to my head.

Make you keep kissing me

Get you to help me understand why I have to go

ASTROV
If you had told me about her feelings a month
or two ago, I might have thought about it . . . but
if she is sick at heart because of me, then I guess
there's no other recourse. . . .]
[(*Pause*)
But tell me, why is it that *you* had to ask me?

(*He looks at her a moment.*)

Ohhhh, I get it!

Make you admit you like me

YELENA
What are you talking about?

ASTROV
You know. Sure, Sonya may be in love, but
why is it you're asking the questions? Why do
you look so surprised? You know why I come
every day. You're very well aware of the effect
you have on me, you lovely "bird of prey."]

YELENA
[Bird of prey! What are you talking about?!

Make you run into my arms and have your way with me

ASTROV
You are a gorgeous, frisky rascal . . . and I am your
victim. Well, you win. You can have me.

(He opens his arms and bows his head like a martyr on a cross.)

I give in. I'm here and ready to be consumed!]

YELENA
[Have you gone mad?!

ASTROV
Oh, you are so coy.

Make you play the game with me

YELENA
I'm not as cunning or as cruel as you're making
me out to be. Honestly, I'm not.]

[(She tries to leave. Astrov rushes to block her way.)]

Stop you from leaving

ASTROV
[I'll leave and I won't return. Just tell me . . .

(He takes her hand and glances about to see if anyone is looking.)

Make you commit to a time and place (so you can't back out)

Where should we meet? Hurry, someone may
catch us—please tell me where.]

[(Whispering lustfully)
Your hair smells wonderful. One little kiss, please
let me kiss you.

Get you turned on sexually

YELENA
I beg of you . . .

ASTROV
(Stops her from talking)
No need to beg, I'm yours. You are so beautiful.
And your lovely hands, I need to kiss your hands.

(He kisses her hands.)

YELENA
Stop it, please stop . . . go . . .]

[(She pulls her hand away.)

ASTROV
You know it's inescapable. We are meant to be
together.

Make you admit you love me

(He kisses her, and at that very moment, Uncle Vanya shows up, carrying a dozen roses, and stops just inside the door. Neither Astrov nor Yelena sees him.)

YELENA
Don't. We shouldn't be doing this. . . .

(She lays her head on Astrov's chest.)]

ASTROV
[At two o'clock meet me at the plantation. *Make you promise*
Promise me you'll come.]   *to meet me*

[*(Yelena sees Vanya looking at them.)*

YELENA
Let go of me!   *Make you want to stay*
                                                    in my arms

(She forcefully pulls away from Astrov.)] [(Then she goes to the window.)
                      (Muttering to herself)   *Make Vanya believe in our*
This is just awful.   *innocence and therefore*
                                                 become your (Yelena's)
                                                          hero

(Vanya carefully puts the roses on a nearby chair. Yelena continues to look out the window, trying to figure out what she's going to say or do next, as Astrov looks painfully guilty and attempts to cover up.)]

ACTIONS and BEATS give you the colors and specificity
of how your character wins the scene.

Tool #7: MOMENT BEFORE

This is the event that takes place before the scene begins.

The MOMENT BEFORE gives you a dire reason for you to want to win your SCENE OBJECTIVE. It tells you *where* you're coming from and *why* you need your SCENE OBJECTIVE so badly right now. You use events that include *present* unresolved issues that are based on real or what-if-my-worst-fear-were-to-come-true situations.

Remember: The MOMENT BEFORE is a visceral reliving of the event just before you launch into the scene; it should take no more than thirty to sixty seconds. As always, write in pencil, putting your MOMENT BEFORE choice on the top of the first page of the scene.

Yelena's MOMENT BEFORE.

In the scene from Act III of *Uncle Vanya*, the scripted MOMENT BEFORE is Yelena ruminating about her utter boredom with life as she speaks to Vanya and Sonya. She explains that she is without purpose or direction. Vanya and Sonya make some helpful suggestions. They offer solutions like running the home, teaching children, caring for the sick and less fortunate. These are worthy endeavors for anyone, but Yelena declares that these activities are for heroines in a novel. She, of flesh and blood, will leave charity work to those that are charitable. She thinks all those activities would be dull and uninteresting, so what would be the point? Vanya exits, leaving Sonya and Yelena alone. Yelena insists that she is Sonya's really good friend, and new friendship always requires a tell-all session. Sonya, in the spirit of friendship and floodgates gone wild, confesses that she loves Astrov. She goes on to say how hopeless she feels and that she fears that her affections will never be returned. Sonya's new best friend, Yelena, offers to help her find out exactly how Astrov feels about her. Sonya is so tortured by her unrequited love that she agrees. Yelena tells Sonya that she will use the ruse of telling Astrov that she has an interest in his drawings, and that she will seek an immediate audience with him. After Sonya goes to fetch Astrov, Yelena muses about what she's about to do, admitting to herself that she feels a tad guilty because she, too, has an attraction to him. While she waits for Astrov to show up, she forgets her guilt as she develops a hearty appetite for the doctor.

Considering the script's MOMENT BEFORE, you have to emotionally correlate it to real events from your own life that make the SCENE OBJECTIVE more honest and important to you. Yelena's SCENE OBJECTIVE is *"to get you to fall in love with me to get my power back."* Yelena is bored stiff and Sonya's unrequited love is an intriguing game for Yelena to play. Wouldn't it be exciting to set up a competition between her and the unknowing Sonya, with Astrov being the prize? What better way to win the competition and prove self-worth than to get her SCENE OBJECTIVE.

Bottom line: Yelena feels like a loser and a nobody because she does nothing with her life. Being able to win the affections of Dr. Astrov over Sonya will validate her importance, essentially making her a winner, a somebody. Therefore, getting Astrov (who becomes quite the catch by virtue of Sonya's obsession with him) to fall in love with her becomes more than just the petty manipulations of an idle woman. It becomes crucial for helping her feel like she has a purpose in her life, an importance of being.

**Keep in mind: The MOMENT BEFORE should have
something to do with your SCENE OBJECTIVE
and your SUBSTITUTIONS for Astrov and Sonya.*

MOMENT BEFORE Suggestions for Yelena

- **MOMENT BEFORE:** Think about a specific event in which you had some form of a competition with your SUBSTITUTION for Sonya and she won (for example, she got better grades, a better job, a better home, a better man, a better review or better financial opportunities, or she won an athletic event, etc.). This will make you want to win today's competition with enormous enthusiasm. Relive this event (where you were the loser and your SUBSTITUTION for Sonya was the winner) in your mind as if it just happened, and then launch into the scene.
- **MOMENT BEFORE:** Think about your SUBSTITUTION for Sonya, a person with whom you have an inherently competitive relationship and who is rarely a good sport about it, gloating and bragging at your expense. Your SUBSTITUTION for Sonya has been regaling you with her constant woes about some man she loves (a conversation that seems to take place more frequently between *girl*friends). Whether you like this guy or not doesn't matter. Going after him and getting him would make you the victor in your own mind, because she'd never have to know about it. As your MOMENT BEFORE, relive the event where your SUBSTITUTION for Sonya was particularly broken up about some-

thing that happened with the object of her obsession, and launch into the scene with the mission—maybe she can't get him, but *you* can.

- **MOMENT BEFORE:** You feel that your SUBSTITUTION for Sonya has betrayed you, diminished you or shown a blatant lack of respect (and she has a boyfriend/husband.) Using the event that exemplifies this, relive it in your mind as if it's currently happening and launch into the scene using her boyfriend/husband as your SUBSTITUTION for Astrov. Making her boyfriend/husband fall in love with you, then, becomes a form of righteous payback.

- **MOMENT BEFORE:** You feel that your SUBSTITUTION for Astrov has betrayed you, diminished you or shown a blatant lack of respect. Getting this culprit to *fall in love* with you would give you the power back in this relationship. Using an event that you felt was the most egregious as your MOMENT BEFORE will make you need to help this rogue feel what you felt and hurt like you hurt. Use his present girlfriend as your SUBSTITUTION for Sonya.

Astrov's MOMENT BEFORE.

In Astrov's case, there is no scripted MOMENT BEFORE. For all we know, he's floating around the house someplace, thinking thoughts only Astrov would be privy to. Although we don't have an actual scene that takes place directly before this one that includes Astrov, we can surmise from previous scenes that he is probably consumed with thoughts about Yelena. After all, he does come to the home daily, and before her arrival, he hardly ever showed up. He also goes on and on about how lonely he is and how hopeless he feels about fixing his bachelor status. He is also readily available when she summons him.

*Keep in mind: The MOMENT BEFORE should have something to do with the SCENE OBJECTIVE for Astrov and your SUBSTITUTION for Yelena.

MOMENT BEFORE Suggestions for Astrov

- **MOMENT BEFORE:** Fantasizing the particular kind of fantasies that you entertain about your SUBSTITUTION for Yelena. For instance, the fantasy sequences in your head could include your SUBSTITUTION for Yelena smothering you with kisses and telling you she loves you more than life itself. Thus, when you find out she wants to see you, you can entertain the idea that maybe your fantasy is about to come true.
- **MOMENT BEFORE:** Fantasize sexually about the actress who is playing Yelena; then launch into the scene. This will make you aroused and physically needy for Yelena's love.
- **MOMENT BEFORE:** Relive an event in the relationship you're presently in that went terribly awry. Replay this horrid event in your mind and launch into the scene. This will make you need your SUBSTITUTION for Yelena to fall in love with you, because she seems so much better in comparison to your mate.
- **MOMENT BEFORE:** Recall an event that typifies your loneliness. It could be imagining your place of residence, staring at four walls and feeling all alone and empty. Or you could use a WHAT IF event like seeing yourself old and dying and there's no one there to mourn your passing. Live it for a few moments and then launch into the scene. This will make you work harder to get Yelena to fall in love with you so you can avoid these horrible pictures from either continuing or ever taking place.

The MOMENT BEFORE gives you the urgency to accomplish your SCENE OBJECTIVE immediately. A strong MOMENT BEFORE choice catapults you into real time and real need.

*Write your MOMENT BEFORE in pencil at the top of the scene beginning.

Tool #8: PLACE and FOURTH WALL

Endowing the PLACE and FOURTH WALL that you're acting in with a PLACE and FOURTH WALL from your own life.

After applying information from the inner story you have created from your OVERALL OBJECTIVE, SCENE OBJECTIVE, OBSTACLES, SUBSTITUTION, INNER OBJECTS and MOMENT BEFORE, ask yourself the question "What PLACE from my life would best inform and add conflict to the choices I've already made?" Once you make the choice of what PLACE you're using, endow the FOURTH WALL with what would be there when you look in that direction. *Uncle Vanya* may take place in the nineteenth century, but your PLACE and FOURTH WALL will not, because this play is not *your* reality. It's difficult to feel private in entirely make-believe surroundings. On the other hand, if you infuse the set with an appropriate PLACE and FOURTH WALL from your own life, the audience will believe you are from this bygone century, because you'll look so at home in your nineteenth-century surroundings.

Keep in mind that when you are making your PLACE and FOURTH WALL choices for both Astrov and Yelena, there is the reality of your SUBSTITUTION for Uncle Vanya lurking around the outskirts of your PLACE. This person can easily enter the PLACE and interfere with you accomplishing your SCENE OBJECTIVE.

*Write, in pencil, your choice for PLACE and FOURTH WALL at the top of the scene's script page.

PLACE and FOURTH WALL from Yelena's P.O.V.

Choose a PLACE and FOURTH WALL that would be highly charged and that lines up with the circumstances you have created with the other tools. The PLACE and FOURTH WALL will also have to instill a danger in accomplishing your SCENE OBJECTIVE of *"to get you to fall in love with me to get my power back."*

PLACE and FOURTH WALL Suggestions (Depending on Your SUBSTITUTION Choices for Astrov and Vanya)

- **Your living room or bedroom:** Where your mate (or parent, sister, brother, friend—anyone who hates your SUBSTITUTION for Astrov) can show up and, as a result of what they see, sever all ties with you.
- **Your boss' office:** (When the boss is your SUBSTITUTION for Astrov.) His wife (or his secretary, a fellow employee, his boss) could enter any minute, causing you to lose your job, promotion possibilities, respect from coworkers, etc.
- **A classroom at your school:** (When a student is your SUBSTITUTION for Astrov.) It would be devastating both morally and maybe even legally to be caught by the dean or the principal (or a fellow teacher or another student).
- **Your friend's bedroom:** (When using a friend's boyfriend/husband as your SUBSTITUTION for Astrov.) There's a huge potential for your friend to unexpectedly arrive home early and catch you in the act.
- **Your mate's apartment:** (When using a mate's good friend or relative as your SUBSTITUTION for Astrov.) This is perilous by virtue of the fact that your mate can walk in uninvited at any time—walking into your own home doesn't usually require an invite.

PLACE from Astrov's P.O.V.

Choose a PLACE that you would feel the probably disruptive presence of a person who would be hazardous to your achieving your goal of *"to get you to fall in love with me."*

PLACE Suggestions (Depending on Your SUBSTITUTION Choices for Yelena and Vanya)

- **Your friend's living room or bedroom:** Where your friend can come in from another part of the house and discover you trying to seduce his woman.
- **An office space:** Where your boss (or your fellow employee, Yelena's mate, etc.) can catch you in the act of seduction, creating the possibility of losing your job or your life.
- **A classroom at the school you attend:** Where a teacher (or a fellow student, Yelena's mate, the principal, the dean, etc.) is capable of interrupting your attempt to achieve your SCENE OBJECTIVE and possibly capable of putting a damper on your school career.
- **Her bedroom:** Where her mate (or friend, father, mother, sister, brother—anyone who is adversarial to your getting together with your SUBSTITUTION for Yelena) can barge in at any time.
- **Your living room:** Where your mate (or father, mother, friend, sister, brother, roommate—anyone who would be hostile to you about your SUBSTITUTION for Yelena) can come in and wreak havoc on your life.

In script analysis, PLACE and FOURTH WALL are easy elements to overlook. But don't skip using them. They truly augment and reinforce your character's emotional life and goals.

Tool #9: DOINGS

DOINGS are the handling of props to produce behavior.

The handling of props allows you to behave naturally, as if you were really in the environment your character is inhabiting. And all of the technique's other tools will temper *what* and *how* you handle the props—whether you pick up a book with anger, with lust or with the intent of impressing someone. As a result, using props informs the audience about what you are really thinking and feeling.

Remember: What you DO in the scene isn't only prescribed by the DOINGS described in the text of the scene. It's up to you, the actor, to bring in more of the character's life and behavior by introducing more than what is literally called for in the script.

In *Uncle Vanya*, the DOINGS must relate to the fact that the story takes place in a fairly wealthy country home in nineteenth-century Russia. You must also consider that Yelena and Dr. Astrov are well educated and socially savvy.

The following are suggestions for possible DOINGS. These suggestions are here to whet your imagination. As you read, try to come up with some DO-INGS of your own.

DOINGS should be handwritten (as always, in pencil) and located to the left of the dialogue, where the DOINGS will most likely take place.

Possible DOINGS from Yelena's P.O.V.

UNCLE VANYA
by Anton Chekhov
(A scene from Act III)

Eating a ripe peach.
(There is a non threatening sexuality in eating something that's drippy and pulpy.
When the juice drips on Yelena's chin, Astrov will likely "help" wipe it off with his finger—making him feel safe in starting a seduction.)

ASTROV
[Enters with drawing]
Hello, I understand you wanted to see some of my artistry?

YELENA
Yesterday, you assured me you would show me your drawings. Are you available now?

ASTROV
I'd love to!

[He spreads the drawing on a nearby table and fixes it with stickpins. She helps him.]
Where were you born?

Help him spread the drawing.
(In this way you have a legitimate excuse to "accidentally" touch.)

YELENA
In Petersburg.

ASTROV
And where did you go to school?

YELENA
At the conservatory.

ASTROV
I doubt very much this will intrigue you in any way.

YELENA
Why not? You're right in assuming I don't know
much about the country, but I'm well-read.

*Examine the drawing
closely as he points out each item.* ASTROV
(This is   Look here. It's a map of this area as it was fifty
a way to   years ago. The green color indicates the forest.
appear   Half of the area was surfaced with forest. Where
engrossed   you see the red over the green—deer, wild goats
and to be   and all sorts of wildlife were prevalent. Look at the
physically   third part and you'll see my rendition of how it is
close.)   today. There's green, but it's sporadic. There is no
    wildlife.

[Pause]
You might say it's progress and I'd agree if the
destroyed forests were making way for factories or
schools. But, no, there is a lot of unusable muddied
land filled with disease and people who are
destitute.

[He looks at her askance. . . .]

It seems to me that you have little interest in any
of this.

YELENA
No, it's simply that I don't comprehend much of it.

ASTROV
It doesn't take much to comprehend it. I just
don't think you're all that interested.

Pick up a photograph of
Sonya   YELENA
from a   Please excuse my lack of concentration, as my
nearby table mind is someplace else. To be honest I wanted to
or chest, stare at it with ask you something but I don't know how to begin.
concern.   *[Pause]*
Touch the   It's a question about someone you know. Like
photo with   friends, let's talk, being totally open with each
love and pathos. other and then forget we ever had this
conversation. What do you say?

ASTROV

All right.

YELENA

It's about Sonya, my stepdaughter. What do you think of her? Do you like her?

ASTROV

I can admire her spirit.

YELENA

But do you like her as a woman?

ASTROV
[Pause]

No.

Kissing his hand at the same time that you are telling him to go away sends a mixed message. Your lack of predictability is appealing.

YELENA
[Kissing his hand]
You don't love her. I can see that from your eyes. You know, she's suffering. Try to understand that you must stop coming here.
[Pause]
Ouch! I hate this. I feel like I've been carrying the weight of the world on my shoulders. Anyway, it's done, thank God, so now we can forget we ever had this conversation and move on. You're a smart man. I'm sure you realize why you must . . .
[Pause]
I feel all the blood rushing to my head.

Loosening up your collar or unbuttoning your blouse in order to get some air (and doing so reveals more skin and is provocative).

ASTROV

If you had told me about her feelings a month or two ago, I might have thought about it . . . but if she is sick at heart because of me, then I guess there's no other recourse. . . .
[Pause]
But tell me, why is it that *you* had to ask me?

[He looks at her a moment.]

Ohhhh, I get it!

YELENA

Pulling out a fan that is tucked snugly in your bodice and frantically fanning yourself.
What are you talking about?

ASTROV
You know. Sure, Sonya may be in love, but
why is it you're asking the questions? Why do
you look so surprised? You know why I come
every day. You're very well aware of the effect
you have on me, you lovely "bird of prey."

YELENA
Bird of prey! What are you talking about?!

ASTROV
You are a gorgeous, frisky rascal . . . and I am your
victim. Well, you win. You can have me.

[He opens his arms and bows his head like a martyr on a cross.]

I give in. I'm here and ready to be consumed!

YELENA
Have you gone mad?!

ASTROV
Oh, you are so coy.

YELENA
I'm not as cunning or as cruel as you're making me
out to be. Honestly, I'm not.

[She tries to leave. Astrov rushes to block her way.]

*"Accidentally" run into a piece of furniture
on the way out. (Fall if you must—buy as
much time as possible so Astrov has time
to stop you. Also, things that are on the
furniture are bound to fall. Astrov's attempt
to help you up or help you pick up what fell will
give him legitimate close proximity and an
opportunity to create legitimate intimacy.)*

ASTROV
I'll leave and I won't return. Just tell me . . .

[He takes her hand and glances about to see if anyone is looking.]

Where should we meet? Hurry, someone may catch
us—please tell me where.
[Whispering lustfully]
Your hair smells wonderful. One little kiss, please
let me kiss you.

YELENA
I beg of you . . .

unbutton another button
(because you're so flustered).

ASTROV
[Stops her from talking]
No need to beg, I'm yours. You are so beautiful.
And your lovely hands, I need to kiss your hands.

[He kisses her hands.]

YELENA
Stop it, please stop . . . go . . .

[She pulls her hand away.]
(. . . in a way that makes him want
to take it back.)

ASTROV
You know it's inescapable. We are meant to be
together.

[He kisses her, and at that very moment, Uncle Vanya shows up,
carrying a dozen roses, and stops just inside the door. Neither
Astrov nor Yelena sees him.]

YELENA
Don't. We shouldn't be doing this. . . .

[She lays her head on Astrov's chest.]

ASTROV
At two o'clock meet me at the plantation. Promise
me you'll come.

[Yelena sees Vanya looking at them.]

YELENA
Let go of me!
Angrily buttoning up your blouse (as if to imply that Astrov
is the one who unbuttoned it in the first place).
[She forcefully pulls away from Astrov. Then she goes to the window.]

[Muttering to herself]
This is just awful.
Playing with the window cord or latch
(so it looks like you have a real reason
to be there).
[Vanya carefully puts the roses on a nearby chair. Yelena continues to
look out the window, trying to figure out what she's going to say or
do next, as Astrov looks painfully guilty and attempts to cover up.]

Possible DOINGS from Astrov's P.O.V.

UNCLE VANYA

by Anton Chekhov
(A scene from Act III)

A briefcase held protectively under your arm.

ASTROV
[Enters with drawing]
Hello, I understand you wanted to see
some of my artistry?

YELENA
Yesterday, you assured me you would show
me your drawings. Are you available now?

ASTROV
I'd love to!

*[He spreads the drawing on a nearby table and fixes it with
stickpins. She helps him.]*

Where were you born?

*Manipulate spreading
the drawing in a way that enables
you to legitimately touch her.*

YELENA
In Petersburg.

ASTROV
And where did you go to school?

YELENA
At the conservatory.

ASTROV
I doubt very much this will intrigue you in any way.

YELENA
Why not? You're right in assuming I don't
know much about the country, but I'm well-read.

*Point at the different items
displayed in the drawing in a
way that
forces her to
have to
move in
close to you.*

ASTROV
Look here. It's a map of this area as it was
fifty years ago. The green color indicates the
forest. Half of the area was surfaced with
forest. Where you see the red over the green—
deer, wild goats and all sorts of wildlife were
prevalent. Look at the third part and you'll see

my rendition of how it is today. There's green,
but it's sporadic. There is no wildlife.
[Pause]
You might say it's progress and I'd agree if the
destroyed forests were making way for factories or
schools. But, no, there is a lot of unusable muddied
land filled with disease and people who are
destitute.

[He looks at her askance. . . .]

It seems to me that you have little interest in any
of this.

YELENA

No, it's simply that I don't comprehend much of it.

Pour some vodka from a
nearby table
and down it
(as if to say, "You've upset me.").

ASTROV

It doesn't take much to comprehend it. I just don't
think you're all that interested.

YELENA

Play with
a box
or any item
that's displayed on top of a table
or chest
(so Yelena
won't see
your fear
of her question).

Please excuse my lack of concentration, as my
mind is someplace else. To be honest I wanted to
ask you something but I don't know how to begin.
[Pause]
It's a question about someone you know. Like
friends, let's talk, being totally open with each
other and then forget we ever had this
conversation. What do you say?

ASTROV

All right.

YELENA

It's about Sonya, my stepdaughter. What do you
think of her? Do you like her?

ASTROV

I can admire her spirit.

YELENA

But do you like her as a woman?

ASTROV
[Pause]

No.

YELENA
[Kissing his hand]
You don't love her. I can see that from your
eyes. You know, she's suffering. Try to
understand that you must stop coming here.

Packing up the drawing   *[Pause]*
and putting   Ouch! I hate this. I feel like I've been carrying
it back in   the weight of the world on my shoulders. Anyway,
your   it's done, thank God, so now we can forget we
briefcase   ever had this conversation and move on. You're
(call her   a smart man. I'm sure you realize why you
bluff, make it look like you're   must . . .
leaving).   *[Pause]*
           I feel all the blood rushing to my head.

ASTROV
If you had told me about her feelings a month or
two ago, I might have thought about it . . . but if
Abruptly   she is sick at heart because of me, then I guess
stop   there's no other recourse. . . .
packing up your   *[Pause]*
drawing to   But tell me, why is it that *you* had to ask me?
make a
point.
[He looks at her a moment.]

Ohhhh, I get it!

YELENA
What are you talking about?

Take a comb out of
your pocket and groom   ASTROV
yourself.   You know. Sure, Sonya may be in love, but why is it
you're asking the questions? Why do you look so
surprised? You know why I come every day. You're
very well aware of the effect you have on me, you
lovely "bird of prey."

YELENA
Bird of prey! What are you talking about?!

ASTROV
You are a gorgeous, frisky rascal . . . and I am your
victim. Well, you win. You can have me.

[He opens his arms and bows his head like a martyr on a cross.]
Pick a grape, a piece of
candy, or   I give in. I'm here and ready to be consumed!
a nut out of a bowl on a
nearby table and pop
it into your mouth—to illustrate "consumed."

YELENA

Have you gone mad?!

ASTROV

Oh, you are so coy.

YELENA

I'm not as cunning or as cruel as you're making me
out to be. Honestly, I'm not.

[She tries to leave. Astrov rushes to block her way.]

ASTROV

I'll leave and I won't return. Just tell me . . .

[He takes her hand and glances about to see if anyone is looking.]

Where should we meet? Hurry, someone may catch
us—please tell me where.

Play with her hair—
lift it, smell
it, twirl it.

[Whispering lustfully]
Your hair smells wonderful. One little kiss, please
let me kiss you.

YELENA

I beg of you . . .

ASTROV

[Stops her from talking]
No need to beg, I'm yours. You are so beautiful.
And your lovely hands, I need to kiss your hands.

[He kisses her hands.]

YELENA

Stop it, please stop . . . go . . .

[She pulls her hand away.]

Pull her hand back to
you (just because it's
not written
in the
stage directions, doesn't
mean you can't do it).

ASTROV

You know it's inescapable. We are meant to be
together.

*[He kisses her, and at that very moment, Uncle Vanya shows up,
carrying a dozen roses, and stops just inside the door. Neither
Astrov nor Yelena sees him.]*

YELENA
Don't. We shouldn't be doing this. . . .

[She lays her head on Astrov's chest.]

Kiss her head, play with her hair, pull her in close.

ASTROV
At two o'clock meet me at the plantation. Promise me you'll come.

[Yelena sees Vanya looking at them.]

YELENA
Let go of me!

[She forcefully pulls away from Astrov. Then she goes to the window.]

Maniacally eat what's in the bowl, trying to appear innocent.

[Muttering to herself]
This is just awful.

[Vanya carefully puts the roses on a nearby chair. Yelena continues to look out the window, trying to figure out what she's going to say or do next, as Astrov looks painfully guilty and attempts to cover up.]

People are complex by nature, and it's the actor's job to duplicate that complexity. There's a layered effect to your characterization when you're using DOINGS because words can lie, but behavior always tells the truth.

Tool #10: INNER MONOLOGUE

INNER MONOLOGUE is the dialogue going on inside your head that you don't speak out loud.

Our minds are one continuous scroll of thoughts when we're speaking and listening and even when we're alone. INNER MONOLOGUE is a way to replicate this innate mind-processing system.

Remember: INNER MONOLOGUE is defined paranoia. It's all those thoughts you can't say out loud because they will make you seem insecure, vulgar, crazy, stupid or prejudiced. The INNER MONOLOGUE should be written the way your mind really thinks. This means that the INNER MONOLOGUE should be stated not as introspective musings, but as a way to communicate with the other people in the scene. When crafting your INNER MONOLOGUE always use "you" instead of "he" or "she." Acting is all about creating relationships—it is never a self-indulgent, it's-all-about-me exercise.

The INNER MONOLOGUE you write is just a guideline. It is not additional dialogue to memorize. What you write is a base that provides the initial spark for your thoughts and the direction for them to naturally flow. Whether you're rehearsing or performing, the INNER MONOLOGUE will vary slightly each time you run the scene.

Your guide for your INNER MONOLOGUE should be handwritten in pencil between quotes and under the dialogue so that you can distinguish it from the other choices you've already made.

INNER MONOLOGUE from Yelena's P.O.V.

Once again, Yelena's OBJECTIVE is *"to get you to fall in love with me to get my power back"* to give her a purpose and a reason for being. Therefore, her INNER MONOLOGUE must be colored by her need to feel enhanced by Astrov's falling in love with her so as to ultimately validate her existence. The INNER MONOLOGUE will also include her weaknesses, vulnerabilities, crudeness, modus operandi and neuroses.

The following are suggestions that are geared toward the character of Yelena in the script. When writing your own INNER MONOLOGUE, always make it personal to your life and thoughts.

INNER MONOLOGUE starts before the scripted dialogue.

UNCLE VANYA
by Anton Chekhov
(A scene from Act III)

"I hope I like his drawing. It's so hard for me to pretend when I don't like something. I'm not a good liar. . . . Uh-oh, here he comes. . . . I'm gonna strike that pose that displays both 'come hither' and 'pure innocence.' It's a surefire winner. . . ."

ASTROV
[Enters with drawing]
Hello, I understand you wanted to see
some of my artistry?

"Oh, yeah, I'm just chomping at the bit to see your crude and amateurish attempts. . . ."

YELENA
Yesterday, you assured me you would show
me your drawings. Are you available now?

"Of course you're available. You don't do anything all day except drool whenever I walk by. . . ."

ASTROV
I'd love to!

"That was easy. It's gonna be fun watching you sweat as I accidentally on purpose expose my cleavage to you as I bend down to help spread your drawing on the table. . . ."

[He spreads the drawing on a nearby table and fixes it with stickpins. She helps him.]

"Whoops, I dropped one of the stickpins. So I'm just going to have to bend down to pick it up, making sure I bend in such a way so as to make sure my firm buttocks are in your full view. . . ."

ASTROV
Where were you born?

"What a weird thing to ask. Usually, the sight of my butt and breasts doesn't inspire talk of my birthplace. Except, if you really think about it, one can't be born unless you have sex, so it does make sense, kind of . . ."

YELENA
In Petersburg.

"You're looking at me strangely. Why? Does the fact that I'm from a cosmopolitan, sophisticated, cultured city and you're a hick from the sticks have something to do with it? . . ."

ASTROV
And where did you go to school?

"Not a good line of questioning. I'm going to tell you and it's just going to make you feel bad. I mean, it's real hard to beat out having gone to the conservatory. But I'm not a liar (at least not about my credentials) so . . ."

YELENA
At the conservatory.

"There's that disgruntled face. I knew you wouldn't like the answer. My suggestion, my dear Astrov, is to stop asking leading questions. You'll be a lot happier for it. . . ."

ASTROV
I doubt very much this will intrigue you in any way.

"You got that right. I don't know about the country, nor do I care about the country . . . but I'm really good at making men feel virile and smart. . . ."

YELENA
Why not? You're right in assuming I don't
know much about the country, but I'm well-read.

"Nobody does better 'sincere' than me. You believe me, don't you? That I care about what you care about and I'm excited about learning at your scholarly feet, O wise and boring one . . ."

ASTROV
Look here. It's a map of this area as it was fifty
years ago. The green color indicates the forest.
Half of the area was surfaced with forest. Where
you see the red over the green—deer, wild goats
and all sorts of wildlife were prevalent.

"Green, red, deer, goats, forests . . . who cares?"

Look at the third part and you'll see my rendition
of how it is today. There's green, but it's sporadic.
There is no wildlife.

"Speaking of wildlife, I'm hungry. . . ."

[Pause]
You might say it's progress and I'd agree if the
destroyed forests were making way for factories or
schools.

"Whatever. I'll just keep nodding my head and make you believe I'm really listening. . . ."

But, no, there is a lot of unusable muddied land
filled with disease and people who are destitute.

"I hate disease and poor people. . . ."

[He looks at her askance. . . .]

"I hope there won't be a pop quiz later, because I haven't been listening. . . ."

It seems to me that you have little interest in any
of this.

"Ya think?!"

YELENA
No, it's simply that I don't comprehend much of it.

"You know, I'm highly educated, so I hope the ignorant defense is convincing to you."

ASTROV
It doesn't take much to comprehend it. I just don't
think you're all that interested.

"Yikes, you caught me. I've got to find another way to keep you bonding with me. Perhaps I've underestimated you. You've got spunk. I find that sexy. . . ."

YELENA
Please excuse my lack of concentration, as my
mind is someplace else. To be honest I wanted to
ask you something but I don't know how to begin.

"I'm going to string you along for a while. That always makes men nervous. You don't have a clue what I'm going to ask. It could be anything. Boy, do you look nervous. Gee, this is fun. . . ."

[Pause]
It's a question about someone you know.

"I'm really going to milk this. Hmm . . . let me make it sound ominous. . . ."

Like friends, let's talk, being totally open with each
other and then forget we ever had this
conversation. What do you say?

"I am so brilliant. Look at you squirm. You look like a worm on the end of a fishing hook. Either that or you're suspicious and I'm reading you all wrong. I love a good challenge. This is better than chess. . . ."

ASTROV
All right.

"This could easily backfire. It's a risky question to ask you. What if you do love Sonya? Then I would be the fool. . . ."

YELENA
It's about Sonya, my stepdaughter. What do you
think of her? Do you like her?

"You're taking a long time to answer. This is not a good sign. . . ."

ASTROV
I can admire her spirit.

"What the hell does that mean?! Are you messing with my mind? You're better at this than I thought. God, you're cute. . . ."

YELENA
But do you like her as a woman?

"Now you can't wriggle out of answering this question. There's no obtuse way you can answer my genius choice of words. . . ."

ASTROV
[Pause]

No.

"Yes! I knew it! Sonya's the loser. LOSER!! And now that that homely skank is out of the way, there's nothing keeping you from falling head over heels in love with me. . . ."

YELENA
[Kissing his hand]

"We've come to the point of the game, my love, called 'mixed message.' I'm gonna get you all turned on by kissing your hand in that special Yelena way (I should have it patented) . . ."

You don't love her. I can see that from your eyes. You know, she's suffering. Try to understand that you must stop coming here.

". . . and then tell you to go away. What am I really trying to say to you? Can you figure it out? Every man loves a mystery woman, and they don't get any more mysterious than me!"

[Pause]

Ouch! I hate this. I feel like I've been carrying the weight of the world on my shoulders.

"It's so hard being the kind of person that cares about others so much. Don't you think? I'm so compassionate. . . ."

Anyway, it's done, thank God, so now we can forget we ever had this conversation and move on. You're a smart man. I'm sure you realize why you must . . .

"Here comes the never-fails money move. . . . Ooooh, I feel so faint, I might fall and you must hold me up, you big hunk of man, you . . ."

[Pause]

I feel all the blood rushing to my head.

"Come to me, you moron. Can't you see I'm about to faint?! Why aren't you moving? It can't get any simpler than this. This is your cue to have a legitimate reason to touch and hold me. . . ."

ASTROV
If you had told me about her feelings a month or

"Hold me, come to me. . . ."

two ago, I might have thought about it . . . but if she is sick at heart because of me, then I guess

"Hold me, kiss me . . ."

there's no other recourse. . . .

[Pause]

But tell me, why is it that you had to ask me?

"Uh-oh, good question. You're really good at this game and that really turns me on. How should I answer? I want to inspire you with my clever response. What

should I say? Nothing's coming to my mind. . . . Hurry up brain. Do your stuff. . . ."

[He looks at her a moment.]

Ohhhh, I get it!

". . . I'm just gonna play innocent. That should work. . . ."

YELENA
What are you talking about?

"Are you buying my innocent act? You're not looking too sold on it. . . . Uh-oh, better come up with another tactic. . . ."

ASTROV
You know. Sure, Sonya may be in love, but why is it you're asking the questions? Why do you look so surprised? You know why I come every day. You're very well aware of the effect you have on me, you lovely "bird of prey."

"Bird of prey? Whoa, good word usage to describe what I'm doing. Good for you. Bad for me. New ploy: indignant and offended . . ."

YELENA
Bird of prey! What are you talking about?!

"I can't look at you. If you see my face, you'll know I'm full of it. . . ."

ASTROV
You are a gorgeous, frisky rascal . . . and I am your victim. Well, you win. You can have me.

"You're going for it. Good move! You're so sexy when you're winning. . . ."

[He opens his arms and bows his head like a martyr on a cross.]

"What's with the Jesus bit?! Talk about mixed messages. Is this about sex or religion?"

I give in. I'm here and ready to be consumed!

"You want me to come to you?! You're supposed to be all over me!"

YELENA
Have you gone mad?!

"No one's ever outsmarted me before. I'm really at a loss . . . and that gets me so hot. . . ."

ASTROV
Oh, you are so coy.

"You're relentless. How do I counter?!"

YELENA
I'm not as cunning or as cruel as you're making me
out to be. Honestly, I'm not.

"Believe me. Please believe me. . . . You're such a good player and I'm feeling the
heat, in more ways than one. . . . I'd better get out of here before it ceases to be a
game and we're rolling all over the floor making mad, passionate love. All I've
been used to is old-man sex, and I bet you can last longer than three seconds. . . .
Oh, boy, I gotta get out of here!"

[She tries to leave. Astrov rushes to block her way.]

ASTROV
I'll leave and I won't return. Just tell me . . .

[He takes her hand and glances about to see if anyone is looking.]

"You grabbing me is so strong, so arousing. I want you. I'm married. I can't. Yeah,
I'm married to an old, old man. There are wrinkles in places you don't even want
to know about. . . . Look at your clear skin—sure you've got broken blood vessels
from way too much vodka, but who cares? I want you badly! What if we get
caught? Oh, that thought gets me even hotter. I'm doomed. . . ."

Where should we meet? Hurry, someone may catch
us—please tell me where.
[Whispering lustfully]
Your hair smells wonderful. One little kiss, please
let me kiss you.

"Help me to be strong. I don't know how much longer I can pull away. . . ."

YELENA
I beg of you . . .

"I'm not kidding. Help me get out of here before I get to that place where I can't say
no any longer. . . ."

ASTROV
[Stops her from talking]
No need to beg, I'm yours. You are so beautiful.
And your lovely hands, I need to kiss your hands.

"No, not the hands. I'm so sensitive there. . . ."
[He kisses her hands.]

"It feels so good, too good. Stop. Please stop. I'm losing control. . . ."

YELENA
Stop it, please stop . . . go . . .

"I gotta be strong. I can't lose control. Then I'll lose everything. . . . What if
someone shows up?!"

[She pulls her hand away.]

"I've got to get it together. I'm totally out of control! . . . Oh, I want you. . . . I won't rest 'til I have you. Oh, my God . . . you've got to stop! . . ."

ASTROV
You know it's inescapable. We are meant to be together.

". . . Oh, what the hell? Come here. Take me. . . ."

[He kisses her, and at that very moment, Uncle Vanya shows up, carrying a dozen roses, and stops just inside the door. Neither Astrov nor Yelena sees him.]

YELENA
Don't. We shouldn't be doing this. . . .

"Don't stop! This feels way too good! Hold me, touch me, engulf me. . . ."

[She lays her head on Astrov's chest.]

ASTROV
At two o'clock meet me at the plantation. Promise me you'll come.

"What's wrong with now?! Oh, I want you so much. Take me. . . . Wait a second. I feel eyes on me. . . ."

[Yelena sees Vanya looking at them.]

"Oh, no, this looks really bad. I've got to get away from you. . . . It's not my fault, Vanya. Astrov forced me! . . ."

YELENA
Let go of me!

[She forcefully pulls away from Astrov. Then she goes to the window.]

"Should I lie? Should I cry rape? My husband is going to find out and divorce me and I'll have no money. Should I say I was drunk? Or, better yet, Astrov hypnotized me and made me do his bidding? I'll be left with nothing. . . ."

[Muttering to herself]
This is just awful.

". . . Temporary insanity? Or sleepwalking? Maybe I should come on to Vanya. He's always wanted me. Oh, no, what if Vanya kills Astrov?! Or, worse, what if he tries to kill me?!!!! . . ."

[Vanya carefully puts the roses on a nearby chair. Yelena continues to look out the window, trying to figure out what she's going to say or do next, as Astrov looks painfully guilty and attempts to cover up.]

"... Amnesia? That's good. I could say I bumped my head or something. But if he doesn't believe me, I'll be homeless and without a clothing allowance! Maybe I can convince Vanya he didn't see what he thought he saw. My head was resting on Astrov's chest because he was checking for head lice. . . . I mean, he is a doctor. He could've been doing something doctory. . . . Ahhh jeez, the world's gonna see me as a slut and a whore. . . ."

INNER MONOLOGUE from Astrov's P.O.V.

Astrov's SCENE OBJECTIVE is *"to get you to fall in love with me."* Astrov's SCENE OBJECTIVE is steeped in obsession and liquid courage made possible by means of imbibing much alcohol. Create your INNER MONOLOGUE for Astrov with this in mind. Again, the following thoughts are merely suggestions based on what the character in the script might have as an INNER MONO-LOGUE. You, however, *must personalize* your INNER MONOLOGUE to what makes sense to your inner work. How you manifest your specific INNER MONOLOGUE will fluctuate depending upon how you individually deal with life—your thoughts will emanate from your own unique history and background.

UNCLE VANYA
by Anton Chekhov
(A scene from Act III)

"I hope you like my drawings, and please don't think they're stupid and crude. I mean, you're more sophisticated than me, and my drawings may make me look like a rube. . . ."

ASTROV
[Enters with drawing]
Hello, I understand you wanted to see some of my
artistry?

"Maybe 'artistry' is too strong a word. Sounds like I'm full of myself. Maybe you were patronizing me yesterday when you said you wanted to see my drawings. Maybe you have no interest at all and I'm looking way too desperate."

YELENA
Yesterday, you assured me you would show me
your drawings. Are you available now?

"Oh, yeah, I always just stand around with my drawing in my hand. Of course I'm available. I think that they're pretty damn good. Maybe you'll be so impressed that you'll like me, maybe even fall in love with me, marry me and have my babies. . . ."

ASTROV
I'd love to!

"Whoa, whoa, whoa, way too eager . . . and too desperate, eager and desperate. Now, that's an appealing combo. How can she resist? Just call me 'El Blurto'! . . ."

[He spreads the drawing on a nearby table and fixes it with stickpins. She helps him.]

"You're hovering over me and accidentally touching me. Do you want me sexually, or are you just being helpful and the touches are truly incidental? Well, I'd better figure it out soon because the conversation has stopped and I'm looking really dumb. I'd better say something, but I don't know what to say. What to say? What to say? . . ."

Where were you born?

"Well, that was really stupid. I'm a stupid, stupid man. 'Where were you born?'! Could I have asked anything more boring? Note to self: Next time, bring my brain. . . ."

YELENA
In Petersburg.

"You come from the city. You're cosmopolitan and sophisticated and let's not forget married . . . and I'm not. Why would you want to be with me?! As far as you're concerned, I'm just a country bumpkin. Although I am a doctor. Perhaps I can outdo you with my educational background. . . ."

ASTROV
And where did you go to school?

"Oh, yeah! There's no way you're going beat me, no way in hell. . . ."

YELENA
At the conservatory.

"Ohhhkay, maybe not. Why couldn't it have been any place but the heralded conservatory?! Boy, oh, boy, a shot of vodka would feel real good right about now. . . ."

ASTROV
I doubt very much this will intrigue you in any way.

"How can anything that interests me interest you?! Why should it? You're young and hot and I'm drunk and sweaty. Why did I start this conversation?! I must be more interesting than your wrinkled, crotchety, impotent (and I should know—I'm his doctor) husband. What am I doing?! You're married and my best friend is in love with you. God help me, I'm a louse . . . a very horny louse . . . but a louse nonetheless. . . ."

YELENA
Why not? You're right in assuming I don't know much about the country, but I'm well-read.

"Are you patronizing me? Huh? Huh?! Ah, what does it matter? As long as you're here and I'm here, who knows? Maybe you'll like what I have to say. I mean, it is exciting to me. So here goes. . . ."

ASTROV

Look here. It's a map of this area as it was fifty
years ago. The green color indicates the forest.
Half of the area was surfaced with forest. Where
you see the red over the green—deer, wild goats
and all sorts of wildlife were prevalent.

*"This is good stuff. I love talking about it. It's controversial yet benevolent. Makes
me look real smart . . ."*

Look at the third part and you'll see my rendition
of how it is today. There's green, but it's sporadic.
There is no wildlife.
[Pause]

"This is the best part. You're gonna love this. . . ."

You might say it's progress and I'd agree if the
destroyed forests were making way for factories or
schools. But, no, there is a lot of unusable muddied
land filled with disease and people who are
destitute.

"You look so bored. Why did I go on and on? You must think I'm a babbling loser.
You hate me. I hate me. . . ."

[He looks at her askance. . . .]

It seems to me that you have little interest in any
of this.

"How could you have any interest in this? Why did I think you would? What am
I, nuts?! Ooooh, I love the way your breasts jiggle when you walk. . . ."

YELENA

No, it's simply that I don't comprehend much of it.

"Yeah right. It's not like I'm explaining rocket science here. . . ."

ASTROV

It doesn't take much to comprehend it. I just don't
think you're all that interested.

"That's telling ya. No fool I. Now you're going to think I'm strong, not a wuss,
because I stood up to you. On the other hand, what if you take it badly and leave?!
Oh, no, I wish I could take it back. Don't go. Please don't go. . . ."

YELENA

Please excuse my lack of concentration, as my
mind is someplace else. To be honest I wanted to
ask you something but I don't know how to begin.

"This question could be really, really bad. . . . Maybe you're going to ask me,
'Why do you keep coming to visit so often when nobody is ill? Doesn't anyone
else require your services?' Why am I here all the time? 'Cuz you got me wrapped
around your nasty little finger, you . . . Okay, Astrov, that was a little harsh.
Wait to see what she's gonna ask. Don't assume anything. . . ."

[Pause]
It's a question about someone you know. Like
friends, let's talk, being totally open with each
other, and then forget we ever had this
conversation. What do you say?

"You want to forget we had this conversation? This can't be good. . . ."

ASTROV
All right.
"Please don't prolong the agony. I'm dying here. Ask me already. . . ."

YELENA
It's about Sonya, my stepdaughter. What do
you think of her? Do you like her?
*"Is this a trap? What if I don't answer in the right way? Then you'll hate me.
Should I lie? Tell you I like Sonya and make you jealous? . . . That could backfire
big-time. Or should I tell the truth and let you know I'm available? More than
available—desperate, in fact. Oh, that's real attractive. Every woman loves the
stank sweat of a desperate man. Yeah, right. Think, Astrov, think. . . . Okay, here
goes—I'll try to respond in a way that's real vague. . . ."*

ASTROV
I can admire her spirit.
*"That's good. Nice but noncommittal. Please accept this and change the subject to
something else, like how handsome and sexy you find me. . . ."*

YELENA
But do you like her as a woman?
*"What do you want me to say? Give me a hint. Why can't you make this easy on
me? My life is hard enough. What if I make the wrong choice? I suck at tests. Oh,
boy, could I use a shot or two of vodka. . . . Okay, answer now, vodka later . . . I'll
tell you the truth and hope it flies. . . ."*

ASTROV
[Pause]
No.
"Do you like my answer? Do ya, huh, do ya?"

YELENA
[Kissing his hand]
You don't love her. I can see that from your eyes.
You know, she's suffering. Try to understand that
you must stop coming here.
*"Nothing like the ol' mixed message. You kiss my hand yet you tell me to leave.
What do you want and how should I respond?!"*
[Pause]
Ouch! I hate this. I feel like I've been carrying the
weight of the world on my shoulders. Anyway, it's

done, thank God, so now we can forget we ever
had this conversation and move on. You're a smart
man. I'm sure you realize why you must . . .

"This can't be good. You see me as a weight on your shoulders, not as a virile man. . . ."

[Pause]
I feel all the blood rushing to my head.

"Yet you seem to want me to hold you . . . but what if I'm wrong and you push me away?! Woman, you are so hard to read and I am so aroused. . . ."

ASTROV
If you had told me about her feelings a month or
two ago, I might have thought about it . . . but if
she is sick at heart because of me, then I guess
there's no other recourse. . . .

"I'm babbling and babbling. I sound like a stupid moron, but wait a minute. . . . You didn't have to ask me this question. . . . Maybe you do like me . . ."

[Pause]
But tell me, why is it that you had to ask me?

"Come on. Admit it. You like me. You want me just as much as I want you, right?! . . ."

[He looks at her a moment.]

"You're not answering. That means you're too afraid to answer. I hope this means you want me as much as I want you. I'm going for it. . . ."

Ohhhh, I get it!

"Just say it. You have the hots for me! Oh, yes, you do. . . ."

YELENA
What are you talking about?

"Don't pretend you don't know. You know what I'm talking about. You want me. You want me bad. . . ."

ASTROV
You know. Sure, Sonya may be in love, but why is it
you're asking the questions? Why do you look so
surprised? You know why I come every day. You're
very well aware of the effect you have on me, you
lovely "bird of prey."

"I'd like to feel my lips against yours, hungrily tasting you, you wanting me like the tigress that you are. . . ."

YELENA
Bird of prey! What are you talking about?!

". . . I want you squirming against me, begging me for more and more, grrrrr. . . ."

ASTROV
You are a gorgeous, frisky rascal . . . and I am your
victim. Well, you win. You can have me.

[He opens his arms and bows his head like a martyr on a cross.]

"... Come to me. Hold me. Touch me. Eat me up. ..."
I give in. I'm here and ready to be consumed!
"... What's taking you so long? I'm starting to look insane just standing here,
arms akimbo, looking like Jesus on the cross. And how the hell do I get out of this
position?! ..."

YELENA
Have you gone mad?!
"... Uh-oh, you <u>do</u> think I'm nuts. Or maybe you're just playing hard to get. ..."

ASTROV
Oh, you are so coy.
"That gets me even hotter. Oooooh, I want you soooo much. ..."

YELENA
I'm not as cunning or as cruel as you're making me
out to be. Honestly, I'm not.

[She tries to leave. Astrov rushes to block her way.]

"You can't leave. If you do, I'll never get another chance. I've gotta stop you or else
I'll never get another chance to make you mine . . . and besides, I'm so horny. ..."

ASTROV
I'll leave and I won't return. Just tell me . . .
"I'll promise you anything you want. ..."

[He takes her hand and glances about to see if anyone is looking.]

"... Uh-oh, what if someone walks in and interrupts? I hate when that happens.
Hurry up. We don't have much time. Tell me. Where do you want to go to get down
and dirty? ..."

Where should we meet? Hurry, someone may catch
us—please tell me where.
"Is that perfume or you? Oh, baby, I want to eat you up. ..."

[Whispering lustfully]
Your hair smells wonderful. One little kiss, please
let me kiss you.
"Your body, your hair, your luscious lips are really getting to me! Press your full
lips against mine. Kiss me like you've never kissed anyone before . . . please,
please, please, please. ..."

YELENA
I beg of you . . .

"Oh, yeah! You're begging now, huh? You want me, huh? . . ."

ASTROV
[Stops her from talking]
No need to beg, I'm yours. You are so beautiful.
And your lovely hands, I need to kiss your hands.

"I could get away with saying 'hands.' That's safe to say, but what I'd really like to wrap my lips around is . . ."

[He kisses her hands.]

"Oh, yeah, don't stop now. . . ."

YELENA
Stop it, please stop . . . go . . .

[She pulls her hand away.]

"No, no, no, don't do that! Don't pull away! You're a Leo and I'm a Scorpio—astrologically we're supposed to be together!"

ASTROV
You know it's inescapable. We are meant to be
together.

"What if I'm wrong about you wanting me?! And what if you tell Alexander and Vanya that I've been coming on to you?! What to do? What to do? . . . Oh, those luscious lips. I want to devour them, suck them, lick them. . . . Oh, what the hell? I'm going in!"

[He kisses her, and at that very moment, Uncle Vanya shows up, carrying a dozen roses, and stops just inside the door. Neither Astrov nor Yelena sees him.]

YELENA
Don't. We shouldn't be doing this. . . .

"Come to me. Be with me. Come on. You want to. You know you do. . . ."

[She lays her head on Astrov's chest.]

"Ahh, a little taste of heaven . . ."

ASTROV
At two o'clock meet me at the plantation. Promise
me you'll come.

"I'm so close. I can see it in your eyes. You can't wait for two o'clock. You love me and I love you. And, Astrov, you stud, you are gonna get lucky. . . ."

[Yelena sees Vanya looking at them.]

"... Wait. What are you looking at? Oh, no, it's Vanya. He's got rage issues and is gonna kill me and then what will I do?! ..."

YELENA
Let go of me!

"How am I gonna explain this?! This looks really, really bad. ..."

[She forcefully pulls away from Astrov. Then she goes to the window.]

"Why are you making me look like the bad guy, like I forced you or something?! ..."

[Muttering to herself]
This is just awful.

"I gotta claim innocence, but I look guilty as hell. What should I say or do that will fix it for both of us?! Vanya, what have you seen? What have you heard? When the hell did you come in and how'd I miss it?! It's gotta be that last shot of vodka because otherwise I'm usually very observant. ..."

[Vanya carefully puts the roses on a nearby chair. Yelena continues to look out the window, trying to figure out what she's going to say or do next, as Astrov looks painfully guilty and attempts to cover up.]

"I could say I was so drunk that I didn't know what I was doing. He's witnessed some of my infamous blackouts. Or I could say it was a parlor game we were playing. Or she came to me with some aches and pains and I was just examining her. Being the family doctor that could fly. Except what I was doing didn't look very medicinal ... I gotta come up with something believable so that I can be Yelena's hero and still have a chance to get her to love me. ... There's gotta be a way. Here's one that just might work. I could say, 'I was warming her up for you ...'"

Continue the INNER MONOLOGUE until the director yells, "Cut!" or until the curtain comes down or until after you finish your exit.

Tool #11: PREVIOUS CIRCUMSTANCES

This is a character's history that makes them the kind of person they are today.

With PREVIOUS CIRCUMSTANCES you must first discover your character's history as it relates to the script. Then you connect the script's PREVIOUS CIRCUMSTANCES to parallel emotional experiences from your own life so that you can identify with your character with such insight and depth that you ultimately "become" the character.

PREVIOUS CIRCUMSTANCES for Yelena

The Script's PREVIOUS CIRCUMSTANCES

In late nineteenth-century Russia, being married to a wealthy and well-regarded man was the best a woman could aspire to. Despite her beauty, upper-class education and manners, Yelena didn't marry at the age most young women did. For some reason, she waited. As a result, with the feared label of "spinster" nipping at her heels, she married Alexander. A man at least twice her age, he is a retired professor and hypochondriac who is acerbic, stubborn and asexual. And to Yelena's dismay, her husband chooses to move back to the country, a place she considers to be backward and remote.

Alexander has the means to be quite comfortable, but he is not uberrich. So Yelena's motivation for marrying him would not be to amass huge sums of money. Nor is she with Alexander for his looks. If Alexander was ever handsome, his appearance has withered away with age. Then why would she marry this particular man? We must assume that Yelena is drawn to him because he is well respected. Why is respect something that Yelena craves? Given her behavior over the time that elapses in the script, we can say Yelena is willful, self-centered, obstinate, mischievous, spirited, unrestrained, fiery—a she-devil. What brought this behavior on? Obviously, something she did or something done to her has colored her fortunate beginnings, making her somehow disreputable and no longer worthy of getting a good husband. So she married the best man she could—someone who may be old and ugly but who was once a highly regarded professor, someone from whom she can earn vicarious respectability through association and someone who can help her get her power back in a world that doesn't value women.

Here Are Some of the PREVIOUS CIRCUMSTANCES You Must Personalize

1. Script's PREVIOUS CIRCUMSTANCE: Yelena's history of self-destructive behavior.

Personalized PRIOR CIRCUMSTANCE suggestions: Because of one's zest to live life to the fullest, one often jumps in headfirst without considering any ramifications. Looking back at some of those specific events when you have personally experienced backlash as the results of attempts to create excitement in your life, see becoming Yelena as a continuation of your misadventures. What Yelena does in the time frame that takes place in *Uncle Vanya* is not new behavior. She has been getting herself and those foolish enough to be around her in hot water for a long time. The PREVIOUS CIRCUMSTANCES you parallel to the scripted character could be:

- A history of numerous sexual liaisons
- A history of stealing
- A history of irresponsible partying
- A history of drug and/or alcohol abuse
- A history of pathological lying
- Getting pregnant and having abortion(s)
- Getting caught having an affair or having numerous affairs with married men

Now, consider what happened as a result of your undisciplined behavior. This may have meant getting a bad reputation, jail time, pregnancy, a lack of trust from those around you, the loss of a mate, the loss of friendships, the loss of a job, others seeing you in a bad light and not even giving you a chance to have a friend, a mate or a job opportunity.

2. Script's PREVIOUS CIRCUMSTANCE: The time period's expectations of a woman's need to be married.

    Personalized PRIOR CIRCUMSTANCE suggestions: You have to duplicate the kind of high pressure to get married that would force the need to enter a loveless marriage, as well as bring about the need for "extra-curricular" activities (wink, wink). The following are some possibilities for creating similar PREVIOUS CIRCUMSTANCES from your own life:

    - Social demands haven't changed that much since the late nineteenth century. There's still huge social status associated with having a boyfriend, fiancé or husband. Friends and family make too big a deal over the proposal, the engagement ring, the bridal shower and the marriage ceremony. If you are a woman who is unattached, who has never been married or who doesn't have any prospects of getting attached, it's likely you're looked down upon as someone to pity, and put in the category of a don't-invite case or as a must-set-up-with-a-nice-doctor-or-lawyer emergency case. This set of PREVIOUS CIRCUMSTANCES will give you the need to change your single status A.S.A.P.

• You are married but you got married because of the pressure of PREVIOUS CIRCUMSTANCES such as you were pregnant; there was no one else around; the person you really wanted wasn't available; your marriage was arranged by your family; you and your spouse were expected to wed because you had been going together for so long; or all your girlfriends were married, so you said yes to the first guy who asked you. If any of these examples applies, use that PREVIOUS CIRCUMSTANCE from your life as the impetus to risk everything to go after your SUBSTITUTION for Astrov.

• Perhaps your present relationship sprang from love, but now you and your partner have grown apart and you've become different from each other and bored. If so, use the past events that illustrate this as the PREVIOUS CIRCUMSTANCES that would make you feel it necessary to get your SUBSTITUTION for Astrov to fall in love with you so you can mix it up. . . .

• Maybe the PREVIOUS CIRCUMSTANCES in your life don't include the importance of a long-term marital relationship, but in your case, you do have the need to prove your worth in a long-term job. Useful personal PREVIOUS CIRCUMSTANCES for this option could be a history of problems holding on to jobs, a history of being skipped over when it comes time for raises or promotions or a history of interviewing (auditioning) many times but the tally sheet for jobs booked is still at zero. This would make you want to risk your marriage with Alexander (who would be a SUBSTITUTION for a boss, producer or some work-related authority who isn't presently satisfying you) and pursue Astrov (who would be a SUBSTITUTION for someone that could give you a job or the kind of career that you dream of).

3. Script's PREVIOUS CIRCUMSTANCE: Yelena's past of being shocking, outrageous, scandalous, shameful and socially out of control as a way to feel alive.

    Personalized PRIOR CIRCUMSTANCE suggestions: What is it that you have a history of doing that might risk your security, but you feel compelled to do it anyway so as to keep your life from being dull and monotonous? This could be a PREVIOUS CIRCUMSTANCE of your own such as:

    • Having extramarital affairs
    • Gossiping in massive doses
    • Having a problem with kleptomania (thievery can produce adrenaline)
    • Blurting out shock speak
    • Being prone to inordinate amounts of swearing
    • Being loud and obnoxious in inappropriate places
    • Joking brazenly (and you may even be funny, but too much of a good thing . . .)
    • Dressing indecently or simply for shock value

4. Script's PREVIOUS CIRCUMSTANCE: Yelena's background of manipulation and game playing in relationships.

    Personalized PRIOR CIRCUMSTANCE suggestions: Relationships aren't solely motivated by love. We've all had PREVIOUS CIRCUMSTANCES in which we sought out a relationship for other purposes that were reasonable to us but unclear to those looking in from the outside. Reasons such as:

    • Security
    • Money
    • Employment
    • Social position

- Power
- Competition for a partner
- Good looks
- Loneliness

In order to make the part of you that is manipulative come from a real place when you are becoming Yelena, look at some of the friendships and relationships you have formed because of PREVIOUS CIRCUMSTANCES other than undying love.

5. Script's PREVIOUS CIRCUMSTANCE: Yelena's inordinate need to make men love her. Whereas alcohol is Astrov's addiction, *love*—and bushels of it—is Yelena's drug of choice. Yelena has Alexander, who loves her; Vanya, who is clearly smitten with her; Sonya, who is caught under her spell as a friend and confidante; and Astrov, whose constant presence in the house since Yelena's arrival can mean only one thing—he loves her, too. The other characters' attraction to Yelena didn't occur by accident—Yelena needs people to fall for her, and she's obsessed with the drive to make that happen.

    Personalized PRIOR CIRCUMSTANCE suggestions: What are your PREVIOUS CIRCUMSTANCES that make you personally *need* people to fall in love with you? Could it be:

    - you had abandonment events?
    - you had emotionally undemonstrative parents?
    - you were the "reject" kid when you were growing up?
    - you had a previous mate relationship where you were the one *more* in love and you got severely hurt because you were?
    - you've always thought you're ugly and you need constant attention to prove otherwise?
    - you were horribly abused as a child?

Remember events and PREVIOUS CIRCUMSTANCES in which you were especially needy to get your SCENE OBJECTIVE of *"to get you to fall in love with me to get my power back."* Let this motivate you to make it necessary to win as Yelena.

PREVIOUS CIRCUMSTANCES for Astrov.

The Script's PREVIOUS CIRCUMSTANCES

Astrov comes from Russia at a time when changing your career or social position was nearly impossible. He is a country doctor who is always going to practice and live in the country. In the nineteenth century, it was normal to make calls to houses that were often miles apart, and the constant traveling made a doctor's social life difficult. In this era, age was also an issue. Astrov's having been a confirmed bachelor for a long time doesn't bode well for a future with matrimony in it. All the good girls his age are spoken for, and the other women—spinsters—are unmarried for a reason. He is alone with no prospects for change. But he still wants a wife and family, and this desire is growing. Unfortunately, despite this desire, Astrov thinks his chances for a happy domestic life are slim. This makes him cynical. Because of his ever-growing pessimism, Astrov has transferred his primal need to love and protect a family to a focus on loving and protecting the environment.

We can presuppose that Astrov probably had commitment issues at the key marrying junctures in his life. It's also important to note that he has the opportunity to have a wife and child with the clearly available Sonya, but he chooses instead to fall in love with the unattainable Yelena.

The other characters in the play talk about how much he drinks, and he indeed appears to have a drinking problem, something that clearly isn't new to him. Alcoholism is usually learned or genetically motivated from primal sources. Here it may also be a way for him to manage his desires and his reality.

Here Are Some of the PREVIOUS CIRCUMSTANCES That You Must Personalize

1. Script's PREVIOUS CIRCUMSTANCE: Astrov chose medicine as his career path.

    Personalized PRIOR CIRCUMSTANCE suggestions: Whatever career we choose, we do so for a reason. Our careers define us. You must find events from your past that would drive you to want to become a doctor. Perhaps:

- You have a parent or mentor in the field of medicine, and you want to please and emulate someone whom you love and respect.
- You have had a loved one (a parent, sibling, friend, etc.) die from an illness, and at the time of that death, you felt helpless to do anything about it. Becoming a doctor would satisfy you by offering you the ability to do something about that death if it were to happen again today.
- You have a parent who has a blue-collar job and who wants you to have more out of life than just a daily grind. Becoming a doctor would give that parent a sense of pride in you because you have risen above the family blue-collar legacy.

2. Script's PREVIOUS CIRCUMSTANCE: Stuck in a low social stratum—geographically, educationally and socially. This will affect Astrov's ability to go after Yelena, who bests him in all these areas.

  Personalized PRIOR CIRCUMSTANCE suggestions:

- You came from or still live in a small backwoods town. Think about past experiences that remind you of your feelings of social inferiority (such as times you were humiliated for your way of speaking or dressing or for your lack of savvy).
- You came from or still live in a part of a city that would be considered poor, the ghetto or ethnically segregated. Remember events when being poor or ethnic caused you emotional pain or perhaps even caused you to get into physical battles.
- Your family came from or you and your family still live in a city or town in which you were castigated because you were the sole residents representing an unpopular racial or religious group (the only Black family in an all-white neighborhood, the only Muslim family in your community, etc.). Recall the degradation that you've experienced.
- You are a member of a minority group that has experienced prejudice (African American, Hispanic, Asian, Arabic, Jewish, etc.). Use the history of the bigotry you've experienced.

- You grew up in poverty. Remembering the events of your past that affect you today (going to bed hungry, being made fun of at school because of your shabby clothes, etc.).
- You had issues with school. Think of the specific PREVIOUS CIRCUMSTANCES that caused you shame, such as having been constantly tutored, having been mocked by fellow students and teachers, having been consistently given bad grades that made your parents berate you, etc.

3. Script's PREVIOUS CIRCUMSTANCE: Past opportunities to meet women were limited, creating a currently desperate and lonely Astrov.

   Personalized PRIOR CIRCUMSTANCE suggestions: You have to find emotionally similar PREVIOUS CIRCUMSTANCES from your life that make you feel that you have limited opportunities.

- You have a history of feeling unattractive in some way (too fat, too skinny, blemished skin, bad hair, racial differences, too short, too tall, too plain or homely, etc.).
- You had a long relationship or marriage that broke up and you're out of practice meeting other women, so you feel unprepared and awkward.
- You have a history of knowing women who just want to be friends, excluding any other kind of relationship.
- You were in a long-term relationship that was so abusive that you feel insecure and believe that all future mates are going to treat you the same way.
- You are homosexual, and being around a woman in that way makes you feel uncomfortable.
- You haven't had a relationship in a very long time and you don't have a lot of hope that that's going to change.

4. Script's PREVIOUS CIRCUMSTANCES: The 1890s in Russia—age issues revolving around finding a mate have produced Astrov's present hopelessness.

   Personalized PRIOR CIRCUMSTANCE suggestions:

- Even today, it is a common perception that the older you get, the fewer options you have—that as you age, the fields of choices for mates, careers and improved social circumstances narrow. Take any age-related event that has caused you to feel hopeless about making changes in your life, and elaborate on what change you'd like to make and how difficult it would be to do so given your current age. For example, you've been working as an electrical engineer, which took some time to train for. In order to make a change to be an actor, you'd have to start from the bottom, and you'd always be fearful that younger actors would take precedence over you in the casting process. Use PREVIOUS CIRCUMSTANCES from your own life—actual experiences that make this true.

- What if your actual age is not your problem? Hopelessness doesn't have to necessarily stem from age. Your personal PREVIOUS CIRCUMSTANCES may include the experience that no matter how hard you've tried, you've failed at most of your attempts to succeed: getting consistently bad grades in school, having friends who always seem to turn on you, meeting girls who time after time ridicule you and won't give you the time of day, being fired from job after job. Use personal PREVIOUS CIRCUMSTANCE events from your life that seem to thwart you at every turn.

5. Script's PREVIOUS CIRCUMSTANCE: Astrov's history of commitment problems.

   Personalized PRIOR CIRCUMSTANCE suggestions: Personalize how commitment has been a problem for you by looking at important events and experiences that may have caused you to have a sense of leeriness and fear when it comes to making the "Big C" (otherwise known as "commitment").

   - Perhaps you have been brought up in a family that went through a messy divorce and you don't want to repeat in your life what you witnessed growing up, and therefore commitment scares you.
   - You watched your parents stay together but not get along. You

don't want to commit to someone and feel smothered in a bad relationship the same way your parents were, so you avoid commitment.

- You personally have had a history of bad relationships and don't want to repeat history with yet another painful, devastating commitment.

- You watched your parents, who are loving and amazing, give up their dreams and aspirations to support a family, and you don't want that to happen to you. Because of this, you subconsciously feel that commitment will always equal drudgery and the sacrifice of your dreams.

6. Script's PREVIOUS CIRCUMSTANCE: Astrov's background and the reason for his obsession with environmental issues.

   Personalized PRIOR CIRCUMSTANCE suggestions:

   - Astrov's love and concern for the country is not new to him. A devotion like his increases over time, largely because he doesn't have anywhere else to put all those feelings of passion. People are not caught up in an issue unless they feel motivated by personal PREVIOUS CIRCUMSTANCES. You have to look at yourself and consider what you are obsessed with rectifying and why you are obsessed. A person who is caught up in changing drunk-driving laws is usually someone who's had some past tragedy caused by a drunk driver. A person who is troubled by the way the mentally handicapped are dealt with usually has a disabled family member and has witnessed their abuse firsthand. Whatever issue you have chosen as an INNER OBJECT for the theme contained in Astrov's drawings, think about what in your own personal history (PREVIOUS CIRCUMSTANCES) would cause you to be as concerned about your own issue as Astrov is about his.

7. Script's PREVIOUS CIRCUMSTANCE: Astrov's alcoholism.

   Personalized PRIOR CIRCUMSTANCE suggestions: First, you have to identify the "drug" that is an addiction for you. What is the thing you do to endure life's torments? Food? Drugs—prescription or street? Sex? Cutting? Isolation? Pathological lying? Social media obsession? Then elaborate how and why you have a problem in this area by looking at your own PREVIOUS CIRCUMSTANCES.

- If you're a Valium addict, remember the event that triggered the first time you ever took it and what specifically happened later to create an escalating problem. Was it trauma, or was it just rising insecurity coming from daily events that became increasingly harder to deal with? How did you know about Valium in the first place? Was your mother, a role model, someone predisposed to taking it? Or did a friend or lover have a problem with it and it seemed to work for him or her? Did your addiction begin as a peer-group activity and end with you being the only one who continued after the phase was over for everyone else? Understanding and knowing your PREVIOUS CIRCUMSTANCES in this area will determine how your personal addiction was learned and/or genetically induced.

PREVIOUS CIRCUMSTANCES put the final layer in becoming a living, breathing, three-dimensional human being. You are Astrov. Or you are Yelena. At this point there should be no distinction between you and the character. All that's left to do is to . . .

Tool #12: LET IT GO

Trust the work that you've done.

Trust that you've created a strong foundation for spontaneity to emerge. Trust the choices you've made. Trust . . . and LET IT GO.

Epilogue:
And Now a Word or Two
About Auditions

There's so much myth and mystique around the auditioning process. People think anyone who can cast a role (the casting director, director, producer) might somehow lift their royal scepters and grant eternal stardom. I hate to break it to you, but they are mere mortals just looking for the best so that they can create the greatest project. They want to excel and be successful (or more successful) via their casting choices.

How do we present the best to the people who hold the key to us booking or not booking a role? Here are some points that can help you be more effective in the auditioning process.

1. DO THE WORK

Following the twelve steps of the Chubbuck Technique, do script analysis with enough details to trigger an organic performance. Don't be lazy. Prepare! Hard work pays off in every aspect of your life.

2. DON'T PAPER-PLEASE

Paper-pleasing is like people-pleasing, but it's about pleasing the script. What this means is that you mindlessly follow the instructions written on the page on how to act the scene, or make choices based on *how* you *think* the casting director (or director or producer) wants to see you perform it. Paper-pleasing, just like people-pleasing, rarely works. It comes off as needy and uninteresting and lacks the specialness that your authentic self can bring. When I used to be in casting, working with directors and writer-producers to help them cast, it was fascinating to see how many different actors did exactly the same read because they were trying to give the performance they thought the casting people wanted to see. The actors who bring their authentic selves to their choices and go after their OBJECTIVES in an effective way (not necessarily in the way you think "they" want it done) generally get the job. Even if you don't get the job, they remember you for future jobs. Good auditions get rewarded at some point. Be yourself. You are unique, so there's no one else out there like you. Bringing yourself and the ways in which you negotiate life to get what you want (OBJECTIVE) will express that something special that everyone is looking for.

Odelya Halevi, who plays ADA Samantha Maroun on *Law & Order*, studied with me for years. When she was given the audition for this part, the description was for a Southern girl with a Southern accent. Seemed pretty clear what they wanted. Odelya is from Israel. English is her second language, and she has an Israeli accent. Instead of trying to become a girl from the American South and trying her best at a Southern accent, she decided that she is who she is, and she would go after the OBJECTIVES and establish the inner work based on her own life. This was a self-tape, and thinking she didn't have a shot, because, again, the casting breakdown simply wasn't her, she still did all the work and sent it off.

A few weeks later, her agent told her the producers wanted to have a Zoom meeting with her. She assumed it was a callback, but when she got on the Zoom call, they told her she had booked the job and wanted to talk to her about her own life so they could rewrite the character with that in mind. They also said they had been looking for a Southern girl for months, and after seeing hundreds of tapes, when they got hers, they knew that Odelya was right for the part. It is quite rare to get booked on a big job from just one self-tape. Normally there are callbacks before you get a job. This is my way of proving the point that you can take the risk of being your most authentic self for the job, no matter what the description says. As an artist, you have the freedom to cross boundaries, take risks and think outside the box.

Speaking of which . . .

3. MAKE BOLD CHOICES

Physicalize. Choose highly triggering inner work when doing your script analysis. Take chances; don't play it safe. Feel comfortable to physicalize. I am not talking about enthusiastically miming the behavior described in the script but don't be afraid to be visually expressive. When you listen, make strong choices so that behavior is allowed to emerge (see chapter 25, "ACTIVE LISTENING").

When directors or producers show me the tapes of the choices they've made for casting, they almost always explain why they chose those people by telling me to watch their behavior or to watch how they listen with strong INNER MONOLOGUE (which creates behavior). It's rare that they mention how the actors said a line.

When Charlize Theron and I worked on her audition(s) for the movie *The Devil's Advocate*, she had at that point in her career done only a couple small roles in small movies. The character was described as a plain thirty-year-old woman from Florida. Charlize was way too young and way too pretty, and she was from South Africa. No matter how hard you tried, there was no way to make her plain, even if she was au naturel. I also told her that if decision makers really wanted a true Floridian accent, they would get her an accent coach. What they were looking for was the best actress, not an accent. Among Charlize's competition were women who had greater résumés and who were the "right type." Also, this was a coveted role, as it was a big studio movie starring Al Pacino and Keanu Reeves.

She was given two audition scenes. The first one involved her coming home, where Keanu's character greeted her. Since their characters had been married for five years, Charlize determined that they would have a fun relationship, not a formal one. Her idea was that as she was doing the dialogue in the script and entering their home, she would take off her sweater (underneath which was a modest bathing-suit type of bra) and pretend she was doing a striptease. This was not in the script at all—the script had just husband-and-wife type of dialogue. But the inner work we did alongside some fun behaviors established a solid, playful, loving long-term relationship, so when they had severe problems later in the script, it would create a strong story arc.

The second audition scene took place after Al Pacino as her father-in-law (a.k.a., literally the devil) aborts the fetus in her womb. The character had a monologue, and we used a profoundly upsetting event from Charlize's life as her inner work. We also decided she would do this scene on the floor, rocking herself in the fetal position in an attempt to calm herself.

The bold choices she made in this audition in front of some very important people left a big impression—so big that even though she was wrong for the role as they had envisioned it, they couldn't get her audition out of their heads. After the first audition, those very important people told her manager that they loved her but they weren't going to go any further in the process because she wasn't the right type. They auditioned more people and . . . then decided to have Charlize return to audition again. Charlize and I got together and upped the stakes even more before the next audition. Yet again, her people were told that they loved her audition, but they weren't going any further because she wasn't right for the role—and frankly, her previous credits were meager.

Of course, the casting process didn't stop there. They brought Charlize in for callback after callback after callback . . . and following each callback, they phoned her management to say, "It's not going any further." I ran into her manager at a party around this time and I told him I had a feeling she was going to get the role. She was making choices that made her a force that could not be denied.

And in the end, she wasn't denied. Even though she was too young and too pretty and not a typical American type, she got that part. Charlize's career has been filled with bold choices, and that's part of the reason for her iconic success. Don't be afraid to take risks!

4. HAVE A LAST THOUGHT

A last thought encourages casting directors (producers, directors, etc.) wanting to see what you'll do next, which they will find out only if they cast you. They stop believing you're the character if you just drop out at the end of the scene (generally when the dialogue is over). The last thought enables you to continue the character's journey from a strong INNER MONOLOGUE point of view. It helps the people who have the power continue to believe you are the character and thus they will be more prone to want to cast you.

You will find that while these four major points make for a great audition, they <u>are also effective in your script analysis for work that you are actually performing.</u> So keep in mind:

1. DO THE WORK
2. DON'T PAPER-PLEASE
3. MAKE BOLD CHOICES (TAKE RISKS)
4. HAVE A LAST THOUGHT

TEN PIECES OF ADVICE
FOR ACTORS

1. Make sure that your OVERALL OBJECTIVE provides a primal human need that creates a universal journey, one that everyone can support and cheer for. In this way, people/audiences from every corner of the world and every segment of society can relate to the OVERALL OBJECTIVE and therefore change and grow because of the experience.

2. Don't play the character. *BE* the character. Find your personal connection to the character on the page so you can always be present and in the moment. Your need will come from a truthful and necessary place.

3. Never play the victim. We never support a person in real life who feels sorry for themselves. We always love and support people who—against all conflicts and obstacles and no matter how horrible their circumstances—will still fight to overcome and attempt to WIN!

4. Celebrate your flaws, fears and insecurities—they are what make you interesting and special.

5. Never color the underbelly of your work with sadness. Sadness creates lethargy and inertia—the inability to make moves. Instead, find the anger. Anger is a fuel that makes us do things that in normal circumstances we would never do. Anger creates passionate behavior. I always say, "Anger moves mountains. Sadness digs a hole."

6. Humor, even in the darkest of dramas, is important to bring into your work. You can't see darkness without the comparison to light. Humor also makes the experience of watching a play, movie or television show a more enjoyable experience. Chekhov's plays are filled with satire

(humor) alongside profound drama. This is why he is such a celebrated playwright and has stood the test of time. You'll find this is true of Shakespeare, Tennessee Williams, David Mamet, August Wilson, Noël Coward, Samuel Beckett, Sophocles, Oscar Wilde, Aristophanes, George Bernard Shaw, Harold Pinter, Lillian Hellman, Jean-Paul Sartre and all the great playwrights that have historical value!

7. Chemistry is key in a great performance. And chemistry, or lack of it, can make or break the success of a movie (or a TV show or a play). Chemistry is also something that everyone all over the world understands and relates to, no matter what their religion, geography, language, moral priorities, intellect, socioeconomic stature or occupation. Making other cast members *and* your audience feel that you are accessible is part of what makes a star. All people everywhere would rather spend time with someone whom they are attracted to and whom they have a crush on than with someone whom they are not interested in.

8. Take risks. Never play it safe. There's more satisfaction for the actor and the audience when choices are made from fearlessness. Bottom line: Fear is antithetical to art.

9. Greatness is in the details. It takes a lot of work to create the details. But if we're duplicating real human behavior, we have to duplicate the complicated nature of being human, too.

10. Have a strong work ethic. Success in ANY field takes time and work. Laziness is for losers. The people who work really hard on their script analysis, who rehearse a lot and who take the vast amount of time necessary to create a real three-dimensional human being out of a character are the winners.

THE CHUBBUCK TECHNIQUE 12-STEP CHECKLIST

1. OVERALL OBJECTIVE:

2. SCENE OBJECTIVE:

3. OBSTACLES:

4. SUBSTITUTION:

5. INNER OBJECTS:

6. BEATS and ACTIONS:

7. MOMENT BEFORE:

8. PLACE and FOURTH WALL:

9. DOINGS:

10. INNER MONOLOGUE:

11. PREVIOUS CIRCUMSTANCES:

12. LET IT GO:

Acknowledgments

· ·

I'd like to thank, first of all, Farrin Jacobs for helping me forge my way through all the updates I've accumulated over the twenty years since the first edition of *The Power of the Actor* was published. Brian DeFiore for being a really great agent who made excellent decisions to create a more enhanced and empowered journey for me. And Linda Kaplan, Brian's colleague in his company, for having the idea to do a "refresh" of the book for the twenty-year anniversary. Hannah Steigmeyer for your editorial prowess and the rest of the team at Avery for enthusiastically supporting this new and improved edition. Halle Berry for being a friend, an ally, a kindred spirit, an unwavering support system for my family and me—and a key element in my writing the original book. My friend and cohort Deryl Carroll for making me feel loved and covered and for making all things complicated become simple in my day-to-day in the Chubbuck Technique / *The Power of the Actor* business. And my lovely friend and support system Cameron McCormick for taking over when Deryl retired. My family, the Gottfrieds, for their creative and often hilarious dysfunction, which aided in making the technique relatable and accessible. The Gottfrieds consist of Helene and Bernard (Mom and Dad) and Nan, Linda, Heidi, Hagen, Joe and Erika (my siblings). The thousands of students I've taught over the years for dedicating yourselves to our beloved craft—we've learned and grown together. My husband, who has passed away, for having the idea that I should write the book in the first place—and then for insisting I do it. And finally, my daughter, Claire Chubbuck, for being my inspiration for everything and for being true legacy as a prolific and talented person I am proud to say is my spaw

About the Author

Ivana Chubbuck created the widely adopted Chubbuck Technique, an acting method taught in universities and in officially accredited Chubbuck Technique studios all over the world. Ivana's students have gone on to win major awards, including Oscars, Emmys and Tonys. *The Power of the Actor* has been translated into more than twenty different languages.

Through her technique, Ivana pursues her mission to facilitate Empowerment Through the Arts. She lives in Los Angeles, where she runs the Ivana Chubbuck Studio. Her daughter, Claire Chubbuck, an award-winning and talented filmmaker and Chubbuck teacher, is the legacy for furthering Ivana's mission.